Generation X Rocks:
Contemporary Peninsular Fiction,
Film, and Rock Culture

HISPANIC ISSUES • VOLUME 33

Generation X Rocks:
Contemporary Peninsular Fiction, Film, and Rock Culture

Christine Henseler

AND

Randolph D. Pope

EDITORS

Vanderbilt University Press

NASHVILLE, TENNESSEE

2007

This book is printed on acid-free paper
made from 50% post consumer recycled paper.
Manufactured in the United States of America

The editors gratefully acknowledge
assistance from the College of Liberal Arts and
the Department of Spanish and Portuguese Studies
at the University of Minnesota.

*The complete list of volumes in the
Hispanic Issues series begins on page 263.*

Library of Congress Cataloging-in-Publication Data

Generation X rocks : contemporary peninsular fiction,
film, and rock culture / Christine Henseler
and Randolph D. Pope, editors.—1st ed.
p. cm.—(Hispanic issues ; v. 33)
Includes bibliographical references and index.
ISBN 978-0-8265-1564-3 (cloth : alk. paper)
ISBN 978-0-8265-1565-0 (pbk. : alk. paper)
1. Spanish fiction—21st century—History and criticism.
2. Motion pictures—Spain. 3. Rock music—Spain.
4. Popular culture—Spain. I. Henseler, Christine, 1969-
II. Pope, Randolph D.
PQ6144.G44 2007
306.0946—dc22
2006034924

Contents

Introduction: Generation X and Rock:
The Sounds of a New Tradition
Christine Henseler and Randolph D. Pope   xi

PART I
Rocking the Academy: Generation X Narratives

1   A Distopian Culture:
    The Minimalist Paradigm in the Generation X
    Gonzalo Navajas   3

2   The Pistols Strike Again! On the Function
    of Punk in the Peninsular "Generation X" Fiction
    of Ray Loriga and Benjamín Prado
    Paul D. Begin   15

3   What We Talk About When We Talk About
    Dirty Realism in Spain
    Cintia Santana   33

PART II
Can Anyone Rock Like We Do?:
Sex, Drugs, and Rock & Roll, Then and Now

4   Can Anyone Rock Like We Do? Or, How the Gen X
    Aesthetic Transcends the Age of the Writer
    Samuel Amago   59

5   Apocalypses Now: The End of Spanish Literature?
    Reading *Payasos en la lavadora* as Critical Parody
    Luis Martín-Cabrera   78

6   Not Your Father's Rock and Roll:
Listening to Transitional/Eighties Writers
and Generation X
Elizabeth Scarlett   97

PART III
Historias del Kronen *on the Rocks*

7   Between Rock and the Rocking Chair:
The Epilogue's Resistance in *Historias del Kronen*
Randolph D. Pope   115

8   Realism on the Rocks in the Generational Novel:
"Rummies," Rhythm, and Rebellion
in *Historias del Kronen* and *The Sun Also Rises*
Matthew J. Marr   126

PART IV
Rocking the Road with Ray Loriga

9   Reckless Driving: Speed, Mobility, and Transgression
in the Spanish "Rock 'n' Road" Novel
Jorge Pérez   153

10   Television and the Power of Image in
Caídos del cielo and *La pistola de mi hermano*
by Ray Loriga
Kathryn Everly   170

11   Rocking around Ray Loriga's *Héroes:*
Video-Clip Literature and the Televisual Subject
Christine Henseler   184

PART V
The Soundtrack of Gender:
Violating Visions and the Psychological Power of Rock

12 Watching, Wanting, and the Gen X Soundtrack
of Gabriela Bustelo's *Veo Veo*
Nina Molinaro   203

13 Saved by Art: Entrapment and Freedom
in Icíar Bollaín's *Te doy mis ojos*
Linda Gould Levine   216

Afterword:
The Moment X in Spanish Narrative (and Beyond)
Luis Martín-Estudillo   235

Contributors   247

Index   251

◆   **Introduction**

**Generation X and Rock:
The Sounds of a New Tradition**

Christine Henseler and Randolph D. Pope

While various labels have been used, discussed, and in many cases rejected, it is evident that in the 1990s several Spanish writers, who are significantly different from their predecessors and from many of their contemporaries, became famous and attracted critical attention: among others, Lucía Etxebarria (b. 1966), José Ángel Mañas (b. 1971), and Ray Loriga (b. 1967). The stories they have to tell have been told before. The three sisters of Etxebarria's *Amor, curiosidad, prozac y dudas* (1997), are similar in their choice of very different life paths to those found in Carmen Martín Gaite's (1925–2000) *Entre visillos* (1958); the group of friends rattling away in Mañas' *Historias del Kronen* (1995) as they spend a day of idle revelry that ends in tragedy has reminded many readers of Rafael Sánchez Ferlosio's (b. 1927) *El Jarama* (1955); while Loriga's self-absorbed characters and his criticism of the media in novels such as *Lo peor de todo* (1993) and *Héroes* (1994) have a family resemblance to Juan Goytisolo's (b. 1931) novels. Yet the older writers emerged from the post-Civil War repressive society with their main concern being the still looming presence of a tragic conflict and the strict control of the dictatorship. A dance at the town's social club would at most be accompanied by cigarette smoke and wine; an outing to the countryside took place on bicycles, music was aired from a phonograph; and to live openly as gay and smoke hashish one had to migrate to France or

Africa. In comparison, by the time the younger writers, born in the 1960s and 70s, came to adulthood, society had become permissive, cars zoomed through crowded cities, music was everywhere 24/7, drugs were easily available, and the country was immersed in conflictive projects of national affirmation and fragmentation, as well as in an accelerated blending into Europe. The thrill of a new democracy gave way to the indifference of the young to the posturing and jockeying for personal advantage among politicians. The novelists who described this new Spain that emerged after the transition to democracy are known as the Generation X. The label is borrowed from an American and British designation and its context is provided in several of the essays included in this volume. The fact that the term "Generation X" comes from abroad, though, does not reduce its validity, as in their time the terms Baroque, Romanticism, Realism, or Surrealism were perfectly appropriate to describe an international cultural stage in which Spain participated. Of the many characterizations Generation Xers have received, the most appropriate for our book is the one that Daniel Grassian provides in *Hybrid Fictions: American Literature and Generation X*:

> Generation X is not completely eclectic or indeterminate. Rather, there is some cohesion amongst the generation, especially in terms of the central and common ground of media-focused historical and political events, as well as television shows, films and music that frequently serve as their common frames of reference. (14)

> (What defines, then, this generation is not only the common references they use, but also the media through which these references circulate and the social economy into which they are integrated; not the book, but film, not opera, but rock music, not the exclusive, but the open and shared in youth culture.)

Twice before in Spanish literary history, a small number of significant writers has been called a generation. In both cases, not all the writers of a similar age who are actively participating in the cultural life of their period get included into a generation, as the term has been used in relation to the Generation of '98 and of '27. Antonio Machado (1875–1939) and Miguel de Unamuno (1864–1936) belong to the Generation of 98, which excludes Manuel Machado (1874–1947) and Ramón María del Valle-Inclán (1866–1936). Federico García Lorca (1898–1936) and Rafael Alberti (1902–1999) belong to the Generation of 27, while Juan Ramón Jiménez (1881–1958) and José Ortega y Gasset (1883–1955) are included in neither of these generations. The classification, therefore, may seem arbitrary and it has not always emerged with the same importance.[1] While literary critics have labeled some writers as Generation of

1950 and of 1970, these labels have not become as general or as contested as those of the Generations of 27 and 98. Richard Cardwell complains rightly that the division of writers of the same period between those belonging to the Generation of 98 and those marked by Modernism is an "altogether false picture [that] has bedeviled any proper assessment of the real identity and role of Spanish *modernismo*" (502). In fact, the recent and important book that contains Cardwell's essay, *The Cambridge History of Spanish Literature*, does not devote a chapter either to the Generation of 98 or to the Generation of 27, but rather the authors classify them under other more general categories. And yet there is a reason why one can safely predict that the Generations of 98, 27, and the Generation X, will not be abandoned. To understand why, we must see how Ortega explained the generational method in his influential *En torno a Galileo* (1933, *About Galileo*).

For Ortega, human life is always relational and therefore human beings are not only just situated in a society as observers of history, but are also a questioning mind, a project, and more than an isolated self:

> Cada uno de nosotros se encuentra, en efecto, sumergido hoy en un sistema de problemas, peligros, facilidades, dificultades, posibilidades e imposibilidades que no son él, sino que, al contrario, son aquello en que está, con que tiene que contar, en manejar y luchar con lo cual consiste precisamente su vida. Si hubiésemos nacido cien años hace, aun poseyendo el mismo carácter e iguales dotes, el drama de nuestra vida hubiera sido muy distinto.
> La pregunta radical de la historia se precisa, pues, así: ¿qué cambios de la estructura vital ha habido? ¿Cómo, cuándo y por qué cambia la vida? (27)

> (Each one of us finds oneself, in fact, immersed today in a system of problems, dangers, advantages, difficulties, possibilities and impossibilities that are not what one is, but, on the contrary, is where one is, that which one must take into account, since one's life consists precisely in dealing and struggling with this situation. If we had been born a century ago, even if we had the same personality and equal gifts, our lives' drama would have been very different.
> The most profound question of history becomes, thus, formulated as follows: What changes have there been in the structure of living? How, when, and why does life change?)

This question about the structure of one's life resonates in periods of deep transformations, as was the end of the nineteenth century and the period right before the Spanish Civil War, and again after the transition from the Franco dictatorship to a democratic society was relatively completed. Not all writers in those critical periods deal with the question that Ortega formulates so clearly: How, when, and why does life change? Those writers who do ask this question are those who come to form the generation, because they reflect intensely their own time. There had been a quiet transformation of the Spanish society before 1975—as is well described by José Carlos Mainer in "Spanish Literature between the Franco and post-Franco Eras"—but even the most innovative novels, such as those of Juan Goytisolo or Juan Marsé, remained mostly centered on the political issues of an oppressive history and the presence of a strong and censorial central government.[2] By the late eighties a significant part of a new young society is not only enjoying different material conditions, political structures, and freedoms, but the luxury of forgetting the past and being able to concentrate in living an exuberant, consumerist, drug-imbued, sex-abundant life.[3] Spain had drastically and profoundly changed, but also had the world, where the fall of the Berlin wall in 1989 had been symbolic of the collapse of old regimes.[4] Some would see this turn of the youth towards their own present as the consequence of a pact of forgetfulness, but much of this younger generation had only vague memories of the dictatorship and the Civil War, passed along to them by their parents and an elder society they saw as out of touch with the contemporary age.

Ortega adds a characteristic of generations that is useful here. He affirms that any present period is a compendium of the past, since our situation would be different had the past been otherwise (45). But generations do not always simply succeed each other: some accept their past and then take over to assure continuity of a society they have come to like, while others reject the past as an unwelcome inheritance and do what they can to change the way of life. Clearly, the Generation X belongs to this second group. Therefore, as rock music begins to appear in many novels studied in this book we are not seeing a simple ornament or marginal addition, but instead the manifestation of a radical choice to be different, joining the international music that Americans and British bands had brought to most of the globe, aided by the electronic revolution, which had liberated music from geography and, with the electric guitar, especially, had left the home or the concert hall to take over the large arenas where multitudes could feel transported in a communal frenzy.[5]

At the end of the nineteenth century, Walter Benjamin observed that a boom in the textile trade, the advent of building in iron, and the presence of crowds created a situation in the city that directed "the visual imagination, which ha[d] been activated by the new, back to the primeval past" (148) and to the illusion of a classless society. At the end of the twentieth century in Spain, the explosion in music, the advent of new electronic methods of production and distribution, and the presence of crowds dedicated to Dionysian dance and leisure in discotheques and stadiums (frequently with the aid of alcohol and drugs), also produces the illusion of a classless society. In the novels we study, the social issues that were frequent in the fifties and survived through the seventies are but faint echoes: class recedes, history fades, money is not a serious issue, and traditional politics are distant and disdained. And yet, rock sends a loud message of individual and social restlessness, inviting to a defiance of social traditions and obligations. There is no doubt that sexual mores changed during this period, that women asserted their rights and gay issues emerged defiantly, and that it all came with the impulse of international and local bands that played a music which flowed from the double young tradition of American musicians such as Nirvana and the bands of the British invasion.[6]

Rock music, which had been known in Spain since its origin in the fifties, emerged in the nineties' novels with a new centrality. By then, decades had created layers of canonical rock music to which one could refer, knowing that most of the hip public would recognize the lyrics, remember the melodies, and share their significance. While in *Entre visillos* references are to Juan Ramón Jiménez and in Juan Goytisolo's *Count Julian* to Luis de Góngora, we are confronted in the newer authors' works with Bob Dylan, Nirvana, and David Bowie. This does not just demand of critics more necessary footnotes if their students are to grasp all the implications of the text, but an attentive listening to what characters in these novels hear through their headphones.

As critics, the first obstacle to overcome is the frequent association of rock with popular music, and therefore with a cultural element residing on the low end of the distribution system or spectrum between high and low. In fact, the novel has always incorporated all expressions of human activity; Miguel de Cervantes has his narrator in *Don Quixote* read pages he finds on the ground at marketplaces, and Benito Pérez Galdós has great fun in *Fortunata y Jacinta* with the titles of books sold by door-to-door salesmen. Placed into historical perspective, there was even a time when the novel was described as a frivolous avocation next to the time-honored epic poem, drama and poetry. When eventually the novel reached its peak, film began contending a position that made the academic study of movies respectable, while television only recently gained a foot into the door and the study of *telenovelas* is in its infancy. It is high time to realize that rock music attracts so many people for a reason: it can play powerful music, contain striking lyrics, and retain memorable performances, therefore meriting our full critical attention.

A second point to consider is the assumption that because rock is marketed by an international entertainment industry it is therefore extraneous to the most vital concerns of Spanish youth. Obviously, a foreign language and fame never presented any difficulty when it meant acknowledging the importance of Petrarca for Garcilaso de la Vega, of the Italian neo-realist films for the fifties in Spain, or of jazz and even opera for many novels of previous generations.

A similar point is that commercial products, as most of the famous groups usually become, are alien to authenticity and conserve only weak tremors of their original shattering power. How can anything remain oppositional which is a bestseller or at the top of the charts?[7] The most appropriate comparison is with religion, which makes radical demands for life transformation that are heard by many but followed by few. For most, religion is only a Sunday feel-good activity, but for some it has deep transformative effects.

Yet we must understand that there is a wave of rejection that comes from these novels to the orderly social life that we share as scholars. There is a vast gap that is not easy to overcome. Rock still has questioning power: questioning us. Kurt Cobain wrote in his notebooks, not long before his death by suicide (even if there is a theory that he was murdered), the following:

> Hope I die before I turn into Pete Townshend. [The lead guitarist of The Who.]
> At this point in our uh, *career* [underlined in the original], before hair loss treatment and bad credit. I've decided that I have no desire to do an interview with *Rolling Stone*. We couldn't't benefit from it because the Average *Rolling Stone* reader is a middle aged ex hippie—turned hippiecrite who embraces the past as "the glory days," and has a kinder, gentler, more adult approach towards liberal conservatism. The average *Rolling Stone* reader has always denied the underworlds musical options unless it becomes an obviously safe commodity. (269)

We hope we are not presenting here safe commodities, but live intellectual wires such as Etxebarria, Mañas and Loriga. Therefore, in this book, we wish to explore the very perspicuous confluence of novel, film, and rock that takes place in Spain in the nineties and after, but without claiming this as a general and defining characteristic of all writers of the period. The claim, instead, is that rock in literature and the movies is a new and significant cultural event requiring close study and placing new demands on literary and cultural criticism because, as explained above, it is the most salient expression of a generation that has entered into a radically different world.

Gonzalo Navajas' essay which opens this book describes the transition from the solidarity of humanism, represented by Jean-Paul Sartre, to an anti-ethical and individualist search, as seen in Mañas and Loriga. Also the register of language has changed, becoming more inclusive and tending towards the minimalism that we associate in the United States with Bret Easton Ellis, Frederick Barthelme, Ann Beattie, and Raymond Carver.

One could fall into the temptation of attributing a point of origin to novelists such as Ellis—his *American Psycho* (1991) is invoked frequently in *Historias del Kronen* (1994), even if perhaps Ellis' *Less than Zero* (1985) is more of a model—and seeing the Spanish scene as derivative. But Paul Begin in his essay, "Music and Subculture Practice in Peninsular Gen X Narrative," indicates we should not conceive of the rock and youth culture in Spain as a subculture of the British Invasion and the globalization of the United States and British music industry, but instead use Lawrence Grossberg's terms of "affective alliance" or "hyperalliance," which better convey the appropriation and rapid integration into Spanish culture of these international movements. Begin sees most of rock, but especially punk, as a rebellion against the cultural reaffirmation of power of the higher classes, what Antonio Gramsci accurately described under the term "hegemony." One can easily confirm this aggressive oppositional nature of punk by reading Craig O'Hara's *The Philosophy of Punk: More than Noise*, in which he affirms, for example, that "punk is gut rebellion and change . . . Punk is a formidable voice of opposition" (41). The excitement punk generated can still be faintly perceived in the many outrageous (for their time, but some still for today) photographs found in *Punk: The Definitive Record of a Revolution*, by Stephen Colegrave and Chris Sullivan. Alaska brought to Madrid the punk spirit after a visit to London, as is well documented in Rafa Cervera's *Alaska y otras historias de la movida*, with a prologue by Pedro Almodóvar. The problem, as Begin sees it, is that any form of rebellion and vanguard easily becomes co-opted and looses power when successful; nevertheless, punk did have an impact in Spain and was creative, offensive, transgressive, and fun. Punk's effect in Spanish culture can be compared to waves crashing on the shore: while each wave fizzles away in foam and recoils into the sea, it is only to return with renewed vigor.

With the British invasion of rock music, came the flood of books translated from United States' authors associated with Dirty Realism, such as Raymond Carver, Jayne Anne Phillips, and Tobias Wolff. Cintia Santana's essay, "What We Talk About When We Talk About Dirty Realism in Spain," insightfully shows that we should be cautious when speaking of the presence of these writers in Spain, since the translations, in spite of being of what was called *Dirty Realism*, used a standard Spanish that erased from the original all indexes of class, race, and region, always difficult to convey and perhaps more politically charged in Spain than in the United States. This essay raises the question not only of how insufficiently known models can still exert a decisive influence, but also suggests that an examination of novels in this period may in fact encounter fewer examples of class conflict than in the novels of the fifties.

Yet there are also continuities (as Ortega knew) in what appears as a radical generational break. Samuel Amago, in "Can Anyone Rock Like We Do? Or, How the Gen X Aesthetic Transcends the Age of the Writer," studies how the culture of sex, drugs, and rock and roll can be traced in Spain earlier than the Generation X, and finds an important role for controlled substances in the works of Juan Goytisolo, Carmen Martín Gaite, Juan José Millás, and Carlos Cañete. To these names one could add José María del Valle Inclán and endless drinking among many poets of the fifties. In Amago's essay it is important to perceive that the model offered by rock is embraced not as a foreign lifestyle, but as reaffirmation of what had already native roots in the Spanish peninsula. When Carlos in *Historias del Kronen* wants to speak only of "de sexo, de drogas y de rocanrol" (205) (of sex, drugs, and rock-and-roll), he has much in common with previous writers—sex and drugs—as proven by Amago, but Carlos introduces the differential element that completes the Generation X's sacred trilogy: rock-and-roll.[8]

One difficulty in approaching the novels we study here is that they can be ironical, satirical, or parodical, as many of the acts put on by rock bands among fire and smoke. Luis Martín-Cabrera, in "Apocalypses Now: The End of Spanish Literature? Reading *Payasos en la lavadora* as Critical Parody," provides an excellent example of a novel in which traditional values are shattered, but within a rhetoric of complicity and evasive implication. In Geoffrey T. Holtz's well-known book, *Welcome to the Jungle: The Why Behind "Generation X,"* he writes:

> Some notable changes in the message of rock music have also sprung up. Rock-and-roll songs have long featured an us-against-them theme, with the idea that through perseverance, ideals, or love, people can change the world. But one notion that runs through many of today's new music acts is me-against-myself . . . What hits home with such extremes of self-deprecation is that the listener isn't quite sure if the singer is serious or just putting us on. (201)

While *Payasos en la lavadora* shows an author who makes us doubt if he is serious or just pulling our leg, Elizabeth Scarlett's essay, "Not Your Father's Rock and Roll," provides two detailed examples of how rock appears in two authors not usually associated with this music, in Antonio Muñoz Molina and Manuel Rivas. In these cases, though, one can notice the difference that Holtz indicated: Muñoz Molina and Rivas echo the earlier era of rock music. Scarlett's close reading of several texts reveals how rock music becomes so charged with meaning—social, emotional, ideological—that very brief references to it are crucial to grasp the complexities of the interactions described definitely in a serious manner in these texts.

Randolph Pope, in "Between Rock and the Rocking Chair," reminds us of how careful we must be in extending an anecdote, as it appears in a novel, into a general historical representation. He discusses the epilogue of *Historias del Kronen,* arguing that one of its functions is precisely to work against a totalizing interpretation and the reduction of a whole generation to the characteristics of a few of its members. At the same time, by stressing the importance of the transition from the main text of the novel to its epilogue, he shows how the individualistic project of the Generation X was frequently absorbed back into society, failing to transform its basic structure, even if eroding it.

Matthew Marr also writes about *Historias del Kronen* in "Realism and the Rocks," comparing Mañas to Ernest Hemingway, and the Generation X to the Lost Generation. He establishes deep diachronic roots for *Historias*, while reminding us that the apparent slackers in the nineties are fighting for individual rights and resisting the government's attempts to control their behavior. Both Mañas and Hemingway are reacting against legislation that has made the consumption of alcohol and drugs harder—Prohibition in the case of Hemingway and new laws to control the use of drugs and alcohol in Spain, after an early period of *laissez faire.*

A good number of novels are about being in a car, driving long distances, and feeling the thrill of the slim and relative freedom of speed and choosing directions in a map. Here again, there is a long tradition of travel literature in Spain that includes the *Quixote* as well as novels by Pío Baroja, Camilo José Cela and Juan Goytisolo. But Jorge Pérez, in "Reckless Driving," describes how the road rock 'n' roll novels created a unique space outside the routine of daily life, even if being on the road seldom can offer a transformative social experience and it actually can bring to the fore gender issues.

Kathryn Everly, in "Television, Violence and Power," explores the importance of television for this generation, which has grown up in its glow, becoming familiar with the medium and indulging in the virtual travel it allows, but also capable of insightful criticism. By counterposing Loriga's development of a story he wrote as a novel, *Caídos del cielo,* and then directed as a movie, *La pistola de mi hermano,* a story in which television is a muffled protagonist, Everly shows the strengths, weaknesses and even dangers of all three genres and modes of production. Many questions, of course, remain open, since the ever-growing variety of offerings leaves space for exceptions while the freedom one must allow for readers and spectators to choose their poison should make us very aware of the differences between description, opinion, and normativity.

The previous essay is complemented by Christine Henseler's "Rocking Around Ray Loriga's *Héroes*," an examination of how video clips provide not just material to sample, but a mode of conceiving existence which has radically transformative consequences for the novel, where the real and the virtual mix in a narrative in which the usual chronological line has been shattered as inconsequential and alien to the youthful experience of reality.

We conclude the book with a section that examines two instances of the visual, of crucial importance for the Generation X. Curiously in Gabriela Bustelo's *Veo veo* (I See I See), as Nina Molinaro explains, vision is meshed with rock music which is constantly accompanying the action and providing a commentary in an updated version of the Greek chorus.

Similarly, Linda Gould-Levine, in "Saved by Art?" on the 2003 movie *Te doy mis ojos* (I Give You My Eyes), examines how images, in this case museum paintings, serve as a catalyst to present the topic of domestic violence and highlight gender issues. The movie had great public success, indicating a strong support for the still needed reaffirmation of women's freedom from the patriarchal domination which long prevailed in Spain. Above all, this essay shows how the characters make paintings in a museum—an earlier form of virtual reality—part of their lives, threatening or inspirational, according to the points of view of the struggling couple, since ultimately these images on canvas become decisive in their lives.

The times, they are a'changing. The open and blunt expression of their rock-immersed lives by several key writers of the Generation X may have exhausted itself as fireworks that lasted too long, yet it opened up a scene of revelation that created new possibilities, not only for culture, but also for the life of the generations that will follow us, if we can light their fire.

Notes

1. In his very detailed study of how the Generation of 27 was formed, Andrew Anderson shows conclusively that what began as a vast group of poets became decanted into a few by the power of anthologies, especially by Gerardo Diego's *Poesía española: Antología 1915–1931*, a book published in 1932. See especially p. 81 of Anderson's *El veintisiete en tela de juicio*.

2. Part IX of the *Cambridge History of Spanish Literature* is appropriately called "In and Out of Franco Spain," with almost every chapter referring to what Ortega would have

called the structure of living under a dictatorship: "The Literature of Franco Spain, 1939–1975," "Prose in Franco Spain," "Poetry in Franco Spain," "Theatre in Franco Spain," and "Film and Censorship under Franco, 1937–1975." Innumerable other books and articles express this condition, such as Jordi Gracia García and Miguel Ángel Ruiz Carnicer's *La España de Franco (1939–1975)*, which highlights the many complexities of the Franco period, rich in ambiguity, and with many undercurrents that continued the culture of the first part of the century and prepared the future democratic society. But the fact remains that the title still speaks of a united country dominated by one figure, which was the dominant ideology to be shattered in the late seventies and eighties, as superbly described by Teresa Vilarós in *El mono del desencanto: Una crítica cultural de la transición española (1973–1993)*.

3. Teresa Vilarós, in "The Novel Beyond Modernity," puts the relation with the past as follows: "Novels of the democratic state negotiated the rift between the two former, antagonistic constructs of Spanish difference by wiping them out" (254).

4. Tara Brabazon cites the Pet Shop Boys, "My October Symphony," which speaks about an international change "from revolution to revelation." She comments: "This lyric traced a movement away from credible, authentic, public domain politics to the realm of affect, identity politics and change-fatigue" (1).

5. Hank Bordowitz in *Turning Points in Rock and Roll*, devotes a chapter to 1946–55, the period in which "Les Paul Invents the Solid-Body Electric Guitar, Close Miking, the Multitrack Studio, and a Bunch of Other Stuff" (23–33). Bordowitz explains that "As the technology revolutionized the instrument, it started to change the way players—especially young players—approached the instrument. With the guitar amplified, it changed the need for large bands to generate the volume required for groups to entertain dancers (and compete with drummers). Beyond that, the guitar, which had primarily been a rhythm instrument, now could develop an expressive voice as a solo instrument" (27). Another chapter, of course, is "1965: Bob Dylan Goes Electric at the Newport Folk Festival" (125–33). Added to the improvements in television (where Alaska introduced in the 80s some glorious songs in La Bola de Cristal), radio, and portable players, the change was technologically driven and international in scope. In Spain the time of the lonely poet singing political songs accompanied by his acoustic guitar, as the members of the *Nova cançó* or the Latin American *nueva canción*, was over (Boyle 294).

6. Not all agree, of course, with the ample tolerance and unconcern with moral values that the novels of the Generation X reveal. A chapter in a book by Sebastian Neumeister, which includes examples of German, American, British, and Spanish novels, is titled "Bankrott der Moral: Die Generation X und der Untergang des Abendlandes," ("The Bankruptcy of Moral: The Generation X and the Decline of the West"), beginning with references to Nietzsche's concept of beyond good and evil, Paul Feyerabend's "anything goes," and ending with an ominous reference to Oscar Spengler's classic book on the forthcoming decline of the West. The collection of his essays, published in 2004, celebrated Neumeister's 65th birthday.

7. Leslie Haynsworth states that 'the various artists—like the members of R.E.M., Nirvana, and Green Day—who have emerged from subcultural enclaves into the national spotlight generally insist that this shift in status and positioning has not altered their identities or their artistic vision in any significant way" (43). But she adds: "The increasing absorption of Gen X values and practices into mainstream youth culture signifies a perhaps irrevocable loss of pure countercultural status, which is troubling for a movement that is self-defined through its oppositional stance" (57).

8. For this topic there is ample and irrefutable evidence in *The Mammoth Book of Sex, Drugs & Rock'n'Roll*, edited by Jim Driver.

Works Cited

Anderson, Andrew. *El veintisiete en tela de juicio*. Madrid: Gredos, 2005.

Benjamin, Walter. "Paris, Capital of the Nineteenth Century." *Reflections*. Ed. Peter Demetz, Trans. Edmund Jephcott. New York: Schocken Books, 1986. 146–62.

Bordowitz, Hank. *Turning Points in Rock and Roll*. New York: Citadel Press, 1994.

Boyle, Catherine. "The Politics of Popular Music: On the Dynamics of New Song." *Spanish Cultural Studies: An Introduction*. Ed. Helen Graham and Jo Labanyi. Oxford and New York: Oxford University Press, 1995. 291–94.

Brabazon, Tara. *From Revolution to Revelation: Generation X, Popular Memory, and Cultural Studies*. Aldershot, England: Ashgate, 2005.

Bustelo, Gabriela. *Veo veo*. Barcelona: Anagrama, 1996.

Cardwell, Richard. "The Poetry of *Modernismo* in Spain." *The Cambridge History of Spanish Literature*. Ed. David T. Gies. Cambridge and New York: Cambridge University Press, 2004. 500–12.

Cervera, Rafa. *Alaska y otras historias de la movida*. Barcelona: De Bolsillo, 2003.

Cobain, Kurt. *Kurt Cobain Journals*. New York: Riverhead Books, 2002.

Colegrave, Stephen and Chris Sullivan. *Punk: The Definitive Record of a Revolution*. New York: Thunder's Mouth Press, 2001.

De la Iglesia, Alex. *Payasos en la lavadora*. Barcelona: Planeta, 1997.

Diego, Gerardo. *Poesía española. Antología 1915–1931*. Madrid, Editorial Signo, 1932.

Driver, Jim, ed. *The Mammoth Book of Sex, Drugs & Rock'n'Roll*. New York: Carroll & Graf Publishers, 2001.

Ellis, Bret Easton. *American Psycho*. New York: Vintage Books, 1991.

_____. *Less than Zero*. New York: Simon and Schuster, 1985.

Etxebarria, Lucía. *Amor, curiosidad, prozac y dudas*. Barcelona: Plaza y Janés, 1997.

Gracia García, Jordi and Miguel Ángel Ruiz Carnicer. *La España de Franco (1939–1975): Cultura y vida cotidiana*. Madrid: Editorial Síntesis, 2001.

Grassian, Daniel. *Hybrid Fictions: American Literature and Generation X*. Jefferson, NC, and London: McFarland & Company, 2003.

Haynsworth, Leslie. "'Alternative' Music and the Oppositional Potential of Generation X Culture." *GenXegesis: Essays on "Alternative" Youth (Sub)Culture*. Ed. John M. Ulrich and Andrea L. Harris. Madison, WI: University of Wisconsin Press, 2003. 41–58.

Holtz, Geoffrey T. *Welcome to the Jungle: The Why behind "Generation X."* New York: St. Martin's Griffin, 1995.

Loriga, Ray. *Caídos del cielo*. Barcelona: Plaza y Janés, 1997.

_____. *Héroes*. Barcelona: Plaza y Janés, 1993.

_____. *Lo peor de todo*. Madrid: Debate, 1992.

Mainer, José Carlos. "Spanish Literature between the Franco and post-Franco Eras." *The Cambridge History of Spanish Literature*. Ed. David T. Gies. Cambridge and New York: Cambridge University Press, 2004. 687–93.

Mañas, José Ángel. *Historias del Kronen*. Ed. Germán Gullón. Barcelona: Destino, 1998.

Martín Gaite, Carmen. *Entre visillos*. Barcelona: Destino, 1958.

Neumeister, Sebastian. *Literarische Wegzeichen: Von Minnesang zur Generation X*. Heidelberg: Universitätsverlag Winter, 2004. 319–32.

O'Hara, Craig. *The Philosophy of Punk: More than Noise*. London: AK Press, 1999.

Ortega y Gasset, José. *En torno a Galileo*. In *Obras completas*, vol. V. 7th edition. Madrid: Revista de Occidente, 1970.

Pérez Galdós, Benito. *Fortunata y Jacinta*. 2 vols. 6th edition. Ed. Francisco Caudet. Madrid: Cátedra, 2000.

Sánchez Ferlosio, Rafael. *El Jarama*. Barcelona: Destino, 1956.

Vilarós, Teresa. *El mono del desencanto: Una crítica cultural de la transición española (1973–1993)*. Madrid: Siglo XXI, 1998.

_____. "The Novel Beyond Modernity." *The Cambridge Companion to the Spanish Novel: From 1600 to the Present*, Ed. Harriet Turner and Adelaida López de Martínez. Cambridge and New York: Cambridge University Press, 2003. 251–63.

Part I

Rocking the Academy: Generation X Narratives

◆ 1

A Distopian Culture:
The Minimalist Paradigm in the Generation X

Gonzalo Navajas

The Humanist Framework

In 1946, Jean-Paul Sartre published a controversial and highly influential work, *L'existentialisme est un humanisme* (*Existentialism Is a Humanism*), in which he provides a comprehensive foundation to his philosophical program, which is based on the rejection of universal axiological principles. In the book, he attempts to link his program to the humanist project that has been a central focus of modern thought from Goethe and Voltaire to the present. Sartre does not pretend to restore and save the classical tradition of thought, but he, none-theless, establishes a connection between the nihilism and solipsism of his philosophy and the history of humanism, which, at least theoretically, posits a common and solidary destiny for all humanity. Without renouncing his negative critical methodology, Sartre inserts his philosophy within the modern paradigm in which the humanist ideal supplies the central justification.

From this perspective, Antoine Roquentin, Sartre's nihilist figure of *La nausée* (*Nausea*), would ultimately propose a renovated and more genuine view of the human condition. His critical examination of the philosophical tradition takes on an extraordinary dimension since, after assuming the burden of a past that he considers false and illegitimate, he undertakes the task of exploring new venues that would be exempt from prior metaphysical presuppositions. He thus claims to uncover a freer form of humanism that potentially can provide a more valid path for a self that, in a Nietzschean manner, has overcome the restrictions of the past. For Roquentin, the old version of humanism is dead, but he can still act according to a new version of humanism in which the only framework of reference is absolute freedom without limits: "l'homme, sans aucun appui et sans aucun secours, est condamné à chaque instant à inventer l'homme" (*L'existentialisme* 38) (Man, without any support and without any assistance, is doomed to invent man at every moment). More than fifty years later, this radical proposal still resonates actively in the foremost critical movements of the end of the twentieth century that derive from the negative hermeneutics of the Sartrian model: deconstruction and postmodernity. In them, negation is an initial phase that eventually leads to the exploration of new forms of ethical and axiological assertion. Thus, these developments make apparent that the humanist horizon, albeit reconfigured and redefined, cannot be excluded from the contemporary philosophical and aesthetic debate.

The Sartrian parallel is useful to frame conceptually significant segments of the current contemporary cultural condition. In particular, it provides a suggestive methodological tool for the analysis of the works of the authors of the so-called Spanish Generation X that produce their works in the last decade of the twentieth century and the beginning of the new century. For these authors, the Sartrian dichotomy between old and new humanism is irrelevant. That opposition implies a dialectical exchange between past and present cultural paradigms in which one is bound to prevail over the other. However, for these authors, one component of the dialectical opposition is missing and thus the confrontation cannot take place. As the narrator of Angel Mañas's *Ciudad rayada,* Carlos, asserts, those who remain concerned with the cultural tradition are "fossils" that lack the conceptual and vital instruments to understand the current cultural situation and adapt creatively to it. Roquentin rejected the conventional humanist project because it relied on values that had become a subterfuge used to mask a strategy of ideological domination, but his rejection was the consequence of a rigorous examination of the cultural tradition. On the other hand, for the narrator of Mañas' novel, that humanist enterprise is not even worthy of consideration since he has never been exposed to it and he lacks the motivation to know it: "A veces, cuando me encuentro con alguno [humanista], tengo la impresión de que vivimos en planetas diferentes, como si nunca hubieran sido como yo . . . Siempre he pensado que los fósiles son unos hijosdelagrandísimaputa" (*Ciudad rayada* 145) (Sometimes, when I run into one of them [humanists], I have the impression that we live in different planets, as if they had never been like me . . . I have always thought that those fossils are real big sons of bitches).

In the narrator's language, the "fossils" are attached to a cultural paradigm that is obsolete and does not deserve his attention. Roquentin communicated actively with the icons of the humanist tradition and, at least partially, he could appropriate portions of their work and thought in order to transform them and modify them according to his own conceptual proposals. The cultural unconscious of Roquentin—who in this case functions as Sartre's alter ego—is nourished by a vast repertoire of texts that include, among others, the works of Hegel, Marx, Bergson, and Husserl as well as Flaubert and Proust. He differs from them, but he is aware of their significance in cultural history and, in the case of Marx and Flaubert in particular, he sees in them a seminal inspiration for his own ideas. For Sartre, the conventional systematization and evaluation of western intellectual history is deficient and it needs to be corrected radically. His project is comprehensive since it attempts to replace a disqualified system with new principles that serve as guidelines for a new mode of reinsertion of the existential self within a reconfigured world. The existential negative dialectic involves a complex process of analysis and examination as well as a definition and characterization of the new mode that emerges after that process of epistemological and ethical reconstruction. The negativism of the process is only preliminary since it involves a complete *Aufhebung* of the cultural past but at the same time it implies an acknowledgment of the necessity of its existence. In fact, that recognition also implies that the Sartrian self, including its most solipsistic expression, Roquentin, cannot exist without its link to the past. The break-up between past and present modes is, therefore, not complete since, in order to exist, the new self depends, in a Hegelian manner, on that which it denies and from which it separates itself.

The relation of the Generation X to the humanist tradition is different. The narrator of Mañas's *Historias del Kronen*, Carlos, defines it graphically when he refers to "las viejas historias del pasado" (the old stories from the past) and he asserts that "el pasado es siempre aburrido" (*Historias* 83) (the past is always boring). Unlike Roquentin, Carlos cannot dissect and reject systematically the humanist paradigm because he lacks familiarity with it and he acknowledges its existence only through sporadic allusions without engaging in a dialogue with it. His position, which matches the position of the rest of the authors that comprise his generation, is the consequence of the dissolution of the great paradigms of history that the existentialist, post-Marxist, and deconstructionist epistemologies have brought about. Those schools of thought took a combative stance against what they viewed as delegitimized and obsolete systems. In a different manner, Carlos's generation adopts a passive and noncommittal position towards what they simply see as an accomplished fact that is beyond debate. Sartre's nothingness and Derrida, Althusser, and Balibar's critical unmasking of historical ideologies originate in a confrontation between an isolated self and an overwhelming cultural history and they imply a process of intellectual and personal struggle between contrary positions. For the writers of the Generation X, negation is devoid of all attributes of ethical greatness and it has become a customary and banal *Lebensstil* that does not need further elaboration.

A self without attachments to history and deprived of ethical expectations is destined to be situated in a time framework that is located strictly in the present, deprived of bonds to the past, and not motivated to project himself or herself toward the future. The characters of the novels of Mañas and Loriga lack a program of action and they move through the streets of big cities such as Madrid without any specific design about their lives. They know that the present replicates the past and that the future will not differ from previous times. They display a self that is deprived of all the traces of history and that has itself as its only point of reference.

That *presentness* or strict placement of the text in the present time is reflected in the narrative mode of these works in which temporal multidimensionality is absent. In the case of *Historias del Kronen*, for instance, the text often eliminates the distance between the time of narration and the chronological time of the events that are being narrated and it develops a close overlap between the two, thus minimizing or eliminating the narrator's conscience that in the novel appears as being an empty and flat surface on which nothing seems to leave any imprints. Carlos observes events and situations in a neutral and remote manner without ever making value judgments about them and without establishing connections between those events in the present and others that happened at another time. For him, events certainly take place, but they do not seem to have any ontological or signifying entity and thus they do not remain in his memory. Carlos reveals a thorough amnesia of both time and space that produces an amalgamation of facts and information lacking well-defined structure and direction: "Me levanto y miro el reloj: son las once y veinte. Voy al salón y cojo el teléfono. ¿Sí? Oye, Carlos, que soy yo, Miguel. ¿Te he despertado? . . . ¿Llamas tú a Roberto? . . . Sí, yo le llamo . . . Pues hasta las siete . . . Cuelgo el teléfono y me meto otra vez en la cama. Tres horas más tarde me vuelvo a despertar. Abro los ojos y me quedo mirando el techo un buen rato. Luego me masturbo" (49) (I get up and I look at the watch: it is eleven twenty. I go to the living room and I answer the phone. Hello? Listen, Carlos, it is me, Miguel. Did I wake you up? Are you calling Roberto? . . . Yes, I call him . . . Then until seven . . . I hang up the phone and I get once again into bed. Three hours later I wake up again. I open my eyes and I remain looking at the ceiling for a long while. Then I masturbate). Carlos accurately transcribes the reality around him as if it took place without him apparently contributing to its outcome and as if he and his environment were permanently divorced from each other.

The reductionism of time and the individual conscience is associated with the minimization of the cultural dimension. Carlos does not appear to have a personal history or a consistent biographical trajectory and at the same time he does not seem aware of the repertoire of signs that shape the community in which he functions. Thus, the "weakening of Being," the ontological devaluation that, according to Gianni Vattimo, characterizes the core of the contemporary cultural condition reaches in Mañas a well-defined actualization (Vattimo, 36). Self, narrative voice, time, space, and language have been reduced to their most schematic expression. Furthermore, unlike in other discourses of the negation of the self, in this case, this reduction is viewed as a fatal and unavoidable fact without the subject seemingly expressing its disagreement or protest.

The textual focalization on a devalued and trivialized present does not prevent the emergence of small realms of assertion where the self can find immediate satisfaction of his or her desires. For example, the narrator of Ray Loriga's *Tokio ya no nos quiere* shares with the narrator of *Historias del Kronen* a narrow but nonetheless real horizon of expectations. Within these limitations, he is able to create a small but privileged space where he can realize his program of gratification for his senses and his conscience: "Estamos borrachos de sake, rodeados de zapatillas de colores y perfectos cortes de pelo, no se ve el rastro de ninguna religión, sea la que sea, a más de quince calles, nadie dice nada que podamos comprender, las tiendas están abiertas y los bancos están todos cerrados. El cielo debe ser en realidad algo muy parecido a esto" (243) (We are drunk with sake, surrounded by colorful slippers and perfect haircuts, there is not a single trace of a religion of any kind, at a distance of more than fifteen streets, no one says anything that we can understand, the stores are open and the banks are all closed. Heaven must be in fact something very close to this). This diminished version of Eden does not promise access to a heightened state of bliss, but it offers instead a reversal of the values and principles that may be conventionally associated with paradise and personal satisfaction. The elimination of religion, as well as of money and routine human communication may originate, by default, the only possible paradise that this philosophy of limits can offer. The narrator is resigned to the impossibility of affecting the contemporary cultural wasteland and instead he only aspires to carve a small but personal niche within it.

In *Héroes*, also authored by Loriga, this search for an individualized Eden follows the troubled journey of the leading character after he has forsaken his previous marks of identity and he has rejected as an unacceptable burden the realization of a new configuration of himself. Once again, the scope of this personal Eden is narrowed to a minimal configuration. The protagonist of the novel only searches for a small space where he can listen to his music and where he can attempt to pursue his undefined goals. Unlike that of other travelers, his journey does not lead to a new continent or country in a way that would replicate the conventional path followed by many other travelers or immigrants in the past. His expectations have been drastically reduced and, instead of a new nation and society, he only dreams of the smallest of places: "decidí que lo único que necesitaba era una habitación pequeña donde poder buscar mis propias señales" (15) (I decided that the only thing that I needed was a small room where I could look for my own signs of identity). This "small room" does not even need to correspond to a concrete physical space and may be just a construction of his mind. In fact, the character identifies this room as an essentially shifting and unstable space, a subliminal *locus* that he visualizes ideally as a song. The immaterial sounds and lyrics of popular music prove to him more reliable than any other possible space. It is not surprising that David Bowie appears as the emblematic icon of this territory, a figure with whom he can identify and that he sees as endowed with redeeming attributes. The utopian dimension reappears tentatively, reconfigured here not according to abstract concepts and terms—like in the twentieth-century versions of utopia—but within the more immediate and accessible realm of rock and roll music: "Si pudiera vivir dentro de una canción para siempre todas mis desgracias serían hermosas" (127) (If I could live inside a song forever all my misfortunes would be beautiful).

The search for an epistemological and ethical *Heimat*, which has guided the trajectory of central segments of twentieth-century thought from Unamuno and Bloch to Vattimo, Eugeni Trías and Cioran, is reconfigured, in the case of *Héroes*, as a powerful yearning for a provisional relief from the misfortunes of everyday life (see, for instance, Bloch, *Spirit* 277; Cioran *History* 107). The pursuit of the above-mentioned thinkers does not achieve a resolution and it ends typically in indeterminacy and ambiguity. However, the process of the search *per se* is illuminating and it expands the horizons of the searcher because it uncovers areas of the human conscience that were not known before. The legitimacy of the search is found in the process itself rather than in the final outcome. The narrator of *Héroes* as well as of the other figures of the Generation

X does not aspire to acquire new knowledge, but only to appease an anguished mind that, despite its efforts, is set adrift in a turbulent myriad of signs that elude its understanding and control.

The New Economy of Language

Supported by this view of the self and its position within a diminished world, the novelists of the Generation X generate a new cultural mode that is opposed to the established world of high culture, strictly dominated by the canonical written and literary medium. This new mode can be characterized as a counter-paradigm of minimalist culture and it is constituted by several features that define its nature. The first one is the redefinition of the iconic figures and constitutive signs of classical culture. The rare allusions that are made to that culture occur in a parodic or ironic manner. *Ciudad rayada*, for instance, engages in a process of defamiliarization with regard to the most central text of Spanish literature, *Don Quixote*, which is visualized through the eyes of a young man for whom the protagonists of Cervantes's masterpiece are absurd and incomprehensible. For instance, when referring to the teaching of the book in his class in high school, he says: "aparte de que el que un pavo [Don Quijote] se raye y vea molinos de viento y cosas así no es algo que me parezca fascinante. Pavos así de rayados los hay a patadas. Vamos, y mucho más" (189) (Besides that a weirdo [Don Quixote] becomes mad and sees windmills and things like that it is not something that I find fascinating. Weirdos crazy like that you can find them by the hundreds, I mean, and much more).

The well-known formula by Shlovski to create a new kind of socially critical fiction is used in this instance in order to reconstitute the dimensions of the undisputed classical icon to within the limits of contemporary human types that are commonly found in the streets of Madrid. A similar defamiliarizing procedure is used when referring to the monuments of the city that for him lack aesthetic or vital appeal: "el centro [de la ciudad] estaba lleno de edificios monumentales kon estatuas ke no pintan nada encima de los tejados: kaballos kon alas, gordas kon kasko y lanza, kabezas de kokodrilos; kosas ke parecen de tripi y demuestran lo rayados ke estaban los madrileños de antes" (*Ciudad* 177) (The center [of the city] was full of monumental buildings with meaningless statues on their roofs: horses with wings, fat ladies with a helmet and spear, crocodile heads; crazy things that show how out of it were the Madrid people from the past). The *V-Effekt*, the separation between the artistic object and the spectator, which in the Brechtian aesthetic paradigm serves the purpose of highlighting the inequities of history, is presented here as a technical device to make apparent the complete disconnection that Carlos thinks exists between a glorious historical past and the trivialized but to him more authentic and vital present. The lack of continuity between past and present is thus foregrounded and the narrator deliberately does not display any desire of ever bridging the gap between the two.

Another feature of the minimalist cultural mode of the Generation X is its adherence to a linguistic economy that fits appropriately the more schematic and narrower conceptual repertoire within which it operates. Since this mode rejects the norms and texts of the classical canonical paradigm, its linguistic model places itself outside the literary medium and it creates its own defining terminology and procedures. Its representative texts use a superabundance of dialogue that reproduces faithfully the speech of the different street subcultures of the young and in particular the one linked to pop music. It is a speech characterized by its lack of conceptual abstraction and directness and by a fluid combination of Spanish and English which produces a new hybrid language that defines the cultural reality of the group and its icons: "El primer puente musical es un break-beat a 147 BPM. Luego llegan las melodías de bajos super ácidos que he sampleado de un viejo TB303, es flipante pensar que el 303, con el que el diyéi Pierre inventó el Acid House, había ya salido en Japón en 1977 cuando todavía estaban Dylan y sus colegas dando la vara en las radios . . . Poco a poco voy metiendo ritmos más machacones, con percusiones bien bestias" (*Ciudad*, 115). (The first musical number is a break-beat at 147BPM. Later it is the turn of the melodies with super acid bass tones that I have sampled from an old TB303, it is awesome to think that the 303, with which the DJ Pierre invented the Acid House, had already been out in Japan in 1977 when Dylan and his pals were still the big names in the radio . . . Little by little I begin to put on noisier rhythms, with really brutal percussions). Terms as "samplear," "flipante," "diyéi," which are direct adaptations from English, reveal that, for Carlos, the world of popular music has removed the barriers of linguistic purity that constrain the nature and environment of high academic culture. To him, that culture resists the inclusion of what it views as "barbarian" cultural manifestations that need to be opposed in order to preserve what Pierre Bourdieu calls the "rites d'institution," the prerogatives of the masters of cultural institutions (114). In its simplicity and immediacy, the texts of the young generation display a more flexible and inclusive concept of language, one that corresponds to a global view that is attuned to the reality of the instant and universal communication of the electronic age.

This economic view of the language in which expediency of communication prevails over aesthetic or stylistic criteria is also found in the characterization of fictional figures and the context in which they are situated. Physical descriptions and biographical profiles are kept to a minimum and thus the characters are transformed into schematic types with few individual traits. This responds to an anti-psychological view of characterization in which analytical depth is considered with suspicion as a mechanism to disguise reality. Thus the characters become interchangeable and they function as replaceable pieces in a network of signs in which they are another component among others without special significance. The texts of the Generation X signify the final step in the long process of fragmentation and dissolution of the self that follows the crisis of the principles of the classical representational novel in which the individualized completeness and distinctiveness of the characters was considered an essential component. The characters of Mañas, Loriga, and other writers of their group would represent the final stage of the undoing of the nature of the subject that begins with the criticism of Unamuno, Proust, and Pirandello about the identity of the self.

Since functionality and immediacy are the superior guiding principles, it is not surprising that the audiovisual means of communication become paramount in these texts. The shift to film, television, and the visual media in general as the emblematic media of our time signifies another reversal in the cultural hierarchy since for the characters of these works the written literary medium has lost the last remaining attributes of the aura that Benjamin attached to the aesthetic objects of high culture that he saw as being threatened by popular art. What Benjamin perceived as the emergence of a powerful process beginning with avant-garde art, has grown, with the advancement of the new technologies, into a fully established cultural and aesthetic condition that defines our time. All the characters and events of these novels clearly lack the aura that accompanies the monumental literary works of the past. The texts favor instead the objects and signs of the culture of the ephemeral that is prevalent in contemporary aesthetics.

The narrator of *Héroes*, for instance, openly declares its abhorrence of the mechanisms of conventional thought and reflexivity that he associates with intellectual routine and physical and mental decrepitude. The classical paradigm for him offers only restricting structures for a self that thrives on individual freedom and absolute opposition to rules and universal norms. His position is an assertion of personal liberation and an affirmation of his right to dictate his own rules in a cultural world that he considers limiting and obsolete because it does not seem to respond to the new premises of the contemporary condition. The highlighting in the novel of the images of television with its uninterrupted bombarding of objects and signs of an undifferentiated cultural wasteland devoid of meaningful signifiers is an illustration of the attachment of the new minimalist culture to provisional principles and values lacking any ontological dimension. The narrator's mind reproduces the fragmentation and triviality of the language of commercial television where the hierarchies, taxonomies, and evaluative principles of the high-culture literary medium are absent. In the following illustrative passage, his mental trajectory replicates a typical session of commercial television where the only criteria for selection are commercial and economic excluding any other consideration: "enfermedades, muertes, suerte, millones por casi nada en la televisión, disparos en la cabeza en la televisión, vendedoras de alfombras y de remedios contra la impotencia . . . , bancos, dinero, comisiones, intereses . . ." (78) (diseases, deaths, luck, millions for almost nothing on TV, shots in the head on TV, saleswomen of rugs and cures against impotence . . . banks, money, commissions, interests . . .).

This is the cultural framework where the narrator's mind moves. Although he is aware of its uselessness and absurdity, he is at the same time incapable of detaching himself effectively from its overpowering influence and thus he feels impotent to create a different language that would overcome the insufficiencies of the paradigm that, despite his efforts, still nurtures him. Like the central characters in other parallel texts, he is aware of the degrading nature of the visual medium that feeds him, and he uses various ironic procedures to establish a distance between himself and his environment. The quoted passage is an example, among others, of his capacity to evaluate critically the predominant cultural option which is also his own, but, at the same time, it is impossible for him to create alternatives with which to counter a language and concepts that, although he uses extensively, he does not consider genuinely his. It is precisely this lack of alternative proposals or venues what determines the axiological nature of the new culture. The general conceptual and linguistic minimalism is complemented by an anti-ethical orientation.

The Antiethical Counterproposal

The exploration of the validity of the moral option has been a predominant trend of thought since Nietzsche began, in *The Genealogy of Morals,* his critical analysis of conventional morality that he perceived as being based on submission to the tenets of privileged discourses (in particular, Christianity and the different rationalist systems). The evolution of intellectual history in the twentieth century has been determined to a considerable extent by the critical analysis of the concept of morality and, in particular during the second half of the century, the trend has been to pursue further Nietzsche's negation of moral normativity and to take it to its ultimate expression. From existentialism to deconstruction and postmodernity, philosophical and cultural discourse undertook a progressive devaluation of the previous foundations of moral principles and proposed the ultimate denial of the moral option as a disguise for ideological constructs. The last ramification of this gradual devaluation of the moral option can be seen in the works of the Generation X. As an alternative to the undoing of the mythical and false structures of traditional morality, Nietzsche created an ideal and utopian figure, the *Übermensch*, who supposedly was capable of overcoming the submissiveness and inertia of previous moral icons. Thus, Nietzsche negates, but he is also able to advance an ethical alternative that, in fact, becomes a more imperative axiological proposal than all the prior ones because it is centered on the excellence of a superior being who prevails over all other options.

No such alternative exists in the texts of the Generation X. In *Historias del Kronen*, Carlos scorns the weaknesses of his friends, ("sois todos unos débiles, en el fondo os odio a todos" (223) (you all are weaklings, the truth is I hate all of you), but he does not see himself as potentially incarnating the attributes of a singular figure that would not be subject to the frailties of his friends. He despises his friends, but he also has a negative view of himself and he is incapable of creating or imagining new ways of the configuration of human nature. Therefore, Carlos is only a partial and minimized *Übermensch*. He acknowledges the vacuity and inanity of the axiological options that contemporary culture makes available to him and the young members of his group, but he is not able to entertain the task of visualizing a counter-figure to *Das Man*, which is the debased contemporary human being, anonymous and without distinctive personality. Carlos is critical of the values, behavior, and language of the common man, but he remains one of them and he can only oppose to it his negation without any feasible alternatives. His only act of assertion is the violence against his friend Fierro, who suffers the consequences of his weakness and his inability to be like the rest of a group dominated by Carlos's strength and power: "Carlos tuvo la idea . . . él le golpeó la cabeza contra el lavabo. Si no le paramos, le hubiera destrozado la cabeza, . . . quería matarle, . . . luego se volvió loco, gritando que nos odiaba a todos, que éramos unos débiles . . ." (*Historias* 233) (It was Carlos's idea . . . he hit him on his head against the bathroom sink. If we do not stop him, he would have destroyed his head, . . . he wanted to kill him, . . . then he lost control, yelling that he hated all of us, that we were weak . . .).

Carlos acts according to a dystopian view of humanity and of the group to which he belongs. Gratuitous violence and rage are the symptoms of his scorn toward a prevailing cultural mode from which he feels alienated. With Theodor Adorno and Max Horkheimer, who were the first to unmask critically the banality of contemporary media culture, he refuses to recognize himself in a confusing repertoire of signs that are not his own (Adorno, 167). Those signs belong to an Other with whom he does not share any points of contact. However, differing from Adorno, who never abandoned the utopian humanist perspective as a counterweight to a determinist view of history, Carlos's ethical revolt ends in itself. It reveals the absolute lack of appeal of contemporary culture to the young generations. It also makes apparent that, unlike the Sartrian Roquentin, Carlos and his companions lack the sense of historical destiny to conceive a parallel alternative venue that could potentially rescue the humanist project from its final dissolution.

Works Cited

Adorno, Theodor and Max Horkheimer. *Dialectic of Enlightenment.* New York: Continuum, 1996.

Bloch, Ernst. *The Spirit of Utopia.* Trans. Anthony A. Nassar. Stanford: Stanford University Press, 2000.

Bourdieu, Pierre. *Homo Academicus.* Paris: Minuit, 1984.

Cioran, Emile M. *History and Utopia.* Trans. Richard Howard. Chicago: University of Chicago Press, 1998.

Loriga, Ray. *Héroes.* Barcelona: Plaza Janés, 1993.

_____. *Tokio ya no nos quiere.* Barcelona: Plaza Janés, 2000.

Mañas, Angel. *Ciudad rayada.* Madrid: Espasa, 1998.

_____. *Historias del Kronen.* Barcelona: Destino, 1994.

Sartre, Jean-Paul. *L'existentialisme est un humanisme.* Paris: Nagel, 1968.

_____. *La nausée.* Paris: Gallimard, 1994.

Vattimo, Gianni. *After Christianity.* Trans. Luca D'Isanto. New York: Columbia University Press, 2002.

◆ **2**

The Pistols Strike Again! On the Function of Punk in the Peninsular "Generation X" Fiction of Ray Loriga and Benjamín Prado

Paul D. Begin

The Clash, the Ramones, and the Sex Pistols, especially Sid Vicious—these are just some of the references to 1970s British and U.S. punk music that have made their way into Peninsular Generation X fiction of the 1990s. If this penchant for 1970s punk seems strange, contrived, or even "inauthentic," it is because these groups are often linked to a specific time and milieu. Meanwhile, these groups and their music are often examined as tightly bound subcultural units, whose subversive practices can be localized and explained within their specific contexts. Dick Hebdige's seminal study, *Subculture* (1979), is instructive in this respect. Now, however, these groups, representing as they do the "origins" of punk, are internationally recognized, commodified, and thus no longer constitute a "threat" to the status quo. Accordingly, a subcultural lens is not entirely helpful when considering the use of punk within a contemporary Peninsular context. Given the current "post-punk" context and the location (Spain), a more productive point of entry will be to examine how punk informs Generation X in general and how this confluence is manifested within Spanish cultural production. Specifically, this essay explores the intersection between punk, Generation X, and Spanish youth culture in two novels, *Lo peor de todo* (The Worst of All) (1992) and Benjamín Prado's *Nunca le des la mano a un pistolero zurdo* [Never Shake Hands with a Left-handed Gunman] (1995). What one finds in these works is an ad hoc appropriation of certain aspects of punk (its "blank" quality, the social critique, its negationism and nonconformity), qualities which speak to the more diffuse, international, and apolitical attitude of Generation X.

Punk, of course, is not a new phenomenon in Spain during the 1990s; it was already an influential force throughout the *movida*.[1] However, the *movida*'s appropriation of punk was selective. For example, one of punk's most significant impacts was on music and the music industry itself, but this did not transfer to Spain, since the state of rock was (and remains) significantly different than in the U.S. and Great Britain. Rock and roll is generally considered an "import" to the Peninsula, and John Hooper writes that, "in the field of pop and rock . . . Spain lags" (352).[2] Hooper is not alone: music critic Jesús Ordovás writes that the changes in taste in Spain are directly (albeit slowly) influenced by the popular styles in Europe and the United States (354). In the early years of rock in Spain, it was the Dúo Dinámico (Dynamic Duo) who introduced to the music of Paul Anka and Elvis, but these were covers, not even originals inspired by Elvis or others (Ordovás 355). Los Bravos had some international impact with their hit, "Black is Black," but the presence of other Spanish groups on the rock charts has been fleeting if at all. The only autochthonous rock to come out of Spain and have any impact are the hybrid forms of flamenco rock and flamenco pop, with groups such as El Último de la Fila (The Last in Line), Triana, Ketama, and La Terremoto (Earthquake). But apart from this, British and U.S. music is what controls the charts (Ordovás 359). In other words, Johnny Rotten's famous declaration—"The Pistols finished rock and roll. That was the last rock and roll band. It's all over now. Rock and roll is shit. It's dismal. Granddad danced to it"—would have had little meaning to participants in the *movida* (quoted in Szatmary, 237).

What did translate well into the *movida* was punk's do-it-yourself attitude toward art and its employment of an avant-garde style *bricolage* without the political overtones. Mark Allinson observes that Spanish youth culture in the 1980s followed punk's playful and corrosive attitude toward art, but that it "is distinct in that its emergence from the heady excesses of a suddenly liberated post-Franco Spain deprives it of the social signification as deviance or resistance often associated with youth subcultures" ("Construction" 265). Punk, in effect, became primarily an *aesthetic* influence throughout the *movida*. Alaska is an important figure in this respect. In comparing Spain's 1980s manifestation of punk with the British version, Allinson observes:

> The position of Madrid's underground version of punk culture is different in several important aspects. First, it is derivative, finding its inspiration in British punk and attempting to copy it. [. . .] Second, the *movida* is selective in its appropriation of

punk's cultural baggage. The aesthetic of punk and the element of bad taste and corrosive humor are taken up, but largely without the political or moral significance. ("Alaska" 227)

Throughout the *movida*, punks challenged the orthodoxy of expression and broke taboos, but with humor. Spanish punk, unlike its Anglo-American counterpart, also attracted people from all social classes (Allinson, "Alaska" 225). While punk was a strategy for protesting social conditions and mainstream values in Britain during the seventies, it actually helped the *movida* to move in the opposite direction during the eighties. The *movida* version of punk is not disquieting, but kitschified and fun. By 1984, the *movida* and its punk stylings were fully integrated into the mainstream, to the extent that the popular children's television program, "La bola de Cristal," featured Alaska as a sort of postmodern witch ("El librovisor") along with a group of puppets (akin to Jim Henson's Muppets) called the "Electroduendes," whose linguistic tics and ironic commentary more than hinted at their hedonistic excesses.[3] Allinson sums up well when he writes:

> The example of Alaska . . . demonstrates that, in the Spanish context, the commodification of subculture by the dominant culture is such that the labeling of subculture as deviant is rendered unnecessary. This in turn can be related to the precise social, historical, and cultural context of the irruption of punk onto the Spanish cultural scene. ("Alaska" 223)

Punk, as a commercial commodity, is stripped of its political potency and neutralized. It is decontextualized from its so-called working-class opposition. It is used only as an aesthetic device; it is trouble as fun.[4]

Then, in the 1990s, punk resurfaces, not just in Spain but also throughout North America and Western Europe within the context of "Generation X," as both a reference to a specific "generation" of youths as well as to a form of cultural production. It is not within the scope of this particular essay to offer a detailed genealogy of the term Generation X; however, some knowledge of its development will help shed light on how it informs the works in question.

The term itself, "Generation X," was first used by Robert Capa in the 1950s, as the title for a photojournalism spread which covered the lives of several twenty-somethings following World War II.[5] According to Capa, the project was "intended to present the problem of a generation . . . which has as its main problem 'going to war or not'" (qtd. in Ulrich 5). Nevertheless, the responses collected were not unanimous; Capa discovered that, in spite of their indifference to politics and the "adult" world as a whole, several respondents were positive about their individual futures (Ulrich 8). Ulrich concludes:

> In this way, Capa's use of the term "Generation X" carries with it no particular connotation beyond the fact that this particular generation remains 'unknown' [. . .] the letter X is meant here to function primarily as a placeholder, a variable or blank to be filled in later. (8)

This "unknown" quality of Generation X would later translate into a desire to avoid being identified, or "known." In 1964, Charles Hamblett and Jane Deverson seize upon the work of Capa (as well as Bertrand Russell) to publish a paperback book, entitled *Generation X*, about British mods and rockers with the aim of depicting a generation of youths that must grapple with what Douglas Coupland will eventually call an "accelerated culture," that is, a culture in which subjects will have "no unique, well-defined identity," partly because of their inability to stay ahead of the information curve (Ulrich 10). By now, the term Generation X is linked specifically to a loosely connected mass of youths who, in response to modernity's crushing pace and seemingly false values, have willingly placed themselves on the fringe of mainstream society.

It is no surprise that the term Generation X should interest participants in 1970s punk, where it begins to accrue more specific connotations, building upon this notion of blankness. In 1976, Billy Idol (William Broad), Tony James, John Towe, and Gene October form a punk band and name it Generation X, after the paperback by Deverson and Hamblett. Songs by Generation X, such as "Wild Youth" and "Your Generation," highlight a growing generational schism. While generational conflict is nothing new, what is unique in this case, observes Ulrich, "is the way the punk subculture repeatedly defines its generational identity in terms of 'blankness' or 'emptiness'" (13). For example, in "Pretty Vacant," the Sex Pistols sing:

> There's no point in asking us you'll get no reply
> Oh just remember and don't decide
> Got no reason it's all too much
> You'll always find us
> Out to lunch!
> We're so pretty, oh so pretty va—cant
> We're so pretty, oh so pretty va—cant
> Now and we don't care
>
> Don't ask us to attend cause we're not all there
> Don't pretend cause I don't care

Don't ask us to attend cause we're not all there
Don't pretend cause I don't care

Richard Hell, a punk rock musician from New York, along with his band, the Voidoids, famously expressed this feeling of absence in a 1977 song entitled "Blank Generation." In it, Hell clearly places himself within said generation, with the lyrics of "Blank Generation" gradually becoming more and more elliptical; the singer seeks to avoid being labeled by leaving empty spaces where modifiers would normally sit: "I belong to the generation _____ / but I can take it or leave it each time."[6] Generation X becomes defined, then, by its substantive lack, its desire to remain undefined, and thus demonstrates an evasive attitude toward any ready-made signifiers with roots in mainstream values. Blankness, or vacancy, thus arises as a form of rebellion against the values of the parent culture.

Perhaps the most important value eschewed and even mocked a propos of the parent generation is a sense of work ethic—the idea of maintaining a steady job, paying one's dues and following certain codes of conduct, and eventually retiring with a small pension, i.e., the traditional career arc. It is well-documented that British punk emerged in large part as a response to high unemployment, which was exponentially worse among the youth quarter; however, this is not to say that those who subscribed to a punk philosophy were hoping for a piece of the working world of their parents.[7] In fact, the case is quite the opposite; punks viewed such a world as oppressive, arbitrary, and ultimately unfulfilling.[8] Looking back, Johnny Rotten quips that, "there was no hope as far as any of us were concerned. This was our common bond. There was no point in looking for a normal job because that would be just too awful. There was no way out." (qtd in Szatmary, 227–28). The Pistols' "Pretty Vacant" clearly responds to this skepticism toward the working world and its mores, while "Wild Youth," by Generation X, figures to be an outright rejection of such a seemingly antiquated system: "I got no money, but that's okay / Because I live from day to day / And I'm free to come and go just as I please." Here one can observe how the issues of work ethic and expectations of the parent generation are intertwined with notions of space, that is, blank space.

Blank space is a way by which a subject can avoid being sucked in by mainstream values and labeled while seeking an alternative route to personal fulfillment (an extension of punk's do-it-yourself ethos). In the U. S., the term Generation X will almost instantly conjure up images of listless, blank youths, often referred to as "slackers," who are seemingly unmotivated (although financially backed) by the working-world of their Baby-Boomer parents. One can observe how, for example, in Douglas Coupland's seminal work, *Generation X: Tales for an Accelerated Culture* (1991) the reader is confronted by a group of youths who move out to the desert in California so as to avoid the typical yuppie lifestyle that can be found in the suburbs:

> There is no weather in Palm Springs—just like TV. There is also no middle class, and in that sense the place is medieval. [. . .] Nonetheless, the three of us chose to live here, for the town is undoubtedly a quiet sanctuary from the bulk of middle-class life. (10)

These characters adopt an alternative lifestyle, working McJobs, playing spontaneous games that test their reservoir of arcane, even useless knowledge (naming things people do in the desert, for example), and generally try to do things differently.[9] As one character puts it: "We live small lives on the periphery; we are marginalized and there's a great deal in which we choose not to participate" (Coupland 11). These characters evince what is a defining value, or lack thereof, among "Gen Xers," the idea that work should not impede life, and that less is often better than more. Gen Xers refuse to conform to the traditional bourgeois value of productivity.

As a reaction to a mainstream, homogenized society, practices such as thrift-store shopping and acquiring fluency in B movies and underground music become important to Gen Xers, as an indicator of their nonconformism. If the bourgeois signs of success are a name-brand suit, a well-manicured house, a luxury car, and the latest in multi-media gadgetry, then Gen Xers go in the opposite direction. The "stuff" and the rigidity of middle-class culture are swapped out for the unstructured lifestyle and peripheral values of Gen X adherents. In this respect, one of the most pivotal Gen X referents is Nirvana, whose members struck a chord, so to speak, with youth audiences by offering a dynamic style of music that contains exploding choruses and a merciless employment of distortion, producing feedback and reverb in a manner previously unheard in mainstream music. Also, by avoiding pretentious designer brands in favor of worn-through jeans, second-hand shirts and Converse One Star tennis shoes, Nirvana appealed to Generation X's rebellion against the parent culture's seemingly arbitrary notions of success, propriety, and taste.

It is no wonder, then, that in the 1990s Nirvana became such an important cultural reference in Peninsular "Gen X" narratives.[10] The group first arrived on the Spanish scene in late 1991. In January of 1992, the group's second album, *Nevermind*, which had garnered world-wide attention, was released in Spain and subsequently reviewed in *El País*'s cultural supplement, *Babelia*, in an article entitled, "La penúltima generación" (The Latest Generation), indicating that this most recent novelty is just part of a growing list. With that, Generation X arrived in Spain (Lev 26).[11] The arrival of Nirvana's ironic anti-anthem, "Smells Like Teen Spirit," then coincides with a new trend in Peninsular cultural production. Publishing houses such as Anagrama and Suma de Letras were already publishing translations of works by North American authors Coupland (Canadian), Bret Easton Ellis (*American Psycho, Less Than Zero*), and Elizabeth Wurtzel (*Prozac Nation*), so that this Gen X sensibility which was introduced via grunge music and blank fiction managed to create an aperture for a new style of literary discourse in Spain.[12]

It is no coincidence that in May of 1992, only months after Nirvana's triumphant entry into Spain, Ray Loriga publishes his first novel, *Lo peor de todo*. The subsequent reviews offer a telling commentary. On 1 May 1992, the conservative *ABC Literario* begins its review of the novel by writing that Loriga "aparece como un joven escritor sin biografía en el saturado panorama literario de nuestros días" (*Lo peor* 9) (appears like a young writer with no biography in the saturated literary panorama of our times), expressing optimism that the then 24 year-old Loriga would offer a fresh perspective within a rather stagnant literary market.[13] Unfortunately, though, for the critic, Loriga's text is defective; there is "escaso interés prestado a la elaboración constructiva y estilística de un texto bastante descuidado en todos sus niveles" (9) (hardly any interest paid to constructive and stylistic elaboration in a text which is rather carelessly written on every level). Furthermore, the narrative contains, "oraciones simples en párrafos cortos y en la concatenación de palabras empleadas como medio principal de relación en una sintaxis muy sencilla" (9) (simple sentences in short paragraphs, and with the concatenation of employed words as the principal means of relation within a simple syntax). According to this same reviewer, *Lo peor*'s (lack of) formal aspects correlate with a prevailing attitude among several young people:

> Con todo, no debe descalificarse por entero esta narración que, sin duda, pretende acercarse a la distinta sensibilidad e indiferencia reinantes en la conducta de numerosos sectores juveniles del momento. (9)

> (Given all this, one should not discredit this narration entirely which, undoubtedly, attempts to approximate the distinct sensibility and indifference which dominates the conduct of numerous sectors of today's youth.)

Another reviewer, Ignacio Echevarría, who is writing for *Babelia*, echoes this sentiment, noting that Loriga's work reflects:

una sensibilidad notoriamente representativa de un sector social ocupado principalmente por la juventud, que de común esquiva la parcela literaria y se expresa por la vía del comic y del rock. En este punto, es algo más que anecdótico el hecho de que Ray Loriga debutara como escritor en las páginas de una revista underground. (14)

(a sensibility notoriously representative of a social sector populated mostly by youths, which normally side-steps the area of literature and is expressed through comic books and rock. On this point, the fact that Ray Loriga would debut as a writer in the pages of an underground magazine is more than anecdotal.)

In fact, Loriga's first work, which will be considered forthwith, has a great deal in common with other products of this "latest generation," especially in the way in which it engages punk philosophy at an international level.

Lo peor is similar to Loriga's other novels which were published in this early period, works such as *Héroes* (1993), *Días extraños* (1994), and *Caídos del cielo* (1995). Briefly, some of their linking features are an interest in youth culture, (self)marginalized protagonists who are preoccupied with questions of authenticity, contained violence, an appropriation of Anglo-American cultural products—especially rock, and a "blank" narrative structure.[14] In fact, out of these four works, *Caídos* is the only one that offers what may be considered a standard plot. All four works, including *Caídos*, contain very brief, elliptical chapters, to the extent that the aforementioned reviewer from *ABC Literario* commented that *Lo peor* is in reality a short story containing "muchas deficiencias de un texto primerizo" (many of the defects of a first work). While the novel may indeed suffer from certain "freshmen" mistakes, the novel's paucity and cryptic manner should not be looked down upon as evidence of an authorial lapse. Rather, the novel's sparse, and seemingly forgetful structure pairs well with its content, which, given the framework put forth above, can be viewed as being on par with other Generation X products that ignore precedent and mainstream expectations, but instead support the notion that "less is more." The proper view is that *Lo peor* "dresses down," so to speak, and refuses to conform, structurally speaking, to any traditional literary standard. This, again, is punk's do-it-yourself attitude manifesting itself in Generation X production, this time within the context of Spain.

Lo peor, though, dresses down in other ways, and the legacy of punk is likewise important for understanding the cultural references offered in *Lo peor*, which range from serial killers to the Vietnam War. One reference is of particular importance—that of Sid Vicious. Elder Bastidas, the protagonist of *Lo peor*, is a youth with a troubled past and inauspicious future. He has been expelled from school indefinitely for violent outbursts while also being involved in other altercations. Given his fragile temperament, Elder obsesses over how miserably unfair life has been to him. Statements such as, "La mayoría de las veces las cosas no salen como uno espera, salen mucho peor" (78) (Most of the time things don't go as one plans, but much worse) and "Algo ha salido mal" (105) (Something has gone wrong) provide insight into Elder's mentality. He feels ostracized, with the world against him, yet he takes no responsibility for his present condition. He is agitated and imbalanced, stating that "tarde o temprano, voy a tener que matar a alguien" (93) (sooner or later, I will have to kill someone). He even selects a symbolic date, January 22, for his first "acción de guerra" (124) (act of war). On that same day in 1879, the British Army suffered its greatest defeat in Africa, when 24,000 Zulu warriors invaded a British camp of 1,700 near the Isandlwana Hill. Over 1,300 of the British force were killed, with only 60 Europeans surviving. In other words, it marks the overpowering of a dominant (colonizing) culture by a supposedly subordinate subculture.

Elder, needless to say, finds himself on the fringe, in spite of the fact that he hails from a comfortable middle-class family which afforded education and opportunity. But like the character's in Coupland's *Generation X*, Elder has trouble conforming and instead accepts low-paying "McJobs." He sets his sights, not on a corner office suite, but on becoming the employee of the month at the local burger joint. Here, again, punk and Generation X are conjoined. Elder's job prospects are reflective of the economic situation in Spain at the time of *Lo peor*'s publication, when there existed an equally high unemployment rate, a problem that was quantitatively worse for the young as it was in England in the 1970s. In Spain:

> the education of many young people up to the university level created an expectation of similar access to appropriate employment which the 1980s and 1990s have spectacularly failed to deliver. [. . .] The response to the frustrations of the expectations of youth has been apathy and evasion. (Allinson, "Construction" 267)

Whereas the response to unemployment took a very playful tone (or was simply ignored) during the *movida*, within Peninsular Generation X production, a different posture is taken. The post-Franco euphoria has worn off—the deceased dictator is never even mentioned—and Elder and those like him still have little hope of finding satisfactory jobs, to the point that the narrator of *Lo peor* observes with disdain: "Tanto dinero gastado en colegios para ministros y lo más que consigo es apilar cajas" (87) (So much money spent on private schools and the most I can get is a job stacking boxes). Elder's attitude is not identical to the attitudes vis-à-vis working that are observed in Coupland's novel, however, there is a similar skepticism toward traditional work and in particular the idea of "working your way up." Elder is frustrated, first, because there are few good jobs available, and, second, because even if there were a good job, it would not appeal to him. In short, it is readily evident throughout *Lo peor* that the job situation in Spain and Elder's attitude toward work are the primary sources of his angst.

Subsequently, it is no surprise to find Elder aligning himself with Sid Vicious and inscribing himself into a tradition of deviance. While Vicious had little, if any musical talent, his public display of destructive, anti-social behavior propelled him to a legendary status within the world of rock. He made a name for himself precisely by not conforming, and through violence. It is therefore disturbing to find Elder comparing his situation, along with that of his girlfriend, "T," to that of Sid and Nancy, at one point saying, "las cosas no están puestas aquí para T, ni para mí, por eso de vez en cuando me acuerdo de Sid y Nancy" (45) (things here are not meant for T, nor for me, for this reason I sometimes think of Sid and Nancy). Elder is referring specifically to the pernicious relationship between the bassist and Nancy Spungen, which ended with the former murdering the latter and committing suicide shortly thereafter.[15] Since Elder cannot find social acceptance and recognition through conventional means, he goes in the opposite direction, aiming to do so by cultivating an "alternative" set of tastes while plotting public acts of violence, employing Vicious as a spiritual accomplice along the way. The brooding, cynical youth marks a clear change from the aesthetic, fun version punk of the *movida*. In short, *Lo peor* extracts for its own use the more serious, socially-conscious side of British punk, where the term was first employed for its many connotations: "punk" as literally someone or something unimportant and worthless, but also a young ruffian or hoodlum. The term also refers to a young (often coerced) male partner of a homosexual, symbolic of the youth situation in the working-class ghetto of London's East End.

The aforementioned connotations are indicative of how Elder feels vis-à-vis his social situation. Within punk, chains and collars became homologous to being in a state of bondage. In particular, the iconic Sid Vicious appeared filthy and beaten, and would use broken beer bottles to gouge himself during performances, and Elder sees himself in this way. Taking his cue from Vicious, Elder willfully places himself on the periphery by plotting a violent attack, although he misses his opportunity. In short, as a reaction to social stagnation and the economic situation encountered in Spain during the early 1990s, *Lo peor* adopts a nihilistic, "vacant" posture while deploying a series of erstwhile "punk" referents as a means of escape from mainstream values and expectations. In this vein, the novel can be read, within the Peninsular literary canon, as an alternative path, or what Paul Fussell calls the "The X Way Out" (179).

This "X Way Out" is typified in Benjamín Prado's novel, *Nunca le des la mano a un pistolero zurdo*. The work's very title evinces a Gen X affinity for peripheral cultural production, swiped as it is from a single line in the film *Johnny Guitar* (1954), a low-budget, cult classic Western about a woman named Vienna who built a saloon outside of town and ends up defending herself and her rights alongside Johnny Guitar, a mysterious gun-slinging guitar player. There are other obscure references to popular culture in the work, such as *Straight-Jacket* (1964) and the slightly more renowned *High Sierra* (1941) with Humphrey Bogart. In fact, Israel, the main protagonist in *Nunca*, insists on conversing with his pals through quotes from B films, punk music (The Sex Pistols, Blur, Nirvana, Dee Dee Ramone, the Velvet Underground, Patti Smith, Muffs, the Clash, and Sonic Youth), and little-known detective novels, to the extent that the novel, at times, evokes an almost Borgesian quality.[16]

As mentioned earlier, this display of peripheral culture is a quintessentially Generation X strategy, which is employed to distance oneself from mainstream, suburban middle-class life and values. As the novel opens, Israel is listening to "Country House" by Blur, a post punk band that is decidedly more concerned with social minutia. The song is a "sad story" whose lyrics satirize the bourgeois individual ("a successful fella") who takes a rest from the stresses of modern life in his country cottage because he feels that he is "caught in a rat race terminally." There, "he's reading Balzac, knocking back Prozac / It's a helping hand that makes you feel wonderfully bland / Oh it's the centuries remedy / For the faint at heart, a new start." As with *Lo peor*, the more prominent intertextual reference is to the Sex Pistols and Sid Vicious in particular. Israel emerges as a precocious youth, with a solid education, both academically and culturally speaking, attending law school per his father's instructions, while being weaned on jazz music (Bud Powell, Thelonious Monk, John Lewis, Duke Ellington, Art Tatum) and classic literature (Dickens, Twain, Conrad, Auden, and others). As a boy, Israel was taken with his father's tastes, acting out the adventures from his books, and caring to learn about history and music. He could read, understand, and internalize works by authors such as T.S. Eliot and Federico García Lorca. But this "tasteful" upbringing was eventually overshadowed by his father's physical and mental abuse. Eventually, while still living at home, Israel began to rebel, but not through conventional delinquent activities. His rebellion took symbolic form. Israel acquires his own set of tastes which counter his father's phony high-brow pedagoguery. One friend remembers how suddenly, "Israel saltó de T.S. Eliot a los Sex Pistols y yo me quedé donde estaba" (61) (Israel jettisoned T.S. Eliot for the Sex Pistols and I stayed right where I was).

It is precisely this interest in the Pistols, as part of his unusual affiliations and interests, which symbolically reinforces Israel's challenge to his father's dominance and the bourgeois culture practices to which he subscribed. Like Sid, Israel is willfully self-destructive. After an argument with his father, Israel gouges his own arm with a broken bottle, mimicking Sid Vicious's live acts of self-mutilation. He claims to be a mix between Phillip Marlowe and Johnny Rotten: "uno de ellos me está matando y el otro está intentando descubrir al asesino" (139) (one of them is killing me and the other is trying to find the killer). When his father finally dies (and Israel is by now living elsewhere), the youth does not move into his father's home or maintain his father's precious possessions, his Rolex watch, the Mercedes Benz, and his house on the water. Instead, Israel sells the car and buys an R.V., which he parks in the front yard and uses as his primary residence while the house degrades, effectively rejecting any form of middle-class comfort. He also refuses to use his law degree, opting instead to work low-wage, no-future jobs with the hope of someday purchasing a boat and becoming self-employed. The question of work, both available and desirable, is, again, an important one. He sustains himself on Red Wolf beer and scraps from the neighborhood pub, and he refuses to wake up before 11a.m.[17] In sum, his living situation is quintessentially punk: "a room, bare save for a mattress, a few bottles, a few books" (Marcus 433).

Israel's rejection of bourgeois tastes and values is on par with other 'X People,' who, as Paul Fussell writes, "tend to be self-employed, doing what social scientists call autonomous work" (180). Fussell adds that, "if, as Mills has said, the middle-class person is 'always somebody's man,' the X person is nobody's, and his freedom from supervision is one of his most obvious characteristics" (180). These Generation X people avoid conformity at all levels, in the way they work, dress, eat, live, and especially in how they learn. While Fussell's depiction is often too prescriptive, he accurately identifies some attributes of Gen Xers within U.S. that are also applicable to Gen Xers in Spain, as they are studied here. In particular, Generation X people are "entirely self-directed" to "pursue remote and uncommonplace knowledge" (184). This information is very often international in character, demonstrating a keen sense of global awareness and, in some cases, creating a form of solidarity among fellow Gen Xers, that is, other "slackers." In fact, it is at this point where we can delineate a fundamental difference between punk subcultures of the 1970s and a Generation X ethos. Ulrich writes:

when mainstream society looks at slackers, what it perceives is a lack of structure—the lack of that 'career arc' that maps the trajectory of a normative lifestyle.
Without that structure, mainstream society can find nothing to value; such lives
seem worthless and wasted at best, and at worst, they seem to be an affront and an
insult to everything 'productive' society stands for. It is the realm of (in)activity—
everyday live—that the work world has structured, colonized, and marginalized.
Slacker seeks to reclaim that space, to occupy it as a realm of *creativity* rather than
waste. (18)

In this way, a slacker is not a rebel, seeking to usurp a stable society. Rather,
he is one who simply wants to remain apart. Whether out of a feeling of inad-
equacy or for ideological reasons, the slacker actually relies on the mainstream
culture in order to cultivate an opposing set of alternative values, effectively
avoiding the consumerist "competition" but somehow entering another competition of wits and obscurantism.

As with *Lo peor*, this Generation X ethos can be found in the very structure
of Prado's novel. *Nunca*'s insistence on imported and often occult references
to music, literature, and film is actually a staple in Prado's other works, such as
Raro (1995). In fact, in one metafictional moment, the narrator of *Nunca* alludes
to *Raro*, all the while claiming to be Benjamín Prado, who is then referencing
one of his own books. Once Israel skips town, he takes on a more prominent
role in the narrative by interrogating the other characters in an attempt to "crack
the case." At this point, the work appears to lose focus, as Israel is relegated to
an almost secondary status while the characters and their "author" converse in
an attempt to figure out what happened to him. The novel, at this point, begins
to unravel, much like Unamuno's *Niebla*; however, this unraveling is devoid of
ontological questioning—it is more playful than serious. The ending of *Nunca*
is appropriately left "blank," so that the reader can decide what happened to
Israel. The very structure of the work then reflects the decentered, "alternative"
spirit which Generation X inherits from punk.

Finally, there is one major difference between punk as it relates to the
specificity of the 1970s and subcultural theory and how it is appropriated by
Generation X. Toward the end of *Nunca*, when Israel goes missing, his friends
realize that something is awry only when they discover that his Sid Vicious t-
shirt is left behind in the R.V. According to Gaizka, "nunca se habría marchado
sin llevarse a Sid y Nancy" (88) (he never would have left without wearing
Sid and Nancy). That is, he would never leave the house without this external
display of his subcultural ideology. The shirt, along with music by the Pistols,
Nirvana, and Blur, reinforces his identity as a loner, as though he is indeed participating in "un maldito partido" (a hellish game) in which, "la mayoría de la

gente llevase el uniforme del equipo contrario" (42) (the majority of people are wearing the other team's uniform). It is curious to note that, rather than wearing slashed shirts and jeans, piercings, and tattoos (as would Vicious), Israel simply wears a shirt bearing the likeness of his favorite punk rocker. In other words, the Sex Pistols and, by extension, the whole of punk appear already commodified within the work. Clearly, Israel does not pose a threat to any establishment, but simply cultivates an affinity for groups who project an outlook with which he agrees. Because of his convictions apropos of bourgeois society, Israel finds comfort in rebelling against his father and his culture while taking solace in a symbolic, even ironic, position of self-marginalization—a position largely informed by punk. Still, there is no call for destruction, he makes no claims to being the antichrist, as Johnny Rotten so famously did (Marcus 1). He seeks instead only a small space, alone, away from and outside of everything. His connections to the rest of society are loose and variable. This marks an important difference between the destructive mission of the punks and the "affective alliances," to borrow Lawrence Grossberg's term, forged by Generation X subjects.

This brings us back to the problem articulated at the outset of this essay: what does punk mean in Spain in the 1990s? The answer is undoubtedly multiple, but one of the main obstacles impeding an honest look at this question is the fact that punk is usually analyzed through a strict subcultural lens, resulting in binary perspective of authentic versus inauthentic. Spanish writers who favor Anglo-American products over Spanish products certainly raise the question.[18] Allinson has written that "the late eighties and the decade of the nineties are marked by something of a deficit in national youth cultures at the expense of imported cultural products" ("Construction" 270). This may certainly be part of the equation; however, as we have seen, it is also part of larger Generation X's strategy to look beyond national cultures and take interest in *lo ajeno* (that which is outside) as a means of distancing oneself from routinized, mainstream culture.

As Israel's shirt indicates, if there is any rebellion in these works, it is contained within the system, and is therefore a simulacrum of rebellion—something that can be put on as a source of differentiation, or empowerment. In this sense, Lawrence Grossberg is right to question subcultural explanations which are rooted in politics in order to move towards a view that places rock and roll in the lives of youths as source of affective alliance, or what he also calls a hyperalliance: "Thus, the music's popularity depends less on its place within specific alliances than on the construction of hyperalliances as venues for other sorts of affective relations and activities" ("Is Anybody Listening?" 56). In this vein, punk style and music only has different meanings within given contexts. After all, as Simon Frith notes, "the question raised by punk wasn't who consumed music, but how they did it [. . .] the questions punk focused on were about leisure opportunity, about the relationships of choice *and* restraint" (267). This helps us understand the use of punk in Peninsular Generation X narrative, whose subjects seek distinction and empowerment through their modes of consumption within capitalist culture; they choose the music that corresponds to their tastes and which they view as compatible with their social outlook, and which sends a message vis-à-vis the "parent" culture, albeit in a less threatening manner. Finally, they find in the Sex Pistols and punk rock a temporary escape from the boredom and alienation of everyday reality.

Notes

1. The "movida" as it is called in Spanish, was a cultural movement in Madrid which took place during the 1980s after the death of Francisco Franco and the economical rise of Spain. As a cultural movement, it is best characterized as hedonistic, as a time in which adherents challenged Catholic mores, sexual and otherwise.

2. While I agree with Hooper's general observation, his reasoning is untenable. He writes: "Rock is a product of youth culture which is in turn the result of a rejection of established social values. In societies where family ties are still strong, it is impossible to create such a youth culture" (353). He is basically working backward from a subcultural view which sees rock as the product of a ruptured family structure—if societies with disrupted families is the precondition for rock, then strong families will not produce rock. He also points to the fact that Spain has traditionally been more rural than urban. These factors may contribute to the situation, but his analogy is overly simplistic and lacking in empirical evidence.

3. Allinson writes that "as far as the *movida* is concerned, most interested parties signal its death between 1984 and 1985" ("Construction" 270).

4. The British punks were not free from the tensions between politics and commodification either. While presenting an ethos of anti-consumerism, they simultaneously acknowledged it as necessary—since their destructive task required reaching the largest possible audience. They toured America and Europe, while selling thousands of records along with other merchandise. Tom Robinson was one of the first punks to recognize the contradiction between leftist politics and his label's money-making goals. He recognized that one has "to use the capitalist media to reach the people. And I do feel that pop music is the way to reach people. Ideally, I'd like to be played on AM stations rather than FM stations, rather than the rarefied atmosphere. I'd rather be played in taxis, in factories, for housewives working at home" (qtd. in Szatmary 234).

5. It seems ironic that Capa first attained fame through his photography of the Spanish Civil War, while Generation X Spaniards, as they are portrayed in literature, are largely uninterested in what took place between the years of 1936 and 1939 and the ramifications of that war.

6. Hell quips: "To me, 'blank' is a line where you can fill in anything. It's positive . . . It's the idea that you have the option of making yourself anything you want, filling in the blank. And that's something that provides a uniquely powerful sense to this generation" (qtd. in Szatmary 223).

7. Szatmary notes that "between 1974 and 1977, the British unemployment rate shot up 120 percent, increasing by more than 200 percent among the young, and the rate of inflation neared 30 percent" (226).

8. In "Your Generation," by Generation X, the parent generation is told that their way of viewing no longer makes sense: "You know all the ways when in what I see / The ends must justify the means / Your generation don't mean a thing to me."

9. In *Generation X*, Douglas Coupland defines a McJob as: "A low-pay, low-prestige, low-dignity, low-benefit, no-future job in the service sector. Frequently considered a satisfying career choice by people who have never held one" (5).

10. Nirvana is featured prominently in several works by Peninsular writers: *Caídos del cielo* (1995) by Ray Loriga, *Historias del Kronen* (1994) by José Ángel Mañas, *La muerte de Kurt Cobain* (1997) by Care Santos. The group is also mentioned in the works that are to be discussed here. This is not to mention Lucía Etxebarría's well-documented interest in Courtney Love, the wife (now widow) of Cobain.

11. *El País* is Spain's major daily, akin to *The New York Times* in the U.S.

12. Some critics, such as Germán Gullón, refer to works by authors such as José Ángel Mañas, Ray Loriga, Benjamín Prado, Lucía Etxebarria, and others as "Realismo Sucio" (Dirty Realism); however, it is my conclusion that these works share more in common with Generation X production, such as *Generation X* by Coupland and *Prozac Nation* by Wurtzell, or what is called minimalism, *Less Than Zero* by Bret Easton Ellis. The use of the term Dirty Realism to describe the works being discussed within this volume is a misapplication, or, as Cintia Santana has so insightfully pointed out, a mistranslation. See Cintia Santana. *Influence in Translation: Dirty Realism and the Spanish Novel and Short Story* (1985–2000). Diss. Harvard University, 2004. Ann Arbor: UMI, 2004.

13. All translations from Spanish to English within this essay are mine.

14. One could make the case that *Lo peor de todo*, *Héroes*, and *Días extraños* are all driven by the same narrative voice, one which offers a compilation of daydreams, pseudo-philosophical meditations, social commentary, and narrative bits. Also, the protagonist's love interest, "T," reappears in *Días extraños*. On the other hand, though, there are subtle differences in personality and even narrative structure. *Héroes* is more self-conscious. For example, by conjuring up the figure of Bowie the novel plays with ideas of superficiality and ritual. *Días extraños*, for its part, contains illustrations, an even more uneven structure, and certain details that cause the reader to questions the

distance between author and narrator. The narrator, for example, discusses being a writer and performing journalistic work.

15. On the morning of October 12, 1978 Vicious allegedly awoke from a drug-induced stupor to find Spungen dead in their Room 100 apartment, at the New York Hotel Chelsea. She had been killed by a single stab wound to her abdomen. Vicious was arrested and charged with her murder, although he claimed to have no memory at all of the previous night's incidents. Later however he claimed to have "killed her because I'm a dirty dog", although there are also theories that the murder may actually have been committed by a third party, possibly one of the many drug dealers who frequented the apartment.

16. "Eran esas novelas policíacas que él siempre . . . bueno, de hecho no iba a ningún sitio sin una de ellas y le gustaba que yo también lo hiciera porque . . . decía que dos hombres que no han leído el mismo libro no tienen nada de que hablar. Lo cierto es que después todo su juego giraba en torno a eso; quiero decir, estabas en un bar y llegaba una chica y entonces Israel decía: ella era tan bonita como el demonio y dos veces más peligrosa, y si tú sabías quién había escrito eso . . . bueno, estabas a este lado de la línea. Yo siempre los elegía por los títulos, ya sabes, *El hombre que murió tres veces*, *El caso de la lata vacía* y otros de ese tipo. Pero normalmente era él quien me los daba y la verdad es que solían gustarme; los de Chester Himes, Jim Thompson y cosas así. Aquella mañana cogí *Todos muertos* y *Algodón en Harlem*" (20).

17. Red Wolf Beer (an Anheuser Busch product) became popular in 1990s along with other "red" beers.

18. There did exist some Spanish punk groups: Alaska and the Pegamoides, Paraíso, Tos (later, Los Secretos), Nacha Pop, Mamá, Radio Futura, and Siniestro Total (Allinson, "Construction" 268).

Works Cited

Allinson, Mark. "Alaska: Star of Stage and Screen and Optimistic Punk." *Constructing Identity in Contemporary Spain*. Ed. Jo Labanyi. Oxford: Oxford University Press, 2002. 222–36.

_____. "The Construction of Youth in Spain in the 1980s and 1990s." *Contemporary Spanish Cultural Studies*. Ed. Barry Jordan and Rikki Morgan-Tamosunas. London: Arnold, 2000. 265–82.

Blank Generation. "Wild Youth." *Generation X*. EMI. 2002.

Blur. "Country House." *The Great Escape*. Virgin, 1995.

Coupland, Douglas. *Generation X: Tales for an Accelerated Culture*. New York: St. Martin's, 1991.

Deverson, Jane and Charles Hamblett. *Generation X*. Greenwich, Connecticut: Fawcett, 1964.

Echevarría, Ignacio. "Elder Bastidas, el extranjero." Review of *Lo peor de todo*, by Ray Loriga. *Babelia* 16 May 1992: 14.

Fussell, Paul. *Class: A Guide Through the American Status System.* New York: Touchstone, 1992.

Grossberg, Lawrence. "Is Anybody Listening? Does Anybody Care? On 'The State of Rock.'" *Microphone Fiends.* Ed. Tricia Rose and Andrew Ross. London and New York: Routledge, 1994. 41–58.

Hebdige, Dick. *Subculture.* London: Methuen, 1988.

Hell, Richard. "Blank Generation." *Richard Hell and the Voidoids.* Sire, 1990.

Hooper, John. *The New Spaniards.* London and New York: Penguin, 1995.

Lev, Michael. "La penúltima generación." *Babelia* 25 Jan. 1992: 26.

"Lo peor de todo." Review of *Lo peor de todo,* by Ray Loriga. *ABC Literario* 1 May 1992: 9.

Loriga, Ray. *Caídos del cielo.* Barcelona: Plaza y Janés, 1995.

_____. *Días extraños.* Madrid: El Europeo & Canto de la Tripulación,1994.

_____. *Lo peor de todo.* Madrid: Debate, 1992.

Marcus, Greil. *Lipstick Traces: A Secret History of the Twentieth Century.* Cambridge, Massachusetts: Harvard University Press, 1989.

Ordovás, Jesús. "Cuarenta años de música popular en España." *España Hoy II: Cultura.* Ed. Antonio Ramos Gascón. Madrid: Cátedra, 1991. 351–66.

Prado, Benjamín. *Nunca le des la mano a un pistolero zurdo.* Barcelona: Plaza y Janes, 1996.

_____. *Raro.* Barcelona: Plaza y Janés, 1995.

Sex Pistols. "Pretty Vacant." *Filthy Lucre Live.* Virgin, 1996.

Szatmary, David P. *Rockin' in Time. A Social History or Rock-and-Roll.* New Jersey: Prentice Hall, 2000.

Ulrich, John M. "Generation X: A (Sub)Cultural Geneology." *GenXegesis: Essays on "Alternative" Youth Subculture.* Ed. John M. Ulrich and Andrea L. Harris. Madison: University of Wisconsin Press, 2003: 3–37.

◆ 3

What We Talk About When We Talk About Dirty Realism in Spain

Cintia Santana

In recent decades, the object of literary studies (i.e. a once upon a time Canon) has come into question resulting in a foregrounding of the political valuations attached to "literary value." The notion of the narrative text that is discussed within literary studies has broadened to include texts that are verbal only in part (e.g., film, television, song, *zarzuela*). Material translations, however, continue to be considered little more than the subject of marginal critical inquiry within literary studies. A critique of Western metaphysics' phonocentricism and the less privileged position occupied by writing when compared to speech, or "arche writing," does not exempt the field from its own hierarchies; translated literature vis-à-vis literature in the original language is considered derivative and imperfectly representative, as is writing alongside speech when considered through a Derridian lens. The underexploration of translated literature continues to be the case within Spanish literary studies, despite Spain's long-standing tradition of literary borrowings across linguistic borders and, in recent decades, Spanish editors' fervor to publish translations: Spain is second only to Germany (and ahead of France) among countries that publish the highest number of translated works per year (UNESCO). While translation studies has come to constitute a field in its own right, the translated text as the focus of scholarly endeavor continues to be relegated almost exclusively to the aforementioned field, where it is also marginalized among other areas of inquiry more often involved with technical or "practical" text translations, rather than "literary" texts.

The present essay is governed by the understanding that translated texts, the study of their material production and their literal, that is, linguistic transformation, constitutes a valuable, if often overlooked point of entry for critics citing "influence," "intertextuality," "literary interference," and "appropriation" attributed by way of translation. In the analysis that follows, the source and target texts constitute a primary text, its recto and verso. The aim is not simply to evaluate the "deviation" of the translation from the original but rather to read the target text as yet another version of the source text as Jorge Luis Borges proposed ("Las versiones homéricas" 239). In so doing, the transformations of a text across languages can illuminate the various currents that communications navigate between initial utterance and subsequent receptions.

In 1983, fiction editor Bill Buford marketed the spring issue of the literary magazine, *Granta*, under the title "Dirty Realism: New Writing from America." In 1986, in the same year that Spain entered the EU, consolidating its democracy according to some, Spanish publishing houses took an avid interest in publishing the works of Dirty Realist writers such as Raymond Carver's short story collection *Catedral* (*Cathedral,* Anagrama) and Tobias Wolff's *De regreso al mundo* (*Back in the World,* Alfaguara). The brisk syntax and set of cultural references said to be characteristic of Dirty Realism began entering contemporary Spanish writing soon after: Ray Loriga's *Lo peor de todo* (1992), José Ángel Mañas' *Historias del Kronen* (1994), and Benjamín Prado's *Raro* (1995) became the paradigm of a new generation of Spanish writers. The authors self-consciously and insistently associated themselves with the United States, and were often grouped by critics under the literal translation of the English term: *Realismo sucio*.

Discussion of Spain's *Generación X, Generación Kronen, Realismo duro*, and *literatura de la cloaca,* inevitably makes mention of their Anglo precursors, especially that of Raymond Carver's work.[1] Rather than distancing themselves from the "father's" influence, as so many writers are eager to do, the writers of *Realismo sucio* (Dirty Realism) eagerly claimed their fathers, albeit foreign fathers. *Realismo sucio* writers' self-conscious insistence on their association with a global (i.e. primarily Anglophone) culture, often carried with it an adamant rejection of an autochthonous tradition: in response to an interviewer's question about the relationship of the protagonist of *Historias del Kronen*, Carlos, to *Lazarillo de Tormes*, Mañas answered, "El Lazarillo es un pan y Carlos es hielo" (Fidalgo). In an interview in *El País*, Loriga stated, "Mi generación convive con referencias culturales más globales: este es un libro que podía haber escrito un tipo nacido en Liverpool. Para nosotros el folclor no supuso nada. A mí Carmen Sevilla no me dice nada. Ya no se puede hablar de raíces" (My generation lives among more global cultural references: this is a book that could have been written by a guy in Liverpool. Folklore didn't mean anything to us. Carmen Sevilla doesn't speak to me at all. You can't talk about roots anymore). If since the 1960s it had been proclaimed that "*España es diferente*," (Spain is different) Spain was anything but different by the 1990s according to its newest generation of writers.

The heterogeneity of literary production in Spain in the 1990s is evident, even among those writers who found their way into print for the first time during this decade. Jordi Gracia has cautiously divided the novelistic production of the 1990s into at least three groupings: consecrated writers and those recently established in the 1980s who continued to publish throughout the next decade (e.g., Juan Benet, Camilo José Cela, Miguel Delibes, Juan Goytisolo, Gonzalo Torrente Ballester, Ana María Matute, Juan Marsé, Manuel Vázquez Montalbán and the more recent, Javier Marías, Juan José Millás, and Antonio Muñoz Molina); "El memorialismo y la literatura del yo," which included autobiographies, ever-numerous memoirs, and diaries; and "La nueva tradición" which gathered writers published for the first time in the 1990s and who were born after 1965. Among those authors classified as *escritores jóvenes* were the writers of *Realismo sucio* as well as those who had little in common with these other than their youth (e.g., Belén Gopegui, Juan Manuel de Prada, Luis Magrinyà, and Juan Bonilla). Nonetheless, publicity campaigns and some reviewers sought to lump them together, in part, because of the dominant perception throughout the 1990s that youth was a marketable asset from an editorial standpoint (Grijalba; Santos Alonso; Carlos Bernadell; C. A.; Ortega).

The names associated with *Realismo sucio* are also far from an invariable grouping: Ray Loriga, José Ángel Mañas, Benjamín Prado, Roger Wolfe, Pedro Maestre, Lucía Etxebarria, Tino Pertierra, Daniel Múgica, Félix Romeo, José Machado, Eduardo Iglesias, Gabriela Bustelo, and Francisco Casavella. Nonetheless, the various studies and literary dictionaries that discuss this generation unfailingly point to Loriga and Mañas as writers of *Realismo sucio*, most consistently followed by mentions of Wolfe's poetry and prose, and Benjamín Prado's novel, *Raro*.

Despite the much touted influence of U.S. "Dirty Realist" writers on the works of Spanish *Realismo sucio*, the similarities are not readily obvious. While the protagonists of Dirty Realism drink and listen to country music, the characters of *Realismo sucio* are obsessed with sex, designer drugs, and rock and roll. Dirty Realism depicts the lives of blue-collar men and women through minimal prose and plot, while *Realismo sucio's* protagonists tend to be privileged, young men in their late teens and early twenties, fascinated with spectacular violence. They live comfortably at home with their parents, as does the protagonist of Mañas's *Historias del Kronen*, or the narrator of Loriga's *Lo peor de todo* who states, "Yo no soy un niño de la calle ni nada por el estilo. De niño estudié en los colegios más caros y mi casa tenía jardín y piscina particular" (14–15) (I'm not a child of the streets or anything like that. As a child, I studied in the most expensive schools and my house had a yard and a private pool). The behavioral acts of violence that characterize *Realismo sucio*, are also absent in the *Granta* writers' work. The gender of protagonists, the social class represented, and the level of violence constitute the most salient differences between Dirty Realist writers' work and that of Spanish *Realismo sucio*, yet they have gone virtually unmentioned in criticism thus far.

The *El País* article that first introduced a Spanish audience to Dirty Realism featured photographs of several of the American writers (Carver, Ford, Wolff, Bobbie Ann Mason, Richard Russo, and Elizabeth Tallent) and brief bios under the headline *"Los protagonistas."* The heading is a useful one, both as an indication of the direction the Spanish publishing industry had begun to take (i.e. the "star system" of marketing which conferred the status of an entertainment diva on a writer) but also as a reminder that the grouping, as with any grouping of writers, is a culturally constructed fiction, one that tells the story of a time and place. "Dirty Realism" hardly need be a static term; time, place and the translations that bridged these, resulted in a different understanding in Spain of U.S. Dirty Realism from that of its reception in the U.S. where the writers were better known as "Minimalists."[2] However, the difference in understandings has yet to be explored by critics. Literary movements do not unilaterally spread, rather they metamorphose in their travel through the desires, creative choices, and practical constraints of the differing producers, consumers, and material translations. Dirty Realism and *Realismo sucio* embody such a process and, as I also argue, may be "cleaned" by these very same elements.

This essay documents Dirty Realism's transfer by focusing on the specific challenges posed to translation by Carver's use of literary dialect. How do Carver's characters "talk" in Spanish (for in Spain they also speak Catalan and Euskera, if not yet Gallego) and by extension, what have we come to talk about when we talk about Dirty Realism in Spain? Specifically, I consider how the social class markers present in the English original have been "cleaned out" in the Spanish translations of Carver and other U.S. Dirty Realist writers' works. Ultimately I conclude that these omissions may be said to account, in part, for the differences in class represented by U.S. Dirty Realism and its

Spanish manifestation in the 1990s. Carver's material translation is further complemented by other literal and metaphorical translations that surrounded his introduction in Spain.

The analysis of material translations does not attempt to supplant considerations of the local, Spanish elements that gave rise to *Realismo sucio*, despite many of the writers' (and critics') frequent statements about the global, transnational quality of the movement; if Spanish *Realismo sucio* has been said to be symptomatic of the "globalization of literature," it also illustrates that local receptions and reappropriations persist. These differences are instructive not only as to what the host culture brings to the mix but as to what translates and what remains untranslatable, both literally and metaphorically.[3] By placing textual translations among the central concerns of a scholarly literary investigation, this essay aims to further deepen our understanding of the exportation and importation of dialogues by way of these changes, the cultural and linguistic—often creative—understandings which make for the complexity of interliterary dialogues.

Granta's Dirty Realism

The cover of the *Granta* volume that christened Dirty Realism featured a detail from Grant Wood's *American Gothic*. Instead of the house with gabled window and tracery in the American Gothic style that inspired the painting's title, the farmer and his spinster daughter stood against a background of neon motel signs. As Wood's piece so aptly illustrated, the enclosed stories exposed a skewed American dream. The protagonists of these stories were waitresses, cashiers, and construction workers who were divorced, unemployed, over-weight; the stories they told were set in trailer parks, roadside cafes, and small ranch towns. The issue included Raymond Carver's "Compartments," Tobias Wolff's "The Barracks Thief," Richard Ford's "Rock Springs," Elizabeth Tallent's "Why I Love Country Music," and Bobbie Ann Mason's "Still Life with Watermelon." The issue was such a success that three years later the summer 1986 issue of *Granta* appeared under the title "More Dirt," showcasing the work of Jayne Anne Phillips, Richard Russo, Ellen Gilchrist, and Joy Williams.

Buford's introduction to the first *Granta* issue characterized the new writing as "unadorned, unfurnished, low-rent tragedies about people who watch day-time television, read cheap romances or listen to country western music" (4). He described the writing as "flat, 'unsurprised' language, pared down to the plainest of plain styles" (5). On October 16, 1986, three years after Buford had coined the term "Dirty Realism," Spain's most widely circulated newspaper, *El País,* featured a two-page spread on the cover of its book review section titled, "*¿Sabe usted qué es* 'dirty realism'?" The article was the first in Spain to anticipate Anagrama's publication that same month of Carver's short story collection *Catedral (Cathedral),* the first translation into Spanish of a Dirty Realist writer. A year later, the stories contained in the *Granta* issues were translated into Catalan and gathered into a two-volume anthology (*Dirty Realism/ Realisme Brut*). In addition to Carver, many of the other *Granta* writers were translated into Spanish soon after: Mason (*Shiloh,* Anagrama, 1987), Phillips (*Sueños mecánicos,* Edhasa, 1987), Wolff (*De regreso al mundo,* Alfaguara, 1988), Tallent (*Tiempo con niños,* Alfaguara, 1989), and Ford (*El periodista deportivo,* Anagrama, 1990). Tallent, Ford, Russo, Phillips, and Carver were additionally translated into Catalan, and in 1993, Carver appeared in Euskera.

Carver was the best selling of the *Granta* writers by far, a fact still evident by the number of his titles that continue to be edited more than twenty years later. Dubbed "el Chéjov americano" (Wolfe "Hablar . . ."; Januszczak), he has also been referred to as the "mentor del dirty realism" (de España) and "el padre del Realismo sucio" (García-Posada "¿Quieres hacer . . ." Rato, "Raymond Carver . . ."). With the exception of some of Carver's earlier prose and poetry volumes, all five short story collections published since 1981 have been translated into Spanish and have undergone numerous editions. Carver's poetry is also attributed with the rise of Spanish *Realismo sucio* poetry, independent of such a movement in the United States. Richard Ford and Tobias Wolff are the *Granta* writers who have achieved a close second and third place success in the Spanish literary market.

Carver Talk in Spanish

One of the similarities that Carver's work and that of the Spanish writers of *Realismo sucio* share is the attention paid to their representation of orality. Orality is here defined as the various forms of vernacular everyday speech represented in writing. As used in this essay, the term extends beyond the limits of what is understood as direct speech, or quoted dialogue, so as to include the quality of direct speech that may characterize a first-person point of view. Carver was hailed—and criticized—in the United States for the oral quality of his narratives, his ready ability to reproduce "real" working-class speech. In a review of *What We Talk About When We Talk About Love,* Anatole Broyard states, "It is written in faux-naif Hemingway sentences as they might be spoken

by an illiterate person. There is in every line a loud and self-conscious artlessn
ess . . . . [Carver's work] employs an "I go-she goes" idiom that we reluctantly
associate with children. Mr. Carver uses repetition in dialogue in a manner that
takes us all the way back to the homey sentimentalism of the 30's in which
the proletariat struggles with language and thought like a beetle on its back,
flailing its legs." A review of *Cathedral* by Irving Howe states, "His characters are plebeian loners struggling for speech . . . . Mr. Carver's characters, like
those of many earlier American writers, lack a vocabulary that can release their
feelings . . . [A Small Good Thing reads] a bit like Sherwood Anderson at his
best, especially in the speech rhythms of the baker."

Orality, if a very different one, constituted a notable characteristic of
Realismo sucio as well, a "new" orality, according to some critics, that reproduced the colloquial speech of urban youth at the end of the twentieth century.
(Capanaga, Conte, Dorca: 314, Gullón "Cómo se lee . . ." (31) "Prólogo"
(xxi–xxii), Oleza (42), Platas Tasende (348), Tyras (514–15), Senabre). While
the transcription or representation of colloquial speech is hardly foreign to the
Spanish literary tradition (e.g., literary dialect has served realist as well as more
avant-garde schools of writing such as those undertaken by Galdós, Pio Baroja,
Valle-Inclán, Carlos Arniches, and Sánchez Ferlosio), the characters and the
language portrayed by Mañas, Loriga, Prado, and Wolfe, capture not the speech
of the small town or urban Spanish proletariat, but of young, urban "pijos"
whose speech simultaneously attests to their consumption of North American
cultural products.

As it is represented in literature, orality confounds the traditional dichotomy
of orality and literacy, "the two technologies of the intellect" as Goody and
Watt have referred to them. Orality in a text constitutes a palimpsest of sorts
before the reader in which the oral, human voice, calls attention to itself under
the written word. The complexity of this artifice and the reader's distance from
its "source" (i.e. "real"-life speech) is augmented in translation: literary speech,
extracted from life and represented in writing, has been further removed from
a source language through an additional artifice, that of translation. Writers
often represent nonstandard elements of language to bring into play elements
of geography, socioeconomic class, age, and/or race, which are relevant to the
story. Milton Azevedo uses the term "literary dialect" to describe such writing which aims to reflect regional and/or social linguistic differences through
unconventional orthography, morphosyntax, or lexical choices ("Literary Dialect" 125). This literary dialect stands out against the backdrop of standard
language. The effect may be augmented when the fictional narrative is written
in the first-person point of view of a character so as to foreground the sense of

spontaneous speech (as in Eichenbaum's term "skaz"). This first-person point of view which foregrounds the use of literary dialect is characteristic of Carver's work, and has also been noted of the writers of *Realismo sucio* (Dorca 312, Urioste 460–63).

Like William Faulkner's Yoknapatawpha, or Gabriel García Márquez's Macondo, Carver's fiction and its representation of the United States' working poor were so deftly delineated and recognizable as to earn the name of "Carver Country" among critics (Adelman, Scobie). Critics have noted the central role of orality in Carver's work, and by extension, a concern with portraying the difficulties of communication (Malamet, Gearhart). The majority of characters in Carver Country speak "Carver Talk" and illustrate how speech not only accompanies empires, but also acts to undercut them. While Carver's stories are primarily set in the Pacific Northwest, the literary dialect he employs does not represent a specific linguistic variety (no literary dialect does), but rather displays characteristics of a "general nonstandard" English attributed to a white, working class. It is important to clarify that literary dialect is no more "real" than standard literary dialogue; both are crafted artifices that *suggest* real life and aid in the reader's suspension of disbelief. The prestige value (or lack thereof) that critics' comments attribute to "Carver Talk" is well served by Peter Trudgill's reminder that all dialects are equally "good" as linguistic systems, adequate for the need of their speakers: "Any inferiority is due only to [a sociolect's] association with speakers from under-privileged, low status groups. In other words, attitudes toward nonstandard dialects are attitudes which reflect the social structure of a society" (9).[4]

A broad overview of Carver's work suggests that a minimum of five categories of nonstandard English can be found.[5] The following examples from Carver's work are representative of each category across the gamut of his collections over time. If we take a look at the translations into Spanish of that which in the original was considered "dirty" English by some critics, a significant change is undergone at the morphosyntactic level: almost without exception, the nonstandard quality of the English alluded to by American critics is "cleaned" into "standard" Spanish by both of Carver's Spanish translators.

1.   **Addition of –s inflection to all persons:** (Traugott 330)

"I'm Mr. Palmer," I says. 'Mrs. Palmer is not here now,' I says. ("Sacks" 39)

Soy el señor Palmer, digo yo. La señora Palmer no está en este momento, le explico. (Zulaika 43)

2.   Multiple negation:[6] (Traugott 333, Trudgill 35–36)

"I haven't told this to nobody." ("Sacks" 43)
No se lo había contado a nadie. (Zulaika 47)

"Not me, neither," ("They're Not Your Husband" 23)
Ni a mí. (Zulaika 28)

3.   Nonstandard past tense: (use of the present tense to express a past tense)

"I heard it on the radio before I come." ("So Much Water So Close to Home" 87)
Lo he oído en la radio antes de venir. (Zulaika 91)

"If they said they was sorry and it was the first time, I'd let them go." ("Sixty Acres" 69)

Si dijeran que lo sentían y que era la primera vez, los dejaría marchar. (Zulaika 71)

4.   Nonstandard use of deictic:

"He sleeps in one of them trees." ("Feathers" 18) Duerme en uno de esos árboles. (Gómez Ibáñez 23)

"Take off them coats and empty them out." ("Sixty Acres" 69) Quitaos las cazadoras y vaciadlas. (Zulaika 70)

"I feel like me and her monopolized the evening." ("Cathedral" 222)
Tengo la impresión de que ella y yo hemos monopolizado la velada. (Gómez Ibáñez 200)

5.   Nonstandard verb agreement (and use of deictic):

"I wish me and Cliff was friends again." ("I Could See the Smallest Things" 34)

Desearía que Cliff y yo volviéramos a ser amigos. (Zulaika 38)

Nonstandard English is represented in the work of the other *Granta* writers and is similarly standardized when translated into Spanish.[7] While the *Granta* writers' styles cannot be lumped together, the incorporation of nonstandard English is a constant element in their work, one that often relates the stories of characters who live in rural Montana and New Orleans (Ford), West Virginia

(Phillips) western Kentucky (Mason) and the Southwest (Tallent). Wolff is, perhaps, the *Granta* writer whose work is least tied both to single locations and to nonstandard English. Given that class difference is one of the significant variations between Spanish *Realismo sucio* and United States' *Dirty Realism*, the standardization of Carver's nonstandard speech may be said to account, in part, for the class difference between the movements, a difference which critics have failed to mention thus far.

Realismo sucio's Orality

Not surprisingly, comments regarding a nonstandard "dirty" Spanish, equivalent to "Carver talk," are entirely absent from the Spanish reviews of these U.S. writers. Nonetheless, the orality of *Realismo sucio* writers has garnered its writers a fair share of criticism for its own "dirty" quality. The orality represented in the works of *Realismo sucio* occupies a central position in the debates regarding the "literariness" of the movement. Ana Maria Platas Tasende's *Diccionario de términos literarios* (2000) states that the writers, ". . . se apartan del cultivo de un lenguaje de raigambre literaria" (348) (". . . distance themselves from the crafting of a literary language"). Antonio Ortega makes a similar point, describing the language as "lenguaje desgarrado, coloquial y extremo en su uso, reflejo de jergas juveniles variadas, y *alejado de la escritura*" (32, emphasis added) (course language, colloquial and extreme in its usage, a reflection of various youth slangs, that distances itself from written language). Germán Gullón's summary of the criticism devoted to *Realismo sucio*'s language acknowledges "la pobreza formal, la sintaxis arbitraria, el lenguaje desgarrado y plagado de coloquialismos, es decir, *extraliterario*" (Prólogo, xxi, emphasis added) (a formal poverty, an arbitrary syntax, a course language plagued by colloquialisms, that is to say, an unliterary language). Gullón goes on to describe the language of *Realismo sucio* as "la respuesta del ciudadano al lenguaje de notario, del académico," (the citizen's response to a public notary or an academic's language) that of "[el] ser humano despojado de los privilegios," (Gullón, Prólogo: xxii) (the human being stripped of privileges). Ricardo Senabre characterizes the orality in *Realismo sucio* as "salpimentada con acuñaciones y tics coloquiales de arrabal" (Senabre) (peppered with the colloquial coinages and quirks of the slum). Such remarks suggest that the writers of *Realismo sucio* represent a marginal sector of Spanish society, as Carver was similarly said to represent in the U.S.

Realismo sucio's orality is markedly different from Carver's orality however. The now perhaps famous opening sentence of Mañas's *Historias del Kronen* reads, "Me jode ir al Kronen los sábados por la tarde porque está siempre hasta el culo de gente" (11) (It pisses me off to go to the Kronen on Saturday afternoons 'cause it's just got people coming out its ass). In *Héroes*, Loriga's narrator says "No tengo por qué escuchar a todo el mundo. Puedo decir, sencillamente: QUE TE DEN POR EL CULO" (original emphasis, 156) (I don't have to listen to everybody. I can simply say: FUCK YOU UP THE ASS). In a review of Roger Wolfe's novel, *El índice de Dios*, Ignacio Echevarría writes, "La voluntad de trasgresión se libera mediante expedientes tan infantiles como el gamberrismo verbal ('y culo y coño, y polla, y polla, y polla . . .'). Los intentos de explotar una nueva sintaxis narrativa naufragan una y otra vez en el más primario tremendismo" (The will to transgress is relieved through means as childish as verbal hooliganism ('and ass and pussy and cock, and cock, and cock . . .'). The attempts to exploit a new narrative syntax founder time and again in the most primary *tremendismo*).

The language of *Realismo sucio* is not limited to extra-literary locutions however: *troncos* are friends (Mañas, 25), *cerdas* (Mañas, 95) or *tías* (Wolfe, 14) are women, as men are *tíos* (Bustelo, 14), *talegos* are bills (Mañas, 100), to snort cocaine is to *enfarlopar* (Mañas, 116), and delincuents are *manguis* (Wolfe, 53). The orality of *Realismo sucio* has its roots in *cheli*, a slang that originated in the 1970s and 1980s and that the Real Academia Española's dictionary defines as, "Jerga con elementos castizos, marginales y contraculturales" (642) (Slang with Castilian, marginal and countercultural elements). Francisco Umbral termed the orality in the works of *Realismo sucio*, "argot post/cheli," and saw it as reason to champion their work initially ("De ussías"). Miranda Stewart has pointed to *cheli* as an anti-language, originating in major cities in Spain in the 1970s primarily within criminal subgroups, "spreading over time to a sector of the cultural elite and then among a wider youth community, principally to the *pasotas* but in some instances to Spanish youth in general" (91). Stewart states, "The main linguistic sources for *cheli* were in-group language of criminals and petty delinquents, loans from caló, the language of another marginal group, the gypsies, and borrowings from the language of the lumpenproletariat" (91). One of its principal confluences was drug trafficking culture (Stewart 91; Umbral *Diccionario* 43). The spread of *cheli* was not confined to face-to-face exchanges, however, as is the case with most covert argots (Stewart 91). The flourishing publishing world of underground magazines, fanzines (e.g., *Kallejero*) and the various creative arts of the *movida madrileña* (e.g., its use by pop groups such as *Gabinete Caligari* and characters in the films of Almodóvar of that period) facilitated the dissemination of *cheli* among less marginal groups (Stewart 91).

While serving to undercut hegemony's empire initially, *cheli* did not remain "underground" for long. In 1983, the year in which Umbral compiled the *Diccionario cheli*, *cheli's* status as a language, no matter how anti-language, had become institutionalized to some degree. In 1993, Ramoncín compiled *El tocho cheli: diccionario de jergas, germanías y jeringonzas* and its revised edition, *El nuevo tocho cheli*, in 1996. As "hick became chic" in the U.S. in the 1980s (Yardley), so *cheli* became increasingly co-opted and appropriated by a higher socioeconomic class in the 1990s in Spain. Its incorporation into literature by the works of *Realismo sucio* demonstrates the extent to which it had become popular among not so marginal groups, including the numerous readers that consumed these works.

In her analysis of the language in *Historias del Kronen*, Pilar Capanaga points to neologisms produced by the amalgation of noun phrases (Jenriretratodeunasesino, Lanaranjamecanica), and the "Spanishization" of anglicisms (*Yinkases* (gin + "Kas"), *rocanrol* (Rock and Roll), *De Quiur* (The Cure), *Depesh Mod* (Depech Mode). One might add that the anglicisms contained in the works of Mañas and other *Realismo sucio* writers are also specifically those that attest to the consumption of angloculture. In addition to the two forms of neologisms indicated by Capanaga, the reduction of *cheli* to a smattering of lexicon in the works of *Realismo sucio* mark it as post-*cheli*, while rendering it largely readable, and commodifiable.

Even today, after the dissemination of certain elements of *cheli* (for *cheli* has variations at the structural and phonetic level as well) among a wider audience, *caló*, which differs from standard Spanish virtually through lexical choice alone, remains virtually unintelligible except to user groups (Stewart 92). Stewart points to a recording made in a prison in which two petty delinquents simulate the planning, in a public space, of a burglary (Martín Rojo). The exchange demonstrates just how impenetrable this jargon can be to those outside its ingroup. Luisa Martín Rojo provides a translation of the transcription into standard colloquial Spanish and into English:

> Lacorro, mira, ligueramos a la rachí y asina mucho mejor . . . entrifamos por la perlacha aquella y si no, esparrábamos la burda. (259)

> Chaval, mira, venimos de noche y es mucho mejor, entramos por la ventana aquella y si no, forzamos la puerta.

(Look kid, we'll come here at night and it'll be much better, we get in through that window there, or if not, we'll break the door down.)

The language in Mañas's *Historias del Kronen*, as Raúl del Pozo states, "no es chulesco, ni de sainete, ni siquiera de yonky, ni calorro, ni flamenquista, ni el cheli que tan bien reflejó Umbral, ni argot, sino una jerga más simple, de los jóvenes de hoy que incluso han reducido el vocabulario de la primera movida" (It isn't *chulesco*, nor from a *sainete*, nor even that of a junkie, nor *calorro*, nor *flamenquista*, nor the *cheli* that Umbral captured so well, nor slang, but rather a more simple jargon, of a youth today that has even reduced the vocabulary from the first *movida*). Vázquez Montalbán similarly characterizes the work of Loriga, Mañas, and Prado as that in which "los jóvenes marginados de la burguesía madrileña . . . hablan mediante 40 palabras de argots mezclados" (13) (the marginalized youth of Madrid's bourgeoisie . . . speak by means of 40 words taken from mixed slangs). Thus, it may be argued that the translations of Carver's work were not the only "clean" texts to be found in Spain in the last two decades of the twentieth century: the post-*cheli* slang of *Realismo sucio* may also be argued to be rather "clean," commodified and commodifiable. The inclusion of the literary dialect of a truly marginal element of Spanish society, by the translators of Carver, or by the *Realismo sucio* writers themselves, would have resulted in much "dirtier" fiction than *Realismo sucio's* diluted *cheli* and its "palabras malsonantes" no matter how frequent.

The Translation of "América"

Within the space of this essay, the metaphorical translation of "América" (i.e. so often and problematically reduced to "U.S.A.") can only begin to be touched upon. However, in order to account for the class differences of *Realismo sucio* and Dirty Realism, an analysis of the translation of Carver's nonstandard English, must be complemented with other translations, both metaphorical and literal, that accompanied Carver's entrance into Spain. In a special issue of *Quimera* devoted to U.S. literature, Miguel Riera wrote, ". . . este movimiento [Dirty Realism] aparentemente ha triunfado aquí incluso *antes de que haya sido traducido ni uno solo de sus autores,* quizá con la excepción de *Catedral,* de Raymond Carver" (4, original emphasis) (Apparently, this movement [Dirty Realism] has triumphed here even *before any one of its authors has been translated,* with the exception, perhaps, of *Cathedral,* by Raymond Carver).

"América" in the Spanish imaginary is evidently linked to an urban setting, to youth, and to violence in a number of reviews of the Granta writers despite the particularities of their work. For example, in *El Urogallo*, Javier Goñi's article "Carver-Wolff-Ford; America en el fotomatón" appeared accompanied by a panoramic shot of Manhattan skyscrapers, even while none of the three writers that were the subject of the article had set the works under review in urban settings (*Tres rosas amarillas, Ladrón de cuarteles*, and *Rock Springs*). That Dirty Realism came to be associated with youth is evident in José Blay's statement: ". . . Richard Ford, que pese a sus cuarenta y seis años, bastantes más que los escritores que hemos citado anteriormente [Jay McInerney, Tama Janowitz, David Leavitt] también ha recibido en ocasiones el calificativo de Dirty Realism" (62) (Richard Ford, who despite his forty-six years of age, quite a few more than the writers whom we have cited previously, also has been categorized on occasion under Dirty Realism). As previously indicated, Richard Ford was one of the writers to have appeared in the first *Granta* issue to introduce the term.

In *ABC*, Miguel García-Posada's review of Carver's *¿Quieres hacer el favor de callarte, por favor?* states:

Carver ha inaugurado—se dice—una nueva visión del mundo, con la inmersión en una realidad descarnada, la contemplación sin máscaras ni mediaciones culturales de un universo lacerante, o el encuentro con la violencia de la sociedad urbana avanzada . . . La soledad, la pobreza y la violencia agobian los personajes de Carver . . . con [hipérboles] Carver 'dispara' una vez y otra su mensaje sobre la violencia que es inherente a determinadas estructuras sociales.

(Carver has inaugurated—it is said—a new world vision immersed in a stark reality, an unmasked and unmediated contemplation of a lacerating universe, an encounter with the violence of an advanced urban society . . . Loneliness, poverty, and violence overwhelm Carver's characters . . . with hyperbole, Carver "fires" time and again his message on the violence that is inherent to certain social structures.)

However, the urban violence that García-Posada suggests is mirrored in his word choice more so than it is to be found in the Carver collection reviewed. While Carver's work unveiled the dirt of the American Dream, it was neither urban nor violent (although Carver's writing certainly can be argued to contain verbal, and/or emotional violence). García-Posada's review leads potential readers, however, to expect murders, rapes, prostitution, drug overdoses, and other criminal activity encountered in urban neighborhoods.

Spanish audiences' interest was stirred, however, and the Spanish market was ripe for the publications of the *Granta* and other U.S. writers. As I have argued elsewhere, a translation "boom" characterized the Spanish publishing industry during the 1980s (Santana). UNESCO statistics show that in Spain translations from English into Spanish rose from two works in 1975 to 2036 works in 1990. U.S. writers belonging to generations prior and post the *Granta* writers were literally entering Spain in translation as never before.[8] Within three months of the first translation of Carver into Spanish, the translation of two other novels from the U.S. appeared that indelibly determined the understanding of Dirty Realism in Spain: Bret Easton Ellis's *Menos que cero* (Anagrama, 1987) and Jay McInerney's *Luces de neón* (Edhasa, 1987). Set in Los Angeles and Manhattan, respectively, both were first novels by young authors. *Menos que cero* narrates the story of a college student who returns home to Los Angeles during Christmas break. He has all the money (i.e. his parents' money) he could care to spend on alcohol and cocaine, as do his similarly affluent friends, a generation "que nada en dólares y cocaína en un mundo de Ferraris y jacuzzis; un mundo tan remoto para la mayoría de los mortals . . ." (Baeza) (swimming in dollars and cocaine in a world of Ferraris and jacuzzis; a world so remote to most mortals). McInerney's literary foray tells a similar story, that of a fact checker for a prestigious New York literary magazine who aids in his own self-destruction: a Manhattan described as "sofisticado y culto de los *yuppies*, de los cocainómanos de postín, borrachos caros e impotentes sexuales" (Harguindey) (the sophisticated and cultured Manhattan of yuppies, posh coke-heads, expensive drunks and the sexually impotent). The translation of McInerney and Ellis's novels reinforced images already associated with the United States: violence, youth, and metropolis.

One of the few critics writing at the time to have discerned the differences between Carver and the writers who followed was José Baeza. In *Quimera*, Baeza referred to the *Granta* writers as Minimalists, eschewing Buford's marketing term. In considering whether Ellis and McInerney's novels had "como movimiento precursor a Carver y a sus discípulos minimalistas," responded with a resounding "no." The predominant understanding of Dirty Realism in Spain, however, was a synchronic phenomenon which received the "newest" U.S. writers (new to Spain in translation, that is) as the "latest" (and youngest) generation of U.S. writers.

The generational conflation of U.S. writers is also evidenced photographically in the press. Pictures of Tobias Wolff and Jayne Anne Phillips (both belonging to the *Granta* group) appeared in the first *El País* article devoted to the topic. The photographs that accompanied the second *El País* article, "Las reglas de los sucio," to review Carver's and Wolff's work included photographs of Wolff, Phillips, and three additional writers who had not formed part of the original *Granta* issues and who had not been labeled Minimalists in the U.S.:

Tama Janowitz, David Leavitt, and Jay McInerney (10–11). David Leavitt's picture, alongside the headline, "Sucio y bruto" was the only one to accompany the review published in *La Vanguardia* of the *Dirty Realism/ Realisme brut* anthology, although his work was not included in the volume. He was neither considered part of the Dirty Realist writers in the U.S. nor was his work likened to McInerney and Ellis's. Levitt did, however, approximate Ellis's and McInerney's age. Some editor may have believed that the sexual orientation of his characters was reason to warrant his juxtaposition next to such a headline if, perhaps, only to better promote his work.

Many Spanish writers of the 1990s were subject to similar marketing strategies by their publishers, conflated on the basis of their age and their vocal allegiance to Anglophone influences. In this marketing climate, a picture was worth a thousand books: a review of Luis Magrinyà's *Belinda y el Monstruo*, published in *Quimera*, devoted a fourth of a page to a picture of Magrinyà (Calvo). Magrinyà wore a black leather jacket, leaning slightly forward and looking at the reader in a pose that uncannily echoes one of Raymond Carver's better known images. Magrinyà, had little else in common with *Realismo sucio* writers other than his age, and he is a generation younger than the Granta writer whom his picture aimed to echo.

With time, the "newest generation" of U.S. writers would come in hindsight to include Charles Bukowski (1920–1994), belonging to a generation prior to that of the *Granta* writers, but with whom Spanish readers were already somewhat familiar.[9] In an interview, Roger Wolfe, the bilingual writer of Spanish *Realismo sucio* stated:

> En mi modo de ver, se ha aplicado la etiqueta del realismo sucio de una forma errónea en España. Fue un término que surgió en los años ochenta para describir la obra de una serie de autores norteamericanos (. . .) que hacían una especie de realismo cotidiano. Lo de sucio sería porque se trataba de un realismo manchado por la vida, pero no pretendía ser una historia escatológica, sino historias de todos los días sobre problemas domésticos y cotidianos. (Tapia)

> (As I see it, the Dirty Realism label has been applied erroneously in Spain. It was a term that rose in the 80s to describe a series of North American authors (. . .) who did a type of everyday realism. The dirty part must have been because it was a realism soiled by life, but it didn't pretend to be a scatological history, rather a history of the everyday, about domestic, daily problems.)

Seven years earlier, David. C. Hall's introduction to Roger Wolfe's collection of short stories, *Quién no necesita algo en que apoyarse* (1993) had compared this writer of *Realismo sucio* to Carver, Bukowski, and Hemingway (14).

Realismo sucio was a term that sold in the press and would come to successfully sell books, both foreign and autochthonous, categorized as such. As Jorge Herralde has stated in his editorial memoir,

> La equívoca etiqueta de 'realismo sucio' hizo la fortuna que supongo imaginaba Bill, a costa de no pocos despistes por parte de críticos algo despistados. Así se asoció este presunto movimiento a Bukowski, quizá por lo *dirty* del *dirty old man*, cuando Carver parece, en todo caso, provenir más del lacónico Hemingway . . . (96)

> (The equivocal label "dirty realism" made the fortune I suppose Bill thought it might, at the cost of not a few slip-ups on the part of somewhat absent-minded critics. That is how this alleged movement became associated with Bukowski, perhaps because of the *dirty* of *dirty* old man, while Carver seems in any case, to come from the laconic Hemingway . . .)

The conflation must not have hurt Herralde's pocket either, given that it was Anagrama who first launched Carver and Bret Easton Ellis, then retroactively recovered Bukowski.

Carver's repeated association in the Spanish media with Bukowski, Ellis, McInerney, and Leavitt, is baffling unless one takes into account the publishing conflation and the ways in which, from a foreign perspective, the work of these writers can be argued to illustrate the "dirtyness" of "América." As Borges asserts in "Kafka y sus precursores," it is the emergence of Franz Kafka that changes, in hindsight, how those who preceded him are read, bringing a new sensibility to the form, tone, and mental affinity in the work of those who preceded him.[10] As Kafka creates his precursors, so the Spanish writers of *Realismo sucio* provide new insights into theirs, a fiction that has been a product of its critics as well as its writers.

While publicized as "shocking," "dirty," and "marginal," those young, "rebellious" writers that would appear to be problematic and disruptive were, in fact, achieving success center-stage. If we recall Iain Chambers's statement on the possibilities of art as, ". . . a space that can serve to interrupt the prevailing narrative of cultural subjectivity, citizenship and nation by introducing what refuses to make sense or speak in the prescribed way"(28), the particular incorporation of *cheli*, the marketing apparatus, and the critical reaction to *Realismo sucio* indicate that the disruptive potential of Spanish society represented by this movement was relegated to the sphere of saleable spectacle, a disruption of Spanish society "tamed" from its very birth. *Realismo sucio's* reception, both positive and negative, emphasized its "dirtyness" and "contamination," or alternately "renovation," of Spain's literary tradition by virtue of its "American-ness," while other kinds of "dirt" on Spanish soil remained unresolved. Considerably less commodified and commodifiable was Spain's problematically high unemployment rate, the rise in acts of terrorism by ETA during the first half of the 1990s, and the dirt of much dirtier discourse: the Caso Guerra, the Caso Filesa, the discovery of the government's implication in the counterterrorist organization GAL. The Socialist party also underwent an organic and historical rupture with its union brother the UGT (Juliá 269). The optimism with which the PSOE had been elected to power reached a bitter end fourteen years later. The Spanish worker, in as much as might be expected to be represented by the PSOE, and this worker's "language," (a worker by this time often a North African or Latin American immigrant) as might have been represented in the Carver translations, or in the works of *Realismo sucio*, was not to be found. Those who were truly marginal remained unseen, invisible beyond the optic of the market and the time, a time in which the market is only ever one lens, and which by virtue of its position remains blinded to that which lies outside its range.

Notes

1. For critics who refer to the influence of U.S Dirty Realism see Fortes (27), Gullón ("Cómo se lee" 31), Langa Pizarro (87, 185, 188), Masoliver Ródenas (25), Moreiras Menor (225), Oleza (42), Platas, Tyras (513), and Urioste (472). Carver is not the only Anglo model of writing that the Spanish writers claim or are claimed to appropriate (e.g., Bret Easton Ellis, Bukowski) but the name of the official "padre del realismo sucio" is insistently, if uncritically, referred to, when not also fictionalized within the work of the Spanish writers (e.g., Benjamín Prado's *Raro*, Roger Wolfe's poem, "Raymond Carver").

2. According to British writer and critic, Nick Hornby, the popularization of the terms Dirty Realism and Minimalism in Britain and the United States, respectively, mirrored a difference in critical reception. Hornby maintains that while American critics made much ado about the *Granta* writers' style, British critics concerned themselves with the content of their work (33). He explains that Buford's marketing strategy was meant to sell the new fiction to a well-read English audience, exploiting the fascination with American violence, consumerism, and pop culture iconography. American scholar, Robert Rebein, makes a similar point: "For the British, in short, dirty realism was a kind of truncated documentary naturalism that told the 'truth' about America

in the 1980s, even as imported television shows such as *Dallas* and *Dynasty* traded in 'lies'" (42). While the stories contained in the *Granta* issues do not quite deliver the expectations Buford's term may have aimed to create, Dirty Realism certainly "sold" as a term more so than "Minimalism," not only in Britain but in all other countries (e.g., Cuba, Italy, France, and Mexico) where the *Granta* writers came to be known, including Spain. The United States constitutes the only exception where the term "Dirty Realism" is little known, while "Minimalism" readily conjures Carver and his contemporaries' work.

3.   When comparing the individual *Granta* writers' publication statistics in Spain, for example, it does not come entirely as a surprise that the Spanish writers of *Realismo sucio*, which is almost entirely associated with male writers, have selected the male writers of U.S. Dirty Realism as their precursors. Half of the writers represented in the two *Granta* issues that introduced Dirty Realism were women, women who achieved a measurable level of success on the U.S. market. Yet critics and the writers (both male and female authors) of *Realismo sucio* do not mention these U.S writers when tracing the influences of *Realismo sucio*; the success of these women has neither literally nor figuratively translated significantly in Spain: Bobbie Ann Mason's *Shiloh and Other Stories*, which won the PEN/Hemingway Award, has only seen one edition in Spanish (Anagrama, 1987). Other works by Mason such as *In Country* (1985), *Feather Crowns* (1993), and the collection of stories *Love Life* (1989) remain untranslated into any Iberian language. Elizabeth Tallent's *Time with Children* (1987) was translated into Spanish (*Tiempo con niños*, Alfaguara, 1989). Her novel, *Museum Pieces*, while translated into Catalan (*Peces de museu*, 1988), has not been translated into Spanish. No subsequent editions have been issued, and other works such as *In Constant Flight* (1983)—which includes the *Granta* story "Why I Love Country Music"—and *Honey* (1993), also remain untranslated into an Iberian language. Jayne Anne Phillips is the one exception to the gender rule. Her work has found moderate success both among Spanish and Catalan publishers. *Machine Dreams* (*Sueños mecánicos*) saw two different editions and translations into Spanish (Edhasa, 1987, and Círculo de lectores, 1988), and one Catalan edition (*Somnis de màquina*, Columna, 1988). *Fast Lanes* (*Carriles rápidos*) was translated into Spanish (Edhasa, 1988) and into Catalan (*Vies ràpides*, Columna, 1989). *Shelter* was translated into Spanish in 1995 (*Campamento de verano*, Seix Barral). Interestingly, the debut collection of short stories that placed her on the U.S. literary map, *Black Tickets*, has not been translated into Spanish.

4.   Broyard also complained that nothing happened in Carver's fiction, such as in the story "Preservation" in which a couple's refrigerator stops working. In an interview, Carver's response to Broyard illustrates the socioeconomic gap that separates some critics from the dramatic tension that his fictional characters experience, and which may explain the perception of said fiction as Minimalism versus Dirty Realism within the United States: "Anatole Broyard tries to criticize my story "Preservation" by saying, "So the refrigerator breaks—why don't they just call a repairman and get it fixed?" That kind of remark is dumb. You bring a repairman out to fix your refrigerator and

it's sixty bucks to *fix* it; and who knows how much if the thing is completely broken. Well, Broyard may not be aware of it, but some people can't afford to bring in a repairman" (Ewing 111).

5. Categories of nonstandard English are taken from Traugott and Pratt's *Linguistics for Students of Literature* (1980) and Trudgill's *Sociolinguistics: An Introduction to Language and Society* (2000) where indicated. I thank Milton Azevedo for pointing me towards these texts as well as Miranda Stewart's *The Spanish Language Today* (1999).

6. While multiple negation is a characteristic of most non-standard varieties of English, its usage is standard in Spanish, as is well known.

7. The title story from Mason's collection, *Shiloh*, rich in its usage of nonstandard English, reads: "I've been to kingdom come and back in that truck out yonder," Leroy says to Mabel, "but we never yet set foot in that battleground. Ain't that something?" (Mason: 316). Antonio Mauri and Kosián Masoliver's translation reads: "—Con ese camión de ahí atrás he estado en todos los rincones de este país—le dice Leroy a Mabel—pero todavía no he pisado ese campo de batalla. ¿No te parece curioso?" Other examples include, "Well, facts is facts" (320); "—Bueno, son hechos inegables" (Mauri: 17); "Young folks want to be by theirselves." (322); "—Los jóvenes prefieren estar solos" (Mauri: 20).

8. The first translation into Spanish of the Canadian work by Douglas Coupland, *Generación X,* would not appear until 1993. The supposed influence of this book on the Spanish writers is also far from nuanced among critics as Santiago Fouz-Hernández has pointed out. For one, "Browsing through the more than two-hundred pages of the X Generation's 'Survival Guide' (supposedly one of [Spanish *Realismo sucio's*] key texts), it is interesting to discover that drugs (soft or hard) are hardly (if at all) mentioned" (85). More importantly, ". . . in the American context, this generation's main challenges are to tackle crime, to solve the job crisis, to reform politics, to put an end to homelessness and anti-gay discrimination, and to stop the spread of AIDS. This is very unlike the Spanish youth represented in *Kronen*, if not a complete antithesis of their (lack of) values" (85).

9. Bukowski's works were first published in Spain in 1978 by Anagrama: *Escritos de un viejo indecente, Erecciones, eyaculaciones, exhibiciones*, and *La máquina de follar.* The 1990s would see a resurgence in Bukowski's popularity.

10. Borges writes, "Si no me equivoco, las heterogéneas piezas que he enumerado se parecen a Kafka; si no me equivoco, no todas se parecen entre sí. Este último hecho es el más significativo. En cada uno de estos textos está la idiosincrasia de Kafka, en grado mayor o menor, pero si Kafka no hubiera escrito, no la percibiríamos; vale decir, no existiría" (173–74) (If I'm not mistaken, the heterogeneous pieces I have enumerated resemble Kafka; if I'm not mistaken, they do not all resemble each other. This last fact is the most significant. In each of these texts is Kafka's idiosyncrasy, to a greater or lesser degree, but if Kafka had not written, we wouldn't perceive it; it might well be said, it wouldn't exist).

Works Cited

Adelman, Bob. *Carver Country: The World of Raymond Carver.* New York: Collier Macmillan, 1990.

Altares, Guillermo. "Ray Loriga: 'Para escribir hay que ser radical.'" Interview. *El País* Nov. 22 1993,

Azevedo, Milton. "Literary Dialect as an Indicator of Sociolinguistic Conflict in Juan Marsé's *El amante bilingüe.*" *Journal of Interdisciplinary Literary Studies* 3.2 (1991): 126–36.

_____. "Orality in Translation: Literary Dialect from English into Spanish and Catalan." *Sintagma: Revista de Linguistica* 10 (1998): 27–43.

Baeza, José. "Adolescentes para adolescentes." *Quimera* December 1986: 70.

Bernadell, Carles. "Los que no son de Cuenca: retrato de un artista adolescente." *Quimera.* March 1996: 38–39.

Blay, José. "Una generación en pie de Guerra." *Leer.* June 1990: 51–63.

Borges, Jorge Luis. "Kafka y sus precursores." *Otras inquisiciones.* Buenos Aires: Emecé, 1996. 145–48.

_____. "Las versiones homéricas." *Prosa completa.* Barcelona: Bruguera, 1980. 239–43.

Broyard, Anatole. "Books of the Times." *New York Times* April 15 1981.

Buford, Bill. Introduction. "Dirty Realism: New Writing from America." *Granta* 8. Spring (1983). 4–5.

_____, ed. "More Dirt." *Granta* 19. Summer (1986).

_____. Trans. Javier Alfaya. "¿Sabe Ud. qué es 'Dirty Realism'?" *El País* October 16 1986, sec. Libros: 1+.

Bustelo, Gabriela. *Veo, veo.* Barcelona: Anagrama, 1996.

C. A. "La tribu del Kronen." *Leer* 82 (1996): 30–33.

Calvo, Xavier. "Representación de la representación." *Quimera.* March 1996: 46.

Campbell, Ewing. *Raymond Carver: A Study of the Short Fiction.* New York: Twayne, 1992.

Capanaga, Pilar. "La creación léxica en *Historias del Kronen.*" *Lo Spagnolo D'oggi: Forme Della Comunicazione.* Roma: Bulzoni Editore, 1995. 49–59.

Carver, Raymond. *Catedral.* Trans. Ibáñez Gómez, Benito. 6th ed. Barcelona: Editorial Anagrama, 1999.

_____. *Cathedral.* New York: Vintage Books, 1989.

_____. *De qué hablamos cuando hablamos de amor.* Trans. Jesús Zulaika Goicoechea. 1st ed. Barcelona: Círculo de Lectores, 1988.

_____. *¿Quieres hacerte el favor de callarte, por favor?* Trans. Jesús Zulaika. Barcelona Editorial Anagrama, 1999.

_____. *Tres rosas amarillas.* Trans. Jesús Zulaika. 2nd ed. Barcelona: Editorial Anagrama, 2000.

_____. *What We Talk About When We Talk About Love: Stories.* New York: Knopf, 1981.

_____. *Where I'm Calling From: New and Selected Stories*. New York: Atlantic Monthly Press, 1988.

_____. *Will You Please Be Quiet, Please?* New York: Vintage Books, 1992.

Chambers, Iain. "Citizenship, Language, and Modernity." *PMLA; Special Topic: Mobile Citizens, Media States* 117.1 (2001): 24–31.

Conte, Rafael. "Historias del Kronen." *ABC Cultural* March 4 1994: 11.

_____. "De qué hablamos cuando hablamos de amor". *ABC literario*. Oct. 3, 1987: 14.

de España, Ramón. "Carver, pequeños fragmentos del horror." *La Vanguardia* Sept. 29, 1988, sec. Libros: 35.

de Paola, Luis. "Luces de neón." *ABC literario* March 21 1987: 10.

del Pozo, Raúl. "'Kronen,' la novela-magnetofón." *El Mundo* April 12 1994: 37.

Dorca, Toni. "Joven narrativa en la España de los noventa: la Generación X." *Revista de Estudios Hispánicos* 31 (1997): 309–24.

Echevarría, Ignacio. "El lobo feroz; Roger Wolfe novela las andanzas de un psicópata." *El País* December 11 1993, sec. *Babelia*.

Ellis, Bret Easton. *Menos que cero*. Trad. Mariano Antolín Rato. Barcelona: Anagrama, 1986.

Fidalgo, Feliciano. "'Venga, rulamos un porrito.'" Interview. *El País* Feb. 27 1994.

Fortes, José Antonio. "Del 'Realismo sucio' y otras imposturas en la novela española última." *Ínsula*. 589–90, (1996): 21+.

Fouz-Hernández, Santiago. "Generación X? Spanish Urban Youth Culture at the End of the Century in Mañas/ Armendáriz's *Historias del Kronen*." *Romance Studies* 18/1 (2000): 83–98.

Frank, Thomas and Matt Weiland. *Commodify Your Dissent*. New York: W.W. Norton, 1997.

García-Posada, Miguel. "¿Quieres hacer el favor de callarte, por favor?" *ABC literario* Sept. 17 1988: 3.

_____. "Tres rosas amarillas." *ABC literario* December 9 1989: 9.

Gearhart, Michael William. "Breaking the Ties that Bind: Inarticulation in the Fiction of Raymond Carver." *Studies in Short Fiction* 26/4 Fall (1989): 439–46.

Goñi, Javier. "Carver-Wolff-Ford, América en el fotomatón." *El Urogallo*. May (1990): 82–84.

Goody, Jack and Ian Watt. "The Consequences of Literacy." *Comparative Studies in Society and History* 5 (1963): 304–45.

Gracia, Jordi. "Prosa narrativa. Introducción." *Los nuevos nombres: 1975–2000*. Ed. Jordi Gracia. *Historia y crítica de la literatura española*. Vol. 9/1. Barcelona: Crítica, 2000. 208–44.

Grijalba, Silvia. "Se busca joven escritor." *El Mundo* Jan. 17 1996: 41.

Gullón, Germán. "Cómo se lee una novela de la última Generación (Apartado X)." *Ínsula* 589–590 (1996): 31–33.

_____. *Prólogo a J.A. Mañas, Historias del Kronen*. Barcelona: Destino, 1998.

Halliday, M.A.K. *Language as a Social Semiotic: The Social Interpretation of Language and Meaning.* London: Edward Arnold, 1978; Stewart, 91.

Harguindey, Ángel S. "Lucidez y cinismo." *El País* January 15 1987: 3.

Herralde, Jorge. "Raymond Carver Memorial en Londres." *El observatorio editorial.* Buenos Aires: Adriana Hidalgo, 2004.

Hornby, Nick. *Contemporary American Fiction.* New York: St. Martin's Press, 1992.

Howe, Irving. "Stories of Our Loneliness." *New York Times* September 11, 1983.

"Index Translationum." <http://databases.unesco.org/xtrans/stat/xTransStat.html.>

Januszczak, Waldemar. "America's Chekhov." *The Guardian* August 19 1988.

Juliá, Santos. *Un siglo de España; política y sociedad.* Madrid: Marcial Pons, 1999.

Langa Pizarro, M. Mar. *Del franquismo a la posmodernidad: la novela española (1975–1999).* Alicante: Universidad de Alicante, 2000.

Loriga, Ray. *Héroes.* Barcelona: Plaza & Janés, 1993.

_____. *Lo peor de todo.* Madrid: Editorial Debate, 1992.

Malamet, Elliot. "Raymond Carver and the Fear of Narration." *Journal of the Short Story in English* 17 Autumn (1991): 59–74.

Mañas, José Ángel. *Historias del Kronen.* Barcelona: Ediciones Destino, 1994.

Martín Rojo, Luisa. "The Jargon of Delinquents and the Study of Conversational Dynamics." *Journal of Pragmatics* 21.3 (1994): 243–89.

Mason, Bobbi Ann. *Shiloh and Other Stories.* New York: Harper & Row, 1982.

_____. *Shiloh.* Trans. Antonio Mauri and Kosián Masoliver. Barcelona: Anagrama, 1987.

Masoliver Rodenas, Juan Antonio. "Encuesta a los críticos." *Ínsula* "Narrativa española al filo del milenio." 589–590. January-February (1996): 25–26.

McInerney, Jay. *Luces de neón.* Trans. Elena Rius. Barcelona: Edhasa, 1986.

Moreiras Menor, Cristina. *Cultura herida: literatura y cine en la España democrática.* Madrid: Ediciones Libertarias, 2002.

Oleza, Joan. "Un realismo posmoderno." *Ínsula* Jan./Feb. (1996): 589–90.

Platas Tasende, Ana María. "Generación de 1995." *Diccionario de términos literarios.* Madrid: Espasa-Calpe, 2000: 281.

Prado, Benjamín. *Raro.* Barcelona: Plaza & Janés, 1997.

Real Academia Española. *Diccionario de la lengua española.* Madrid: Espasa Calpe, 1992.

Rato, Mariano Antolín. "Digno ante la vulgaridad, y decente." *El Urogallo* 1988: 62–63.

_____. "Raymond Carver: padre del realismo sucio." *El Urogallo* 1988: 60–62.

Rebein, Robert. *Hicks, Tribes, and Dirty Realists: American Fiction after Postmodernism.* Lexington: University of Kentucky Press, 2001.

Riera, Miguel. "Muchas voces, muchos ámbitos." *Quimera.* Nov. 70/71 (1987): 4–5.

Santana, Cintia. "The Elephant in the America's Room." *Going Transatlantic: Towards an Ethics of Dialogue.* Ed. Marina Pérez de Mendiola. [forthcoming in *Chasqui*]

Santos, Alonso. "Ser joven para triunfar." *Leer* 82 (1996): 23–29.

Scobie, Brian. "Carver Country." *Forked Tongues? Comparing Twentieth-Century British and American Literature.* Ed. Ann Massa and Alistair Stead. London: Longman, 1994: 273–94.

Senabre, Ricardo. "Héroes." *ABC literario* December 24 1993: 9.

Stewart, Miranda. *The Spanish Language Today*. London: Routledge, 1999.

Suñen, Juan Carlos. "Las nuevas generaciones." *El País* September 18 1988.

———. "Las reglas de lo sucio." *El País* September 18 1988, sec. Libros, 1+.

Tapia, Juan Luis. *Ideal*. April 5, 2001: 50.

Traugott, Elizabeth C. and Marie Louise Pratt. *Linguistics for Students of Literature*. New York: Harcourt Brace Jovanovich, 1980.

Trudgill, Peter. *Sociolinguistics: An Introduction to Language and Society*. London: Penguin, 2000.

Tuneu, Miquel, (ed.) *Dirty Realism/ Realisme brut: nova narrativa nord-americana*. Trans. Hortènsia Curell i Gotor. 2 vols. Barcelona: Eumo, 1987.

Tyras, Georges. "Figures De Postmodernité." *Los nuevos nombres: 1975–2000; 9/1*. Ed. Jordi Gracia. Barcelona: Crítica, 513–15.

Umbral, Francisco.

    <http://www.elmundo.es/papel/hemeroteca/1996/10/13/opinion/171679.html>

———. "De ussías, garzones, aznares y Valle-Inclán." *El Mundo* Oct. 13, 1996.

———. *Diccionario cheli*. Barcelona: Grijalbo, 1983.

Urioste, Carmen de. "La narrativa española de los noventa: ¿Existe una 'Generación X'?" *Letras Peninsulares* 10.3 Winter (1997): 455–76.

Vázquez Montalbán, Manuel. "La 'Generación x, y, z.'" *El País* September 2 1995: 12–13.

Wekker, Gloria and Herman Wekker. "Coming in from the Cold: Linguistic and Socio-Cultural Aspects of the Translation of Black English Vernacular Literary Texts into Surinamese Dutch." *Babel: Revue Internationale de la Traduction/International Journal of Translation* 37.4 (1991): 221.

Wolfe, Roger. "Hablar, hablar, hablar." *El Mundo* Oct. 26 1996, sec. Libros: 17.

———. "Raymond Carver." *El invento*. Málaga: Cuadernos de Trinacria, 2001. 62–63.

———. *Quién no necesita algo en que apoyarse*. Alicante: Aguaclara, 1993.

Yardley, Jonathan. "Chic to Chic: The Country Way of Life." *Washington Post* March 25 1985.

Part II
Can Anyone Rock Like We Do?
Sex, Drugs, and Rock & Roll, Then and Now

◆ **4**

Can Anyone Rock Like We Do?
Or, How the Gen X Aesthetic Transcends
the Age of the Writer

Samuel Amago

Criticism of the emerging canon of Generation X writers has emphasized the importance of a sex, drugs and rock and roll aesthetic linked to Anglo-American popular culture. What has tended to elude study is the prevalence of controlled substances in works by previous generations of Spanish novelists. Indeed, some of the foundational works of the post-Franco period are steeped in their own drug culture. Juan Goytisolo's *La reivindicación del Conde don Julián* (1970), for example, cannot be understood fully without a consideration of the importance of hashish to the narrator's ever-deteriorating mental state, while in Carmen Martín Gaite's *El cuarto de atrás* (1978), the hallucinogenic pills that C. ingests with the Man in Black play an important structural role. These novels' adversarial critical stances vis-à-vis some of the most ingrained commonplaces of Spanish cultural history make them fine models for the Gen X project of the 1990s, which on both sides of the Atlantic has taken an iconoclastic approach to cultural tradition.

Inspired in part by Robert Spires's recent article, "Depolarization and the New Spanish Fiction at the Millennium," in which the author problematizes generational shibboleths, this essay investigates how the Generation X aesthetic that came to the fore in the early 1990s might be profitably expanded to include work by writers born in the 1940s and 1950s. In the following pages, I explore some of the points of contact between younger Gen X writers and the more "mature" (Gracia 238) generation of Spanish writers that continues to write and publish alongside them—authors such as Nuria Amat (b. 1950), Carlos Cañeque (b. 1957), Juan Madrid (b. 1947), Eduardo Mendoza (b. 1943), Juan José Millás (b. 1947), Antonio Muñoz Molina (b. 1956), and Manuel Rivas (b. 1957). From this admittedly broad and varied range of writers—all of whom have drawn in one way or another upon some of the styles and themes that we now associate with Gen X literature—I focus here on Juan José Millás and Carlos Cañeque because of the critical acknowledgment that they received in the 1990s both in the form of the Premio Nadal—a prize that served to legitimize at least two Gen X authors—and that they continue to receive in the pages of academic journals and scholarly monographs.

Juan José Millás is routinely recognized as one of the most popular and critically acclaimed authors writing in Spain today, sharing his position on the bestseller lists with younger writers such as Lucía Etxebarria, Ray Loriga, and José Ángel Mañas. Among other literary awards, he won the Nadal prize for *La soledad era esto* in 1990, and the Premio Primavera for *Dos mujeres en Praga* (2002). He is the author of more than thirteen novels, seven collections of short stories and essays, and he has been a regular contributor in the Spanish press. Carlos Cañeque has not enjoyed the same kind of success as some of his contemporaries, although he has recently begun to receive deserved critical attention for his first novel, *Quién* (Premio Nadal 1997) (Amago; Kunz). Cañeque has since published two other novels with major Spanish publishing houses, *Muertos de amor* (1999) and *Conductas desviadas* (2002); two books of nonfiction: *Dios en América* (1988) and *Conversaciones sobre Borges* (1995); and two books about Borges for children, *El pequeño Borges imagina el Quijote* (2003) and *El pequeño Borges imagina la Biblia* (2002); and several co-edited scholarly volumes.

Taking as my point of departure these two Premio Nadal-winning novels of the 1990s, Millás's *La soledad era esto* (1990) and Cañeque's *Quién* (1997), I argue that the aesthetic that we have come to associate with Gen X is not entirely unique to younger authors such as Mañas, Etxebarria, and Loriga, but rather, that this aesthetic transcends the chronological paradigm of the literary generation and brings together a wide group of writers of varying ages who published novels in the 1990s. Like the Gen X writers with whom they share the pages of literary supplements and academic journals, older authors like Millás and Cañeque draw upon sex, drugs, rock and roll, and literary criticism as methods not only to reexamine our contemporary experience of reality but also to propose new ways of representing it through the use of self-conscious narrative strategies, a critical examination of "canonical" texts, the fusion of popular and literary cultures, and the exploitation of a 1990s poetics of disaffection that functions as a critical response to economic, social and political discontent.

While my purpose here is not to define the Generation X aesthetic or to explain its provenance—critics such as Toni Dorca, Christine Henseler, Jason Klodt, and María Pao have made important contributions on this theme already in the Peninsular context—I should like to offer a brief synthesis of some of the themes and forms that have come to be associated with Gen X fiction in order to analyze later the work of Millás and Cañeque within the larger literary context of the 1990s. In addition to the sex, drugs, and rock and roll paradigm I mention above, Gen X narrative is typified by some of the following themes: a sometimes nihilistic stance of resistance to dominant cultures; marginalization and estrangement, either self-imposed or imposed by society; inability or unwillingness to engage in meaningful social intercourse with partners and/ or peers; vitriolic antiestablishment attitude, often in terms of a perceived or desired generational conflict and/or misunderstanding; emphasis on achieving or maintaining personal authenticity, usually through oppositional strategies of identification; slackerism, boredom, depression and self-pity; protracted interest in the materiality of the body; and a well-articulated awareness and acknowledgment of foreign literatures and cinematic traditions. Related to these themes are narrative forms that may be called a poetics of disaffection: ironic commentary on the trappings of literary representation; critical distance; complexity; fragmentation; use of vernacular language and emphasis on dialogue (and, conversely, a predominance of first-person narration); intertextuality, usually through references to popular culture, rock music and punk; self-referentiality; intermingling of reality and fiction / abstraction from reality; drug and alcohol abuse as structuring elements; communal production through multiple narrators and/or the illusion of collaborative literary production; open-ended resolutions (Dorca; Gracia; Henseler; Pao; Ulrich and Harris).

In the following two sections, I discuss *La soledad era esto* and *Quién* in terms of these Gen X poetics of disaffection and propose that many of the formal and thematic characteristics that exemplify youth narrative of the 1990s transcend the "Generation X" moniker and in fact infiltrate much of contemporary Spanish literary production by writers born not just in the 1960s and 1970s, but also in the 1940s and 1950s.

La soledad era esto

In a music review published in the *New Yorker*, Sasha Frere-Jones writes that "rock bands, like people, are living longer" (94). Discussing several big ticket rock concerts of 2004, Frere-Jones points to the continuing success and relevance of aging rock stars and bands such as Bob Dylan, REM, The Pixies, U2 and David Bowie, who have continued to tour and release popular, critically acclaimed albums well into and beyond middle age. To varying degrees, these musicians represent important influences on subsequent popular music and literature and have been involved in contemporary inter-generational cultural production. We may recall, for example, the collaboration between Pearl Jam and Neil Young—the de facto elder statesman of grunge—on his "Mirror Ball" album released in 1995, a record that demonstrated how two generations of rock musicians might collaborate and challenge each other in the production of a recording that, for lack of better words, really rocked. Similarly, Spanish novelists born in the 1940s and 1950s such as Rosa Montero, Manuel Rivas, Antonio Muñoz Molina, Carlos Cañeque and Juan José Millás have all continued to rock the literary establishment in novels published coetaneously with those produced by a younger generation of writers by pushing the limits of the novelistic genre; engaging critically with conventional ideas about high and low brow cultural production; self-consciously exploring the boundaries between reality and fiction, self and other, and received notions of literary tradition.

Juan José Millás, whose novels can be read and understood within the context of Gen X narratives of the 1990s, is, like Neil Young, an elder statesman of the same kind of anomy and alienation that pervades transatlantic cultural production of the 1990s. Among the principal themes of his fiction are the individual's alienation by contemporary society and his or her search for a more authentic existence; the exploration of the processes of constructing and representing personal identity; and the examination of the writer's attempt to understand reality through writing. I begin this essay with *La soledad era esto* because of the critical acknowledgement it received with the Premio Nadal and because the novel appeared at the beginning of what would later become the Gen X decade. Millás's stature in the Spanish literary world makes him a propitious beginning example of how older writers can rock just as hard as we do. *La soledad era esto* in particular shares many thematic and structural elements—an emphasis on drugs and rock and roll, a fragmented multivocal discourse, a marginalized slacker protagonist, protracted generational and familial estrangement, social and mental disconnection—with Gen X works written around the same time in the United States and Spain, and consequently serves to demonstrate how this aesthetic permeates Spanish narrative of the 1990s regardless of the age of the writer.

La soledad era esto, like many other Millás novels and many Gen X works of fiction, is about alienation and the search for personal authenticity. The protagonist, Elena Rincón, is estranged from her surroundings: she remains ignorant of her grown daughter's pregnancy and is at odds with her increasingly distant husband, whom she suspects of having an affair. Perhaps because she has no profession, Elena spends most of her days smoking hashish and strolling about her northeast Madrid neighborhood known as "Prosperidad." Elena is not only disconnected from her daughter and her husband, but she also avoids family responsibilities upon the death of her mother and thereby creates further emotional distance from her brother and sister.

Elena Rincón is an angsty, neurotic forty-year-old who meanders without points of reference through her geographic and personal spaces. The free indirect style of the novel's first part focalizes on her consciousness as she struggles to come to terms with her self-imposed solitude and estrangement. Having just learned of her mother's death, Elena becomes aware of generational continuity and conflict through the reading of her mother's diary, and although she realizes that she shares more with her mother than she thought, she eschews meaningful contact with her daughter in order to submerge herself in her own personal development. Like Lucía Etxebarria's protagonists in Amor, curiosidad, prozac y dudas (1997) and Beatriz y los cuerpos celestes (1998) published later in the decade, Millás's novel explores the ebb and flow of a feminine subjectivity and "the estranging effects of individual autonomy and the failure of intimacy" (Klodt 3), all the while embracing the Gen X notion that depression, introspection, and solitude may be cathartic methods of walking a path to possible redemption. La soledad era esto documents the process of Elena's gradual personal metamorphosis as she comes to terms with her alienation, following the pattern of the Kafka tale from which Millás draws his epigraph. From monstrous disaffection Elena seeks to become more authentically human and finally come to terms with her self-imposed solitude and alienation.

Millás's novel is composed of a variety of textual elements: Elena's mother's diaries, her own diaries, reports from the private detective she has hired, a letter from her husband, and a transmogrified Beatles song. In part one, Elena is both protagonist and reader; she is the object of the overarching narrative of the novel in which she has a more passive role while she reads her mother's diaries and the detective's reports. In part two, Elena assumes the role of narrator of this novel about herself, creating her own discourse from her own point of view while commenting directly upon the construction of the other narratives that comprise the text. Elena's disjointed experience of reality is reflected in the fragmented discourse that communicates her story. Her interior life is documented by an impersonal, unknown omniscient narrator, while her movements in the city are painstakingly recorded by the private detective she had hired earlier to follow her husband. This personal and textual fragmentation also reflects the generational separation that Elena perpetuates by distancing herself from her better-adjusted daughter, her mother before she died, and her brother and sister.

Acknowledging that she is alienated from her own life (20) and from the lives of her family (146), Elena is trapped in a self-perpetuating downward spiral of drug and alcohol abuse that further exacerbates her alienation and misanthropy. As she points out variously throughout the novel, hashish (sometimes combined with whisky) allows her to control the images that comprise her life (94) and alter in some way her reality: "sometimes a joint modifies my vision of reality. The bad thing is that lately it accentuates the reality I'm trying to escape from" (153).[1] Nevertheless, she does assign marijuana a positive role in her personal transformation, saying that "thanks to hashish I was able to access a new perception of reality and escape from the prison that awaits so many women" (177). At the same time, however, Elena realizes that her drug use was also an important part of her self-destructive behavior and she consequently vows to stop smoking so much. Related to her drug habit are Elena's hygiene and intestinal problems. After attending the burial of her mother, Elena wanders through the streets of Madrid, unshowered and unshaven. She has not showered or shaved her left leg in several days because of a mental association she has created between her mother's passing and the bathroom. Elena's hygienic tics reflect the total loss of symmetry and order from Elena's perception of space and time, while simultaneously pointing to the extent to which she embodies a slacker/stoner persona. In the novel's final chapters, the detective she has hired to follow her and write reports about her activities notices that she must have quit smoking so much weed because of her improved personal hygiene and physical appearance, two common casualties suffered by the habitual stoner.[2]

Elena's excessive use of hashish is linked structurally to the Beatles' tune, "Lucy in the Sky with Diamonds," a song that has been commonly associated with the drug culture of the 1960s.[3] The song is imbedded in the novel's first part, and the fact that the tune appears here translated into Spanish points to a nearly unconscious appropriation of British-American rock music by contemporary Spanish culture. As she enjoys a beer at a cafeteria, the sound system pipes in the Beatles song that she translates mentally. In Elena's mind, the lyrics cross national and linguistic boundaries to become immediately relevant to her own situation, and while the song initially improves her mood, Elena quickly loses her sense of well being as all the images that constitute her perception of reality become confused. As her ability to distinguish between what is real and unreal begins to collapse, she realizes that she is literally living in a world like that of the Beatles song. Elena wanders through a nearby neighborhood and sees juxtaposed images that whirl through her brain: her unshaved leg, the wet streets, a broken streetlight, a plastic minister, a marmalade river with caramel boats, the cadaver of her mother wrapped in green and yellow cellophane (32). This schizophrenic apparition of images is a technique exploited by many Gen X writers, especially Loriga (*Tokio ya no nos quiere* 1999), and serves to represent emblematically the conflicting facets of her fragmented perception of reality. This collapse of reality and fiction—a melding of psychedelic song imagery, quotidian Madrid, and reminders of personal loss—lead Elena back to her previous nihilistic vision of a "reality condemned to death" (*Soledad* 30). Searching for a bathroom to relieve her chronic colic, she enters a kindergarten and passes out with her underwear around her ankles. This is perhaps the lowest point to which Elena will fall, and from this moment to the end of the novel she struggles to reconcile her slacker attitude, the generational conflict that she has constructed between herself and her daughter and dead mother, her unwillingness to settle things with her husband, and her growing self-awareness and reconciliation with her previous identity crisis.

What distinguishes Elena's alienation from that of a younger generation is that she devotes much of her social criticism not to a previous generation but to the corruption that she sees in her own cohort. While her critical stance does not approximate the vitriol that characterizes Jesús, the narrator of Millás's *Tonto, muerto, bastardo e invisible* (1995)—another novel that picks up and amplifies Gen X static—her identity crisis is very similar.[4] Elena, for her part, is appalled by people like her husband, a low-level government bureaucrat who has been embezzling funds and investing them abroad. He is a cynical, self-identified sell-out (86–87) who has given up his youthful idealism in favor of making money. Elena's husband has become a corporate phony much like the television studio executive played by Ben Stiller in *Reality Bites* (1994), who packages the images of youthful idealism for an MTV-style television show. Elena's husband, on the other hand, cynically acknowledges that he no longer has to identify with the losers in the struggle between the classes because he has become a winner. Having worked his way up in the ranks of corporate Spain, he now believes that the very corruption that he has come to embrace is an important, even necessary, part of any system (122). While Elena finds his attitude disgusting, she also realizes that he, at the very least, may rely on his status within this corrupt socio-economic system as a way to certify his existence and define himself (128), while she has no such method of self-definition. Elena Rincón is a woman without qualities, and faced with forming a part of a corrupt, diseased social order, she chooses to opt out rather than sell-out. As a reader of Kafka's *Metamorphosis*, Elena seeks to reconcile her inner and outer selves and achieve personal authenticity, while her husband picks up the story and rereads it, not from the perspective of the victim Gregor Samsa, but from the point of view of Gregor's family and his boss (86–87) in order to understand his own newfound position as a "winner" in the contemporary class struggle.[5]

As she herself indicates in the second part of the novel, Elena views her husband and daughter as if they were two fragments of her identity that have been separated from her being. Consequently, she regards her life as useless and mutilated (117), her experience of the world is a collection of unrelated fragments. The solitude to which the novel's title alludes is a direct result of Elena's sense of generational and economic alienation and subsequent search for a personal, inner understanding as she undergoes her transformation. Solitude, she says, is an amputation that she can barely perceive (135), a fragmentation of the body and the body politic.

Much like the reader finds in Mañas's *Historias del Kronen*, the protagonist of *La soledad era esto* inhabits a markedly specific geographical and cultural milieu that is contemporary Madrid. Taking into account the geographic language (concrete street names and numerous cartographic references) that pervades Millás's text, it becomes apparent that the key to Elena's eventual metamorphosis will be the dual activities of reading and writing, both of which function as symbolic cartographic acts that orient and situate Elena in a more concrete physical and emotional space and allow her to reconstruct her own identity through an oppositional strategy of self-identification: she is *not* like her husband, she is *not* like her mother, she is *not* like her daughter.

Having discovered that her husband has been cheating on her and that she does not really care after all, Elena hires a private detective to follow and write reports of her activities. These reports form an important part of the novel's discourse, and as she becomes more comfortable with her narrator for hire, Elena begins her *literary* criticism of them. This technique represents a key characteristic of postmodern metafiction, which seeks to break down "the distinctions between 'creation' and 'criticism' and merges them into the concepts of 'interpretation' and 'deconstruction'" (Waugh 6). Although she does not reach the extreme of Antonio López, the protagonist of Cañeque's *Quién*, Elena's role in the novel becomes that of an alienated critic who attempts to create something through criticism. A careful reading of the work reveals that as her story continues, Elena's directions to the investigator become increasingly narrative—indeed, critical. With the help of her private investigator, Elena goes about the work of self-centeredly and self-consciously producing what ultimately amounts to a novel about herself. The private investigator's third-person narrative complements her own first-person account of her life. This illusion of collaborative critical production functions as an important structuring principle; it is a method of de-centering the self and converting it into a text that may be read, interpreted, commented upon and understood. Gen X narrative culture, as Traci Carroll writes in an intriguing discussion of *Beavis and Butt-Head* and *Mystery Science Theater 3000*, draws heavily upon this kind of communal critical production. Carroll notes that one of the main thematic concerns of Gen X writing and criticism has to do with "making something out of nothing, of creating something out of an ever-shrinking economic security that is perceived as a nothing, an empty set, an 'X'" (Carroll 201). Alienated from her family, her husband, her society in general, and having no economic opportunities or adequate social alternatives of her own, Elena is similarly forced to fashion a new self out of nothing by cobbling together all of the various texts that are, in some way, about her.

As she goes about the business of re-writing her self, Elena essentially promotes her private investigator into a narrator-for-hire, and thus she becomes both an object of investigation and a discerning critical subject. This self-conscious collapse of traditional distinctions between subject and object effectively transforms Elena Rincón into her own shrink while complicating the tradition of the noir P.I. This self-conscious game between subject and object is very much a part of the postmodern narrative culture of the 1990s, in which conventional hard-and-fast binary distinctions are complicated in order to draw attention to the importance of multiple perspectives to the representation and interpretation of reality.

Carroll writes that, in many ways, "Generation X rhetoric reproduces Beat generation clichés about white alienation, but instead of taking the alienated artist as its emblem, Gen X culture focuses on the textual consumer—the alienated critic" (205). Much criticism of Gen X culture points to the widespread dearth of economic opportunities, the dehumanizing effects of some aspects of postmodern cultures, and the ills of contemporary social, cultural and economic reality as generative causes of its generational anomy. Faced with selling out like her husband, Elena chooses to take control of her life (180), find an apartment, and stop smoking so much weed. She realizes that perhaps no one ever really finishes constructing his or her personal identity (166), and that perhaps identity is *supposed* to be tenuous (156, 159). Like the younger generation that would come of age in the 1990s, Elena Rincón must come to terms with the idea that perhaps our identities are composed of nothing more than a seemingly random conglomeration of stories, sound bites, songs and film clips. Although Millás suggests that personal identity is provisional, the novel nevertheless ends with a possibly positive open-ended conclusion in which Elena takes control of this novel about herself and begins the introspective, contemplative life of a writer. But she still does not appear to have found a job.

Quién

Carlos Cañeque is a titular professor of political science at the Autonomous University of Barcelona, but the bulk of his published work is literary. While he has only recently begun to be recognized for his fiction, the author's first novel, *Quién*, is particularly noteworthy because of its ingenious engagement with many of the commonplaces of literary postmodernism. Further, the novel represents an important example of how Jorge Luis Borges has grown in importance in the contemporary Spanish literary sphere. Its biting irony, humor and pure enjoyability make the novel arguably Cañeque's best work to date, in spite of the fact that his two subsequent novels touch on some of the same themes—the literary marketplace, social estrangement, narcissistic nihilism, narrative self-consciousness—and the protagonists of *Quién* appear in his later novel, *Muertos de amor*.

Quién not only appeared in the midst of the Gen X decade—three years after José Ángel Mañas was chosen as a finalist for *Historias del Kronen* in 1994 and one year before Lucía Etxebarria won the award for *Beatriz y los cuerpos celestes* in 1998—and the novel embodies much of the alienation and anomy that typifies 1990s narrative fiction. In these ways, the novel represents a prime example of how the Gen X aesthetic has tended to transcend generational taxonomies, bringing together writers born in the 1940s, 1950s, 1960s and 1970s as they use sex, drugs, rock and roll and literary criticism to represent their multiple experiences of contemporary reality.

Quién shares many formal characteristics with the tradition of Gen X novels written by younger writers. Its defeated nihilistic protagonist, Antonio López, is very much like Mañas's narrator Carlos of *Historias del Kronen* in his egocentric misanthropy, antiestablishment attitude, and acute critical acumen—while Carlos is well-versed in the language of cinema and film criticism, Antonio is a well-read professor and critic of literature. In addition, *Quién* offers a protracted ironic commentary on the many traditions of literary representation through a carefully constructed critical distance that brings the novel in line with many other Gen X works. This self-conscious distance is created through the use of multiple and mutually aware narrators, critics, scholars and readers, all of whose voices converge in the novel in order to create the illusion of a collaborative literary production. Indeed, *Quién* is about creation through criticism; all of the voices that appear in the novel belong to critics of one kind or another. Cañeque's work shares with the youth narrative of the 1990s a formal complexity derived through fragmentation, self-conscious intertexuality, and use of drugs and alcohol as important structuring elements.

Quién is made up of first person stream of consciousness; third person omniscient points of view; transcripts of conversations; letters; scholarly prologues to critical editions of the novel; fictional reviews of *Quién* taken from newspapers and scholarly articles; and footnotes which comment upon the novel even while it is being "constructed." There are at least three possible narrators: Antonio López, Gustavo Horacio Gilabert, and Luis López (Antonio's estranged brother), although many other narrative voices appear throughout. Composed of such varied textual elements, the novel's title alludes to the indeterminacy that characterizes the entire narrative: Who is the real author of this novel?

Antonio López, the first person narrator of chapter one and ostensibly the novel's principal protagonist, is a defeated, unsuccessful, nihilistic college professor trapped in what he characterizes as a loveless marriage. Nevertheless, this numbingly banal married life is useful to Antonio in at least one way, as it allows him the peace and quiet he needs in order to begin his novel (25). Many of the work's unnumbered sections deal directly with Antonio's narcissistic desire to write something that will save him from his "painful anonymity" (14), for he believes that to publish a great novel represents his only chance for personal redemption. Antonio constantly reiterates that the only way to escape his spiritual and emotional malaise would be to write a critically acclaimed novel, but, as *Quién* progresses, it becomes increasingly apparent that he lacks the willpower and focus necessary for the completion of his project. The novel therefore becomes the documentation of both his desultory preparations and, to a lesser degree, his actual writing of the novel, in spite of the fact that he believes that he arrived much too late to the distribution of literary *savoir faire* (12-13).

Antonio López's novel will be about an older book editor named Gustavo Horacio Gilabert, who is in turn writing a novel about a failed college professor named Antonio López, who is writing a book about a book editor named Gilabert, and so on. Regardless of who narrates, however, it is clear from the beginning that Antonio is a loser in just about every sense of the word, and is very poorly suited to his profession as a scholar of literature. Recalling Beck's iconic Gen X anthem, "Loser," from 1994, Antonio is a self-conscious "perdedor" who pins his hopes on a novel that he will never write. He has many ideas for titles, possible plot lines and scenarios for a work that will in essence be an extended Borges tale, but he knows that his dream is perhaps unattainable: he confesses that the terrible process of writing the novel will probably result finally in making him a "definitive loser" (89).

The novel that Antonio writes—basically a diary that documents his desire to write the novel and his various ideas as to what it could be about—is peppered with admissions and justifications as to his own laziness: "today I have arrived at the conclusion that I am extraordinarily lazy" (120); "only the lazy can contemplate the world as it truly is" (123); and he even proposes that "absolute relaxation" might be gainfully declared the new national pastime (124). Antonio's slacker attitude is related perhaps to the fact that he has failed so miserably as an academic. For example, his book on Borges titled, *La morfología de los cuentos de Borges* [A Morphology of the Stories of Borges] has sold only 116 copies in ten years. In a passage that may be read as a critique of scholarly publishing in general, Antonio suggests that authors such as himself be cited and fined for taking advantage of a system that requires a book for tenure; only by imposing a fine would the authors of scholarly books stop writing unnecessary works (95). And for academics who insist on continuing to write books even after they have been fined, he suggests a mandatory jail sentence, although he admits that even then "the imbeciles would probably keep writing [. . .] To produce a book without a readership is a capricious extravagance that, like water dripping into water, calls for oblivion" (95). Antonio's protagonist/narrator Gilabert, for his part, criticizes the commercialism of the publishing industry on a radio show whose transcript is included as part of *Quién*'s discourse. He likens his own project to Marcel Duchamp's ready-mades: by making Antonio López the author of his book, Gilabert says that he seeks to problematize deepseated notions about authorship and artistic creation (227–32).

The painfully self-conscious Antonio López is completely unable to engage in meaningful social intercourse with his wife, his family, his coworkers or even his character/narrator Gilabert. The disaffected distance that he creates between himself and the world places him squarely into the more masculine discourses of Gen X literature of which *Historias del Kronen* is a prime example. Antonio refers to his life with his ever-suffering wife as a "simulacrum of happiness" (24) that only barely dissembles a marital routine based upon "matrimonial hatred" (88). Their lovemaking is a mind-numbing mechanical activity that produces only boredom (41–42). Similarly, Antonio's professional life is completely bereft of meaning. He teaches the classics, works by Homer, Virgil and Dante that over the years have become more and more boring: "everyday their works become more boring because what I read day after day from my rancid notes is boring" (42).

Antonio also disdains his father for his one-dimensional bourgeois life (65) and deems his brother "an insipid uninteresting character, a bourgeois conservative who 'plays the system'" (62), just like Elena Rincón's husband and any one of the older pro/antagonists that appear in novels such as *Historias del Kronen*. Perhaps not surprisingly, a third-person narrator (who may or may not be Gilabert) traces Antonio's disaffection and perceived estrangement from his family to his young adulthood when he began smoking hashish habitually and listening to early symphonic rock. Drugs, after all, have become a cornerstone of the thematic triad that has traditionally been understood to comprise Gen X cultural identity. Antonio, again like Loriga's and Mañas's characters, is only able to meaningfully communicate with *anyone* via the consumption of large quantities of drugs. He smokes hashish and/or swallows poppers before having sex with his wife, and he is only able to reconcile himself with his father after slipping him some LSD during a trip they took together a few years before (66). Drugs represent for Antonio the only viable access to authenticity and communication with his father (67). At an academic conference devoted to the work of Borges, an overdose of hashish allows Antonio to finally converse with his hero on a hotel balcony (102–3), although having swallowed massive doses of the stuff, he begins to hallucinate that Borges can fly. Controlled substances are arguably the only *real* thing in Antonio's life. One of his favorite rituals involves soaking in a hot bath while smoking a joint, listening to jazz musician Bill Evans under the watchful eye of a poster featuring Marilyn Monroe. These are the essential elements that comprise his "growing philosophy of laziness and sloth" (23) on which he disserts so often. Faced from the beginning with personal and professional failure, Antonio always opts for a good soak in the tub.

At the same time that drugs and alcohol allow Antonio to suffer his way through dissatisfying social encounters, professional failures, and familial estrangement, hashish offers him a heightened perception that, coupled with poppers (amyl nitrate) and his many literary readings, allows him to confront his literary forebears in the novel's antepenultimate chapter. Just before his death, Antonio participates in dreamlike conversations between Cide Hamete Benengeli, Avellaneda, Cervantes, Don Quixote, Pierre Menard, Unamuno, and Augusto Pérez and converses with his own character/author Gilabert, who plays Don Quixote to his Sancho. Virtually the entire tradition of Spanish self-referential writing appears in this chapter, alongside the authors and characters of great works from the western canon. Gilabert becomes Virgil and Antonio is Dante, and at the gates of hell they see various sinners playing with a globe; nearby are Fernando Savater and E. M. Cioran, while Charles Foster Kane repeats "Rosebud" over and over, accompanied by several characters from Dante's *Inferno*–Pier della Vigna, Ugolino and Ruggieri degli Ubaldini. In this respect, I would say that *Quién* is markedly different from much of the work of younger writers of the 1990s who draw upon more rigorously contemporary cultural referents in the construction of their narratives. Cañeque most often draws upon the classics of world literature and largely leaves contemporary cinematic and popular literary references out.

When Antonio wins the prestigious "Galaxia" prize for his novel—in spite of the fact that he never entered the competition—he dies of a heart attack. Having fortified himself with tranquilizers washed down with whisky in order to make it through the stultifying pleasantries of a literary dinner, when his name is announced as the winner of the "Galaxia" prize, Antonio expires. His final words are, "this is a bad joke . . . I never presented . . . a . . . novel . . . to any . . . fucking prize competition" (36). It later becomes apparent that his girlfriend Teresa had collected his diaries and notes, put them together in manuscript form, and submitted them to the competition as a novel. Thus, not only are Antonio and Gilabert alternately posited as possible authors throughout the text, but Teresa's editorial instincts and savvy are also required for the completion of Antonio's manuscript. Further, with a Unamunian twist, the novel ends with the possibility that Antonio's brother may in fact be the "true" author of the text. Cañeque himself is also drawn into the game of authorial identities, for he appears in several of the novel's footnotes to proffer an erudite quip or two. It is the collaboration and exchange between multiple mutually-aware narrators that conspire together and against each other that gives the novel its form. Because no one author rises above any other to claim ultimate responsibility for the text, *Quién* functions also as a critique of conventional notions of authorship.

Quién can be read as a philippic against academe, the publishing industry, yuppies and the bourgeoisie, authorship, religion and marriage. In this way, Cañeque's novel is very much of its time. Antonio holds back none of his invective, and even criticizes Nietzsche, the ultimate iconoclast, for his formulation of the superman, what he calls "the most naive utopia conceived in the history of humanity" (115), and he describes Dante's poetry as a combination of a "hippy and Don Juan" (118).[16] Indeed, his antipathy is very reminiscent of any one of the hypercritical Gen Xers portrayed in *Reality Bites* or Kevin Smith's *Clerks* (1994), or (again) Carlos of *Historias*. But *Quién* is not all vinegar and vitriol. It is at once an entertaining ode to literature and the literary life and a critical attempt to demystify Literature in general and put some fun back into the critical process. As Patricia Waugh reminds us, contemporary metafictional novels seek to "[examine] the old rules in order to discover new possibilities of the game" (42). *Quién* is a game in which metafiction is stretched to its extremes, parodying all metafictional texts, premodern, modern and postmodern, in order to draw attention to the creative process and the dynamic nature of the reader's reconstruction of the written text.

Criticism has become a creative vehicle that textual consumers may use in order to deconstruct traditional discourses and, in the process, build new ones from the rubble. As Traci Carroll affirms, "rather than trickling down to the culture at large from the vantage point of the university, critical thinking both inside and outside centers of learning derives from a postmodern aesthetic of creative textual consumption" (206). These novels by Millás and Cañeque demonstrate how anyone can become a writer, a critic, a literary creator, regardless of their academic formation, social status, or professional success. Millás offers a sensitive reflection on the power of narrative in one woman's reconstruction of her life, while Cañeque's novel takes a more extreme, decidedly masculine approach to the representation and repudiation of the western academic establishment and literary tradition. Carlos Cañeque shows how even a graduate education does not guarantee success in the contemporary world. The postmodern aesthetics of creative textual consumption serve, in the end, as a reassuring alternative to pure nihilistic fatalism: "Doubtful about the possibility of a profound political shift, Gen X criticism is nevertheless an attempt to respond to our culture with intelligence, wit, hope, and a sense of fun" (Carroll 206).

How the Gen X Aesthetic Transcends the Age of the Writer

In his introduction to the section on narrative in the first supplement to the *Historia y crítica de la literatura española. Los nuevos nombres: 1975–2000*, Jordi Gracia asserts that while they are certainly newer and younger, there really is no difference between Gen X writers—Mañas, Etxebarria, Loriga, et al—and the more mature writers born in the 1940s and 50s (known also as the generation of 1968) that preceded their appearance on the literary scene (Gracia 237–38). While Gracia acknowledges the thematic and formal diversity of contemporary Spanish literary production, he nevertheless lumps Gen X writers together with older authors such as Mendoza, Muñoz Molina, Rivas, Montero and Millás.

Am I advocating the same kind of undiscriminating association of all writers of the 1990s? My answer is a qualified, "not exactly." Returning to Robert Spires's essay on "Depolarization," the author points out, rightly I think, that the whole idea of the literary generation has a propensity to be problematic because it tends "to be simultaneously all-exclusive and all-inclusive" (485). On the one hand, as the essays included in this volume attest, even those members who are associated with a generation from the very beginning often "convey ethical attitudes and narrative styles that are both similar to and in conflict with not only those of other designated members, but also those of several writers born within the same decades but not generally recognized as charter members of the category" (486). To prove his point, Spires mentions first the divergent styles and themes that separate the work of Etxebarria, for example, from the "blatantly sexist discourses found in Mañas and Loriga" (486). Spires devotes the bulk of his study to the work of Javier Cercas (b. 1962) and José Ángel Mañas, two writers born within the parameters that normally define Generation X, but whose work is, on the surface, very different. The tricky thing about the literary generation—a "disputable classificatory term" (Epps 723) to begin with—is that

> once the initial membership has been determined, the tendency is to create closed societies; a given writer either is or is not considered a member, new constituents are almost never admitted, and old ones are seldom rejected. Once the designation is assigned, the category usually becomes all-exclusive. (Spires 485–86)

This second point about exclusion brings me back to the issue that I have sought to address here. By looking beyond the canonical group of young Gen X writers, I have explored how the Gen X aesthetic can be seen to function in the work of other writers not immediately associated with that generation. Through their critical use of the interrelated themes of literature, criticism, music, sex and drugs, Juan José Millás and Carlos Cañeque participate in the oppositional cultural work of 1990s fiction along with a cadre of younger writers such as Etxebarria, Loriga and Mañas. Nor are Millás and Cañeque alone; I think that it is safe to say that the Gen X aesthetic can transcend the age and personae of the writers who embrace it. Juan Madrid's novel *Días contados* (1993), for example, and Manuel Vázquez Montalbán's *El estrangulador* (1994) arguably stand out also for their explorations of the Gen X violence, death, and criminality that characterize some of the most well-known fiction of Mañas and Loriga.

In spite of the fact that Elena Rincón and Antonio López are in their forties, both are self-absorbed slackers who are perhaps even more confused about their situation in life than are their twenty-year-old counterparts. But rather than dwell in a space of nihilism and defeatism, both characters embrace their status as losers and turn their disaffection into literature. The dynamic, indeterminate nature of Antonio's novel explores new possibilities for the game of writing fiction even while it exposes the arbitrary nature of traditional notions of authorship. Similarly, by decentering her own narrative and incorporating multiple points of view into her discourse, Elena succeeds in constructing a viable alternative to her unfulfilling identity as the trophy wife of a morally corrupt executive. From their marginalized positions outside of mainstream economic, political, academic and familial cultures, Elena Rincón and Antonio López search for the same kind of personal authenticity that has variously obsessed younger Gen X characters. Their hair is just a little grayer.

Notes

1. It is worth remembering also that Millás is fond of Freudian allusions. Elena's rejection of socially established notions of cleanliness and good grooming may also be read as symptoms of a late anal expulsive stage of her personal development as she comes to terms with her changing, marginalized place in society.
2. In a recent interview with *Uncut* magazine, Paul McCartney finally admitted that "Day Tripper" was about acid and that it was "pretty obvious" that "Lucy in the Sky with Diamonds" was inspired by LSD ("Sir Paul Reveals Beatles Drug Use").
3. Jesús's nihilistic world-view springs from his dissatisfying, trite existence in a society populated by people he calls "social democrats," a term with pejorative connotations that he uses to describe any one of the bourgeois drones who live and work in the contemporary Spanish workplace. Dale Knickerbocker has pointed to the dual structure of *Tonto, muerto, bastardo e invisible*, which is based upon the protagonist's alienation from his surroundings and an acute social criticism of an inhumane, dehumanizing Spanish society of the early nineties (230).
4. In this respect, Elena's sell-out husband is much like José Antonio, the cousin of Carlos's mother in *Historias del Kronen*, whom the narrator describes as "one of the finest of the 1968 vintage, a millionaire owner of a publishing company affiliated with the Communist Party" (162).
5. To avoid prolixity, I have chosen to leave out the rest of the novel's implicit and explicit intertextual references, criticisms and critiques of the literary tradition simply because the novel is filled with them.

Works Cited

Amago, Samuel. *True Lies: Narrative Self-Consciousness in the Contemporary Spanish Novel*. Lewisburg: Bucknell University Press, 2006.

Cañeque, Carlos. *Conductas desviadas*. Madrid: Espasa-Calpe, 2002.

_____. *Conversaciones sobre Borges*. Barcelona: Destino, 1995.

_____. *Dios en América: Una aproximación al conservadurismo político-religioso en los Estados Unidos*. Barcelona: Ediciones Península, 1988.

_____. *Muertos de amor*. Barcelona: Destino, 1999.

_____. *El pequeño Borges imagina el Quijote*. Barcelona: Zendrera Zariquiey, 2003.

_____. *El pequeño Borges imagina la Biblia*. Barcelona: Sirpus, 2002.

_____. *Quién*. Barcelona: Destino, 1997.

Carroll, Traci. "Talking out of School: Academia Meets Generation X." *GenXegesis: Essays on "Alternative" Youth (Sub) Culture*. Ed. John M. Ulrich and Andrea L. Harris. Madison: University of Wisconsin Press, 2003. 199–220.

Dorca, Toni. "Joven narrativa en la España de los noventa: La generación X." *Revista de Estudios Hispánicos* 31 (1997): 309–24.

Epps, Brad. "Spanish Prose, 1975–2002." *The Cambridge History of Spanish Literature*. Ed. David T. Gies. Cambridge: Cambridge University Press, 2004. 705–23.

Frere-Jones, Sasha. "When I'm Sixty-Four: Aging Rockers Onstage. " *New Yorker* 17 January 2005: 94–95.

Goytisolo, Juan. *Reivindicación del Conde don Julián*. Madrid: Cátedra, 1995.

Gracia, Jordi. "Prosa narrativa. " *Historia y crítica de la literatura española. Los nuevos nombres: 1975–2000. Primer suplemento*. Ed. Jordi Gracia. Vol. 9/1. Barcelona: Crítica, 2000: 208–54.

Haynesworth, Leslie. "'Alternative' Music and the Oppositional Potential of Generation X Culture." *GenXegesis*. Ed. John M. Ulrich and Andrea L. Harris. Madison: University of Wisconsin Press, 2003. 41–58.

Henseler, Christine. "Pop, Punk, and Rock & Roll Writers: José Ángel Mañas, Ray Loriga, and Lucía Etxebarria Redefine the Literary Canon." *Hispania* 87.4 (2004): 692–702.

Klodt, Jason Edward. "Sex, Drugs, and Self-Destruction: Reading Decadence and Identity in Spain's Youth Narrative." Diss. Michigan State University, 2003.

Knickerbocker, Dale F. "Búsqueda del ser auténtico y crítica social en *Tonto, muerto, bastardo e invisible*." *Anales de la Literatura Española Contemporánea* 22.2 (1997): 15–16, 211–33.

Kunz, Marco. "*Quién*: Cañeque, Borges y las paradojas de la metaficción." *Iberoamericana* 4.15 (2004): 61–77.

Loriga, Ray. *Tokio ya no nos quiere*. Barcelona: Plaza & Janés, 1999.

Mañas, José Ángel. *Historias del Kronen*. Barcelona: Ediciones Destino, 1994.

Martín Gaite, Carmen. *El cuarto de atrás*. Barcelona: Destino, 2001.

Millás, Juan José. *Dos mujeres en Praga*. Madrid: Espasa Calpe, 2002.

_____. *La soledad era esto*. Barcelona: Ediciones Destino, 1990.

_____. *Tonto, muerto, bastardo e invisible*. Madrid: Alfaguara, 1995.

Pao, María T. "Sex, Drugs, and Rock & Roll: *Historias del Kronen* as Blank Fiction." *Anales de la Literatura Española Contemporánea* 27.2 (2002): 245–60.

"Sir Paul Reveals Beatles Drug Use." (Wednesday, 2 June, 2005): *BBC News UK Edition*. 2 June 2005. <http://news.bbc.co.uk/1/hi/entertainment/music/3769511.stm>.

Spires, Robert C. "Depolarization and the New Spanish Fiction at the Millennium." *Anales de la Literatura Española Contemporánea* 30.1–2 (2005): 485–512.

Ulrich, John M., and Andrea L. Harris, Ed. *GenXegesis: Essays on "Alternative" Youth (Sub) Culture*. Madison: University of Wisconsin Press, 2003.

Waugh, Patricia. *Metafiction: The Theory and Practice of Self-Conscious Fiction*. London: Methuen, 1984.

◆ **5**

Apocalypses Now: The End of Spanish Literature?
Reading *Payasos en la Lavadora* as Critical Parody

Luis Martín-Cabrera

> *"La crítica ya no puede ni debe aspirar a fijar cánones, en un desesperado
> intento de poner un cinturón de castidad a la literatura considerada como una
> virgen idiota asaltada por los apetitos de los lectores concupiscentes."*
> —Manuel Vázquez Montalbán. *La literatura en la construcción de la ciudad
> democrática.*

> (Criticism cannot and should not aspire to establish canons, in a desperate effort
> to impose a chastity belt on literature considered as a stupid virgin accosted by
> the readers' desires.)

Specters

The beginning of the 1990's in Spain is distinguished by an unprecedented
flux in the editorial market, together with the irruption of a new mass readership and a group of young writers who have come to be known as "Generation X" (Moret, Gullón, Bernardell etc.).[1] The boom in the Spanish editorial
industry comes at a moment in which, as Eloy Fernández Porta affirms, the
convenient symbiosis between government projects and the world of culture
has disappeared (35). The object of desire, integration to the European Union
or the foundation of the "sociedad del bienestar"—the consumerist notion of
social well-being based entirely on acquisitional power—have been swallowed
into the black hole allegorized by the celebrations of '92 (Moreiras-Menor,
"Spectacle"). In this context, the younger generation of writers—Ray Loriga,
José Angel Mañas, Benjamín Prado, Martín Casariego, David Trueba, and so
on—is perceived by establishment-based criticism as a faithful reflection of
this new era of superficiality and skepticism: *l'ère du vide*, as Gilles Lipovetsky
defined it.

There are countless testimonials and criticisms that comprise a devastating
vision of the "new literature"; I will limit myself to that of José María Martínez

Cachero, since his work on the contemporary Spanish novel is considered to be among the most authoritative of Spanish scholar-critics.

In the three full pages which Martínez Cachero concedes to this genera- tion, under the sonorous title of "jovencitos, no exageremos," (youngsters, let us not exaggerate), he defines Gen X literature as a largely uninteresting form of 'costumbrismo', presented in the form of fragmentary portraits, in a style which is composed of short paragraphs, simple or very simple sentences, and a sadly limited vocabulary (495). Thus, the characteristics of this generation as articulated by institutional criticism would be, first and foremost, an apathetic attitude toward reality, the use of the techniques of collage and direct quotes from U.S. pop culture, the representation of large doses of violence, the exalta- tion of drugs and rock music in an escapist avoidance of unbearable reality, etc. The precursors of the generation, in the Borgesian sense of the term, would be Charles Bukowsky, Jacques Kerouac, as well Bret Easton Ellis, Raymond Carver . . . (Gullón, "Cómo" 31).

While one could debate the accuracy of this and other descriptions of the Generation X writers, what is most striking and relevant for this discussion is the persistence of the use of the "generational method" in both academic and media criticism. The invention of the "generational method" in order to study literature is generally attributed to Julius Petersen and his work *Filosofía de la ciencia literaria* (1930), although it is with the publication of Ortega y Gasset's *El tema de nuestro tiempo* that the method became paramount.[2] As a faithful Orteguian approach to culture, the "generational method" is broadly predicated on the assumption that national literature evolves from one generation (an elite of talented individuals) to another in a dynamic relationship with the masses, that is to say, the generation is in charge of shaping the esthetic and moral values of the "vulgar" and "amorphous" masses.[3]

The perpetuation of such an anti-populist hermeneutical method by con- temporary Spanish critics poses two interrelated problems. On the one hand, it conceives culture in general and literature in particular as the domain of writers and a critics' elite in charge of defining taste, literariness and even what should, and should not be included in a national canon. On the other, this very generational approach results in a gigantic simplification of different writers and works whose ultimate result is the suppression of historicity. According to Cristina Moreiras-Menor, the use of the "generational method" to refer to these young writers does not take into account the historical and cultural transforma- tions that enabled the very production of their texts. She further elaborates:

En este sentido, aun sin quizás proponérselo se dehistoriza la cultura, se deshis-
toriza a los propios autores (. . .) y se les roba su carácter político para dejarles
únicamente un valor estético (es o no es buena literatura, seguirá o no leyéndose
en las próximas décadas) sobre el que emitir juicios casi siempre profundamente
ideológicos. (*Cultura*, 196)

(Thus, perhaps without intending it, culture is removed from history, authors even
are taken out of history . . . and their political characteristics are erased to leave
only their esthetic value (is it or is it not good literature, will we or will we not
continue reading them in the future), about which one can pass judgment, almost
always in a profoundly ideological way.)

In order to account for the historical and esthetical particularities of writers such as Ray Loriga and José Ángel Mañas, Moreiras-Menor has proposed
abandoning the categories of national literary tradition and its springboard, the
concept of literary generation (*Cultura*, 197). This is perhaps to suggest that the
so-called Generation X is not a generation, at least in the Orteguian sense of the
term, because most of these writers count on a mass readership, and above all
their novels blur the distinction between high culture and popular culture (the
common fascination of these writers with rock music is the more visible sign of
this incorporation of popular culture into the realm of literature).

As I will try to demonstrate through this essay, literary critics like Ramón
Acín, José María Martínez Cachero or Miguel García Posada mask their anxiety
about the rise of Spanish popular culture with a vague anti-capitalist discourse
that, in reality, responds to their fear of the democratization of culture brought
about indirectly by mass media. As a Marxist critic, I share the preoccupation
with the increasing commodification of the Spanish literary market, but the
insistence on the "generational method," the apocalyptic tone, and the rejection
of these writers on esthetic grounds make me suspect that its is not capitalism
what the above mentioned literary critics oppose, but rather the specter of the
people taking over the otherwise restricted realm of Literature. As Vázquez
Montalbán graciously put it when he paraphrases the beginning of the *Communist Manifesto*: "Un fantasma recorre desde hace cincuenta años la sociedad
literaria y anuncia el final de la literatura expulsada del paraíso por tentación de
la masificación del lector y la contaminación con los códigos de comunicación
de masas" (159) (A specter has been haunting the world of letters for fifty years
now and it announces the end of literature, expelled from paradise for falling
into the temptation of having as a reader the masses and for contaminating itself
with the communication codes of mass media).

This specter has to be conjured away, because it threatens the privileged position of the critic as the arbiter of good taste and literariness, it threatens to reveal the inherent tensions between high culture and popular culture, and it may even open the doors of culture to the masses of unqualified readers. One may argue that this cultural struggle is not new—in fact, it is as old as the formation of the bourgeois State—what is new, however, is the preeminence that popular culture occupies in the contemporary debate. For instance, in the nineteen century it was probably easier to condemn *folletines* as a form of low culture than to ignore today that rock music and film shape our experience of reality as much as Literature.

Spanish filmmaker Alex de la Iglesia addresses this very same conflict in his first and to date only novel, *Payasos en la lavadora* (1997).[4] The novel tells the story of an unemployed poet, Juan Carlos Satrústegui, who is obsessed with the idea of assassinating the critic who gave his first book of poetry a bad review. The insane monologue of Satrústegui and his adventures are a vehicle to enact a sarcastic parody of the announced apocalypses of art and literature. Against the rigid division between high and low culture, the novel's introductory note clarifies, with a Cervantine wink, that the present work is a manuscript that the author found in an abandoned Macintosh PowerBook at the Bilbao bus station. This fictional editor writes:

Hablé con la familia y me dijeron que (Satrústegui) había sido ingresado en un psiquiátrico. Con su consentimiento me hago cargo de la publicación del texto, confiando en que ello quizá ayude a su pronta recuperación. Lo he dividido en capítulos, he suprimido la mayor parte de los insultos a personas e instituciones, así como los párrafos directamente incomprensibles (. . .). También he considerado conveniente introducir unas cuantas citas que saqué de un diccionario, para darle un tono un poco más universitario, por consejo de su madre. (8)

(I spoke with the family and they told me that (Satrústegui) had been taken to a psychiatric ward. With their consent I took charge of the publication of the text, trusting that this would speed the author's prompt recovery. I've divided it into chapters, I've erased the majority of the insults against persons and institutions, as well as paragraphs which were simply incomprehensible (. . .). I've also felt it appropriate to insert a few quotes which I've taken from a dictionary, to give it a more academic tone, following a suggestion by the author's mother.[5])

In the following pages, I propose to read *Payasos en la lavadora* as a limit to the concept of the Generation X, and therefore as a menace to the normativity prescribed by cultural institutions and establishment critics. Thus, I take Alex de la Iglesia's novel as a starting point for a broader theoretical reflection on the statute of Spanish fiction at the crossroad between high culture and popular culture.

Apocalypse

On various occasions, Satrústegui's delirious monologue proclaims the death of art; the very title of the novel, which translates as Clowns in a Washing Machine, functions as an emblem of the way in which high culture as a discourse has been exhausted through repetition, paralyzed before the logic of the media. The emblem itself of the clowns going around in circles in a washing machine is borrowed from a television commercial from the early nineties. The title, then, remits to the corruption of the supposed purity and autonomy of art: the death of art, in its eternal return, becomes something laughable, a real *payasada*.[6] Take for instance the following quote, in which Satrústegui launches one of his vitriolic attacks on high culture:

> El teatro, el cine, la música, la poesía—menos la mía—están muertos, son fósiles, piezas de museo de provincias, experimentos fallidos de una cultura pasada de moda. Ya nadie hace nada bueno; lo poco que se podía hacer ya está hecho. Sólo quedan unos cuantos payasos haciendo el ridículo. La única posibilidad de triunfo que les queda es que los dos tipos del anuncio se ahoguen en la lavadora y poder así ocupar su puesto. ¿Qué pasa? ¿Os escandaliza? ¡Necios arrogantes! Oídme bien; es un hecho evidente que arrastramos muertos desde hace mucho. Y ya huelen. El teatro, por ejemplo: un grupo de gente chillando en un decorado cutre. ¿Por qué siempre chillan en el teatro? ¿Para que los oiga el de la última fila? (. . .) En cambio, amigos míos, la televisión es innovadora, creativa, joven, fuerte.

> (Theater, film, music, poetry—except mine—are dead, fossilized, they are exhibits in provincial museums, failed experiments of yesterday's fashion. Nobody does anything good any longer; the little that could be done, is already done. We have only a few clowns left, making fools of themselves. The only chance they have of success is that the two guys already in the washing machine drown, so they can then take their places. What? Are you shocked? Pompous fools! Listen to me with full attention: It is evident that we have been dragging corpses for a long time now. The theater, for example: a bunch of people shouting on a shabby stage. Why do they always shout in the theater? So they can be heard from the back seats? . . . Instead, my friends, television is innovative, creative, young, strong.)

Reading this, there is the temptation to view the novel as a discourse on the death of literature, but to declare the death of literature would simply reproduce the reactionary perspective on the end of art that is, in similar terms and in similar circles, the death of history, paralyzing any possibility of transformation (Beverley vii). On the contrary, the novel seems to parody the apocalypse direly predicted by some Spanish scholars: art, bled white and prostrate before the death threats of the parasitic media and the market.[7]

As I pointed out before, Literature is defended on the basis of supposedly progressive postulates that attempt to conserve the essence and purity of literature against the omnivorous logic of the market and its ever-increasing demands. However, this passionate and disinterested crusade "for art" happens to hide a political agenda all of its own. According to Fredric Jameson,

> The very deployment of the theory of the end of art was also political, insofar as it was meant to suggest or to register the profound complicity of the cultural institutions and canons, of the museums and the university system, the state prestige of all the high arts, as a defense of Western values: something that also presupposes a high level of investment in official culture and an influential status in society of high culture as an extension of state power. (75)

Nonetheless, the emergence of so-called Gen X literature, together with the increase in consumers of its cultural products, would seem to undermine the effectiveness of the death of art as a discourse of political hegemony. What, in other words, is the use of a hegemonic discourse which opposes the accumulation of capital by the very media which safeguards the survival of its most authoritative spokesmen, organic intellectuals? How should we understand the schizophrenic workings of media conglomerates, which simultaneously disseminate Gen X novels from their publishing houses and condemn them from the pages of their literary supplements? The PRISA group provides an enlightening example: Alfaguara, a publisher which belongs to the conglomerate, publishes Gen X novelists and creates broad-based publicity for them in its leisure supplement (*El País de las Tentaciones*) while the columnists at *Babelia* (the cultural supplement of *El Pais*) virulently attack these novels for their supposed lack of literary value (Bernardell 39).

The only way to approach this apparent contradiction is to recognize, as Jameson did, the Hegelian substratum which grounds this debate, to focus on the seemingly contradictory relations between the two key apocalyptic discourses: the end of art and the end of history. The discourse of the end of history, understood in its hard-line formulation, that is, in that of Francis Fukuyama, does not imply the dissolution of the so-called great narratives, as Jean Francois Lyotard has proposed, but rather the triumph of Western democracy and the free market over any possible alternative (this is why we say 'neoliberalism' instead of 'postliberalism') or, from another perspective, the triumph of the United States' mode of political and economic hegemony over those of the rest of the world.[8] History ended, for Spain, in 1992: in its post Olympic logic, the sweeping victory of the market would seem to render obsolete the aesthetic hierarchies which once regulated cultural merchandise, establishing an extremist incarnation of exchange-value: that which sells is of value, and that which is of value sells. It is surprising, then, that the hegemonic groups should oppose precisely such a de-hierarchization of cultural merchandise in the name of the end of art, that is, in defense of literature. It is as if the very end of history should require the apocalyptic discourse of the end of art in order to continue fetichizing cultural production: the end of history guarantees that media conglomerates keep accumulating capital; the end of art assures the state that its hegemony remains uncontested.[9]

In the age of globalization and new information technologies, someone must be exercising control over a cultural marketplace that is increasingly multidimensional and chaotic. It seems that the return of aesthetic discourses on beauty and the end of art which Jameson has identified as signs of a certain postmodernity (100) respond to this new need to control the decentralization and relative de-hierarchization of information. The apocalyptic critic, consciously or unconsciously, is complicit in a system of cultural distinction whose purpose is to sustain State hegemony. Alex de la Iglesia may have a similar conception of these apocalyptic critics in mind, because they are the main target of Satrústegui's insane monologue. In the following caustic remarks the reader may appreciate Satrústegui's unforgiving opinion about the literary critic who reviewed his book:

Mi primer libro de poesías, *A tomar por culo,* ha sido bien acogido por la crítica especializada, y las ventas van muy bien, según dice mi editor. Como toda obra de vanguardia, ha suscitado una fuerte polémica, y cierto sector de la crítica—la más rancia—no ha entendido nada, tachando mi obra de zafia. (. . .) Me considero una persona muy madura; estoy ya muy pasado de rosca para que me afecte la opinión de un crítico; un estúpido viejo que publica sus pajas en un periódico y luego va de intelectual, cuando en realidad no es más que un demente senil, un anciano que todavía recuerda el mayo francés, un puto fósil que se tenía que ir a hacer fogatas con mi abuela. (22)

(My first book of poetry, *A tomar por culo* [Piss off], has been well received in literary criticism and is selling well, according to my editor. Like any avant-garde work, its reception has been polemical, and a certain sector of criticism—the most established—hasn't understood it at all, dismissing my work as trite (. . .). I consider myself to be a very mature person; I'm too much out of line to let the opinion of a critic affect me; some stupid old man who publishes his masturbations in the newspaper and then goes around being the intellectual, when in reality he's nothing more than demented and senile, an old-timer still reminiscing about Paris '68, a fucking fossil who should be out making bonfires with my grandmother.)

Satrustegui's novel is not a discourse on the death of literature but a discourse against literature that rebels against the normativity of high culture: against style, against good taste, against literary value . . . all notions of distinction are undermined by a strong irony that parodically rewrites the literary discourse as anti-aesthetic. This deconstruction extends to political discourse and attacks the assumptions of a criticism which continues to proclaim art's capacity for liberation when, in reality, the collective imaginings of '68 have passed away: a majority of the revolutionaries of that May in Paris are now organic intellectuals serving the State. The iconoclasty of the writer-subject in *Payasos en la lavadora* cannot be interpreted as the classic provocative gesture of the avant-garde—this is not one more episode in the quarrel between ancients and moderns—because the discourse is completely dispossessed of any telos. It is writing which breaks with linear temporality—"in a non-linear, non-Euclidian space of history the end cannot be located" (Baudrillard 110)—engulfing the poet in a circular, rhyzomatic and accelerated temporality. In fact, the narration of *Payasos en la lavadora* occurs in the present tense, because, as Satrústegui states in the following quote, the future has been swallowed in a media repetition:

> Escribo en presente, porque todo está ocurriendo otra vez, todo sucede delante de mis ojos de nuevo, limpio y brillante, a todo color. A través de la pantalla de cuarzo líquido se distinguen los lugares, las cosas, las personas. Conocer es recordar; es algo que los griegos tenían muy claro: no hay nada nuevo, todo es como una gigantesca reposición televisiva programada para una entidad metafísica ininteligible, cuarentona y aburrida, sedienta de nostalgia. (12)

> (I write in the present tense, because everything is happening all over again, everything occurs again before my eyes, clean and sparkling, in full color. Through the TV screen I see places, things, people. Knowledge is memory; that's something the Greeks knew well: nothing is new, everything is a gargantuan TV remake,

programmed for an unintelligible metaphysical entity, forty-something and bored, thirsty with nostalgia.)

The difference, given that all repetition implies difference, is that in our global and media age, repetition is increasingly chaotic and vertiginous, to a point at which the end of history disperses at the horizon of the infinite interchange of images. As Baudrillard puts it:

> Perhaps history itself has to be regarded as a chaotic formation, in which acceleration puts an end to linearity and the turbulence created by acceleration deflects history definitively from its end, just as such a turbulence distances effects from their causes. We shall not reach the destination, even if that destination is the Last Judgement, since we are henceforth separated from it by a variable refraction hyperspace. (111)

Perhaps what both Baudrillard and Alex de la Iglesia are suggesting in their narratives is that we have reached the end of the end. For Baudrillard, all of these reflections are colored by a tone which, if not quite catastrophic, is at least pessimistic, since the end of the end would imply, in his terms, the impossibility to keep producing social meaning, the reality disappearing into the black hole of a mass indifference to the violence of our capitalist societies. On the other hand, it seems that Alex de la Iglesia strips the drama from the apocalypse in a much more radical way, based on a notion of parodic performativity as an answer to the disappearance of meaning. In his proposal, the teleological impulse has disappeared, but not all possibility of political meaning, as Baudrillard would insist; there remains the possibility of parodically reiterating the apocalypse in order to reveal the very mechanism of its repetition. And this is precisely what occurs at the end of the novel, when we find Juan Carlos Satrústegui up on top of a Caterpillar excavator, ready to vanquish the antichrist—that is, the literary critic—as he screams from within the crowd:

> Celebramos la pasión y muerte de Occidente. (. . .) Las ruinas de una civilización corrompida y decadente dejarán paso a una nueva era donde el hombre podrá sentir con más intensidad, donde la angustia del Ser se disolverá en placer, el placer de una nueva poesía, de una nueva conciencia . . . (59)

> (We celebrate the passion and the death of the Western World. [. . .] The ruins of a corrupt and decadent civilization will give way before a new era in which man will be able to feel with greater intensity, where the anguish of Being will dissolve into pleasure, the pleasure of a new poetry, a new consciousness . . .)

Of course, none of this actually happens; at the moment when Satrústegui is about to finally kill his literary antichrist, he discovers that the critic has changed his mind and now refers to him as "an authentic writer fully engaged with his time, intelligent and full of sensitivity" (163). The impossibility of articulating counter hegemonic discourses—of symbolically killing off litera-ture—could be read per Baudrillard's theory as the impossibility of producing meaning, a reading of the protean force by which capitalism neutralizes any discourse of resistance and resignifies it according to its own laws: canoniza-tion, museum, literary history . . . but the novel ends when Satrústegui is sent to a psychiatric hospital. Could we read this as the brand of the process of nor-malization upon the abject body of the poet?

Abjection

Payasos en la lavadora can not only be read as a metacritical reflection on the statute of literature and art at the end of the millennium but also as a failed Bildungsroman, as a failed coming of age story of the construction of identity in the globalized, post-capitalist Spain of the nineties. The construction of this new cultural subject allows us to think about the conditions of cultural pro-duction in the nineties, since Satrústegui's novel is the reflection of this new subject constructing himself in the midst of a spectacularized society.

The novel takes place during the *semana grande* in Bilbao and tells of Satrústegui immersed in a festive and spectacular ambiance that blurs the fron-tier between the public and the private. The society of spectacle, as Guy Debord defined the concept in the seventies, is characterized by the replacement of reality and life for a massive accumulation of images, with capitalism in such a state of accumulation that it becomes (*devient*) an image of itself (32). Spec-tacle, conceived in this way, is an instrument of domination that joins together its subjects by converting them into spectators fascinated by the unreality of images, at the same time that it separates them from reality and converts them into passive subjects. Satrústegui's story takes place in the middle of a society that is indifferent to the violence of reality, sucked up by mechanisms of social relations completely stripped of any emotional connection. As Satrústegui wan-ders around the streets of Bilbao he contemplates the following scene against the background of a passive collectivity:

Nos abrimos paso a codazos entre la gruesa capa de cabecitas que nos sirven de colchón y salimos de nuevo al Arenal, cerca del teatro Arriaga. Un par de coches carbonizados arden en medio de la calzada. Nadie les presta demasiada atención, como si se tratase de un montaje, de un acto dramático callejero ya finalizado. (148)

(We elbow our way through the thick layer of small heads that serve us as a mattress and once again come out into the Arenal, near the theater Arriaga. A couple of burnt cars are still glowing in the middle of the street. No one pays too much attention, as if it were all a set from some street theater production that had just ended.)

The violence of reality can no longer be distinguished from its own simulation and thus the subjects of this new society are indifferent to it, the image of the market has occupied everything, reality is an allegory of the market mirrored in images. Satrústegui, as a spectator of this new society of the image, is a subject stripped of affections, an abject subject, expelled and branded by violence.

The marks of the consumerist orgy of the nineties are written on his body (he is constantly being beaten up and expelled from every public or private space); the object of desire—European integration, the illusion of normalcy, economic development, revolution, etc.—has disappeared, swallowed into the society of spectacle. This very absence, this loss of the object of desire is precisely what provokes a narcissistic crisis in Satrústegui and converts him into an abject being. In his own words: "Me gustaría abrirme la cabeza. Y con una cuchara raspar las paredes del cráneo y sacar todos los desperdicios acumulados, toda la roña de ideas podridas, de sueños fracasados . . ." (64) ("I would like to open up my head. And with a spoon scrape the walls of my cranium and get rid of all the trash accumulated there, all the crust of rotting ideas, of failed dreams . . .").

The story of Satrústegui is, then, the adventure of a subject who does not want to ask himself who he is, but rather *where* he is. But there is no place for him; the city is converted into a space dominated by horror, a map empty of meaning, an indolent, inhabitable place. The subject of the postmodern city is condemned to wander indefinitely through its streets, never finding a place. Satrústegui is a decentered, disoriented subject, without either identity or location; bereft of identity, perhaps, precisely because he has no location, expelled from the public sphere: kicked out of his house, of welfare offices, of bars, of the shacks of the homeless, of public institutions, of whorehouses . . .

The impossibility of finding a place in the city makes Satrústegui a fractured subject, incapable of passing through the symbolic, in a Lacanian sense, to articulate himself as "I" because the object, the other, has occupied his place. In the words of Satrústegui:

Al sentir ascopena nos vemos implicados con el objeto, como si nuestro sentimiento, al alcanzar lo otro—lo absolutamente otro—, chocara con él y nos salpicase, manchándonos de horror. (25)

(By feeling *ascopena*, [neologism which combines the words for pity and disgust] we implicate ourselves with the object, as if our sentiment, reaching the other—the absolutely other—should collide with him and splatter us, stain us with horror.)

But what is this other uncanny reality that produces the disappearance of affection? What does that horror consist of, as it displaces and fractures Satrústegui's ego? Where does the violence that appears in every page of the novel, that inscribes itself on Satrústegui's body, come from? It is difficult to name an origin of abjection, because abject writing is a decentered writing, dispossessed equally of origin and telos; but what remains evident is that the residues, the uncanny marks of what remains outside of this enormous media simulation affect one way or another the subject. Satrustegui seems to be aware of how, for instance, the contemplation of a junky may stir up the horror of otherness, the sudden realization of structural violence that affects the subject from outside. This is how he describe the process:

Nos encontramos en un semáforo, confiando en que el disco verde se ilumine lo más rápidamente posible. De pronto surge de la nada un tipo sucio con pinta de yonki. (. . .) Es posible que nos amenace con una jeringuilla, o algo peor. Tienes miedo. Tienes miedo, porque ese canalla que se acerca no huele bien, no le conoces de los anuncios ni de las revistas. Ni siquiera tiene vehículo, como tú. Subimos los cristales del coche, histéricos, por si acaso. (. . .) habla con el de delante mostrando unos paquetillos ridículos. Se trata de kleenex. (. . .) El ser se dirige hacia nosotros. Observamos su rostro—un nuevo rostro lleno de matices—y nos desagrada tanto que apartamos la mirada. La mirada es la clave. Si los miras—al del kleenex, al pobre de la cajita de cartón, al jipi de la flauta—estás perdido, porque has reconocido su existencia. Os miro porque estáis ahí. No sois un fondo amorfo sin precisar, sois algo concreto que yo miro, y con mi mirada os doy vida. Atención: sólo precisan esa fracción de segundo en la que tu mirada choca con la suya para inocularte su veneno, y ya no puedes escapar. (17)

(We find ourselves at a stoplight, sure that the light is about to turn green. Suddenly, out of nowhere appears some dirty guy, looking like a junky. (. . .) He could threaten us with a syringe or something worse. You're afraid. You're afraid, because that freak who's coming over here smells bad, he's not in commercials or magazines. He doesn't even have a car, like you do. We roll up the windows, panicked, just in case. (. . .) He's talking to the guy in front of us, showing him some ridiculous little packages. Kleenex. (. . .) The being moves in our direction. We observe his face—a face full of subtleties—and it's so unpleasant that we look away. Where you look is key. If you look at them—at the kleenex guy, at the homeless guy with the cardboard box, at the hippie with the flute— you're fucked, because you've acknowledged their existence. I look at you because you're there. You're not an undefined amorphous depth, you're something concrete that I'm looking at, and looking at you I affirm that you're alive. Attention: they only need that fraction of a second in which your gaze meets theirs to inoculate you with their venom, and you can't escape.)

The subject of abjection is a liminal subject, installed in a borderland, in a place where meaning is on the point of collapse, but it is not an asymbolic subject, condemned to silence. On the contrary, the impossibility of finding an object of desire turns language itself into a fetish that produces a hallucinated, heterogeneous discourse (Kristeva 42). This symbolic accumulation, symptom of abjection, tends to blur the limits between the conscious and the subconscious and thus it can be argued that, as the novel draws to a conclusion, Satrústegui becomes a kind of postmodern Quixote continually confusing the signs of reality with reality itself; for example, he confuses a radical Basque national-ist demonstration with a *feria* band, a whorehouse with a literary *salon*, etc.

This position precludes any resignification of the residue (that which could not be absorbed into the logic of the spectacle) under the guise of an ethical position formulated on the basis of universal values. Satrústegui is not the *poète maudit* but its inversion, its parody; nowhere in his monologue do we find the mark of metaphysical sentiment, the messianic values of literature have been occupied by the hallucinated discourse of insanity and violence: "Sólo pretendo impartir unas sencillas lecciones de ontología práctica. ¿Qué es el ser? El ser es una hostia que te arranca los dientes" (106) ("I only try to impart a few simple notions of practical ontology. What is being? Being is a punch that knocks your teeth out").

Heterogenesis

Reading *Payasos en la lavadora*, or any of the so-called Gen X novels, within the parameters of literary value or aesthetic beauty is evidently of little use, because the majority of these novels are constructed as a reaction against these ideals of literature. However, the subject of Gen X novels does not celebrate the market and the society of spectacle; on the contrary, it is a marginal, emotionally bankrupt subject who realizes that Literature, in its modern formulation, has become a discourse with no capacity to respond to this new society of the marketplace and the vertiginous image: its literature is another, or perhaps none at all. The traditional functions of literature: the search for beauty or an ethical position in relation to reality, have been outmoded by a reality that is demanding other types of answers. Vázquez Montalbán seems to agree with this position when he affirms:

> El santuario de la literatura y el arte como recintos sagrados legitimados por el idealismo o el materialismo histórico, el uno invocando la alternativa de eternidad de lo bello frente a la muerte y el otro invocando el carácter prometeico del lenguaje robado a los dioses para que los hombres lo utilizaran para apoderarse de y transformar la historia, no resistió la lógica de la evolución interactiva de la escritura y la lectura . . . (Vázquez Montalbán 168)

> (The sanctuary of literature and art, conceived as sacred enclosures made legitimate by idealism or historical materialism, one invoking the eternity of beauty overcoming death, and the other invoking the Prometheic nature of a language stolen from the gods so that human beings could take charge of history and transform it, did not resist the logic of the interactive evolution of writing and reading . . .)

Therefore, it is no longer about knowing whether literature is going to disappear, swallowed into the audiovisual media, or be vulgarized by the mass access of readers to the editorial market. These are questions which belong to the nineteenth century, because the frontiers and the limits among the disciplines are continually destabilized, the once clear separation among literary genres is continually blurred, because discursive heterogeneity is continually intensified.

To classify this situation as apocalyptic would be a simple resistance to the democratization of culture, to assert that not everybody has the right to write, to refuse to read discursive heterogeneity from a political point of view. And if there is something that resists the homogenizing power of the state and the logic of the society of spectacle, it is precisely that radical heterogeneity; to resist it in the name of literature, to defend the disciplines and patrol the borders among genres, is just for the purpose of supporting the homogenizing force of power: "The only insurmountable obstacle that hegemony of the economic genre comes up against is the heterogeneity of phrase regimens and of genres of discourse. This is because there is no 'language' and 'being', but occurrences" (Lyotard, 181).

A performative conception of language and generic heterogeneity is the basis of writing in *Payasos en la lavadora*. Altogether, the novel can be considered a kaleidoscope of quotes coming from the most diverse archives: references to the Quixote, philosophical citations, B movies, comics, etc. This radical heterogeneity does not give the novel a harmonious structure, but rather transforms it into a space in which the conflict between high and low culture is continually being exposed. Although this situation is hardly new (one can obviously point to Cervantes or François Rabelais as examples of heterogeneous writing), the intensity of the conflict between high culture and popular culture have shifted, both because of the emergence of mass culture and because of the status of our post-capitalist societies.

In any case, heterogeneous discursive constructions now and then constitute what Lyotard calls différends (*les différends*), those cases which are beyond the law and the state because they are per se non-discursive, the experience of the subject dispossessed of the ability to articulate his or her own situation of injustice. The abject subject of a heterogeneous discourse is constructed to testify to the residual, to that which has been excluded from the logic of spectacle. This is not a traditionally political position, based on the transparency of language and the existence of a priori ethical values about justice: "You can't make a political 'program' with it" (Lyotard 181); nonetheless, you can go beyond literature and open up to discursive heterogeneity as a cultural practice. In other words, to testify to the experience of the abject subject is to bear witness to the subject's expulsion from Literature.

Notes

1. As all the things I write, all the things that are written, I suppose, this essay is the result of an ongoing open dialogue with many people. It would be impossible to mention all of them, to forget the two who have contributed the most to these pages would be unfair. Thanks, then, to Cristina Moreiras-Menor for generously opening up new ways of thinking and to Claire Solomon, for helping to put my thoughts into English and for always listening critically.
2. For a complete genealogy of the uses of the "generational method" both in Latin America and Spain see Ricardo Cuadros "Contra el método generacional." According to Cuadros, the use of generations as applied to the study of culture was first suggested by Auguste Compte as a consequence of his biological approach to the evolution of humanity. After Compte's suggestion, the method has been used by many critics from Cedomil Goic and Rodrigo Cánovas in Chile to Pedro Salinas and more contemporary critics like Martínez Cachero in Spain.

3. In the first chapter of *El tema de nuestro tiempo*—entitled "la idea de las generacio-nes" ("The Idea of Generations")—Ortega y Gasset, drawing on biology and other life sciences, states that "La humanidad, en todos los estadios de su evolución, ha sido siempre una estructura funcional en que los hombres más enérgicos (. . .) han operado sobre las masas dándoles una determinada configuración. Esto implica cierta comunidad básica entre los individuos superiores y la muchedumbre vulgar" (6) (In all of the stages of its evolution, Humanity has been a functional structure in which the most energetic men have shaped the masses giving them a determinate configura-tion. This implies a certain basic community between the superior individuals and the vulgar mobs). According to Ortega, the way in which these "energetic individuals" shape the masses is precisely through the concept of the generation defined as follows: "Una generación no es un puñado de hombres egregios ni simplemente una masa: es como un nuevo cuerpo social íntegro, con su minoría selecta y su muchedumbre que ha sido lanzado sobre el ámbito de la existencia con una trayectoria vital determinada. La generación, compromiso dinámico entre masa e individuo, es el concepto más importante de la historia y, por decirlo así, el gozne sobre el que ésta ejecuta sus mo-vimientos" (Ortega, 6–7) (A generation is not a few outstanding men nor simply the masses: it is as new and complete social body, with its select minority and a crowd which have been thrown into existence with a certain vital trajectory. A generation, a dynamic negotiation between the masses and an individual, is the most important concept of history and, so to say, the hinge on which it turns). If we translate this into more contemporary terms, what is at stake in the use of generations is nothing less than the relationship between mass culture and literary culture, which in my view is the center of the polemic around the acceptance or rejection of the Generation X.

4. Alex de la Iglesia is one of the most acclaimed young Spanish filmmakers. To date he has directed six movies: *Acción Mutante* (1993), *El Día de la bestia* (1995), *Perdita Durango* (1997), *La comunidad* (2000), *8000 Balas* (2002), and *Crimen perfecto* (2004). In all these films de la Iglesia mixes with great success elements from differ-ent cinematographic genres and traditions—horror movies, B movies, action movies and comedies—in order to render a poignant vision of postmodern Spain. In spite of having been acclaimed by the critics and the public alike his cinematographic debut was anything but easy. Alex's first movie—*Acción Mutante*—was produced by famous director Pedro Almodóvar. In spite of it, or perhaps, because of it, *Acción Mutante* received very harsh criticism from mainstream critics. In many ways, *Paysos en la lavadora* is a literary response to these critics who judged his movies (and per-haps the cultural products of young writers and filmmakers) from outmoded esthetical categories.

5. All translations from the novel are mine.

6. The name of the brand was *Micolor*. In the commercial a couple of clowns intended to wash their clothes, but instead of putting their clothes in the washing machine they themselves get into the machine, and therefore they end up turning in circles inside the machine to prove the effectiveness of the product advertised. Perhaps because of

the absurd edge, the commercial has become part of popular jokes, and contemporary conversations.

7. Examples of this apocalyptic vision can be found, among others, in the following papers: José Antonio Fortes, "Del realismo sucio y otras imposturas en la novela española ultima"; Miguel García-Posada, "Nuevo canon, nuevo público. Las obras de los autores españoles e hispanoamericanos conquistan el mercado"; Santos Sanz Villanueva "El archipiélago de la nueva ficción." In a recent article, Germán Gullón goes as far as to declare that, in fact, the only solution is to accept stoically the end of Literature: "Quejarse carece de sentido, la única solución es aceptar la realidad del estado de la literatura para poder entender la razón de ser de esta enorme masa de títulos que denominamos narrativa española actual. Creo que una primera resolución debe ser comprender que la Era de la Literatura, la del primer cuarto del siglo veinte, ha terminado definitivamente" (3) (It makes no sense to complain. The only solution is to accept the reality of literature's situation so we can understand why there is that enormous number of titles that we call contemporary Spanish literature. I believe we must first decide that we will understand that the Age of Literature, that of the first quarter of the twentieth century, has definitively ended).

8. For a genealogy of the concept of "the end of history" see Perry Anderson. *A Zone of Engagement*. In the last chapter of the book Anderson gives an extensive account of the origins of this concept, examining the works of Hegel, Kojeve, Fukuyama, and the Post historic School.

9. This use of literature as mark of distinction among the elite is a reproduction of the basic contradiction of *franquismo*; that is to say, economic modernization and political conservatism. The ministers of the Opus Dei who, during the sixties, transformed the then-stagnant Spanish economy into a capitalist success story, led Spanish modernity. In general, the promotion of economic development was realized with the full cooperation and support of the most conservative Catholic political figures.

Works Cited

Acín, Ramón. "El comercio en la literatura: un difícil matrimonio." *Ínsula* 589–90 (1996): 5–6.

Anderson, Perry. *A Zone of Engagement*. London: Verso, 1992.

Baudrillard, Jean. *The Illusion of the End*. Trans. Chris Turner. Stanford: Stanford University Press, 1994.

Bernardell, Carles. "Los que no son de Cuenca. Retrato de un artista adolescente." *Quimera* 13.145 (1996): 38–39.

Beverley, John. *Against Literature*. Minneapolis: University of Minnesota Press, 1993.

Bourdieu, Pierre. *Distinction. A Social Critique of the Judgement of Taste*. Trans. Richard Nice. Cambridge: Harvard University Press, 1984.

Cuadros, Ricardo. "Contra el método generacional." *Revista digital de crítica, ensayo e historia del Arte*. <http://www.critica.cl/html/rcuadros_10.ht>.

Debord, Guy. *La Societé du Spectacle*. Paris: Gallimard, 1992.

De la Iglesia, Alex. *Payasos en la lavadora*. Barcelona: Planeta, 1997.

Fernández Porta, Eloy. "Poéticas del prozac. Tres líneas en la novela española de los noventa." *Quimera* 13.145 (1996): 35–37.

Fortes, José Antonio. "Del realismo sucio y otras imposturas en la novela española última." *Ínsula* 589–590 (1996): 21–27.

Fukuyama, Francis. "The End of History?" *WesJones*. <http://www.wesjones.com/eoh.htm#title>.

García-Posada, Miguel. "Nuevo cánon nuevo público. Las obras de los autores españoles e hispanoamericanos cónquistan el mercado." *El Pais (Babelia)* 95 (1995):10.

Gramsci, Antonio. *Selections from the Prison Notebooks*. Trans. Quintin Hoare and Geofrey Nowell. New York: International Publishers, 1971.

Gullón, German. "Cómo se leer una novela de la última generación (Apartado X)." *Insula* 589–590 (1996): 31–33.

_____. "La novela en España: 2004. Un espacio para el encuentro." *Ínsula* 668 (2004): 2–4.

Jameson, Fredric. *The Cultural Turn. Selected Writings on the Postmodern, 1983–1998*. London: Verso, 1998.

Kristeva, Julia. *Powers of Horror. An Essay on Abjection*. Trans. Leon S. Roudiez. New York: Columbia University Press, 1982.

Lyotard, Jean Francois. *The Different. Phrases in Dispute*. Trans. George Van den Abbeele. Minneapolis: University of Minnesota Press, 1988.

Martínez Cachero, José María. *La novela española entre 1936 y el fin de siglo. Historia de una aventura*. Madrid: Cıstalia, 1997.

Moreiras-Menor, Cristina. *Cultura herida. Literatura y cine en la España democrática*. Madrid: Libertarias, 2002.

_____."Spectacle, Trauma, and Violence in Contemporary Spain." Ed. Barry Jordan and Rikki Morgan-Tamosunas. *Contemporary Spanish Cultural Studies*. London: Arnold Publishers, 2000. 134–42.

Moret, Xavier. "Las Editoriales los Prefieren Novatos." *El Pais (Babelia)* 95 (1995): 8–9.

Ortega y Gasset, José. *El tema de nuestro tiempo*. Madrid: Revista de Occidente, 1963.

Petersen, Julius. *Filosofía de la ciencia literaria*. México: Fondo de Cultura Económica, 1945.

Sanz Villanueva, Santos. "El archipiélago de la ficción." Ínsula 589–590 (1996): 3–4.

Vázquez Montalbán, Manuel. *La literatura en la construcción de la ciudad democrática*. Barcelona: Crítica, 1998.

◆ **6**

Not Your Father's Rock and Roll:
Listening to Transitional/Eighties Writers
and Generation X

Elizabeth Scarlett

> *Si alguien se hubiese tomado la molestia de preguntar sabría*
> *que siempre he querido ser una estrella de rock and roll.* (Loriga 21)
>
> (If anyone had bothered to ask they would have known
> that I've always wanted to be a rock star.)

Rock music has a history in Spanish literature that predates Generation X. A comparison of its appearance in narratives of the previous generation of writers helps to define the position it occupies in narratives by authors born between 1963 and 1979. Some of the fiction of the post-Franco/Democratic Transition/ Eighties Boom narrators has been grouped under the rubric of the *noir* novel or *novela negra* on account of close intertextual relationships with American forties and fifties *film noir* and Chandleresque detective fiction. For novels of this type the predominant music tends to be either the melancholic *bolero* or Latin torch song (Rosa Montero's *Te trataré como a una reina* gets its title from a song in this vein) or the syncopated jazz reminiscent of "As Time Goes By" as it is played in *Casablanca* (several characters in Antonio Muñoz Molina's *El invierno en Lisboa* perform in a more improvisational form of this idiom). As we reach the last decade of the twentieth century, even these writers are more likely to feature rock and roll prominently in their writings. Yet they do so with a different perspective from that of the Generation X writers who are just beginning to publish during this decade. The globalization and diversification of rock, as well as its lengthening history, make these divergent approaches possible. For the purposes of conciseness and clarity, this essay looks at several key narratives from each of the two groups, published during the mid-nineties.

The two main tendencies that emerge are that rock, especially in the form of intertextuality and iconic figures, contributes to the project of dissidence, or anti-Franco and post-Franco protest, in fiction by the writers who came of age in the decade prior to Generation X such as Antonio Muñoz Molina and Manuel Rivas, while the Generation X writers Lucía Etxebarria, José Angel Mañas, and Ray Loriga blend rock music into their worldview of *desencanto*, or disenchantment with the post-1992, post-*Felipista* Spanish scene. For the latter group, the approach to rock is tinged with the cynicism of *fin de siglo* young people towards global capitalism and consumerism, without a valid alternative to be advocated. The configurations formed by rock with its inevitable partners, sex and drug use, also stand in contrast from one group to the next.

Muñoz Molina's *El jinete polaco* is a truly generational novel on a grand scale, combining murder mystery, genealogical and ethnic study, political intrigue, Bildungsroman, and love story.[1] It is the fourth novel by the prolific Andalusian, who was to become the youngest member of the Royal Academy of the Spanish Language in 1996 largely as a result of the book's embodiment of the Transitional/Eighties perspective: it was both a bestseller and the winner of two prestigious awards in 1992, the Planeta and the National Prize for Narrative. In the protagonist's formation and personal tastes, classic rock figures such as Jim Morrison (of The Doors), Lou Reed (of Velvet Underground), and Eric Burdon (of The Animals) are elevated to the level of high literary art on a par with Edgar Allan Poe. They are prized as rock rebels and poets whose freewheeling sexual exploits (in the case of Morrison), political leftism (Reed especially), and working-class sensibility (in the case of Burdon) contrast with the memory of Francoist repression for a writer whose adolescence transpired with the dictatorship still in place. The positive value they are assigned stems from their status as role models in the hero's quest for freedom and love, a quest that is eventually fulfilled just as the murder mystery is solved. The teenage rebellion they personify evinces a larger national design of democratization, modernization, and Europeanization, all seen as attainable advances. Although the protagonist, Manuel, may never have acquired the glamour of his idols, he achieved his goal of becoming an interpreter and in the present of the novel moves with ease between New York City, Madrid, and provincial Mágina (modeled on Muñoz Molina's hometown of Úbeda).

From about the age of sixteen Manuel congregated with his friends at the Martos Bar, where tobacco smoke, beer, and fantasies about his favorite girl (who of course barely notices him) combine with rock music as his preferred escape from the humdrum and stifling Andalusian town. His attempts at deciphering the lyrics of American rock songs on the jukebox foreshadow his multilingual career, and he also acknowledges that much of their allure was owed to what he and his pals projected onto the verses they could not yet understand. Clearly Morrison's "Riders on the Storm" is a key intertext as a contemporary, Beat-influenced, and existentialist counterpoint to the Rembrandt painting to which the novel's title alludes more explicitly. The song encompasses both Manuel and his semi-foreign classmate Nadia, who will later be his lover when they are reunited after nearly two turbulent decades apart from each other.

After the first half of the novel concentrates musically on iconic white-male rockers from the sixties and a few of their most relevant songs (Burdon's "We Gotta Get Out of This Place" logically appears repeatedly, as does Reed's "Walk on the Wild Side"), the second half is more diversified. It leans towards pop-rock in its allusions to Otis Redding's version of "My Girl," which becomes the ironic theme song for Manuel's fantasies of Marina and later the real theme of his reunion with Nadia, and Carole King's "You've Got a Friend," which comes to signify the value of loyalty and continuity in his relationship with Nadia. In addition to the variety of rock styles that are nonetheless limited to those of the sixties and seventies, the general musical eclecticism of *El jinete polaco* cannot be overstated; a different kind of music stands for each major character's perspective, much as literary genres do in *El Quijote*. Marina's incompatibility with Manuel is hinted at by her love of sentimental Mari Trini songs, a superficial make-out artist constantly hums kitschy ditties by Los Canarios, Manuel's academically-oriented classmate Félix eschews anything but baroque, the photographers Otto Zenner and Ramiro Retratista wallow in the romanticism of Schubert's *Death and the Maiden* (an ironic reference to the murdered mystery woman), and the pedantic teacher goes for singer-songwriters Serrat and Brel. Nadia's father prefers a time capsule of Spain in the thirties, before his exile: Republican anthems, pasodobles, coplas. Old men in bars listen to flamenco oldies like Juanito Valderrama and Antonio Molina. Even with this rich musical tapestry, however, rock icons of the sixties and their music stand out as the major intertexts in a narrative of liberation. Some of the songs become so interwoven with the narrative, in fact, that they run throughout the text as parallel allusions, a notion developed by Allan Pasco to explain how certain intertexts take on a metaphorical meaning in the texts onto which they are grafted. This could certainly be said of Morrison's "Riders on the Storm" as well as of his "Break on Through (to the Other Side)," Reed's "Walk on the Wild Side," and Burdon's "We Gotta Get Out of This Place."

Manuel Rivas was born in 1957, and thus is much closer in age to Muñoz Molina (b. 1956) than he is to the Generation X writers. However, he became more established as an author of fiction in the nineties rather than the eighties.[2]

His work in journalism has often championed ecological causes, and his popularity as a fiction writer was greatly boosted by the successful motion picture *La lengua de las mariposas* (shown in English as *Butterfly*) that is a compendium of several short stories that are set at the time of the Spanish Civil War in Galicia. Out of the other stories by Rivas that have been translated into Spanish in the volume *¿Qué me quieres, amor?* two develop intergenerational conflicts relying on rock music as an identity marker, but they do so without quoting from either song lyrics or titles.[3] The Galician author uses rock iconography as an offshoot of visual culture in the characterization of one of the protagonists in the story "El míster & Iron Maiden." In this tale of father-son conflict and finally, solidarity, the classic but still popular heavy-metal group Iron Maiden has a devotee in the Galician family consisting of a father-and-son mollusk fishing outfit and a mother who produces traditional lace flowers as a cottage industry. The young son wears one of the band's familiar t-shirts, consisting of a nearly skeletal, longhaired phantom with glowing eyes and arms outstretched, gleefully clutching a high-voltage cable that is electrifying him.

This Iron Maiden fan is an angry young man; he shares his father's devotion to the A Coruña soccer team, but blames the team's loss after a key player is sidelined on a faulty decision made by the team's aging coach. The father, while disappointed by the loss, defends the coach as the one who was responsible in the first place for the team's recent comeback. It becomes evident from the context of family dynamics that the son projects his hostility at his father onto the coach, while his father identifies with the mature athletic professional who has been branded a useless has-been. The story implies that the son on the other hand identifies with the sidelined player, feeling that his own youthful strength and energy are going to waste (understandable, owing to the economic stagnation of Galicia), with his father somehow to blame in the manner that parents are often held responsible for the status quo in which children find themselves. From the mother, who presumably completes this Oedipal triangle, one hears only the sounds of the tools of her trade as she weaves lace flowers in the kitchen.

Following this bitter argument, the second key situation in the story occurs when father and son are engaged in their fishing enterprise, directed at finding *percebes* (goose barnacles) on the shoals of the treacherous Costa da Morte. After a brief flashback relating the near-disaster of a tidal wave that almost washed the older man off of the shoal and out to sea, another such wave heads for him as the son looks on in horror from their boat. When his father braces himself to face the wave in a warrior stance brandishing his fishing spear as if to fend it off, the son jumps from the boat and runs toward the older man along the shoal that is about to be inundated. The narrator compares the way he runs both to a triumphant soccer player and to the Iron Maiden icon on his t-shirt. Their fate is left unresolved and imperiled, frozen in a moment of sudden camaraderie that may result in the salvation or doom of both men.

The story combines soccer and heavy metal as popular aspects of visual culture that form a hyperreality in which these traditionally Galician figures act out their personal and professional struggles. Iron Maiden is chosen for its association with young soccer fans as well as for the vividness of its iconography, which unites vitality and morbidity in a manner that adolescents and post-adolescents of the late twentieth century have found compelling. The symbolism is also especially troubling to parents and others whom Generation X aims to shock and antagonize: for older generations the concept of death as an energy source is contrary to their survival instincts, sharpened by a daily struggle against the aging process. Furthermore, a popular Iron Maiden song is devoted to "The Flight of Icarus" and the ideal of a glorious premature doom, with a twist on the myth: in the song the father entices the son to his death. The narratorial stance on Iron Maiden is not necessarily one of affinity; the iconography of the band culture is useful as a marker of youthful identity, in this case that of a rebellious working-class Gen Xer from Galicia who is also a soccer fan, as would typically be the case. The band's fan base and vivid commercial imagery prove useful for the creation of a powerful vignette of intergenerational conflict in late twentieth-century Galicia, where the globalization of English-language heavy metal bands, like soccer, has broken down the traditional barriers of regional isolation and poverty.[4] Another story, "La luz de la Yoko," in *Qué me quieres* represents an even younger character, a potential member of Generation Y, as totally immersed in the hyperreality of Japanese technological character toys and the animated television programs that feature them. In this child's hyperreal world there is no room left for the Oedipal confrontation featured in "El míster & Iron Maiden," since the characters effectively isolate the child from all of the family's activities.

In "Solo por ahí" both father and son (rather than the son alone as in "El míster & Iron Maiden") are defined and contrasted against one another by their devotion to specific kinds of rock music. The father's tastes are mainstream classic rock (similar to Manuel's of *El jinete polaco*), which for him was the musical accompaniment of his youthful revelries. He would like to see his son exhibit similar tastes and a devil-may-care attitude towards sex and soft drugs such as hashish, but he is vexed instead by the young man's melancholic attachment to brooding and solitary goth music, fashion and lifestyle. The Gen X son, an actual musician, has chosen a newer strain of rock music that expresses *fin de siglo* nihilism in a self-conscious and perhaps artsy manner. Thus, the son's music actually rebels against the earlier rebelliousness of rock, leaving the ex-hippy father longing for his own dissolute past, which now seems ironically healthy and wholesome. Similarly, in terms of cinema the son prefers chainsaw-massacre and slasher flicks, making his father nostalgic for good old-fashioned porn. As a duo, they encapsulate the progression from rock as part of the anti- and post-Franco perspective of dissidence and the later outlook of rock aligned with youthful *desencanto* that is characteristic of Generation X.

The father is exactly what a Gen Xer would consider an *ex-progre* "sell-out": he travels up and down the coast of Galicia selling Superbreasts (akin to Wonderbras) to retailers, satirizing the commodity fetishism of global consumerism. Here as in "El míster" there is "bleeding" of the hyperreal into the real at the story's conclusion. As the salesman drives around, worried about his son's whereabouts on that night as well as about the young man's general outcome, he sees an iconic poster of Steven Tyler in a store and purchases an old Aerosmith tape to listen to in the car. Soon the unmistakable Tyler magically occupies the passenger seat next to the exhausted father. A crash seems likely, since Tyler's appearance coincides with the driver's growing drowsiness, which the reader takes as a sign that the salesman is falling asleep at the wheel. Furthermore, although the song is not mentioned by name, Aerosmith's biggest hit to date is entitled "Dream On," the lyrics of which happen to evoke a nostalgia akin to the father's mood. The combination of concern over his son and nostalgia for his youth becomes potentially lethal for the father, who perhaps should have trusted in his son's ability to work things out (bringing to mind a Who anthem, "The Kids Are Alright," though it is not alluded to in the story) and focused instead on his own situation. Rock music is once again a key marker of identity in generational terms for Rivas; its late twentieth-century diversification allows it to emblematize the positions of (faded) dissidence and Gen X's *desencanto* in conflict within the same family.

Comparing Muñoz Molina's and Rivas's approaches to rock with those of Generation X, one notes a definite loss of reverence for rock stars and bands in the narration of Lucía Etxebarria's *Beatriz y los cuerpos celestes*, especially relative to the privileged place they occupy in *El jinete polaco*. The controversial Basque author won the Nadal Prize in 1998 with this, her second novel. In many spots it seems the music is generic; one artist or group is as good as another: "La música de fondo, creo recordar, podría ser The Cure o cualquier cosa parecida. Algo muy siniestro, seguro, una canción atormentada en blanco y negro, interpretada por algún jovencito vestido de luto de la cabeza a los pies . . ." (13) (The background music, if memory serves, could have been The

Cure or anything else like that. Something very sinister, surely, a tortured song in black and white, performed by some little guy dressed in mourning from head to foot . . .). So much for the rock star mystique; despite the increase in the nineties in female icons like Madonna and Annie Lennox, there are no rocker role models for Beatriz. The absence of rock figures to be emulated corresponds on another level to a deeper parental rejection: in *El jinete polaco* one of the conflicts so successfully resolved is the Oedipal struggle, when Manuel comes to the realization that he and his father are not so different at heart. The alienation from parents for Beatriz and others of her set is more complete and rapprochement appears impossible. The young and the older generations are separated by a huge divide, with the elders compounding the problem by attempting to seem younger with plastic surgery and other image alterations, all of which simply convinces the young that they are the ones to be imitated. Mothers copy the drug use of their offspring in their dependence on antidepressants, Valium, and diet pills. Likewise, the elder statesmen of rock like David Bowie, Iggy Pop, and the Rolling Stones are in the present of the novel hopelessly out of fashion, good only for adorning the walls of tacky neighborhood bar La Iguana or as overblown status symbols when someone scores an expensive concert ticket to hear Eric Clapton or Joe Cocker.

In *Beatriz* rock is viewed at times as a mass-produced spectacle or simulacrum, another consumer good to be flaunted or eschewed, an approach that is conspicuously absent from *El jinete polaco*, which focuses on the era before truly massive recording companies took over. MTV has played a key role in the globalization of rock as big business, and Beatriz's take on televised rock and roll is telling: "En la pantalla, niños británicos deprimidos que reclamaban a gritos un buen peluquero berreaban con desgana sus guitarras" (91) (Onscreen, depressed British boys who were crying out for a decent haircut wailed on their guitars indifferently). A few individual artists escape from Gen X cynicism. Beatriz's girlfriend Cat is a fan of Bjork and Beatriz admires the punk/gloom Siouxsie and the Banshees' cover of the Beatles' "Dear Prudence." As a preteen, Beatriz expressed her nonconformity by hating Miguel Bosé and liking Alaska and other Spanish neo-punk style rockers of the eighties who were considered bizarre. Certain artists are identified with gay men (Barbara Streisand) or with lesbians (K.D. Lang) but are treated with indifference. The badge they provide is more important than the significance of their music or lyrics.

One of the newer strains of rock that is accorded some degree of prominence in this novel is techno, associated with rave or trance dancing. This music is defined as gay-friendly background music for a trendy eatery, performed by such low-profile groups as The Orb, Prodigy, and Shamen: "Atmósferas inquietantes creadas por ordenador, ritmos que se adaptan al latido del corazón. Ambientes hormonales, secuencias ciberchic" (39) (Troubling atmospheres created by computers, rhythms that adjust to the heartbeat. Hormonal ambiences, cyberchic sequences). Intriguing and hypnotic, though nondescript, this music is also linked to the loss of self-consciousness that Beatriz and others of her set search for as an antidote to their narcissism, although Beatriz historicizes the practice as the same one that goes back to the Bacchanalia, the surrender of one's body/self to the gods: "En Cream y en Taste, los dos clubs que se habían convertido en catedrales norteñas del tecno, la masa bailaba en comunión al ritmo de un solo latido, una sola música, una sola droga, un único espíritu que hermanaba a los fieles" (176) (In Cream and in Taste, the two clubs that had become Northern cathedrals of techno, the masses danced in communion to the rhythm of a single beat, a single music, a single drug, a single spirit that united the faithful). For the record, at least one techno band is mentioned more than once (The Orb), however no visual or personalized image of any kind accompanies the references to techno groups, who remain as amorphous as their music throughout the text, up until the final epigraph, from The Beloved, a rare instance of a techno/rave band making a semantic inroad into a Spanish Gen X narrative (in this case, it is an uplifting encouragement to make a celebration out of life, also uncharacteristic of Gen X nihilism).

The impersonality of techno music seems to work at cross-purposes with the insistently inter-subjective aim of this novel. Beatriz attempts repeatedly to identify either her Scottish or her Spanish sweetheart as her true love, and examines her past behavior in the context of each relationship. Illicit drug use is present in both cases, including ecstasy, cocaine, and hashish. Thus her homosexual encounters are coupled with mood-altering drugs and music. However, her Spanish girlfriend is the more manipulative, the more serious drug abuser, and in the end, the less authentic partner (indeed, she never defines herself as lesbian and moves from one unsatisfactory heterosexual liaison to the next). Furthermore, she no longer resembles Beatriz's memory of her, having gotten frumpy while in rehab. Hence Scotland, where techno reigns supreme in the dance clubs, wins out in the reckoning of Beatriz's search for the closest thing to heaven she can find on earth, though at the novel's conclusion it is unclear whether this option is still open to her, just as it is unclear how Cat could be such a "good person" while remaining a fixture on the Edinburgh drug scene. For Jessica Folkart, it is Cat's demand of reciprocity from Beatriz that makes her the best choice in the long run (61). However, Cat and her social circle are involved in the same atmosphere of drug abuse that Beatriz found to be unhealthy in Madrid; only the language and the music styles are different.

This may explain why such an impersonal kind of music as techno figures so prominently in a novel concerned with inter-subjectivity; like Beatriz, it does not go too deep into questions that might trouble the mind. The music, drugs, and relationships chosen by Beatriz may still be escapes rather than solutions to her inner conflicts. Thus the novel leaves one with the sense that the troubled protagonist still has a long way to go in her search for self-fulfillment.

Rock and roll appears in a constellation of still more transgressive behaviors in *Historias del Kronen*, arguably the most emblematic Gen X novel. José Angel Mañas published his first novel when he was just twenty-three, drawing upon a youthful atmosphere with which he was familiar, and it remains his most influential work to date. Street fighting, rough sex, traffic violations, and trespassing are just a few of the pastimes preferred by the near sociopathic protagonist Carlos. This is a far cry from the fellows hanging out in Mágina drinking beer, smoking cigarettes, and thinking about sex (although Robert Spires finds a similarity between the social context of economic stagnation in *Historias del Kronen* and that of another novel related to Muñoz Molina's, *El Jarama*, 488). Unlike *El jinete polaco*, where there is no reason to suspect a lack of basic affinity between the views of the narrator (at times the protagonist) and those of the implied author, Mañas establishes an ironic distance between the author and the protagonist who narrates the majority of the work. This becomes clear upon examining the novel's epigraph, a long quotation from a lyric by The The, a British gloom band formed by the guitarist from the Smiths, Johnny Marr. In the first place the epigraph describes self-alienation, which will be a major part of the explanation for the social problems portrayed in the novel: "I am a stranger to myself/And nobody knows I'm here" (9). The band itself is much more self-reflexive and given to social critique (Carlos would say flaming-gay, a *mariconada*) than the bands alluded to as Carlos's favorites, which tend to be Spanish hard rock bands with fast guitar licks and deafening drumbeats, such as Siniestro Total, Parálisis Permanente, and Los Ronaldos. Hence the epigraph implies that what follows is a critique of the personality of Carlos as one that is fostered by the dehumanizing circumstances of the Generation X social milieu rather than a celebration of the youthful excesses described. The epigraph also implies that the novel will attempt to comprehend what has prompted this group of young people to adopt a lifestyle of immediate gratification at all cost (an objective that Annabel Martín detects at the heart of *Beatriz y los cuerpos celestes*, 51).

Like *Beatriz y los cuerpos celestes*, *Kronen* focuses with disenchantment upon the freedom enjoyed by Spanish youth; freedom to attend hostile rock concerts like that of grunge band Nirvana, where slam-dancing is so brutal it mirrors the bestiality of the song lyrics: "Manolo y yo bailamos como bestias . . . Tan cerca de los bafles y con el mal sonido del pabellón, no oigo más que ruido. Yo salto y choco con todos los cabrones sudados que bailan a mi alrededor . . . UNDERNEATH THE BRIDGE ANIMALS ARE CRAWLING . . ." (106–07) (Manolo and I dance like animals . . . So close to the speakers and with the poor sound in the stadium, I can't hear anything but noise. I jump and crash into the sweaty bastards dancing around me). Despite the uninspiring lyrics from Nirvana quoted here and elsewhere in the text, grunge has disciples in Spain, and the crassness of the latter are wryly satirized: "Lo que hacemos es música simple, lo más simple, sabes, como Nirvana, eso es lo que le gusta a la gente, un ritmillo guapo y unas letras con un poco de tequieroyyotambién y ya está, sabes" (51) (What we do is simple music, the simplest, you know like Nirvana, that's what people like, a pretty little melody and some lyrics with a little IloveyouandIdotoo and that's it, you know). Another lowest common denominator for Carlos and his crowd is the maddening bakalao music. These tunes are typically pumped up so loud in their vehicle that it renders all communication impossible. While grunge and bakalao are fine with Carlos, he finds John Lennon and The Band (along with most other sixties classic rockers, one would imagine) to be a *mierda* (crap). Rock is secondary to the intoxicating effects the characters get from drugs, so Carlos prefers music without intellectually challenging lyrics or intricate melodies that might bring him down from the high. Roberto on the other hand represents a more cultured and open-minded viewpoint; the more contemplative gloom bands do appeal to him and in the epilogue he takes steps to leave the Kronen gang behind. Rock music is also presented as less compelling for Carlos and his set than either television or cinema, where the visual effects of violence and pornography supply immediate sensory gratification.

After the Nirvana performance, a second big concert scene exposes the profit motive that by the nineties is the undeniable driving force behind commercial and so-called independent rock music. And of course it is relevant to note that the Gen X writers themselves have been criticized often for benefiting from certain marketing strategies of the Spanish publishing industry (Henseler 693). When Elton John comes to town on tour (changed to Elton Yon, as most of the foreign artists' names are deformed by the narrator) the bargaining and bickering for high-priced tickets among the scalpers is accorded as much space as the concert itself. Once the artists begin to perform, Carlos cannot stand the corny reactions of the crowd to the superstar, whose songs all sound the same to the protagonist. A bad drug experience, plaguing his date Amalia, cuts short the unsatisfactory, kitschy spectacle. The brevity of their attendance at the concert illustrates the primacy of the drug-induced high for Carlos and his circle; the musical accompaniment is secondary. Carlos views himself as a consumer who has been ripped-off when the exorbitant price he has paid for the concert tickets do not result in the desired outcome of intimacy with Amalia, and upon his next meeting with her he is determined to reap the benefits of his investment, despite her protestations that the time is not appropriate. He immediately forces himself on her in her bedroom, and although it is not quite rape her reaction shows that he has traded the possibility of a continuing relationship with her for a few moments of sexual domination.

Despite the disillusionment and jaded consumer cynicism directed at rock music in these two novels, adulatory exceptions are found in other examples of Generation X fiction. The pages of Ray Loriga's second novel *Héroes* are in fact populated by great figures of classic rock, which are idolized as in *El jinete polaco*. Loriga's fiction may not have enjoyed the extreme popularity of Mañas's in the nineties but critical reception has favored him as the most literate representative from among the Gen X group. He is also noted for his collaboration with Pedro Almodóvar on the script of *Carne Trémula*. The nitty-gritty social realism that is often called *realismo sucio* of Mañas and Etxebarria is absent from his narrative. While Gen X social realism tends to describe in unflinching detail the transgressive and often sordid behavior of the protagonists in interaction with each other, an interior narrative focus prevails in *Héroes*, like that of the earlier *novela ensimismada*, capturing the delirious fantasy life of a young man who hardly ever leaves his room. Without social connections as a corrective, his grandiose dreams, reminiscences, and imaginings naturally seize the larger than life rock stars of the past as objects of hero worship: Lennon, Dylan, Bowie, Jagger. In addition, Loriga's rock allusions include iconic figures that date from between the classic era of the sixties to early seventies and the newer strains of rock of the nineties (neo-punk, grunge, techno, goth, gloom). For example, he refers to late-seventies through eighties stars such as the Sex Pistols, the Clash, and Bruce Springsteen. In this way he exhibits a more archivist approach to rock than most of his contemporaries, even Muñoz Molina, whose references basically cease in the mid-seventies, coinciding with the end of the dictatorship.

More internalized than Muñoz Molina's narration, Loriga's does share the hedonism of his more realist Gen X contemporaries. His prose raises drug abuse and rock-star deification to the pinnacle of religious devotion: "David Bowie es el único capaz de librarte del pánico. Lleva mucho tiempo cuidando de todos los ángeles y puede cuidar de nosotros si aprendemos a confiar en las canciones" (37) (David Bowie is the only one who is able to free you from panic. He has been taking care of all the angels for a long time and he can take care of us too if we learn to place our trust in the songs). Loriga's pseudo-religious discourse juxtaposes the Spanish tradition of heterodoxy in its emphasis on rock rebels against another Spanish tradition, that of religious fanaticism and intolerance. The latter trend is depicted in the hero's single-minded devotion to his idols and his formulation of a new and absolute dogma. Like Roman Catholicism, this new faith privileges itself as the one true religion: "Sentirte como Jim Morrison no te convierte en Jim Morrison, pero no sentirte como Jim Morrison te convierte en casi nada" (37) (Feeling like Jim Morrison does not turn you into Jim Morrison, but not feeling like Jim Morrison turns you into almost nothing).

From their different narrative positions, both Muñoz Molina and Loriga mediate their escapes from Spanish *cursilería* or middle-class social pretensions through English-language iconic rock figures. As Noël Valis has noted in her study of *cursilería* as cultural phenomenon, for Andalucía the problem of *cursilería* has been especially keen, since this region is the most saturated with the false projection of gypsy/flamenco culture, the *españolada*, that pervades many of the kitschy cultural artifacts associated with *lo cursi*. When Muñoz Molina's Andalusian protagonist lip-syncs to the Animals, or Loriga's more metropolitan character dreams of avenging the death of John Lennon by killing everyone around him, their extreme devotion to a foreign rebellious youth culture works doubly to isolate them from the middle-class values of the middle-aged in their respective milieus. However, for the former the protest is positive and leads to a real personal change that mirrors Spain's transformation into a modern democracy, while for the latter it is doubtful that his nihilistic obsessive ramblings, compelling though they may be in the manner of prose poems (or video clips, as Henseler proposes, 697), will lead to any improvement in his life. While the hero-worshipper may be able to walk on water in his own mind (109), he will never find a girlfriend if he never leaves his room. An isolated schizo/nomad whose only recent contact with reality appears to have been a trip to the Seville Expo in 1992 to assist his brother after an accident that cost the latter an ear, his extreme form of hero worship is not represented as compatible with Spanish urban youth culture of the nineties.

From dissidence to *desencanto*, this essay has traced some of the defining features of rock as it appears in the fiction of the Transitional/Eighties Boom writers and Generation X. In Etxebarria and Mañas the characters are presented as enmeshed in interactions with their peers, and for them rock and roll is an immediate sensory experience to be shared with the peer group. Since their overall attitude is disaffected from social and political contexts and given to hedonism, this extends to the treatment of rock music. The hypnotic beat of techno (in Etxebarria) and of bakalao and grunge (in Mañas) pulsates in the background as their major rock references. There is little space for the extended intertextuality, or parallel allusion in Pasco's terms, to develop with particular rock songs, in the manner in which this occurs in *El jinete polaco*. The reverence for iconic figures seen in Muñoz Molina and in Rivas is replaced by a more contingent flavor-of-the-month rock in these two Gen X novelists, and the music serves chiefly as an accompaniment for the headier excesses of sexual and drug experimentation. In Loriga's novel of hallucinatory isolation, the reverence for rock figures returns but takes on a bizarre pseudo-religious significance, almost a deformation of the hero worship described by Muñoz Molina as part of his protagonist Manuel's adolescence during the final years of the Francoist dictatorship.

In the privileged place accorded to rock music by *El jinete polaco*, rock and rollers inhabit the same Parnassian peak as other great literary references, and through parallel allusions the significance of several vintage songs becomes thoroughly interwoven with the plot of the novel. Like other forms of high art, rock is held in esteem as a source of enlightenment and self-fulfillment: the songs seem to guide both lovers on their quest for freedom and for each other. In Manuel Rivas's short stories involving rock, another writer who might be considered a predecessor to Generation X has his characters relate to key rock figures for self-definition. Although the lyrics do not achieve the prominence that they have in Muñoz Molina, the stars and their music play a positive role in identity formation. When we shift our gaze to the writings of Generation X involving rock, the relationship between rock and art has been replaced by the connection between rock and the hedonistic entertainment of postmodern spectacle. In Etxebarria and Mañas rock is seen as part of a global popular culture with a strong underlying profit motive along with television and film that invites the youthful protagonists to lose their sense of self and their consciousness rather than either defining themselves or raising their awareness of the world in which they live. Even when classic rockers present themselves as icons for emulation as in Ray Loriga, they wind up crowding out reality and meaningful identity formation with a hyperreal world of ideals that the reader cannot help but perceive as an illusion and an escape.

Notes

1. See Amann for the surprising connections between *El jinete polaco* and many fictional genres, such as the *novela bizantina*.

2. Rivas published two books of fiction in the nineteen eighties, winning the Premio de la Crítica in 1989. In the nineties he published seven such works, and attained much greater prominence outside of Galicia.

3. Lyrics from the Latin Big-Band style number "Maní" do make a nostalgic appearance in another story in the volume, "Saxos en la niebla."

4. Will Straw traces the origins of heavy metal as a product of late sixties psychedelic rock marketed by the new rock industry elites of the nineteen seventies. The latter had taken the place of the regional managers who were crucial to the earlier history of rock. Heavy metal from its early days was characterized by the super-band with little or no intermediary strata with its audiences, an emphasis on large-scale touring, lack of an archivist relationship to rock roots and other contexts, rejection of other rock subgenres like disco and punk, relatively low socioeconomic status of listeners, satanic and heroic-fantasy imagery on t-shirts and posters, and "the association of masculinity with physical violence and power" (381). While Straw shows that these elements broadened heavy metal's appeal throughout the seventies and eighties in suburban America, they also no doubt contributed to its popularity in Spain from about the mid eighties onward.

Works Cited

Amann, Elizabeth. "Genres in Dialogue: Antonio Muñoz Molina's *El jinete polaco*." *Revista Canadiense de Estudios Hispánicos* 23.1 (Fall 1998): 1–22.

Etxebarria, Lucía. *Beatriz y los cuerpos celestes: Una novela rosa*. 1998. Madrid: Destino, 2001.

Folkart, Jessica A. "Body Talk: Space, Communication, and Corporeality in Lucía Etxebarria's *Beatriz y los cuerpos celestes*." *Hispanic Review* 72.1 (Winter 2004): 43–63.

Henseler, Christine. "Pop, Punk, and Rock & Roll Writers: José Angel Mañas, Ray Loriga, and Lucía Etxebarria Redefine the Literary Canon." *Hispania* 87.4 (December 2004): 692–702

Loriga, Ray. *Héroes*. 1993. Barcelona: Plaza y Janés, 1998.

Mañas, José Angel. *Historias del Kronen*. Madrid: Destino, 1994.

Martín, Annabel. "Feminismo virtual y lesbianismo mediático en *Beatriz y los cuerpos celestes: Una novela rosa* de Lucía Etxebarria." *Convergencias Hispánicas: Selected Proceedings and Other Essays on Spanish and Latin American Literature, Film, and Linguistics*. Ed. Elizabeth Scarlett and Howard B. Wescott. Newark, Delaware: Juan de la Cuesta—Hispanic Monographs, 2001. 47–56.

Montero, Rosa. *Te trataré como a una reina*. Barcelona: Seix Barral, 1983.

Muñoz Molina, Antonio. *El jinete polaco*. 1991. Barcelona: RBA, 1992.

_____. *El invierno en Lisboa*. Barcelona: Seix Barral, 1987.

Pasco, Allan H. *Allusion: A Literary Graft*. Toronto: University of Toronto Press, 1994.

Rivas, Manuel. *¿Qué me quieres, amor?* 1995. Trans. Dolores Vilavedra. Madrid: Alfaguara, 1996.

Spires, Robert C. "Depolarization and the New Spanish Fiction at the Millennium." *Anales de la Literatura Española Contemporánea* 30.1–2 (2005): 485–512.

Straw, Will. "Characterizing Rock Music Culture: The Case of Heavy Metal." *The Cultural Studies Reader.* Ed. Simon During. London and New York: Routledge, 1993. 368–81.

Valis, Noël. *The Culture of Cursilería: Bad Taste, Kitsch, and Class in Modern Spain.* Durham, North Carolina: Duke University Press, 2002.

Part III
Historias del Kronen on the Rocks

◆ **7**

Between Rock and the Rocking Chair:
The Epilogue's Resistance in *Historias del Kronen*

Randolph D. Pope

"All systems leak."
—Edward Sapir

Epilogues present themselves as superfluous (the main events are over) and necessary (since they are included), delivered with a different voice, impatient with details and satisfying the idle curiosity of the reader for the characters' life after the novel itself has ended. Movies resort to a few lines on the screen, novels inscribe a title as shifter, "Epilogue," which is as effective as italics or footnotes in creating a different address, a space for the overflow of information and, sometimes, the minor concluding revelation. José Ángel Mañas' *Historias del Kronen* appears to end with the fourteenth chapter. This frenzied story of a group of young people in Madrid during the summer of 1992, told by one of them, the narcissistic Carlos, closes when another, Fierro, dies after being forced to drink alcohol, which he cannot tolerate for medical reasons. The text continues, but not with a fifteenth chapter. Instead, an epilogue includes three different texts; the first continues Carlos' first-person narration, the second is a third-person narration of a session of Carlos' friend Roberto and his psychoanalyst, and the third, arguably, is the return of the lyrics of a song, "Giant," which had served as an epigraph at the beginning of the novel. What does this epilogue contribute? Does it actually matter? Why is the transition from the chapters to the epilogue important? I propose in this essay that the transition from chapters to epilogue is emblematic of the inevitable failure of the solipsistic aspects of the Generation X project. This illuminates, on the one hand, a precise historical moment in Spain, when the party of the end of the transition begins to be over, and, on the other, the old human frustration, brilliantly described by Freud in his *Civilization and its Discontents*, caused by the need to restrain one's desires if one is going to live in society.[1]

In the first section Carlos is in Santander with his family, enjoying a vacation. It is August. He meets some friends at the beach and they recall that the previous night Carlos was very drunk. He apparently had sex with Rocío, but when he sees her now, fully revealed by the sun, he tells her he remembers nothing of last night. It is a verbal denial presented as a lie, brushing off the inconvenient consequences of his actions. When he leaves the beach, Rocío follows him with her eyes, but he ignores her. His words and actions acknowledge information but make it discontinuous, inconsequent, in perfect consonance with the Generation X's indifference towards history that Gonzalo Navajas describes so well in another essay in this same volume. Carlos gets away. He then receives a letter from Roberto, who had revealed his homosexual attraction for Carlos after they had mutually masturbated right before Carlos incited the group to force Fierro to drink until he died. These are two disquieting secrets, a sexual transgression and a murder. Readers do not see the content of Roberto's letter, but someone who is with Carlos as he reads asks if there is anything wrong. Did he express some emotion? Carlos replies with an excessive and progressive denial, in the three reiterations favored by ritual: "No. Nada importante. Tonterías" (228) (No. Nothing important. Nonsense"). This section concludes when Carlos crumples the letter (perhaps, again, with some emotion?) and throws it into a wastebasket at a pizza parlor, before asking the friend who is with him, Julián, "¿Tomamos algo antes de volver?" (229) (Shall we drink something before we return?"). One can safely assume that the actions that follow will not be different for him, but more of the same, a return of the ignored and the discarded. And yet, these actions are now framed differently, not from the solipsistic first person narrative but with a third-person voice that places them into a context.

The second section begins with the analyst asking Roberto about the letter to Carlos. Roberto believes Carlos will not read it and says he does not really know why he sent it, uttering the first of the fifteen "no sé" ("I don't know") he uses during this conversation. He identifies, though, a series of insights: he has hidden his true self from his friends, especially from Carlos, because he is afraid of being rejected as gay; he was infatuated with Carlos and made him the object of his sexual fantasies; Fierro did not die in an accident, but was murdered by his friends, led by Carlos; Roberto is now afraid of death; the group of friends is now even more tightly knit by their uniform silence about the truth of the events and their participation in a fabricated cover story. Just as in many myths of the origin of societies, such as imagined by Freud or René Girard, the violent sacrifice of an innocent victim creates the bond that assures loyalty to the tribe. Roberto knows he will see Carlos soon, but does not know how he will react when seeing him. Speaking to the analyst is not a breach of silence, since there is a professional rule of discretion that protects the speaker. Since the crime has already occurred and there is no one in immediate danger, the analyst is not under any legal obligation to reveal the truth of the events. And yet, why are we, readers, overhearing this conversation, which as far as the facts go, tells us nothing really new?

A possible clue is in the repetition of the lyrics that open and close the novel, which belong to the song "Giant" of a group, The The, which fizzled into oblivion after the success of this song. Having the lyrics printed twice is another unnecessary reiteration from the point of view of raw information. *Historias del Kronen* mentions the names of many songs and bands, but they are reduced to muffled allusions that one often must decipher from their fanciful spelling. Only at the Nirvana concert do some fragmented lines come through, from "Something in the Way," a song from the album *Nevermind*: "UNDERNEATH THE BRIDGE ANIMALS ARE CRAWLING . . . THERE IS A LEAK . . . IT'S OKAY WITH FISH CAUSE THEY DON'T HAVE ANY FEELINGS . . . UH, UH, SOMETHING IN THE WAY" (107) (capital letters in *Historias* are used to indicate a very high volume of sound). The complete lyrics are:

> Underneath the bridge
> The tarp has sprung a leak
> And the animals I've trapped
> Have all become my pets
> And I'm living off of grass
> And the drippings from the ceiling
> It's okay to eat fish
> 'Cause they don't have any feelings
>
> (x3)
> Something in the way, mmm
> Something in the way, yeah, mmm

Underneath the bridge
The tarp has sprung a leak
And the animals I've trapped
Have all become my pets
And I'm living off of grass
And the drippings from the ceiling
It's okay to eat fish
'Cause they don't have any feelings

(x4)
Something in the way, mmm
Something in the way, yeah, mmm

We have here a series of elements that can find an echo with others presented in *Historias del Kronen*: the speaker seems to be living in a tent under a bridge, eating fish, grass (which perhaps he is smoking), and drinking the water that drips in from the leak in the ceiling. There are animals with him, but he spares them, because they have feelings and have become his pets. It is a picture of solitude and need, of exposure to the elements and openness to feelings. The many r's in the lyrics—bridge, tarp, sprung, trapped, grass—could be heard to represent acoustically the ripping of the tarp, the impossibility of absolute isolation. The leak seems to rhyme faintly with the fish several lines later, which are forms of life that do not recognize the speaker as their friend, since they have not become pets. They are indifferent life, at least for the person in the tent and under the bridge. "Something in the way" never finds a verb and seems stuck in repetition. Is there an obstacle in the way? Are we to hear a faint and displaced echo of the Beatles' 1969 hit, "Something in the way she moves," which includes the lines "You're asking me, will my love grow. / I don't know, I don't know"? Because just as the images in a dream acquire significance for the place in which they appear, this single audible lyric of some extension comes after an event that will be remembered vividly by Roberto in the epilogue. Carlos, during the concert, grabs Roberto by the neck and kisses him on the mouth. Roberto pushes him away: "Le agarro a Roberto del cuello, cosa que sé que odia, y le doy un beso en la boca. Roberto me aparta con un empujón" (107) (I grab Roberto by his neck, something I know he hates, and I kiss him in the mouth. Roberto pushes me away). Carlos' assurance that he knows Roberto does not like to be grabbed in this way allows him to present his sudden approach as a form of playful aggression instead of a homosexual embrace, but the later revelations during Fierro's party and at the analyst make his excuse here not credible. There is indeed a leak in his system of self-containment, the surfacing of the weakness he is often fearing and denouncing, one that the many unfeeling fish evoked by Nirvana could very well connect with phallic desire. The fragmented and distorted recollection of the lyrics do bring in a powerful word absent from the original song, *crawling*, indicating probably how Carlos associates this breach in his protections with debasement. At the same time, the place of the embrace, a rock concert, and the full reality of the lyrics as a song, point to how the individual guilt and isolation is transcended in the ritual of a multitude and the earth-shaking volume of amplified music.

Roberto's session with the analyst will read this scene quite differently. He pushes Carlos away not because he does not like to be grabbed and kissed, but because he believes Carlos is drunk and just making fun of him. Nevertheless, this event remains not just a burning memory, but the matrix of his many sexual fantasies in which he makes love to Carlos. The epilogue, then, in revisiting this kiss into a story of prolonged and secret passion, in binding it to the Nirvana lyrics, which retrospectively are anything but random, does offer a double reading that is nevertheless not stable. Carlos has decided to ignore the letter and its contents, Roberto holds to the mantra of "I don't know" when speaking to his analyst. What is going on under the bridge, will the leak dismantle the tent and wreck the protective system?

The third moment of the epilogue, as I read it, provides an even deeper and more desolate view, when it reiterates the lyrics of a song ironically called "Giant" (from an album called appropriately *Soul Mining*). The first lines provide the setting:

The sun is high and I'm surrounded by sand
For as far as my eyes can see.
I'm strapped into a rocking chair
With a blanket over my knees.

For Carlos and his friends the night is their natural habitat. As we saw in the first segment of the epilogue, Carlos sees too clearly during the day how he deceives himself after midnight and with artificial stimulants. This is high noon and the time of reckoning. Sand is wasted time, while being strapped into a rocking chair is a cruel parody of dancing to rock music. There is a perverse element in the blanket, since the sun is high, so it does not appear to be necessary: old, crippled, infirm, immobile, blanked out. The song continues:

I am a stranger to myself
And nobody knows I'm here.

When I looked into myself
It wasn't myself I'd seen
But who I've tried to be.

Who could this description apply to, if we assume the author did not choose and repeat this song arbitrarily? Is this Carlos, years later? There is a better fit with Roberto, who has made the choice for much of his life to be accepted socially and deny therefore who he actually is. Yet the text is even more poignant: the speaker has actually tried to look into herself or himself, but has found it a difficult task. The self, deep, vast, and real, as it struggles to bridge and negotiate the gap between its desire for pleasure and the impositions of reality is still, as we know well from many years of psychoanalytic thought, as Freud put it, "the most obscure and inaccessible region of the mind" (1). "Giant" now describes the persistence of the past, not to be easily ignored or denied:

I'm thinking of things I'd hoped to forget.
I'm choking to death in a sun that never sets.
I clugged [sic, for "clogged"] up my mind with perpetual grief
And turned all my friends into enemies,
And now the past has returned to haunt me.

The return of the repressed is not to be denied. Suddenly, the text turns up the volume and expresses fear of judgment and collapse:

I'M SCARED OF GOD AND SCARED OF HELL
AND I'M CAVING IN UPON MYSELF
HOW CAN ANYONE KNOW ME
WHEN I DON'T EVEN KNOW MYSELF

This may be the moment in which the text transfers its questions to the reader and critics. Roberto has told his analyst sharply that he does not understand Carlos (230) and he does not understand his friends (233). The epilogue, then, sounds a warning to reductive conclusions about what we have read, presenting an instructive resistance that I would like to explore here briefly, given that it is crucial to understanding the difference between the discourse of individualism and the communal life of Generation X characters.

Music is usually fun, drugs and sex often produce pleasure, transgression can be a thrill, and young people roam modern cities by night, having a blast, without ending up committing a crime, crippled in a rocking chair, or full of remorse. What we see in this novel is just a minor fragment of the historical real, yet from this and other similar novels the tendency has developed to characterize a whole generation in a similar way, as if Roberto's analyst were to extrapolate from him to all his friends. The designation of Generation X is disquieting, since once more, as in the case of the Generation of '98 or '27, we have a small group of people characterized as the standard bearers for all those who were born at a given period; thus, the uniqueness of life is defined away with an all-encompassing label. *Historias del Kronen* reveals these tensions between the group and the individual, since on the one hand it shows friends that appear remarkably attuned in their habits, move together as an urban nomadic tribe, and talk so similarly that their lines often have no attribution, while on the other hand personalities emerge and distance themselves from each other. This may be an ancient story of youth: to come into the world as a group in which or out of which they must find a place and adopt a narrative of their own, as they give birth to their social selves and add their story to history.

Much more is going on than just the story of these Kronen friends. The novel highlights private affairs while providing a background of national 1992 events, such as the Universal Exhibit in Seville and ETA violence, the first a proclamation of Spain's belated arrival to contemporary Europe and the second showing the splintering effect of unresolved nationalist desire. Santiago Fouz-Hernández, in his very fine article on *Historias del Kronen*, affirms that "the country's apparent enthusiasm, however, is not shared by Mañas's characters," and adds, "1990s Spanish youth experienced a ubiquitous and profound pessimism" (84). The opposed subjects, "the country" and "Mañas's characters," are rough shorthand that makes perfect sense in the context, yet is precisely the sort of compact that the novel unravels in its epilogue. Clearly, Mañas's characters are also part of the country and varied in age, since they are not just the youth, but also their parents. As much as Carlos talks of himself as a lonely wolf, as the text switches from first to third person, his uniqueness is diminished and the constraints of living in society are restored. Carlos suffers from the illusion of uniqueness at the same time that he is read as representative of the pessimism of Spanish youth. But can't one conceive of some people in their late twenties who actually experienced real enthusiasm, not just apparent, for Expo 92, or who were optimists? Must they be excluded from their own generation? This is much more than a quibble; it is working with the novel, which from its very title, a plural *historias*, to its epilogue fights back against reductionism. Maria Pao observes that the novel "also presents alternate views to those of Carlos" (250) and "provides abundant, though rapidly sketched, examples of the narrator's peers who do not follow his model" (250). In fact, continues

Pao, "read against the novel's depictions of other young people, their lives and comments, Carlos seems an aberration" (250). This is crucial: The world of the chapters in which Carlos speaks is contained in a much broader society that does not fully share his values.

The desire to be unique within a larger community by joining a smaller dissident group, which then becomes popular and loses its sharp rebellious nature, is not new—one has only to think how the Romantic hero became a fashion. While the opposition between previous generations, represented by the grandfather and father, and Carlos is clear, within these groups there are gender, class, and economic strains, and even quite diverse choices within those categories.[2]

Nevertheless, Nina Molinaro in her masterful and most insightful article on *Historias del Kronen* does affirm that Carlos, "and those of his generation, are unable to remember themselves, to remember that their Being is determined by their relations with the world" (303). And Pao also generalizes by concluding that "*Kronen* may represent a cautionary statement vis-à-vis encroaching North American cultural forms and the consumption they demand" (246). The fact that Carlos lives in La Moraleja may make it tempting to provide a sociological or ethical reading. Pao believes that Carlos has misread *American Psycho*, quoting Annesley's opinion that it "can be read as a novel with an intensely moral agenda" (257), indicating that *Kronen* "also *contains an implicit warning* against the objectifying ethos and consumerist tendencies embodied in its protagonist and stimulated by North American cultural products" (258, my italics). Since this warning is implicit, the reader cannot expect that its existence be proven in any other way than by the authority of the critic. What if one simply denies it is there?

In a footnote that concludes her article, Pao makes a reference to *Tesis*, a 1996 movie directed by Alejandro Amenábar, in which the fascination with snuff movies is central to the storyline and she concludes that the movie assumes "an ultimately moral posture before a society which finds these things somewhat riveting" (260). Indeed, the last images of the film do show numerous hospital patients watching images of the snuff movie in quiet fascination, but it is evident that the small images repeated in the television screens are amplified in the frame of the movie, which most spectators, judging from its success, are watching with equal attention. The movie is a presentation of a representation, a sequence of at least spaces, actions, images, words, and music that will be attractive, indifferent or repulsive to readers regardless of the moral statements that may accompany them implicitly or explicitly.

And yet the bad conscience of Roberto, the distancing of the text from Carlos as a narrator, and the desolate image of the final lyrics do indicate that

the Dionysian sacrifice of Fierro acts not as a redeeming and liberating sacra-
ment, but as a bond that silences into complicity, guilt and the anticipation of
death. Freud saw the wish or the need to sacrifice the father, who represents the
smothering law and phallic system. But he added:

> Whether one has killed one's father or has abstained from doing so is not really the
> decisive thing. One is bound to feel guilty in either case, for the sense of guilt is an
> expression of the conflict due to ambivalence, of the eternal struggle between Eros
> and the instinct of destruction of death. (*Civilization and its Discontents* 89)

In "The Politics of Representation," Michael Holquist classified what
he described as three different conceptions of language, as conceived by de-
partments of literature in the United States, according to "the ownership of
meaning" (163). The *personalist* believes the individual owns meaning; the
deconstructionist view is inclined to the view that *no one* owns meaning;
dialogism, based on Bakhtin's ideas, holds that *we* own meaning, since for this
view "multiplicity and struggle characterize this heteroglot view of language"
(166). There cannot be any doubt that when we reduce the reality of hundreds
of rock bands with thousands of songs to one designation we are only capturing
an abstract distillation far from the daily manifestation of this music in all its
variety, from trivial to sublime. The same song even, in different circumstances
and for different people can be an inspiring anthem, a noisy distraction, a museum piece, or background music, among many other possibilities. In the three
cases distinguished by Holquist, though, it seems that meaning is a given and
we have something to contest ownership about, that is, there is no meaningless
language, or at least, which is more exact, no meaningless literary language.
Equally, actions end up framed by the predominant ideology of a period. A
murder can be exhilarating for Carlos, but this instant will encounter the reality of living among others, with laws and rules of conduct that either punish or
reduce to silence. The daredevil rock anthem is like a tiger in the zoo: wild and
beautiful, dangerous and mind-blowing, yet well contained. Once the party is
over, people go home and all returns to normal.

Bakhtin's admirable and well-known insight, though, is that the novelist
cannot erase and silence with a final conclusion what acquires life and voice in
the pages she or he has written, so a novel resists a moralistic closure. The relay
of narrative voices in the epilogue of *Historias del Kronen*, so different in the
way they consider experiences they have shared, is a clear indication that all
general statements about the "generation" should be taken with extreme cau-
tion. The sudden breaking away from Carlos' voice to a omniscient narrator,

the presentation of private remorse, both in an analytic setting and in a public song, is, following a silent gap, a representation of the transition which had ended by the time of the novel, when the old young rebels and revelers became the new old government, and a corrupt one at that: Carlos' *movida* faces the resistance and drag of being in a vast and complex society that does not fully share his mode of life and into which, as so many heroes of *Bildungsromans*, he will ultimately blend. Rock serves here to begin and conclude a book that takes us from individual gratification to ritual bonding through guilt and music but, as the epilogue brilliantly, even if unobtrusively, demonstrates, outside and beyond the arena where the band plays its discontent, there is a civilization with its constraints and duties, and ultimate old age and death.

Notes

1. One does not need to be a Freudian to recognize that what Freud wrote in 1930 described perfectly the brutal history of the twentieth century: "the inclination to aggression is an original, self-subsisting instinctual disposition in man, and . . . that constitutes the greatest impediment to civilization" (*Civilization and its Discontents* 77).
2. Fouz-Hernández notes that the lifestyle seen most closely in *Historias del Kronen* does not correspond to a "generation": "However, as pointed out (both in the novel and in the film) by his poorest friend Miguel, this luxury of doing nothing and having expensive habits is only possible for a minority of rich kids" (89). He then seems to forget this statement when he affirms that "it is difficult to come across images of young people anywhere in the Western World without spotting clear similarities in their attires, accessories, haircuts or even attitude and speech" (91).

Works Cited

Bakhtin, M.M. *The Dialogic Imagination.* Ed. Michael Holquist. Trans. Caryl Emerson and Michael Holquist. Austin: University of Texas Press, 1981.

Fouz-Hernández, Santiago. "*¿Generación X?* Spanish Urban Youth Culture at the End of the Century in Mañas's / Armendáriz's *Historias del Kronen*." *Romance Studies* 18 (2000): 83–98.

Freud, Sigmund. *Beyond the Pleasure Principle.* Trans. James Strachey. New York: W.W. Norton, 1961.

_____. *Civilization and its Discontents.* Trans. by James Strachey. New York: W.W. Norton, 1961.

Holquist, Michael. "The Politics of Representation." *Allegory and Representation.* Ed. Stephen Jay Greenblatt. Baltimore: Johns Hopkins University Press, 1981. 163–83.

Mañas, José Ángel. *Historias del Kronen*. With a prologue by Germán Gullón. Barcelona: Destino, 1998.

Molinaro, Nina. "The 'Real' Story of Drugs, *Dasein* and José Ángel Mañas's *Historias del Kronen*." *Revista Canadiense de Estudios Hispánicos* 27 (2003): 291–306.

Pao, María T. "Sex, Drugs and Rock & Roll: *Historias del Kronen* as Blank Fiction." *ALEC* 27 (2002): 245–60.

◆ **8**

Realism on the Rocks in the Generational Novel: "Rummies," Rhythm, and Rebellion in *Historias del Kronen* and *The Sun Also Rises*

Matthew J. Marr

> "*Es una discoteca con música entre el After-punk tipo*
> *De Quiur, Depesh Mod, y el bakalao.*
> *Suena el último disco de De Quiur y yo me pongo a bailar.*"
> —Carlos, *Historias del Kronen* (1994: 117)

> (It's a discotheque that plays music ranging from
> Post-Punk bands like The Cure and Depeche Mode to rave.
> The latest record of The Cure begins to play and I start to dance.)

> "i really don't know what I'm doing here /
> i really think i should've gone to bed tonight but . . . /
> just one drink / and there're some people to meet you
> / i think that you'll like them / i have to say we do /
> and i promise in less than an hour we will honestly go /
> now why don't i just get you another while you just say hello . . ."
> —The Cure, "Open" (*Wish*, 1992)[1]

"I have measured out my life with coffee spoons," declares the awkward and withdrawn everyman, J. Alfred Prufrock, in T.S. Eliot's famous 1917 poem (481). His uninspiring days, set as they are to the humdrum rhythm of monotonous deskwork and coffee breaks, are as steady as a metronome. Substances much stronger and more addictive than caffeine, however, soon jolt twentieth-century literature and its protagonists into a rhythm conspicuously unbound by conventional time signatures and social norms. With respect to the genre of the novel, Ernest Hemingway's libationary epic, *The Sun Also Rises* (1925)—published under the more aptly descriptive title *Fiesta* in Great Britain (and later as a Spanish translation entitled *París era una fiesta*)[2]—is a foundational text whose resonance has been internationally widespread and lasting in contemporary fiction. Indeed, this "book about a few drunks" (a quip from the author himself)[3] plays no small role in setting in motion what can be seen as the behaviorally unrestrained, frenetically-paced subgenre of the novel of youthful rebellion and festive overindulgence. Though arguably having certain origins in the Futurists' love of speed, the late nineteenth-century decadents, or even Thomas De Quincey's 1821 *Confessions of an English Opium-Eater*, this literary tradition is ardently championed by Hemingway and his fellow members of the Lost Generation—in part, no doubt, as a response to the American Prohibition movement.[4]

Subsequent up-and-coming novelists shape and diversify this subgenre in accordance with their own respective generational concerns. Indeed, novels which foreground a kind of fast-living out of step with the steady stride of bourgeois realism routinely appear over the course of the century in a succession of countercultural narrative projects, such as those of the Beat Generation (Jack Kerouac's 1957 *On the Road*) or, more recently, in the Generation X novel (Bret Easton Ellis's *Less Than Zero*, published in 1985, is paradigmatic in this regard). The often frenzied tempo of such works is, in more than a few instances, part and parcel of substance abuse. In Spain, however, the influence of authoritarian social mores—in particular, official censorship under Franco—makes this trend less pervasive throughout much of the twentieth century (Juan Goytisolo's experimental novels of the late 1960s, published in Mexico City, are perhaps a notable exception). Still, with the arrival of democracy and the legislation of some of the most liberal drug consumption laws in Europe, controlled substances become more readily available in Spain. Working their way not only onto the streets and into the nightlife—from the *Movida Madrileña* to the *Ruta del Bacalao*, from the glitz of Marbella to the grittiness of the Basque punk scene—they also find a welcome place in the urban iconography of much cultural production in the 1980s and 1990s. The prominence of drug use in Pedro Almodóvar's early films (such as the 1983 heroin-laced farce, *Entre tinieblas*) or in a cinematic drama like Montxo Armendáriz's San Sebastián-based chronicle of addiction, *27 horas* (1986), is clearly indicative of this trend—so too, to return to the realm of the literary, is the frequent inclusion of "recreational" drugs and liberal quantities of alcohol as indispensable ingredients of the nocturnal urban exploits depicted in *postnovísimo* poetry (by such authors as Carlos Marzal, Roger Wolfe, and Almudena Guzmán).

Yet, perhaps an even more extreme take on this "prescribed" aesthetic is cultivated by novelists like Ray Loriga, Lucía Etxebarria, Daniel Múgica, and José Ángel Mañas. In fact, with respect to the recent Spanish novel, nowhere is such a "prescription" more plentifully filled—and refilled again—than in Mañas's *Historias del Kronen* (1994): a novel which has now been afforded, with more than a decade of critical hindsight, a quasi-canonical status as a representative manifestation of Generation X narrative in the Peninsular context. Much of the scholarly attention garnered by Mañas's novel tends to concern the cultural sources and texts which may (or may not) inform the work's aggressively "edgy" stylings, its eclectic allusions, and, of course, its uninhibited content matter. American cinema, international rock music, and the minutiae of a contemporary, globalized, and "commodified" reality in urban Madrid have all been convincingly identified and analyzed as prominent components of the rich referential fabric of the novel. With respect to literary paradigms, more than one critic has linked *Historias del Kronen* with the "blank fiction" narrative model applied by James Annesley to the work of such contemporary American novelists as Dennis Cooper, Lynne Tillman, Bret Easton Ellis, and Susanna Moore, among others.[5] To date, however, comparative approaches to Mañas's novel have rarely ventured away from interpretations bound in one form or another to either "blank fiction" or its forerunner: the dirty realism of writers like Raymond Carver—a literary mode which can hardly be categorized without alluding in the same breath to the narrative stylings of a young Ernest Hemingway.[6]

To posit that significant bonds of literary kinship exist between Hemingway's *The Sun Also Rises* (*Fiesta*) and Mañas's *Historias del Kronen* seems eminently natural. Both works are, after all, phenomenally received debut novels written by twenty-something authors who have since become virtually synonymous with their respective "generations." Both novels share an array of common leitmotifs (bar life in the European urban milieu, male bonding) and narrative strategies (first-person narrator-protagonists; succinct, idiosyncratic, and innovative prose). The relationship between these novels is, in fact, meaningful enough to merit a close analysis—particularly within the context of this collection, which seeks not only to carve out a more definitive place for Spanish Generation X narrative within the emerging picture of recent Peninsular cultural production, but also to position this literature within a critical framework having a solid international and historical footing. Such is the critical objective at the heart of this essay. In specific terms, the pages that follow will show how Mañas's and Hemingway's novels both embrace excessive drinking and drug use as devices that contribute stylistically to a kind of accelerated narrative rhythm. This radical time signature is reinforced, in turn, by both texts' overt thematization of what is tantamount to a changing of the guard—or rather, the coming of a new "generation"—in each author's respective national culture.

The Lost Generation and Generation X, though vastly separated by time and space, coalesce in *Historias del Kronen* and *The Sun Also Rises* around remarkably parallel sociopolitical concerns: anxieties which involve, at their core, government's attempts to curtail time-honored, culturally-inscribed forms of festive overindulgence.

Over the years, critical commentary and popular reception of *The Sun Also Rises* have tended to privilege the aesthetic impact and symbolic significance of those chapters of the novel set in Pamplona and the surrounding Navarrese countryside: that is, the portion of the work Hemingway labels Book II. Yet, with its relentless depiction of the riotous rendezvous, meandering late-night soirees, and binge drinking of a mixed bag of expatriates living in the centre of Paris, it is actually Book I that most fetchingly invites some of the most immediately tenable comparisons to Mañas's *Historias del Kronen*. It is from this point of departure that my comparison of the two works at hand will begin. In Hemingway's text, the narrative attention devoted to the consumption of alcoholic beverages saturates not only descriptive passages, but also the foreground of characters' dialogues and the narrator's own internal monologue. References to drink orders, the physical characteristics of certain drinks, and the effects of potent potables upon Jake Barnes's thought processes and emotions serve as a sort of rhythmic backbeat to the novel. From the end of Chapter II through Chapter IV, the text reads like a play-by-play—or rather, drink-by-drink—transcript of one particular, though not atypical, evening on the town amongst Paris's Anglo-American expatriate crowd sometime in late June of 1925.

For Jake Barnes (a journalist) and Robert Cohn (an aspiring novelist), the night's exploits commence in earnest after enjoying a late-afternoon whiskey-and-soda at the ground-floor café of the former's office (Hemingway 11). Soon thereafter—once Jake has finished a bit of light work upstairs—both men order an additional aperitif at the Café Napolitain, where they "watch the evening crowd on the Boulevard" (13). As the dinner hour approaches, Cohn takes leave of Jake, who remains at the café to imbibe Pernod—the brand name of an imitation absinthe—in the company of a prostitute named Georgette. In the following passage, Barnes-as-narrator disconnects himself from the mindless small talk being exchanged between Georgette and himself to reflect on the properties of the drink before him. This type of comment, which serves as a breath pause in the quickening tempo of the evening, is common throughout the novel:

"Well, what will you drink?" I asked.
"Pernod."
"That's not for little girls."
"Little girl yourself. Dites garçon, un pernod."

"A pernod for me, too."

"What's the matter?" she asked. "Going on a party?"

"Sure. Aren't you?"

"I don't know. You never know in this town."

"Don't you like Paris?"

"No."

"Why don't you go somewhere else?"

"Isn't anywhere else."

"You're happy, all right."

"Happy, hell!"

Pernod is greenish imitation absinthe. When you add water it turns milky. It tastes like licorice and it has a good uplift, but it drops you just as far. (15)[7]

As if to counter just such a "drop" in their dispositions, the couple ventures forth to fortify their intoxication at yet another watering hole. They proceed by horse-cab to a restaurant where Jake's late-night chums, including Robert Cohn, have gathered. There, Barnes and Georgette have "*another* bottle of wine" (16, my emphasis)—a detail implying that at least one bottle had already been knocked back at the Napolitain. After finishing off "the meal and the wine" (17), as well as coffee and some unspecified after-dinner liqueurs (19), a now larger—and much more intoxicated—band of expatriate "rummies" ("drunkards" in the slang of the day) heads for a dancing-club on the Rue de la Montagne Sainte Geneviève. At this locale, while "standing in the doorway and getting the cool breath of wind from the street," Jake tosses down a beer and comments—seemingly between songs—that he is entirely at ease with his surroundings (20). Nonetheless, his state of mind abruptly takes a turn for the worse when Lady Brett Ashley arrives with her entourage of sycophantic dandies and, what is more, with the emotional baggage of her troublesome romantic history. Brett's recent past, of course, includes a troublesome relationship with the narrator-protagonist himself, who has suffered a wound in the war that has apparently rendered him impotent. Her disconcerting arrival, coupled with the oppressive heat of the dance hall, pushes Barnes to take refuge elsewhere and to intensify his drinking:

I walked down the street and had a beer at the bar at the next Bal. The beer was not good and I had a worse cognac to take the taste out of my mouth. (20)

Upon returning to the club, Jake proceeds to down a "*fine à l'eau*" (*sic*), a cocktail consisting of cognac and water. He does so in the company of Robert

Prentiss, a "rising new novelist" whom the protagonist brusquely pushes to drink with a harder and faster pace:

> I asked him to have a drink.
> "Thanks so much," he said, "I've just had one."
> "Have another."
> "Thanks, I will then." (21)

At this point in the text, Jake confides in the reader that he has become "[n]ot drunk in any positive sense but just enough to be careless" (21). Such an admission, even from the heartiest of drinkers, would seem something of an understatement. Indeed, if Barnes's collective bar tab for this particular sequence of the novel were tallied, it would read something along the lines of what follows: one whiskey-and-soda, one unspecified aperitif, one pernod, upwards of one full bottle of wine, at least one after-dinner liqueur, two beers, one cognac (consumed shot-style), and one *fine al'eau*—in total, no less than a dozen drinks. It is only after one last "drink in the pub next door" at the behest of Brett (24), an emotionally turbulent cab ride with her through the city, and then arriving to find yet some more alcohol-induced revelry among the expatriates at the Café Select (27) (around most bars' closing hour [29]), that Jake finally refuses a glass of champagne and declares aloud that he has "a rotten headache" (29). He walks home to retire for the evening (29–30), or rather, to pass out until Brett stumbles into his residence at half past four in the morning for a nightcap of brandy and bit of romantic melodrama. Thus concludes a sample evening amidst the crowd at the heart of Hemingway's *The Sun Also Rises*: a novel that measures itself out not in coffee spoons, but in rounds upon rounds of spirits.

Though set in the Spanish capital and in an altogether different era, the first chapter of Mañas's *Historias del Kronen* follows this same narrative blueprint: reading, as it were, like a box score for substance abuse as sport. The night depicted in this chapter, also in late June, begins innocently enough. As with Jake Barnes's own drinking spree, the reader encounters at the outset of the evening a pair of male friends meeting at a local pub—in this case, after a televised Real Madrid soccer match (11, 12, 13). Carlos, the narrator-protagonist, and his friend Roberto rendezvous just before midnight (14) at the *Kronen*, a neighborhood bar which evidently takes its name from the mass-produced French lager, *Kronenberg 1664*. As they await the arrival of various drinking companions, Carlos imbibes at least one initial "mini" (a full liter of beer in a plastic cup) (11). When other friends begin to show up—in this case, Pedro,

Raúl, and Fierro (who is diabetic)—Carlos urgently pushes for each of them to order a drink before the owner's ringing of a bell signaling last call (13–14). The protagonist's outright doggedness in goading Fierro to drink ("Venga, sólo una cerveza" (13); [Come on, just one beer]) echoes a constant also found in the rhythmic structure of Hemingway's novel: namely, characters repeatedly beseeching one other (or even themselves!) to "have a drink" at each and every turn, no matter what the cost. The following list of comments from Book I of Hemingway's novel, by no means exhaustive, illustrates this recurrent pattern. This particular feature of the work disallows libationary overindulgence from ever sliding away from the fore:

> "I'm going to have a drink." (22)
> "Do stay and have a drink." (28)
> "Come in and have a drink." (37)
> "There's no hurry. Have a drink." (43)
> "Have another port?" (43)
> "I say, Jake, *do* we get a drink?" (54)
> "Let's have a drink, then." (56)
> "How about some of that champagne?" (58)
> "Drink your wine." (59)
> "Have another brandy." (61)

Peer-induced consumption of controlled substances by Mañas's characters is similarly persistent. When the *Kronen* pub does close, Manolo (who had been tending bar) joins the band of revelers. His presence—like that of Brett in Book I of *The Sun Also Rises*—lights up a wildfire of cock-eyed intemperance. The members of the Kronen clan pile into Roberto's car and make their way toward an epicenter of youthful debauchery in Madrid, the district of Bilbao. En route to this destination, Manolo meticulously rolls and lights—to share with the others—a "nevadito" (16): that is, a cigarette filled with cocaine. He subsequently prepares several lines of the same substance for his companions to snort in a parked car. Wired by the drugs, they belt out in unison a song by the speed-metal band Metallica: a befitting musical allusion on the part of Mañas, given the hyperactive tempo that the narrative here begins to assume. Some moments later, the *Kronen* group enters an establishment which is rendered into Castilian by Carlos as *Barflais* ("Barfly," incidentally, is a term that enters American English just prior to Prohibition). At this particular bar, an exercise in something akin to "Heminwayesque" drinking begins.[8] The narrator-protagonist orders J&B whiskey with Coca-Cola all around (17), a gesture (or challenge) that is immediately reciprocated in turn by Roberto (18). Moving onto the dance floor, Carlos bumps into Elena, an old acquaintance—or perhaps a casual old flame—with whom he begins to flirt. He does so at first only halfheartedly, with a markedly tepid degree of interest recalling Jake Barnes's ambivalence upon seeing Brett: "no me hace mucha ilusión verla" (Mañas 17) (I wasn't especially happy to see her). Yet, fueled as he is by the deafening, throbbing beat of house music, and with his pulse stimulated by the euphoric effects of cocaine "tengo el pulso acelerado por la coca" (17–18) (my pulse is quickened by the coke).[9] Carlos indulges Elena in a frenetic dialogue of disconnected banter not unlike the insipid, disjointed conversations amongst Hemingway's inebriated expatriates in Paris. Matts Djos analyzes this alcohol-related aspect of *The Sun Also Rises* in the following remarks:

> Drinking isolates the characters and fragments their relationship, culminating in rebellion, antisocial behavior, and an addiction to fakery and make-believe. Even their conversations are maddeningly incongruent. We sense that each character talks to himself through a muddled backwash of trivia and banality. Connections are short, focused on externals, and filled with nonsequiturs. Most of the talk is centered on [. . .] banalities of an insufferable texture; but we never really know how anyone *really* feels [. . .]. (144)

Djos's observation on *The Sun Also Rises* is perfectly applicable to much of the dialogue Mañas develops throughout *Historias del Kronen*. With specific reference to the scene at hand, the reader encounters a conversation between Elena and Carlos whose incoherence is exacerbated not only by intoxication, but also by music at full volume and the surrounding "gente que baila a ritmo de máquina" (17) (people dancing with machine-like rhythm). Mañas's use of upper-case characters, signaling the acoustic intensity of both characters' utterances, amplifies the reality that, although physically adjacent, Carlos and Elena are essentially cut off from one another:

—OYE, CARLOS, ¿QUÉ TAL ESTÁS?
Me doy la vuelta y me encuentro con Elena [. . .]
¡CUANTO TIEMPO SIN VERTE! ¿CÓMO ESTÁS? ¿QUÉ HACES AQUÍ?
Le doy dos besos y le digo qué tal.
—¿QUÉ?
—¿QUE QUÉ TAL ESTÁS?
—AY, NO GRITES ASÍ . . .
—NO ME ESCUPAS AL OÍDO.
—¿QUÉ?

—NADA
—PUES ESTOY AQUÍ CON UNA GENTE DE MI CLASE [. . .] NO SABÍA
QUE ESTUVIERAS EN MADRID. HACE CASI UN AÑO QUE NO TE VEO
DESDE SANTANDER . . . (17)

(HEY, CARLOS. HOW'S IT GOING"
I turn around and find Elena in front of me.
"LONG TIME NO SEE. HOW ARE YOU? WHAT ARE YOU DOING HERE?
I kiss her on both cheeks and say hello.
"HAT?"
"I SAID 'HOW ARE YOU'?"
"THERE'S NO NEED TO SHOUT!"
"DON'T SPIT IN MY EAR!"
"WHAT?"
"NOTHING."
"ANYHOW, I'M HERE WITH SOME PEOPLE FROM SCHOOL [. . .] I DIDN'T
KNOW YOU WERE IN MADRID. IT'S BEEN ABOUT A YEAR SINCE I SAW
YOU LAST, IN SANTANDER . . . ")

As this conversation unevenly progresses, Carlos-as-narrator comments to
the reader that, "Hablamos los dos al mismo tiempo. Yo apenas oigo lo que me
dice" (19) (Both of us are talking at the same time. I hardly hear what she's
saying to me). As a character speaking aloud, he rants one-sidedly about coming to blows with some "hijo de puta" (son of a bitch) the previous summer in
Santander. Anemically attempting to steer the conversation toward more agree-
able topics, Elena suggests that perhaps this year she will spend the summer in
San Sebastián. Carlos's impertinent response—a continued rehash of his bar-
room brawl—prompts from Elena the perennial antidote in both of the novels
here considered: "BEBE MÁS Y HABLA MENOS" (19) (DRINK MORE
AND TALK LESS).

This prescription is filled and re-filled again on the night in question. In
fact, before pushing to leave "Barflies" for yet another pub, Roberto delivers
each of his companions one more whiskey and Coca-Cola. This cocktail is
speedily followed (within a half page, or what reads as if a minute's time) by
yet another round—in this instance, a drink that is on the house. Sensing his
friends' pressing urge to run along to still another bar, Carlos is forced to take
down this particular libation at an even faster rate than normal:

Unos minutos más tarde, los otros salen, obligándome a beberme la copa de un trago. Yo me despido de Elena y no puedo evitar darle un buen lengüetazo antes de irme. (19)

(A few minutes later, everyone leaves, and I'm to take down the whiskey in one swallow. I say goodbye to Elena and can't resist slipping her a little tongue before taking off.)

The *Kronen* clan's exit from *Barflais* further accelerates the rhythm of their overindulgence.[10] In Roberto's car, Manolo prepares a few more lines of cocaine and Carlos rolls himself a joint (19). Eventually, after a mischievous 2:30 A.M. jaunt into an abandoned building near the Plaza Dos de Mayo, the group winds up at a bar called *Agapo*, where still another "couple of rounds" are consumed (22). The escalating tempo of the remainder of the night might be best described as a fandango. After leaving the *Agapo*, being tossed out of a *7–11* mini-mart by a security guard, and then driving about in an unsuccessful search for prostitutes, Carlos decides to separate himself from his friends and return home. Ever the advocate of living dangerously, the protagonist opts to drive himself home in his own car. In fact, he does so in an inebriated state comparable to that of Jake Barnes upon his walk home from the Café Select. All said, a conservative estimate of Carlos's "prescription" for festive overindulgence on this one particular Saturday night would include: one liter of beer, a cocaine-infused joint, a few lines of powder-form cocaine, four whiskeys with Coca-Cola (the last of which is imbibed as a shot), and at least two unspecified cocktails. Whatever the case, Carlos's enthusiasm for fast-living is portrayed by Mañas as a generational trend among twenty-somethings in early-1990s Madrid. As the following excerpt suggests, Carlos's drunken race home is far from unique. On the contrary, it seems to represent a precarious norm among Madrid's late-night drivers:

Arranco, pillo Avenida de América y salgo a la Emetreinta. Estoy yendo a ciento cuarenta, casi ciento cincuenta, pero hay coches que me adelantan a más de ciento sesenta. Todos llevan la música a tope. (25)

(I start the car, find the Avenue of America, and take off on the M-30. I'm going one-forty, almost one-fifty, but there are cars that are passing me at more than one sixty. Everyone has the music at full volume.)

This passage of the novel is one of several that help to produce a kind of "generational" discourse. Indeed, within this novel that is dedicated to

Mañas' own father—a dedication which in itself hints at the text's generational concerns—we find that clear boundaries have been drawn between the preoccupations, challenges, and tastes of Carlos' cohorts and those of older generations. Mañas's portrait of this group of *madrileño* Generation X youth incorporates comparative references to at least three older generations, or cultural movements, fundamental in the history of contemporary Spain. The first of these allusions is to the *Movida* of the 1980s. In the following passage, the language chosen by Carlos serves to historicize the most celebrated cultural production of the years of the Transition. Its dismissive tone relegates one highly original filmmaker and a well-known progressive rock band to a sphere of virtual irrelevance:

> [Rebeca] mira la tele y dice algo de una generación de los ochenta, Almodóvar, la movida, Alaska, [. . .] las tonterías de siempre. (32)

> (Rebeca watches t.v. and says something about a generation from the eighties, Almodóvar, the Madrid movida, Alaska, [. . .] the same old ridiculous song and dance.)

In another instance underscoring generational differentiation, Carlos's dying grandfather paints a bleak vision of contemporary Spanish society. He decries the lack of civility and common decency that confronts younger members of a culture which he no longer recognizes as his own. He attributes young people's antisocial callousness to rampant drug abuse of a kind heretofore unknown in Spain (80–84). Mañas's text also dives headfirst into the dynamics of discord that exist between Carlos's generation and that of his father. The former dubs his elders as the "sesentiochista[s] pseudoprogre[s]" (67) (*"the pseudo-progressives of '68"*). This label seeks to mock the Generation of 1968's proud rhetoric of socialist triumph over totalitarian oppression, pointing with the prefix "pseudo-" to the fact that such underdog ideals are now voiced from a position of total power. In Carlos's eyes, the ostensible monopoly held by his father's generation on both countercultural *and* official credibility stunts the development of a sociopolitical consciousness among those of his age group. Unable to find their own distinctive countercultural voice, the sons and daughters of the hippie generation are forced to tread upon ground already covered, a condition that leads many to indulge in the say-nothing and do-nothing culture of slackerdom.[11]

Ya estamos con el sermón de siempre. El viejo comienza a hablar de cómo ellos lo tenían todo mucho más difícil, y de cómo han luchado para darnos todo lo que tenemos [. . .] Son los viejos los que lo tienen todo: la guita y el poder. Ni siquiera nos han dejado a nosotros la rebeldía: ya la agotaron toda los putos marxistas and los putos jipis de su época. Pienso en responderle que justamente lo que nos falta es algo por lo que o contra lo que luchar. Pero paso de discutir con él. (67)

(Once again it's the same lecture. The old fart begins to talk about how they had it so much harder, and how they fought to give us everything we have [. . .] Old people are the ones who have it all: the purse strings and the power. They haven't even left us rebellion: the fucking Marxists and hippies of their day used it all up. I think about responding to him that precisely what we need is something to fight for or against. But I decide not to argue with him.)

Despite Carlos's pessimistic view, I would assert that the novel's Generation X characters do ultimately step up to the plate in a politically-minded campaign of dissent. Though civically irresponsible in a myriad of ways, Carlos and the members of his entourage are clearly concerned with the fortification of *individual* liberties in their city and nation. Indeed, unfettered access to drugs and alcohol—as well as the freedom to consume these where, when, and in whatever form one's primal whims may dictate—collectively emerge in the novel as a banner behind which they demonstrably rally. If the intoxicated escapades which comprise the better part of the novel's narrative happenings do not say as much, then one need only turn to what these rebellious exploits nearly bury: namely, the articulation of a discourse of protest. By the early 1990s, of course, the freedom to consume drugs in public (as well as to drink in the streets) had come to be seen in post-Franco youth culture as something of an inalienable right. The government's own actions had contributed significantly to this perception. As John Hooper writes in *The New Spaniards*, "in the year after coming to office," the Socialist administration took as one of "its earliest measures" the legalization of "the consumption of narcotics both in public and in private." This gesture propagated "the impression throughout the eighties [. . .] that 'anything goes'" (203).

Yet, as Spain moved toward more substantial integration with the European economy, the reigning PSOE gradually (and, for some, shockingly) fell into line with more "neo-liberal orthodoxies" (Graham and Sánchez 412). This about-face naturally had policy implications of an economic nature, but there were also cultural repercussions to the government's unfolding program of reform. Alongside the nuts and bolts of moving toward a free-market economy (removing government subsidies for industry, for instance), integration with the

European Community would require that various public health standards and criminal codes come up to snuff with the more developed nations of Europe. This is especially true with respect to those codes having some bearing upon the sale and trafficking of (elsewhere) illicit drugs.

The highly visible drug and alcohol problem among urban Spanish youth was, by 1992, a prickly thorn in the side of an increasingly image-conscious government. Hooper cites estimates indicating that in 1990 Spain had "two [heroin] addicts per thousand [. . .]—twice the estimated level in Holland, a country that is often cited as having one of the worst drug problems in Europe" (204). Additionally, the so-called "cult of the *litrona*" (the drinking of large bottles of beer by groups of raucous youths in the streets) became in the early 1990s all too ominous:

> Just before Christmas 1990, on the days that the schools broke up, [many Spaniards'] fears were given some substance. Reacting to one of those unfathomable common impulses that can move the young, tens of thousands of chanting, singing teenagers converged on the centre of Madrid swigging from *litronas* and blocking the traffic with their sheer numbers. For the most part, it was a good-natured occasion. But by late afternoon a lot were hopelessly drunk. Fights broke out, some windows were smashed and a few of the youngsters ended the day in jail or hospital. (Hooper 201)

For a nation bent on selling to neighbors its viability as a modern nation and economy, such mischief was all too dangerous. After all, Spain's international makeover involved much more than merely an attempt at securing economic treaties with the European Community. In 1992, Spain simultaneously hosted the Games of the XXV Olympiad in Barcelona and the World Expo in Seville. Madrid, too, would have its day in the sun, ultimately being designated as the 1992 European Community Capital of Culture. Thus, in Carlos's Madrid, there existed not only national pressures, but also local pressures within the capital city itself that pushed vigorously for a reversal of lenient policies in regard to public drug and alcohol use.[12] In the end, a national ban on public consumption of drugs went into effect that year, as did a crackdown on drinking in the streets of Madrid. Enforcement of these measures in the city center became more frequent and inflexible: a trend that figures prominently in the conversations that unfold between the whiskey, marijuana, and cocaine enthusiasts of Mañas's novel. Indeed, Mañas's characters relate the crackdown quite explicitly to international political forces. The members of the *Kronen* clan bemoan, for one, the sellout of Matanzo, a prominent city alderman.[13] As they see it, he has caved into foreign demands that are part and parcel of an incipient, culturally emasculating process of wholesale European homogenization:

> Si queréis, os acompaño a pillar . . . No no hace falta, Carlos, Miguel siempre va solo. Dice que al Niñas no le gusta que le vaya nadie que no conozca porque ahora están las cosas muy chungas, sobre todo desde que está el Matanzo. Cada vez somos más europeos . . . Ya ves . . . (29)

> —Perdonad, pero aquí no se pueden hacer porros—dice un barbas con coleta.
> —Pero qué pasa, menda, si sólo es un porrito tronco—protesta Manolo.
> —No, si no es por mí, entiéndeme. Es porque nos han abierto ya expediente y estoy harto de pagar multas.
> —Tranquilo, tronco, que terminamos de rular y fumamos fuera.
> —Bueno, pero la próxima vez que os lo hacéis fuera, ¿vale?
> [. . .]
> —Qué bocas el menda. Y todo esto es culpa del hijoputa del Matanzo. Hay que joderse—murmura Manolo, poniéndose el porro detrás de la oreja. (109–110)

> —Si es que esto es Europa: el cinturón de seguridad, prohibido fumar porros, prohibido sacar litros a la calle . . . Al final, ya veréis, vamos a acabar bebiendo horchata pasteurizada y comiendo jamón serrano cocido [. . .] Encima, todos los españoles contentísimos con ser europeos, encantados con que la Seat, la única marca de coches española, la compre Volksvaguen, encantados con que los ganaderos tengan que matar vacas para que no den más leche . . . Así estamos todos con los socialistas: bajándonos los pantalones para que nos den bien por el culo los europeos, uno detrás del otro . . . (204)

(If you want, I'll go along with you to score some dope . . . That's okay, Carlos, Miguel always goes alone. He says Niñas doesn't like anyone well else to come along he doesn't know because everything is really a mess now, especially because of Matanzo. We're more and more European, you know . . .)

(Sorry, but you can't roll joints here," says a bearded guy with a ponytail.
Why not, dude, if it's just a measly joint?" protests Carlos.
"Listen, it's not because of me. It's because they've got a file on us now and I'm sick of paying fines."
"No worries, man, we'll finish rolling it and smoke it outside."
"Okay, but next time don't bring it in here.
[. . .]
I've had enough from that guy. And all of this is that asshole Matanzo's fault. Can you believe this shit?" murmurs Manolo, placing the joint behind his ear.)

(So this is Europe: the nanny state, illegal to smoke pot, illegal to drink in the street . . . Sooner than you know it we'll be drinking pasteurized horchata and boiled Serrano ham (. . .) And all these Spaniards happy with being European, happy that the Seat, the only Spanish car brand, has been bought by Volkswagen, happy that ranchers will have to slaughter cows just so they don't produce more milk . . . . And we just stand alongside the Socialists, pulling down our pants so the Europeans can stick it up our behinds, one after the other . . .)

Historias del Kronen is, in this light, something more than a picture of empty decadence; it is, in fact, a countercultural protest novel. Though youthful in its articulation, its stance against the encroachment of imposed temperance supersedes a simple, adolescent complaint that getting high will soon be harder. As the aforementioned passages illustrate, the novel contains a politically informed discourse linking government's increased vigilance and control of intoxicating substances to political trends which, as they expand, inevitably promise to erode additional liberties and even the Spanish cultural identity at large. In this way, *Historias del Kronen* clearly follows in the countercultural spirit of *The Sun Also Rises*. Indeed, Hemingway's 1925 masterpiece is a blunt statement against the American Prohibition movement: a Lost Generation theme often overshadowed, in literary criticism at least, by consideration of the existential repercussions of World War I. Hemingway publishes his debut novel not just in the wake of the tragic upheaval of the Great War, but also on the heels of a radical attempt to legislate social change in the United States. Namely, I refer to the passing of both the 18th Amendment to the U.S. Constitution and the Volstead Act (both go into effect in 1920), legislation idealistically prohibiting the production, sale, and transport of alcohol in all American states and territories. A legal reform that arises as the culmination of the nineteenth-century, Protestant teetotaling movement, Prohibition incites widespread protest of various forms. Commercially speaking, it drives a thriving black market served by gangsters such as Al Capone. On a smaller scale, protest comes in the form of expatriation and, for the economically privileged, binge-style holidays abroad such as those depicted in *The Sun Also Rises*.

Hemingway's novel flaunts its rejection of the stateside teetotaling establishment. It does so by foregrounding the libationary pursuits of its characters and through the explicitly anti-Prohibition banter of certain dialogues. Like *Historias del* Kronen, the text is loaded with sardonically derisive commentary directed against the ideologues of a cultural movement: in this case, the fundamentalist politician William Jennings Bryan and Wayne B. Wheeler, the leader of the Anti-Saloon league. Chapter XII recounts the fishing trip of Jake and

Bill, a friend from New York City, on the Irati River in Navarre just prior to San Fermines in Pamplona. While eating lunch on the banks of the river, the quick-witted New Yorker playfully jibes with Jake for having brought just two bottles of wine on their trip. He sarcastically condemns his fishing companion as a tightfisted rationer of alcohol who is "in the pay of the Anti-Saloon League" (123). Within the same chapter, Bill—who is a self-professed champion of ironic humor (113–15)—also mimics the xenophobic, essentially anti-Catholic rhetoric of the American temperance movement's leaders. He mockingly sizes up Jake's lifestyle as a foreign correspondent with a voice imitating the jingo-istic sensibility of heartland devotees of the Anglo-Saxon Protestant ethic like William Jennings Bryan (whose home state, incidentally, is Illinois—that of young Hemingway himself):

> You're an expatriate. You've lost touch with the soil. You get precious. Fake Euro-pean standards have ruined you. You drink yourself to death. You become obsessed by sex. You spend all your time talking, not working. You are an expatriate, see? You hang around cafés." (Hemingway 115)

In a recent article on the relationship between American prohibition, nationalism, and expatriation in *The Sun Also Rises*, Jeffrey A. Schwartz points out that Bryan's post-World War I "rallying cry" for puritanical, homespun values "did not end solely with America" (184). Commenting upon a speech given by Bryan just after Prohibition had been passed, Schwartz signals the politician's clear "desire to force [American] nationalism on other countries" (184). Bryan calls for sweeping cultural change not only in Germany, but also throughout the rest of Europe. He calls for the expansion of an ethos locked in step with the temperate ways of the victors of the Great War. Such a transfor-mation, at its core, would be not unlike the process of cultural homogenization beheld by the *Kronen* group in early 1990s Spain:

> We must turn our energies to other countries until the whole world is brought to understand that alcohol is man's greatest enemy. Thus it is a fortunate thing that the abdication of the Kaiser and the fall of arbitrary power came in the same year as does the fall of the brewery autocracy and that these two evils came down together . . . Now we can go out for the evangelization of the world on the subject of intoxicating liquor. (William Jennings Bryan, qtd. in Schwartz 184)[14]

The fast and free lifestyles of Hemingway's expatriate characters in *The Sun Also* Rises—as well as the avid drinking of the itinerant author himself—

fly in the face of this doctrine of abstemious American nationalism: an ideology that found acceptance among much of the rural, white, Anglo-Saxon,
Protestant middle class of the United States in the 1920s. This very sector of
the population includes the likes of Hemingway's own parents, whose home
was located in the teetotaling stronghold of Oak Park, Illinois (Stanton 24), a
"village" on the outskirts of bootlegging Chicago which remained dry until the
1970s. Hemingway's own relationship with alcohol, influenced as it was by his
stint in Italy during the war and his time in Paris as a foreign correspondent,
defies the values of the Oak Park rank and file. Tom Dardis asserts that young,
well-traveled, "independent minds [such as Hemingway] believed it was their
moral duty to violate the [Prohibition] law on every possible occasion." Writers
like Hemingway actively contribute to a climate in which "drinking was the
socially correct thing to do" (11). The ostentatious drinking of characters like
Jake Barnes in *The Sun Also Rises* thus "actualizes Hemingway's own views"
of a political and cultural nature (Schwartz 196). Like Mañas's sociopolitical
contextualization of drinking and drug-use in 1992 Madrid, Hemingway's novel
embraces the leitmotif of libationary excess as a generational marker; drinking constitutes an act of protest, of affirmation, and of youthful solidarity in
the face of threatened social liberties. With each successive glass, both novels'
characters toast, as it were, the imminent fulfillment of Hemingway's biblical
epigraph: "One generation passeth away, and another generation cometh . . ."
(taken from Ecclesiastes 1:4). Each generation's time of cultural ascendancy
will ultimately arrive.

An urge to move on, to move away, and to move forward is, more generally
speaking, one of the most tenable links between these two "generational" novels.
An extraordinary degree of transiency, impatience, and unrest is inscribed into
the fabric of both works on various levels. Both texts, for instance, habitually
feature harried scenes of geographic flux that pilot the reader—with a barrage
of toponymic details—through the urban landscapes of Paris and Madrid. In
Chapter III of *The Sun Also Rises*, Jake and Georgette travel in a horse-cab "up
the Avenue de l'Opéra" and past the "New York *Herald* building," where they
then turn "off the Avenue up the Rue des Pyramides, move through the traffic
of the Rue de Rivoli, and through a dark gate into the Tuileries"; they then cross
the river Seine before finally "turn[ing] up the Rue des Saints Pères" (15–16).
Similarly, in Chapter VI, the trajectory of Jake's cab ride is prominently described. He rounds "the statue of the inventor of the semaphore," "turn[s] up
the Boulevard Raspail," and finally stops "in front of the Rotonde" (41–43). As
if not to be outdone, Mañas's narrator restlessly conducts the reader from one
neighborhood of Madrid to another. The following passage is representative of

several other descriptions of this variety, which the author scatters throughout the novel (e.g., pp. 16, 31, 69, 70, 71, 112).

> Roberto baja por Goya hasta Colón, cruza la Castellana, sube hacia Bilbao, se desvía a la izquierda en la Glorieta de Santa Bárbara, sigue por Mejía Lequerica, se mete por Barceló y aparca enfrente de Pachá. (16)

> (Roberto goes down Goya to Colón, crosses the Castellana, and goes up toward Bilbao, turns toward the left at the Santa Bárbara traffic circle, follows Mejía Lequerica, turns onto Barceló, and parks in front of Pachá.)

These frequent episodes of spatial flux are, moreover, rarely countered by prolonged scenes that take place in a stationary location. In fact, both novels' jaunts about their respective urban spaces are routinely preceded and followed by exceedingly brief and superficial social encounters. As Matts Djos has commented with respect to *The Sun Also Rises*, such meetings are self-reflexively "preoccupied with making arrangements to meet again sometime" (145). Though one could choose from any number of scenes in the Parisian portion of Hemingway's novel to illustrate this point (e.g., pp. 17, 19, 22, 23–24, 27, 53, 61–62, 74–75, 78), let us consider an especially apt example as selected and analyzed by Djos:

> In one scene, they go to the Lilas; they order whiskey; they talk about travel and promise to meet "later." During the "later" at the Select, they talk about Brett's hat, Michael's nose, and a few other trivialities. Then they break up, go to a fight, meet again the next day back at the Select and start drinking and palavering all over again. (145)

This is precisely the stuff of Mañas's novel. Returning to the initial scene of the novel, for instance, we find that Roberto and Carlos have just met up at the *Kronen*, where they await the arrival of Pedro, Raúl, and Fierro. Upon arriving, Raúl and Fierro announce their impending plans to rendezvous with Yoni at a bar called *Graf* (13). For their part, Carlos, Roberto, Pedro, and Manolo (who had been working the bar), leave for a club called *Riau-Riau* in the Bilbao district, where Pedro has made arrangements to join up with some of his classmates. En route to the car, the latter crew runs into Sofi and Nani, a pair of acquaintances with whom Carlos proceeds to make plans to rendezvous later at a bar called *Siroco*. Once at *Riau-Riau*, the group fails to find Pedro's entourage, so they venture forth to *Barflais*, and so forth. Perpetual motion, in short, is an undeniable hallmark of the novel. Even when Carlos and his friends are not running the streets, they are on the telephone making plans to perpetuate a relentless series of drug-related appointments and nocturnal social engagements. Typically transcribed in the manner evinced in the quotation below, these telephone calls immediately call to mind the letters and telegraph messages related to characters' comings and goings that appear sporadically throughout *The Sun Also Rises*:[15]

> ¿Sí? . . . Oye, Carlos, que soy yo, Miguel. ¿Te he despertado? Pues te viene bien. No es nada, sólo que ya he localizado al Niñas. Le voy a ver a las dos y luego quedo con vosotros a las siete, ¿vale? . . . Bien . . . ¿Llamas tú a Roberto? . . . Sí yo le llamo . . . Pues hasta las siete . . . Hasta las siete. (Mañas 49)

> (Hello? . . . Hey, Carlos, it's Miguel. Did I wake you up? It's good for you. Anyhow, I just wanted you know I just got in touch with Niñas. I going to see him at two o'clock and then I'll meet up with you guys at seven, okay? . . . Fine . . . Are you calling Roberto . . . Yeah, I'll call him . . . I'll see you at seven then . . . See you at seven.)

All of this contributes to a sensation that both works flow with a high-speed tempo. A variety of symbols related to speed, running, and races reinforce just such a notion by peppering the iconic backdrops of both texts. In television news stories overheard by Carlos, the reader finds numerous references to the Olympic torch being run through Spain (122, 132, 177, 198), the results of the Tour de France (141), and the most dangerous running of the bulls ever in Pamplona (100). Hemingway's novel, of course, quite famously features the running of the bulls during San Fermines, and it alludes to the Tour du Pays Basque bicycle race (235–36). The author's description of the former constitutes, in fact, a kind of symbolic portrait in miniature. The language used to describe the running of the bulls evokes the "running" that dominates the frenetic, and ultimately tragic, social lives of the "rummies" at the heart of his novel:

> Then people commenced to come running. A drunk slipped and fell. [. . .] The crowd were running fast now. There was a great shout from the crowd, and putting my head through the boards I saw the bulls just coming out of the street into the long running pen. They were going fast and gaining on the crowd. [. . .] There were so many people running ahead of the bulls that the mass thickened and slowed up going to the gate into the ring, and as the bulls passed, galloping together, heavy, muddy-sided, horns swinging, one shot ahead, caught a man in the running crowd in the back and lifted him in the air. (196)

That speed-related motifs should populate the pages of these novels seems all but natural. Structural pithiness and narrative rhythm at the level of Hemingway's prose itself have become critical commonplaces. In a 1996 review of *Soy un escritor frustrado* (I'm a Frustrated Writer), the contemporary Spanish poet and critic Roger Wolfe categorizes Mañas's prose, too, as being endowed with "un ritmo trepidante" (a furiously-paced rhythm). Wolfe compares this stylistic feature of the young novelist's writing, moreover, to a kind of "eficacia barojiana" (Wolfe 14) (the efficiency of a Pío Baroja). In light of the present essay's comparison of Mañas and Hemingway, the terms of Wolfe's own assessment could hardly be more appropriate. Baroja is the novelist perhaps most intimately associated with a changed time signature in twentieth-century Spanish narrative prose. Having rejected Ortega y Gasset's ideal of "el *ritmo moroso* de la narrativa" (restrained narrative rhythm), the Basque novelist "sintió, más que ningún otro novelista de su tiempo, que los nuevos tiempos requerían nuevo ritmo" (González López 91) ([he] felt, more than any other novelist of his time, that new times required a new rhythm). By cultivating a narrative pace that "respondía a un mayor dinamismo [cuyas] manifestaciones conocidas [son] el cinematógrafo, [. . .] y más tarde el avión, la radio y la televisión" (91) ([that] responded to a greater dynamism whose foremost manifestations are cinema, and later aviation, the radio, and television), Baroja is a watershed figure in Spanish narrative prose. His influence is patent in the work of later innovators like the Nobel laureate Camilo José Cela and, without a doubt, in the Generation X realism of José Ángel Mañas. In fact, although it refers to now decades-old techniques of Baroja, the following description could almost be read as if it were a contemporary review of Mañas's more recent work:

> [Su] ritmo se manifiesta de muy diversas maneras. Una de ellas, la más simple, es en el paso de [. . .] las figuras de personajes y personajillos que andan por las páginas de sus novelas; y otra es el cambio continuo de escenario, de un pueblo a otro pueblo, de un país a otro país, o simplemente de una calle a otra de la misma ciudad.
>
> El héroe deambulante [. . .] le da un paso rápido a la narrativa, pues vemos con él el desfile de personajes y ambientes a veces en una sucesión casi cinematográfica. [. . .] [La vida] no es otra cosa que acción, lucha, movimiento, desplazamiento. Los personajes [. . .] sienten incesantemente la comenzón de moverse, de actuar [. . .] (González López 92)

(His rhythm is produced in a number of ways. One of these, the simplest, is in the passing-by of so many characters, both major and minor, throughout the pages of his novels; another is the constant changing of scene, from one village to another, from one country to another, or simply from one street to another in the same city. The roaming hero endows his narrative with a quick pace, and we see with him a parade of characters and spaces in a rapid succession with an almost cinematic quality [. . .] Life is nothing but action, struggle, movement, displacement. Characters incessantly feel the need to move, to act [. . .])

The same commentary, too, could easily be applied to Hemingway's *The Sun Also Rises*. This should not be all too surprising. Baroja, after all, was Hemingway's acknowledged master. In fact, after winning the Nobel Prize in 1956, the American author even visited Baroja on his deathbed in Spain, presenting him with a copy of *The Sun Also Rises* that was signed with the dedication, "To Don Pío Baroja, from a respectful disciple" (Castillo-Puche 261–62).[16] In this respect, and given the broader relationship between the work of Hemingway and Mañas that this essay has explored, the critical implications could not be clearer. There comes into plain view a remarkable kinship system: discernible literary bonds between the standard-bearers of two, if not three, distinct narrative generations—a marvelous instance of back-and-forth cross-pollination between Spanish and North American literature that has produced, over the course of the twentieth century, a daring breed of novel. In my estimation, a heightened awareness of such connections only serves to strengthen the singular place which criticism has heretofore afforded *Historias del Kronen* in its vision of recent Spanish fiction. Indeed, by recognizing the bonds of literary kinship that unite this touchstone text's form and discourse to the tradition of the modern "generational" novel inclined toward festive excess, speed, and youthful rebellion, our overall appreciation of Spanish Generation X narrative's position in contemporary literary history can only be enriched, deepened, and more meaningfully contextualized.

Notes

1. "Open" is the first track on *Wish*, the album referenced by Carlos in the first epigraph to this essay. A driving and discordant, guitar-driven maelstrom set to alternate tunings, these lyrics and those of subsequent verses are very much in keeping with the drug and alcohol-fueled exploits of the *Kronen* group (and, indeed, of Hemingway's characters).

2. Gabriel Rodríguez-Pazos has recently published an article on a series of problems with the existing Spanish translations of *The Sun Also Rises*. Specifically, he focuses on the following linguistic defects: "1) elisions, slips, and errors at the level of decoding,

2) mistranslations resulting from cultural differences between Hemingway's context and the context of the readers of the translation, 3) mistranslations resulting from mismatches in knowledge of the external field of reference, and 4) deficiencies in the rendering of style, the main problem posed by Hemingway's texts to his translators and one which puts their condition as artists to the test" (Rodríguez-Pazos 47). For comprehensive information related to all existing Spanish translations of the novel, consult his bibliography (64–65).

3. "I wrote, in six weeks, [a] book about a few drunks" (Hemingway, E. *Selected Letters, 1917–1961.* Ed. Carlos Baker. New York: Scribner, 1981: 365–66. [qtd. in Goodman 51]).

4. F. Scott Fitzgerald's martini-fueled *The Great Gatsby*, similarly rife with allusions to immoderate drinking, is also published in 1925.

5. Maria Pao's 2002 article posits that "beyond surface resemblances to its American counterparts, [. . .] *Kronen* may represent a cautionary statement vis-à-vis encroaching North American cultural forms and the consumption they demand" (246). For his part, Annesley prefers the term "blank fiction" to various other labels which have emerged in studies on recent fiction (such as "fiction of insurgency," "new narrative," "blank generation fiction," "downtown writing," and "punk fiction") (Annesley 2).

6. Within his discussion of violence in blank fiction, Annesley obliquely alludes to the aesthetic links between writers such as Hemingway, Carver, and Bret Easton Ellis (12–13)—iconic names habitually associated with the Lost Generation, Dirty Realism, and Generation X, respectively. For a detailed analysis of the intertextual relationship between Mañas's *Historias del Kronen* and Ellis's *Less Than Zero*, see Marr, Matthew J. "An Ambivalent Attraction?: Post-Punk Kinship and the Politics of Bonding in *Historias del Kronen* and *Less Than Zero*." *Arizona Journal of Hispanic Cultural Studies* 10 (2006). (Currently in press).

7. To kick off the last night of San Fermines in Book II, Jake partakes of vast quantities of absinthe: an especially strong liqueur (now illegal in most countries) which is flavored with wormwood, an herb with hallucinogenic properties. After noting point-blank that the "absinthe made everything seem better," Jake's own narration and the transcribed utterances of his friend Bill fill subsequent paragraphs with allusions to the unyielding pace of his consumption. "We had another absinthe" (222); "'Have another' absinthe. Here, waiter! Another absinthe for this señor." (222); "'Drink that,' said Bill. 'Drink it slow.'" (222); "'Have another?'" (223); "'Try it [. . .] Hey, waiter! Another absinthe for this señor!'" (223); "I set down the glass. I had not meant to drink it fast" (223).

8. Tom Dardis presents a compelling study of this much mythologized author's life-long association with alcohol in *The Thirsty Muse: Alcohol and the American Writer.* Dardis asserts that, from a very young age, Hemingway "discovered that he could easily outdrink nearly everyone he encountered." As he aged, he also "became competitive about the amounts he consumed, demonstrating to Morley Callaghan in Toronto that he could lower seven beers to the younger man's three" (157–58).

9. The atmosphere of this bar, where the driving beat of music is a key element in an overall dynamic of excess, recalls a scene that takes place in Zellli's nightclub at the very conclusion of Book I of *The Sun Also Rises*. In this "crowded, smoky, and noisy" club where "the music hit you as you went in" (62), Brett and Jake drink, dance, and make idle conversation to the lively rhythmic stylings of a jazz drummer prominently alluded to several times by the narrator.

10. The text of a later dialogue in the book semantically conjoins excessive drinking with notions of an accelerated time signature. Manolo, at work behind the bar at the *Kronen*, reacts to Roberto's flurry of drink orders by saying, "Qué ritmo, muchacho." (63) (What a rhythm, man).

11. Carlos's underemployment can be seen as a key—though not definitive—feature of "slacker" status (see Annesley, pp. 122–26, for an extensive discussion of this term). Near the outset of the novel he declares, for instance, that "no tengo NADA que hacer durante tres meses" (Mañas 27) (I don't have ANYTHING to do for three months). Carlos depends, of course, on the financial generosity of his parents, a condition of privilege which draws sharp criticism on more than one occasion from his friends Nuria (144–47) and Miguel (205). This position of privilege seems very much in keeping with the life of Jake Barnes, who can hardly be described as a journalistic workhorse—a point underscored by Matts Djos: "[Jake's] work doesn't amount to much. At the 'office,' he reads the papers, smokes, and sits at the typewriter (writing, I assume). Later, he goes out to watch a politico, has lunch, [and] goes back to the 'office later' [. . .] Mainly, we are told that he stumbles off to his hotel, to the Rotonde, to his flat; he has some drinks, he hails his friends, goes to the races, has a scene, or in quiet moments he feels just plain crummy" (149).

12. Incidentally, as John Hooper notes, "[e]ven under Franco, the possession of small quantities [of hashish] for personal consumption was not an offence" (203).

13. According to Carter Smith, Matanzo is "the councilman of the 'Distrito Centro' of Madrid, [an official] who, during the historical time of [Mañas's] narrative, formed part of the mayorship of José María Alvarez del Manzano" ("Social Criticism").

14. Schwartz cites the following text as the source of the excerpt from Bryan: Behr, Edward. *Prohibition: Thirteen Years that Changed America*. New York: Arcade, 1996: 73–74.

15. Perhaps the best example of this sort of exchange can be found on pp. 238–39, where Brett and Jake send each other telegrams which are literally transcribed by the narrator: "COULD YOU COME HOTEL MONTANA MADRID AM RATHER IN TROUBLE BRETT"; "COULD YOU COME HOTEL MONTANA AM RATHER IN TROUBLE BRETT"; "LADY ASHLEY HOTEL MONTANA MADRID ARRIVING SUD EXPRESS TOMOORROW LOVE JAKE."

16. For a full discussion of Hemingway's great esteem for Pío Baroja, see Castillo-Puche's memoir, pp. 256–76. Vázquez-Bigi has also published a critical article on the influence of Baroja in Hemingway and Dos Passos.

Works Cited

Annesley, James. *Blank Fictions: Consumerism, Culture and the Contemporary American Novel*. New York: St. Martin's Press, 1998.

Behr, Edward. *Prohibition: Thirteen Years that Changed America*. New York: Arcade, 1996: 73–74.

Castillo-Puche, José Luis. *Hemingway in Spain*. Trans. Helen R. Lane. Garden City, NY: Doubleday, 1974.

Dardis, Tom. *The Thirsty Muse: Alcohol and the American Writer*. New York: Ticknor & Fields, 1989.

Djos, Matts. "Alcoholism in Ernest Hemingway's *The Sun Also Rises*: A Wine and Roses Perspective on the Lost Generation." *Ernest Hemingway's* The Sun Also Rises*: A Casebook*. Ed. Linda Wagner-Martin. New York: Oxford University Press, 2002. 139–53.

Eliot, T.S. "The Love Song of J. Alfred Prufrock." *The Norton Anthology of Modern American Poetry*. 2nd ed. Ed. Richard Ellman and Robert O'Claire. New York: Norton, 1988. 482–85.

González López. *El arte narrativo de Pío Baroja: Las trilogías*. Long Island City, NY: Las Américas Publishing Company, 1971.

Goodman, David. "A Rejoinder to Matts Djos on Drinking in *The Sun Also Rises*." *North Dakota Quarterly* 64.2 (1997): 48–55.

Graham, Helen and Antonio Sánchez. "The Politics of 1992." *Spanish Cultural Studies: An Introduction*. Ed. Helen Graham and Jo Labanyi. New York: Oxford University Press, 1995. 406–18.

Gullón, Germán. "Introducción." *Historias del Kronen*. By José Ángel Mañas. Barcelona: Ediciones Destino (CCC), 1998. V–XXXIX.

Hemingway, Ernest. *Selected Letters, 1917–1961*. Ed. Carlos Baker. New York: Scribner's, 1981.

_____. *The Sun Also Rises*. New York: Scribner's, 1926.

Hooper, John. *The New Spaniards*. New York: Penguin, 1995.

Marr, Matthew J. "An Ambivalent Attraction?: Post-Punk Kinship and the Politics of Bonding in *Historias del Kronen* and *Less Than Zero*." *Arizona Journal of Hispanic Cultural Studies* 10 (2006). (forthcoming).

Molinaro, Nina. "The 'Real' Story of Drugs, *Dasein* and José Ángel Mañas's *Historias del Kronen*." *Revista Canadiense de Estudios Hispánicos* 27.2 (2003). 291–306.

Pao, Maria T. "Sex, Drugs, and Rock & Roll: *Historias del Kronen* as Blank Fiction." *ALEC* 27.2 (2002): 245–60.

Rodríguez-Pazos, Gabriel. "Not So True, Not So Simple: The Spanish Translations of *The Sun Also Rises*." *Hemingway Review* 23.2 (2004): 47–65.

Schwartz, Jeffrey A. "'The Saloon Must Go, And I Will Take it With Me': American Prohibition, Nationalism, and Expatriation in *The Sun Also Rises*." *Studies in the Novel* 33.2 (2001): 180–200.

Smith, Carter. "Social Criticism or Banal Imitation?: A Critique of the Neo-realist Novel Apropos the Works of José Angel Mañas." *Ciberletras. Revista de crítica literaria y de cultura / Journal of Literary Criticism and Culture.* Vol. 12 (2005). <http://www.lehman.cuny.edu/ciberletras/v12/smith.htm>.

Stanton, Edward F. *Hemingway and Spain: A Pursuit.* Seattle: University of Washington Press, 1989.

The Cure. "Open." *Wish.* Elektra, 1992.

Vázquez-Bigi, A.M. "Introducción al estudio de la influencia barojiana en Hemingway y Dos Passos." *Cuadernos Hispanoamericanos* 265–267 (1972): 169–203.

Wolfe, Roger. "Descenso a los infiernos de las envidias literarias." *El Mundo.* 12 October 1996: 14.

Part IV
Rocking the Road with Ray Loriga

◆ **9**

Reckless Driving: Speed, Mobility, and Transgression in the Spanish "Rock 'n' Road" Novel

Jorge Pérez

The literary production of Spain's Generation X abounds in protean narratives that are open to the influx of other signifying systems.[1] Film, music, and comics merge with literature generating a body of aesthetic codes that illuminates recent fiction in Spain. Unlike avant-garde novelists, who appropriated cinematographic techniques in order to introduce formal innovations in the genre and experiment with other possibilities of expression, contemporary authors encompass them as part of their cultural background, as an assimilated mechanism of story-telling and no longer as a sign of novelty. In addition, these interdisciplinary codes of communication in the Spanish postmodern market place are transnational, since they embody a global network of cultural references in which the United States is one of its most important nodes and a pivotal source of influence in the construction of imaginary landscapes. With this context in mind, this essay will explore the "rock 'n' road novel"—a term that ensues from David Laderman's concept of "rock 'n' road movie" (19)—as a distinctive generic form of Spanish Generation X authors in the 1990s. We will see how this form comprises the transatlantic and multidisciplinary circuit of cultural exchange, as well as explore the politics that lies behind the works of such authors. I will examine the rock 'n' road novel as an emblem of the mobile reconfiguration of the national public space, which

I would like to call "Superhighway Spain," to capture the accelerated pace of the cultural transformations taking effect in the Iberian Peninsula. Imbued by the non-conformist aura of the road movie tradition and the rock universe, rock 'n' road novels are eclectic literary endeavors that have developed against the backdrop of the eulogized socio-economic changes of post-Franco Spain. In so doing, they demarcate the asphalt as a liminal space where high speed and rock music coalesce to express insurgence and to celebrate individual wandering beyond the boundaries of mainstream society.

In his thorough study of the American road movie, David Laderman describes rock 'n' road movies as "road movies about rock musicians or fans on tour, or merely on the road" (19).[2] Drawing on Laderman's concept, I will refer to Spanish rock 'n' road novels as road quests traveling the Spanish highway that are impregnated with the sensory power of rock. Such influence underlines the anti-establishment orientation of road narratives, in that rock music sensibility aggravates the road genre's sense of non-compliance with the system and, more specifically, the "youth rebellion drive" (Laderman 19). Circumscribing myself to the temporal scope of this essay and volume—Generation X literary production—I will focus on three recent Spanish novels that operate along the lines of this sub-genre: Ray Loriga's *La pistola de mi hermano*, initially published with the title *Caídos del cielo* (1995), José Machado's *A dos ruedas* (1996), and Eugenia Rico's *La edad secreta* (2004).[3]

Before I embark on analyzing these three novels, I would like to clarify my hermeneutic framework. To engage with the autonomous cultural practices of film and literature, with their individually-defined genres, languages and conventions, entails the risk of undermining the complexity of the bonds between them, which go beyond mere thematic impact to involve the reciprocal transfer of formal elements. There is a long tradition of mutual symbiosis between film and literature that surpasses the domain of influences and dependency, and is better conceived in terms of areas of convergences between both semiotic systems.[4] These convergent lines materialize, above all, in the narrative dimension of both artistic disciplines. Thus, I argue, along with Millicent Marcus, that "there exists a universal, non-specific code of narrativity which transcends its embodiment in one particular signifying system" (14). From this perspective, films can be appraised as texts, producing textual models that, despite their audiovisual nature, satisfy certain needs of the novel, whether those needs are related to plot structures, character types, or other formal categories (Peña-Ardid 215). Hence, my look at the road movie as a textual paragon for fiction will focus on the localization of narrative correspondences between both disciplines rather than on appropriations of specific techniques of composition and montage.

Similarly, the bonds between film and rock involve a long and complex history that, according to Lawrence Grossberg, still remains to be explored in depth, since "so little has been written on the relations between rock and film, and almost nothing on rock and television (188–89). Bearing in mind the entanglement of these relationships among artistic codes, I aim to examine the kinship among the three manifestations—film, rock music, and literature—in order to illustrate the multi-accented nature of rock 'n' road novels as border-line texts with porous generic margins, as cultural hybrids that juxtapose words, images, and sounds. By integrating rock music, a mass-mediated cultural arti-fact, as a crucial and active component of these novels, the eros of reading and seeing overlaps with the eros of hearing in evoking new layers of meaning that reinforce the aforementioned insurgent impulse of these narratives.

The permeable generic perimeters of these texts correspond to the broader cultural context in Spain in which national borders also become porous. Striving to locate herself in the fluid routes of the global cultural web while simultane-ously undergoing a process of internal redefinition, Spain projects herself as a cosmopolitan country that has overcome Francoist isolation and is willing to participate in the international circulation of goods, images, and discourses. Intertwined with this social milieu, the contemporary Spanish novel evolves as what Teresa Vilarós calls "a smooth cultural artifact of mediation: one that could work as an interface between the symbolic and the economic, between the local and the global, between past and present; and, at the end, between the modern and the post-modern" (253); to put it differently, the novel works as a cultural formation capable of negotiating and mirroring the shifting configura-tion of Spanish national identity. Specifically, the rock 'n' road novel, due to its focus on mobility, may serve as a cogent embodiment of the potential of the literary orbit to arbitrate in the remodeling of the social imagery of a mobile Spain.

In José Machado's *A dos ruedas* (1996), the title already beckons the reader into road culture and the riveting prospects of reckless driving.[5] The opening sentences confirm such an initial token: "He speeds up in the turns. We just saw a sign prohibiting speed over 50km/h. However, he insists on driving the bus on two wheels" (11, all translations in this essay are mine). From the begin-ning, high speed and temerarious behavior are tantamount to freedom and they convey the rebellious energy of the novel. The feeling of existential stagnation of the young narrator in a hostile social environment impels such a mobile impetus: "Stuck. You live in a permanent state of anxiety. Immobile. The hours you sleep can be counted on the fingers of one hand. Paralyzed" (32). These sentences contain the sense of loss and despair of Generation X. The absence of a name or any other individualized information about the narrator invites the reader to make assumptions and regard him as an archetype who stands for all GenXers and their drifting nihilism. Unable to find the right course for an aimless existence—as he insistently wonders, "where the hell will we end up?" (48)—his only certainty is the urge to move forward. This movement does not completely jettison his anxieties and his emptiness; yet, he understands that the only possible orientation is forward, for stability and steadiness are tantamount to standing still.

This ethos of rapid motion with a metaphorical oppositional value must be framed within the context of a general disillusionment with the socialist administration of Felipe González, to which the novel refers as "CorruP$OE" (74), in a blatant reference to the notorious cases of corruption of the Spanish government during 1982–1996.[6] The inclusion of the dollar symbol evinces both the acquiescence of Spanish government to the logic of consumer capitalism, as well as its submissiveness to the leadership of the United States. In particular, the juxtaposition on the same page of the scandal of the FILESA affair (42) and the reference to the legendary Route 66 and the idolized Beat Generation is revelatory.[7] This coexistence in the text carries a diaphanous message: in such a corrupted context new paths and alternatives are necessary. By this account, the road acts as a liberating space with its utopian promise suitable for new adventures and individual success beyond the constraints of society. Similarly, speed acquires a dissident significance by allowing an escape from a rarefied social milieu. Nonetheless, this utopian nature of the road liberation, which Joseph Interrante cleverly conceptualizes as an "autopia" (89), inextricably conveys a sense of futility, a feeling that there is no space to hide from the custody of mainstream society, as the road eventually brings the rider back to the same social reality.

The journey of the protagonist, indeed, is more metaphorical than real. Apparently, the trip is made in a bus that echoes the one used by people like Ken Kesey and the Merry Pranksters for their coast-to-coast adventures. However, except for an initial allusion to Piedrafita (11), the narration lacks references to real places, and there is neither an itinerary nor any kind of geographical mapping. Likewise, there is not a recognizable destination, only wandering. The journey features symbolic movement with no purpose other than the thrill of motion, thus compromising the political implications of this mobility as an emancipatory strategy. Yet, as a metaphor of life itself, the trip signifies the maturing of the protagonist, who recounts his learning experience in terms of miles traveled (105). The different stops in the trip are like the stages of his development, as he travels around his young existence through the pages of this novel. At the end of the road, he confesses that the knowledge he has acquired is only a more lucid perception of the detritus of society accompanied by a nostalgic remembrance of the passing of time and paradise lost: "What do you see now that you have gotten off the bus? Crap. I can see all the grief more sharply, all that sticks to the sole of one's shoes" (171). In other words, the search does not lead to any certainties or accomplishments; in a reversal of the Foucauldian epistemological paradigm, knowledge does not empower the subject, but rather leaves him in a nihilistic cul-de-sac. It accentuates his sense of loss and anguish, and it upholds his skepticism about his possible reintegration into the community.

This pessimistic refusal to participate in the social fabric is reinforced by the diegetic role of the rock universe. From its very genesis, rock developed as a mass cultural form defined in confrontation with the "system." Ubiquitous intertextual references to songs, bands, and rock stars as well as the oppositional aura of rock culture percolate through *A dos ruedas*. The Rolling Stones, Sonic Youth, Pink Floyd, Bob Dylan, and Nirvana, among many others, swarm around the text leaving their trademarks. Two full pages reproduce parts of the lyrics of "Alive," by Pearl Jam (127), and "El blues del autobús," by Spanish rock legend Miguel Ríos (83). Originally written by Víctor Manuel, "El blues del autobús" reflects the melting of music—in this case, a blues song, one of the precursors of rock 'n' roll—and road culture to offer a critical perspective. It is worth reprinting the lyrics that appear in *A dos ruedas*:

> . . . I AM STARTING TO MISS A MINUTE BETWEEN US.
> I LIVE ON THE ROAD, IN A BUS.
> I LIVE ON THE ROAD, AND I ALWAYS LOOK TOWARD
> THE SOUTH.
> I LIVE ON THE ROAD, THE BLUES OF THE BUS. (83)

These lyrics lament the price a rock musician has to pay for his success, in this case the separation from his lover. The lines also comprise the nomadic lifestyle of the rock musician on the road and the ethical dimension of his or her task: "I always look toward the South" signals the abiding concern of rock musicians for social causes, represented metonymically by "the South," which embodies the subaltern spaces, subordinated to the rule of "The North," that is, to spaces with a more prominent geopolitical position.

A dos ruedas borrows this nomadic vein—both in a literal and a figurative sense—of rock culture to verbalize the sense of Spanish youth's desperation at the twilight of the twentieth century: not fully integrated in the social structures, teens occupy a transitional position that makes them marginal. In this way, rock functions as an incubator for alienation and rebelliousness against mainstream society (Altschuler 107). This operative role of the rock ethos might be better fathomed in light of sociologist Henri Lefebvre's well-known critique of everyday life. More than a utensil to enact radical political changes, rock culture is appropriated in this novel as a creative medium to construct a space outside the tentacles of everyday life; namely, the homogenizing forces of ordinary life, conceived as routine, domesticity, and the productivity demanded by the structures of consumer capitalism. Disenchanted by the tough working experience in several jobs such as errand boy for an attorney (67), and indignant about the corruption of public life (74), the protagonist of *A dos ruedas* decides to run away from that existence by taking the road and embracing rock 'n' roll. The transgression of inimical social forces is suggested by the creative alternative spaces enabled by rock culture and the metaphor of the open road where youth can live at a fast pace. Unfortunately, he inevitably inherits the paradoxes and contradictions that accompany both the road as a utopian liberating space and the rock universe as a mass-produced endeavor that is controlled by major corporations embroiled in global economic unevenness and in the homogenization of youth culture.

In this sense, the latent critique of everyday life in this novel is, unlike Lefebvre's, not designed to have a transformative aftermath. Despite unmasking the shortcomings of the system, the agency of this novel is a product of those very structures that it denounces. As the following fragment reveals, the speaking subject does not relinquish the benefits of commodity culture. To counteract the effects of alienation induced by the dynamics of contemporary capitalism, he embraces the pleasure generated by his material possessions:

> But I have a bathroom, a fridge that produces cold beers, a TV with dish antenna that connects me to every home in the world, a VCR and cable channels, and a hi-fi stereo as big as seven rows of seats. [. . .] I have the best thousand records of the history of rock, which never get scratched, and a huge remote with which I control everything that happens to me. [. . .] Basically, I am alone, but I strive to have a blast as best as I can. (42–43)

This passage exemplifies the paradoxical nature of the cultural politics of this novel. It presents an agent who tries to escape the commodification of late capitalism while at the same time being ensnared by it. It is only through leisure—"I strive to have a blast as best as I can"—and, consequently, through the luxury of entertainment using all the technological advances of consumerism—television,

VCR, stereo, and CDs—that he deviates from social conventions. The politics of youth and rock manifest in this novel are a critique of the work ethic and the discipline privileged by the social order through leisure, forming a perspective akin to what Simon Frith designates as "a politics of leisure" (200).

These conflicting politics locate such cultural products in what George Lipsitz regards as "dangerous crossroads" (12). As artistic practices that do not forsake the conduits of commercial culture, rock culture and *A dos ruedas* speak to and through the systems of consumer capitalism. Although Lipsitz refers exclusively to popular music, his point is no less valid for the two-folded ethics of Machado's novel. The protagonist of *A dos ruedas* shows the dark side of the "Spanish Dream" and its alliance with consumer capitalism—the corruption of the government, the high rate of unemployment, and its animosity to youth—but still takes commodity culture for granted. Consumer capitalism is in this novel cynically appropriated yet never fully dismantled. The epitome of this contradictory tension is the figure of Kurt Cobain. The third epigraph that precedes *A dos ruedas*—the first two epigraphs are quotes taken from Henry Miller and Vladimir Nabokov that announce the rebellious tone of the narration—contains the chorus of the song "Smells like Teen Spirit," from the album *Nevermind* by Nirvana. This band, led by Cobain, brought the sound of Seattle grunge to the mainstream rock audience. Grunge, "[a] collision of punk, heavy metal, and hard rock" (Shugart 135), substitutes punk's disobedience with apathy and indifference. The title of the album *Nevermind* and the chorus quoted by Machado in the epigraph exemplify the ambivalent politics of Nirvana and grunge culture. Nirvana stated that they would never get hooked by consumer capitalism, as represented in the dollar bill that appears in the cover of the album. However, the absence of a new ethics that could replace the bourgeois values that they reject undermines the contestatory dimension of their effort. Ultimately, they remain in an infantilized state, with the negative phrase "never mind" as their only response, already suggested by the image of the baby swimming under water that appears on the cover.

Kurt Cobain's charisma also permeates Ray Loriga's *La pistola de mi hermano*, as it serves to cast light upon the main character of the novel.[8] Cobain despised the mainstream and "became famous for not wanting to become famous" (Herzogenrath 135). In a similar fashion, the main character of Loriga's novel hopes "to remain outside of all challenges and all duties, of all the good and the bad" (104), yet he gains instant fame by virtue of the media manipulation of his public persona. Marked, like Kurt Cobain, by the specter of Thanatos, the adolescent protagonist escapes in a stolen car after killing the aggressive security guard of a convenience store; later in the novel, he also kills the worker of a gas station. The outlaw run of the protagonist, who takes a young girl with him, begins ten days after Kurt Cobain committed suicide, and the media creates a false portrayal of the juvenile delinquent by making assumptions about Cobain's and rock's negative influence on youth (30). Indeed, the rock stamp appears in the initial title of the book, *Caídos del cielo*, with an intertextual echo of Neil Young's *Sleeps with Angels* (1994). Entirely devoted to the death instinct, this album, which was recorded when Cobain's suicide occurred, intertextually indicates the tracing of the fallen angel—"ángel de la muerte" (18)—in Loriga's novel. Also, this young devil—fallen angel—on the road parallels Mickey, the murderous driver of Oliver Stone's film *Natural Born Killers* (1994), described throughout the movie as the reincarnation of the demon.

The analogy between Cobain and the protagonist of *La pistola de mi hermano* also reverberates in the epigraph taken from Jack Kerouac that begins the book: "I'd rather be slim than famous," which reiterates the resistance of these anti-establishment cultural icons to fame. This epigraph paves the way and prepares the reader to expect Kerouac's spirit in Loriga's novel and, as a consequence, the hallmark of the road tradition from *On the Road* (1955). *La pistola de mi hermano*, just like *A dos ruedas*, interlaces the road genre and rock culture. In opposition to *A dos ruedas*, though, the road trip in *La pistola de mi hermano* is not a quest for meaning but rather an escape from the law, germane to the primary master narrative operating in this novel: the outlaw American road movie. The protagonist is depicted with traits that belong to the icon of the rebel of the American road movie tradition and of rock culture. In his outfit—black V-neck shirt, black jeans, and black boots (36)—and his sense of marginality and deviance from other youth of the same age, he resembles rebels such as the biker Marlon Brando in *The Wild One* (1953) and James Dean in *Rebel Without a Cause* (1955). Both films feature, like Loriga's text, social rebellion closely tied to mobility, speed and juvenile delinquency. By the same token, the sensual tone of the fugitive escape of the novel, in which the young protagonists reach moments of sexual satisfaction and mad love during their flight, echoes the itinerant and outlaw sensuality of the previously mentioned *Natural Born Killers*, in which media makes, as in *La pistola de mi hermano*, the lovers Mickey and Mallory famous icons. Finally, the flavor of *Easy Rider* (1969), the most popular road movie tied to rock culture, is vivid in the recurrent musical references to Kurt Cobain and Nirvana, but also to Jimi Hendrix (68), John Lennon (70), and Sonic Youth (73). These references are textual devices that emphasize the iconography of disobedience manifest in road culture and rock 'n' roll. Once again, rock and road culture intermingle, in this case, through the filter of the road movie tradition.

Above all, the discursive relevance of the outlaw road movie in *La pistola de mi hermano* unfolds with Ridley Scott's film *Thelma and Louise* (1991). One of the favorite movies of the novel's protagonist (22), this intertextual presence emerges several times, most specifically in the figure of the "cool police officer" who is in charge of chasing the young criminal, for he is described as being similar to "the good cop in *Thelma and Louise*, the one played by Harvey Keitel" (55).[9] Moreover, the plot of the novel coincides in its macrostructure with the movie. Both the novel and the film give emphasis to the joy of driving on the open road and the appreciation of the beautiful scenery. The communion with the ocean in *La pistola de mi hermano* and the desert in *Thelma and Louise* adds a pastoral note to the romanticized runaway criminal. Furthermore, the excitement of motion and speed ends up in tragedy and death in both texts. The women decide to "keep going" toward the cliff to avoid being caught by the cops, while the adolescent of *La pistola de mi hermano* is massacred by a troop of police officers at the beach (162). The result is the same: death for the transgressors of the law and the restoration of social order.

To find a Spanish rock 'n' road novel that does not lead to fruitless nihilism or the punishment of the rebellious character, we have to wait until the publication of Eugenia Rico's *La edad secreta* (2004).[10] Planned after the main character finds out that she only has three months to live due to cancer, the trip is converted into a quest for a new life for a middle-aged woman who seeks to transcend a mediocre life and her broken marriage. When the initial diagnosis turns out to be a false alarm, it is already too late to change her mind. She begins her journey northbound, which metaphorically stands for finding her aim in life—"encontrar el norte"—and departs from the constraints of her routine existence. The car feels like a free zone, where "the phone never rings" (48), that drives away from domesticity and out of social norms. Likewise, the trip will signify coming to terms with certain demons from her past, as she will feel "liberated from the past and the good manners and the rules that came with it" (75). She is finally unshackled from the results of her strict education in a catholic school and her upbringing in an acutely patriarchal family with a misogynist father.

Keeping pace with the road movie tradition, the trip causes a transformation in the protagonist, who confesses that she has rediscovered herself: she has learned to love herself by loving others (201). At the beginning of her journey, she stops at a gas station and picks up a 20 year-old hitchhiker, who will become not only her trip companion, but also her lover. Although the relationship does not work out, she is proud of having been an active driver of her destiny. She decides to let him into her car and life and later abandons him once she realizes that the momentum is over (224). The learning experience is what she calls her "resurrection" (201), as she discerns the emancipatory effects of this relationship, which have brought a sexual and sentimental awakening and, more importantly, a new trust in herself. Similarly, the trip helps her attain a better understanding and appreciation of herself through the contemplation of the landscape. She does not feel that she is moving through the scenery, but rather she becomes part of it. In this sense, she perceives the parallel between her resuscitated subjectivity and the metamorphosis of post-Franco Spain: "From being the most backward country in Europe, we have come to shock the world with our movies, our huge gay neighborhoods and our self-confidence. This new Spain is unknown even to its mother, and so am I" (123–24). Concretely, she sees this correlation in the image of an old lady in mourning sitting on the side of the road in the main street of a small country village. Such a lady is a remnant of Francoist Spain, a time that is visualized retrospectively by the narrator as a plethora of women dressed in black, passively waiting for their husbands (122). By contrast, in the new Spain, women like herself can take to the road exercising her agency and dismissing the reactionary mandatory domesticity. Thus, mobility acts as a vigorous metaphor of the enfranchisement of both women and the nation. Correspondingly, the road becomes a fluid site that stages the redefinition of Spanish national identity during the democratic period. The European-like freeways typify the adjustment of Spain to modernity (115), once the country has surmounted its old hampering isolation and stagnation.

Interestingly enough, rock 'n' roll again contributes to shaping the mobility of this reinvigorated female subject, as she declares that she is "the daughter of rock and roll, of this life style that my mother never knew about (. . .). However, I would not realize it until I got into this car" (169). As in *A dos ruedas* and *La pistola de mi hermano*, rock culture acquires narrative significance within *La edad secreta* as a compelling tool to celebrate mobility and the countercultural verve associated with the road. Nevertheless, this novel appends new elements to the rock 'n' road genre. First of all, the story does not fit into the youth rebellion scenario of the adolescent who refuses to accept the responsibilities of adult life. She is already a mature person who has "performed" well in the system, with a successful career as a tax collector. In addition, the story puts a woman behind the wheel. Previous Spanish road novels—*La pistola de mi hermano* and *A dos ruedas*, but also Ignacio Martínez de Pisón's *Carreteras secundarias* (1995), Eduardo Iglesias' *Por las rutas los viajeros responden a las plegarias* and *Tormenta Seca*, and David Trueba's *Cuatro amigos* (1998)—are masculine-centered and push women to a marginal position within the narrative, usually reduced to a foreseeable supporting role and often portrayed as erotic diversions and sexual objects.[11] Women are also perceived as a hurdle to the male heroes in motion as they restrain them from continuing their trip. In these cases, the reckless driving of the road adventures to which my title refers actually becomes defensive driving that renders the male protagonists as victims of a feared and unknown feminine "other."

Indeed, as a gendered space with a hierarchical disposition, the road in these narratives loses its potential to challenge solidified norms, at least in relation to gender notions. By denying agency to women and displaying overt sexist fictional representations—especially in *A dos ruedas*—these texts inherit the gender inequalities from their two narrative paragons: rock culture and road movies. Road movies have often been criticized for remaining a male domain (Corrigan, Williams, Laderman), and Steven Cohan and Ina Rae Hark define them as "a male escapist fantasy linking masculinity to technology" (3). Rock culture has likewise been excoriated for being a "masculinist mode of cultural articulation" (Medovoi 157) that excludes women from its rebellion (Frith 242). *La edad secreta*, in this sense, is a cultural product as groundbreaking for the genre in Spain as *Thelma and Louise* was for the road movie tradition in the US, because it endows a woman with the defiant ethos of both the road and rock culture. Conversely, this similitude also means that the novel carries the same contradictory messages about the issue of the emancipation of women on the road. Analogous to the open debates by film critics and feminists on the ability of *Thelma and Louise* to portray empowerment of women, one might argue that *La edad secreta*, far from challenging conventional gender roles, reinforces the dependency of women on men.[12] Tantamount to the naïve excitement of Thelma when she picks up the hitchhiker played by Brad Pitt in Ridley Scott's film, the protagonist of Rico's novel soon desists from her longing for self-sufficiency and becomes emotionally attached to the young man she picks up. This dependency becomes inscripted in letting him drive her car: "I have let him drive my car. After all, he also drives my heart" (133). Taking control of her car is equal to taking over her life and, as a result, her agency seems to slip away in the hands of a new male authority.

Despite this temporary disavowal of self-government, the dénouement of the novel brings to the fore the insurgent potential that I claimed at the beginning of my essay. Most dissident road stories end either with the punishment of the rebellious character, as exemplified by the death of the delinquent in *La pistola de mi hermano*, or with his reintegration in the community and, as a consequence, his acceptance of the social norms. It is my contention that *La edad secreta* plays with and parodies such genre expectations. Toward the end of the journey, the lead character and the young hitchhiker see the body of a dead victim of a car accident lying on the ground (189), an episode that functions as a foreshadowing of their own accident when a truck almost kills them (213). The narrative set up with the premonition invites the reader to predict punishment for the transgressor of the (patriarchal) social law. In the first surprising twist of the last pages of the novel, though, she survives the diagnosis of a mortal internal hemorrhage (219). When she recovers, they drive toward Madrid, which signals their return to the core of the system, both in a geographical and an ethical sense. However, in the second twist, she abandons him when she drops him off before reentering the city. Then, while filling the tank in a gas station, she runs into another young man. Although she initially had decided to return home, her last words leave an open door suggesting that she might continue her trip driven by desire: "But then he looks at me" (227).

By perhaps declining her reintegration into the system, the protagonist of *La edad secreta* personifies the deterritorializing profile that Gilles Deleuze and Felix Guatari postulate in their trope of the "nomad": she stays in a "smooth space" and refuses to be reterritorialized, to surrender to the "sendentary space" of the system (410), which in the novel stands for a return to domesticity. Such rhizomatic movement, enacting transitions underground, free from fixed paths and from a regulation of speed, challenges the notion of a unitary center underpinning humanist subjectivity, for she chooses to continue living on the fringes of society. In the same way, the formal configuration of the novel, in lacking a definite closure and a linear structure, purposely deviates from classical narrative frames to convey the same shifting impression and the collapse of settled generic limits.

This nomadic potential embodies the cultural politics that, in my opinion, distinguishes the rock 'n' road novel. By no means do I intend to overlook the contradictions analyzed throughout the present essay that come along with the mobile subjectivity of these narratives, including those of *La edad secreta*. Rather, I want to underscore that it is precisely these inconsistencies, or better, the tension between compliance and insubordination, between deterritorialization and reterritorialization that produces the creative allure of the rock 'n' road novel. Very much like the classical tragedy for Nietzsche in *The Birth of Tragedy*, the rock 'n' road novel contains an Apollonian element, which enforces self-control, regulation of movement, and a return to domesticity, and a Dionysian impulse, which represents the detour toward the transgression of those very principles. Following this analogy, if in Nietzsche's view of Greek theater the transgressive part is emblematized by the musical aspect with the ritual of the singing and dancing chorus, rock music and its utopian rebellious drive encapsulates the Dionysian dimension that I see as dominant in the rock 'n' road novel, imbricated with the impulse of road culture. The legacy of Dionysus in these narratives evolves in their claim for motion without a teleological purpose to overcome social angst and alienation. By "rocking the road," Generation X writers explore new avenues for the Spanish literary scene, but they also offer the asphalt as a fresh mobile locale that allows the circulation of mutable values in this Superhighway Spain. Thus, the road becomes a creative cultural space where national identity as well as gender roles and power relations are sometimes contested, sometimes reinforced, but always renegotiated.

Notes

1. I would like to express my gratitude to Silvia Bermúdez, Jill Kuhnheim, and David Thurmaier for reading previous drafts of this essay and giving me many suggestions to improve it.

2. Manuel Huerga's *Antártida* (1994) stands out as a Spanish rock 'n' road movie. This film narrates the fleeing of a former rock singer, María Soler, who escapes with a young man called Rafa after having stolen nine kilograms of heroin. Rock songs accompany their outlaw run highlighting the dissident nature of their journey as well as serving as the background for flashbacks of María's past that explain her descent from a successful career as a rock star to an alienated drug addict.

3. Eduardo Iglesias's *Aventuras de Manga Ranglan* (1992), *Por las rutas los viajeros responden a las plegarias* (1996) and *Tormenta seca* (2001) are rock 'n' road novels, but this author, born in 1952, belongs to a previous literary generation. Rock music and high speed also pervade the "tetralogía Kronen" by José Ángel Mañas—*Historias del Kronen* (1994), and *Mensaka* (1995), *Ciudad rayada* (1997), and *Sonko 95* (1999). While they share some traits of the genre, these four novels do not constitute in a strict sense road narratives and, consequently, they remain outside the confines of the rock 'n' road novel. I want to clarify that I am using the term Spanish Generation X in its most accepted or generalized sense, which refers to a group of novelists born in the 1960s and 1970s that appeared in the Spanish literary scene in the 1990s, and who apparently share common traits, styles, and influences (see Urioste). I am aware that both the label and the concept of Generation X has been contested (Moreiras Menor 192–205), and that the topic definitely deserves further discussion, especially in relation to its limits—why should we not consider Eduardo Iglesias as part of the group if he shares many thematic and stylistic features in his rock 'n' road novels?—but the scope of the essay forces me to put the issue aside for another venue.

4. For a detailed account of the history of the literature-film relations, see Carmen Peña-Ardid and Jorge Urrutia.

5. *A dos ruedas* was the literary debut of Machado. His second and most recent novel,

Grillo (2003), was awarded the "IX Premio Lengua de Trapo de Narrativa" and obtained a unanimous acclaim by critics.

6. The PSOE administration, which took over with an overwhelming populist support in 1982, lost the support of its voters tainted by numerous cases of corruption. Starting with the FILESA affair, which aired the illegal funding of the PSOE, the list increased with scandals such as the "Guerra" affair, in which the vice-president's brother, Juan Guerra, was proved to be involved in a misappropriation of public funds. Just as controversial was the GAL affair, which revealed the strategies of state terrorism employed by the socialist administration to counter-attack the terrorist actions of ETA. Needless to say, all these scandals damaged the public image of the government, and eventually motivated the triumph of José María Aznar and the conservative Partido Popular in the 1996 elections.

7. Route 66, also known as "The mother of America" and "The main street of America," is certainly America's most famous highway, and it became a legendary path with the success of Kerouac's *On the Road*, and the TV series "Route 66" in the 1960s.

8. Apart from *La pistola de mi hermano*, Ray Loriga has published six novels: *Lo peor de todo* (1992), *Héroes* (1993), *Días extraños* (1994), *Tokio ya no nos quiere* (1999), *Trífero* (2000), and *El hombre que inventó Manhattan* (2004). In addition, he has written a number of short stories that have been included in anthologies such as *Páginas amarillas* and *McOndo*. Finally, it is worth mentioning Loriga's involvement in filmic projects. In 1997 he directed the cinematographic adaptation of his own novel *La pistola de mi hermano*. He has further collaborated in the script of Pedro Almodóvar's *Carne Trémula* (1997), Carlos Saura's *El séptimo día* (2004), and Daniel Calparsoro's *Ausentes* (2005).

9. The police officer in *La pistola de mi hermano* is also compared to Harry Dean Stanton (77–80), the main actor of *Paris, Texas*, directed by Wim Wenders in 1984, another classic road movie that leaves its trademark in Loriga's novel.

10. *La edad secreta* was a finalist for the "Premio Primavera de Narrativa 2004." Rico has published two other novels: *Los amantes tristes* (2000) and *La muerte blanca* (2002), which was awarded the prestigious "Premio Azorín de Narrativa" in 2002. Also, she has written several short stories published in a number of anthologies published in 2003: *Muelles de Madrid, La paz y la palabra, Que la vida iba en serio . . .* , and *Sobre raíles*.

11. Other recent Spanish road novels that portray women driving on the road and depart from the masculinist nature of the genre are Jesús Torrecilla's *En la red* (2004), and Eugenio Fuentes's *Venas de nieve* (2005). In the realm of film, while Cecilia Bartolomé's *Vámonos Bárbara* (1977) constitutes an early and interesting example, we will have to wait until the release of Miguel Hermoso's *Fugitivas* (2000) to find other women taking the road by themselves.

12. This controversial film has received many acclaims but also many objections from both feminists and non-feminists. While the movie features a female couple escaping from the tentacles of patriarchy, and experimenting a liberation and transformation

during their road trip, many critics from both sides of the ideological spectrum claim that the emancipation of Thelma and Louise is at the expense of a sexist portrayal and humiliation of men, thus reaffirming the gender tensions rather than neutralizing or de-naturalizing them. Conservative views have also advocated that the film is so overtly anti-family and anti-child that it alienates many women from identifying themselves with the characters, while some feminist critics dislike the latent pessimism of the end plus the fact that the protagonists gain agency and power only through violence. For insightful studies on the contradictory politics of this film, see Linda Frost, Cathy Griggers, Carmen Indurain Eraso, David Laderman (184–194), and Sharon Willis.

Works Cited

Altschuler, Glenn. *All Shook Up. How Rock 'N' Roll Changed America*. Oxford: Oxford University Press, 2003.

Cohan, Steven and Ina Rae Hark. *The Road Movie Book*. London and New York: Routledge, 1997.

Corrigan, Timothy. *A Cinema without Walls: Movies and Culture after Vietnam*. New Brunswick: Rutgers University Press, 1991.

Deleuze, Gilles and Félix Guattari. *A Thousand Plateaus*. Minneapolis: University of Minnesota Press, 1987.

Frith, Simon. *Sound Effects: Youth, Leisure, and Politics of Rock 'N' Roll*. New York: Panteon Books, 1981.

Frost, Linda. "The Decentered Subject of Feminism: Postfeminism and *Thelma and Louise*." Ed. Michael Bernard-Donals and Richard R. Glejzer. *Rhetoric in an Antifoundational World*. New Haven and London: Yale University Press, 1998. 147–69.

Fuentes, Eugenio. *Venas de nieve*. Barcelona: Tusquets, 2005.

Griggers, Cathy. "*Thelma and Louise* and the Cultural Generation of the New Butch-Femme." Ed. Jim Collins, Hilary Radner, and Ava Preacher Collins. *Film Theory Goes to the Movies*. New York and London: Routledge, 1993. 129–41.

Grossberg, Lawrence. "The Media Economy of Rock Culture: Cinema, Post-Modernity and Authenticity." Ed. Simon Frith, Andrew Goodwin, and Lawrence
_____. *Sound and Vision: The Music Video Reader*. London and NewYork: Routledge, 1993. 185–209.

Herzogenrath, Bernd. "From the Lost Generation to Generation X: The Great Gatsby versus Kurt Cobain." Ed. Hanjo Berressem and Bernd Herzogenrath. *Near Encounters: Festschrift for Richard Martin*. Frankfurt: Peter Lang, 1995. 121–40.

Iglesias, Eduardo. *Aventuras de Manga Ranglan*. Madrid: Libertarias, 1992.

_____. *Por las rutas los viajeros responden a las plegarias*. Madrid: Alfaguara, 1996.

_____. *Tormenta seca*. Madrid: Suma de Letras, 2001.

Indurain Eraso, Carmen. *"Thelma and Louise*: 'Easy Riders' in a Male Genre." *Atlantis* 23.1 (2001): 63–73.

Interrante, Joseph. "The Road to Autopia: The Automobile and the Spatial Transformation of American Culture." Ed. David Lewis and Lawrence Goldstein. *The Automobile and American Culture*. Ann Arbor: University of Michigan Press, 1983. 89–104.

Kerouac, Jack. *On the Road*. Ed. Scott Donaldson. New York: The Viking Press, 1979.

Laderman, David. *Driving Visions: Exploring the Road Movie*. Austin: University of Texas Press, 2002.

Lefebvre, Henri. *Everyday Life in the Modern World*. New Brunswick and London: Transaction Publishers, 1990.

Lipsitz, George. *Dangerous Crossroads*. London and New York: Verso, 1994.

Loriga, Ray. *Días extraños*. Madrid: Detursa, 1994.

_____. *Héroes*. Barcelona: Plaza & Janés, 1993.

_____. *El hombre que inventó Manhattan*. Barcelona: El Aleph, 2004.

_____. *Lo peor de todo*. Madrid: Debate, 1992.

_____. *La pistola de mi hermano (Caídos del cielo)*. Barcelona: Plaza y Janés, 1997.

_____. *Tokio ya no nos quiere*. Barcelona: Plaza y Janés, 1999.

_____. *Trífero*. Barcelona: Destino, 2000.

Machado, José. *A dos ruedas*. Madrid: Alfaguara, 1996.

_____. *Grillo*. Madrid: Lengua de Trapo, 2003.

Mañas, José Ángel. *Ciudad rayada*. Madrid: Espasa Calpe, 1998.

_____. *Historias del Kronen*. Barcelona: Destino, 1994.

_____. *Mensaka*. Barcelona: Destino, 1995.

Marcus, Millicent. *After Fellini: National Cinema in the Postmodern Age*. Baltimore: Johns Hopkins University Press, 2002.

Martínez de Pisón, Ignacio. *Carreteras secundarias*. Barcelona: Anagrama, 1996.

Medovoi, Leerom. "Mapping the Rebel Image: Postmodernism and the Masculinist Politics of Rock in the U.S.A." *Cultural Critique* 20 (1991–1992): 153–88.

Moreiras Menor, Cristina. *Cultura herida: literatura y cine en la España democrática*. Madrid: Ediciones Libertarias, 2002.

Nietzsche, Friedrich. *The Birth of Tragedy and Other Writings*. Ed. Raymond Geuss and Ronald Speirs. Cambridge: Cambridge University Press, 1999.

Peña-Ardid, Carmen. *Literatura y cine*. Madrid: Cátedra, 1999.

Rico, Eugenia. *Los amantes tristes*. Barcelona: Planeta, 2000.

_____. *La edad secreta*. Madrid: Espasa Calpe, 2004.

_____. *La muerte blanca*. Barcelona: Planeta, 2002.

Shugart, Helene. "Isn't It Ironic? The Intersection of Third-Wave Feminism and Generation X." *Women Studies in Communication* 24: 2 (2001): 131–68.

Torrecilla, Jesús. *En la red*. Madrid: Lengua de Trapo, 2004.

Trueba, David. *Cuatro amigos*. Barcelona: Anagrama, 1998.

Urioste, Carmen de. "La narrativa española de los noventa. ¿Existe una generación X? *Letras Peninsulares* 10.2–10.3 (1997–1998): 455–76.

Urrutia, Jorge. *Imago litterae. Cine. Literatura.* Sevilla: Alfar, 1984.

Vilarós, Teresa. "The Novel Beyond Modernity." Ed. Harriet Turner and Adelaida López de Martínez. *The Cambridge Companion to the Spanish Novel. From 1600 to the Present.* Cambridge: Cambridge University Press, 2003. 251–63.

Williams, Mark. *Road Movies.* New York: Proteus Books, 1982.

Willis, Sharon. "Hardware and Hardbodies, What Do Women Want?: A Reading of *Thelma and Louise.*" Ed. Jim Collins, Hilary Radner, and Ava Preacher Collins. *Film Theory Goes to the Movies.* New York and London: Routledge, 1993. 120–28.

◆ **10**

Television and the Power of Image in *Caídos del cielo* and *La pistola de mi hermano* by Ray Loriga

Kathryn Everly

> Other generations had wars and social movements to unite them, but for
> Xers, television is the common experience.
> —Rob Owen, *GenX TV*

Television plays a crucial role in defining popular culture and, as Rob Owen explains, crosses cultural boundaries creating a common perspective. Although Owen is writing about Xers in the United States, his observations pertain to the Spanish Generation X as well. Ray Loriga (Madrid, 1967), considered one of the forerunners of the Generation X literary movement in Spain, tells in his first novel, *Lo peor de todo (Worst of All)* (1992), the story of a disenfranchised youth struggling with family problems in a fast-paced, consumerist society. The first-person narrative, fantasies of violence, and ubiquitous North American capitalism (the protagonist works in a McDonalds) define, in part, the narrative style and content familiar to readers of Spain's Generation X.[1]

Nevertheless, Loriga has developed and expanded Gen X themes of disgruntled youth, family tension, and popular culture. His career has been dynamic as well as prolific.[2] Loriga has successfully tapped into the importance of image, video, and cinematic language in his novels, bringing this consciousness of form to his films. His work as author, screenwriter, and director complement one another and inspire a new literary language. In his works, Loriga criticizes TV's superficiality and the erroneous sense of community it creates. This essay will analyze the ways in which Loriga uses both visual and verbal language to reveal manipulative television ethics. Television produces images that seduce viewers with a created, false reality that shifts power from the actual events to the televised recreation.

Although he focuses on television as a cultural marker, Loriga also addresses the broader context of contemporary Spanish cultural production in his works. The emphasis on the visual, the urban settings, and youth in Loriga's works stems from an artistic tendency to look toward the future, instead of reflecting on past national disasters such as the Spanish Civil War and resulting Franco regime. However, Loriga and the Gen X writers are not apolitical; their politics are enmeshed with an evolving cultural identity that finally allows the freedom *not* to address history or politics in their writing. The climate of criticism in Gen X writing bears a shift from the political to the personal. In the two works studied here, Loriga seeks to tease out the personal conflict between the individual and, what he seems to consider, overbearing cultural production.

In order to better understand Loriga's contribution to the Gen X movement in Spain, I will focus on the relationship between written and visual language in *Caídos del cielo* (*Fallen From Heaven*) (1995) and in the film adaptation written and directed by Loriga, *La pistola de mi hermano* (*My Brother's Gun*) (1997). The novel and its film version exemplify the difference between visual and verbal forms of communication in that while the characters and plot remain the same, the style and tone of each work is markedly different. However, in order to locate these texts within the shifting parameters of the Gen X movement, I will briefly consider the polemics of naming the contemporary literary movement in Spain and of Spanish television.

Christine Henseler points out that Spanish Gen X authors are more concerned with redefining literary language than perfecting it. She describes the cover of Loriga's novel *Héroes* (*Heroes*) (1993), where the author appears holding a bottle of beer and sporting a skull ring and long hair. Loriga appropriates the marketing machine as he sells the relationship between author and text as part of "the territory of virtual reality, worlds infused with simulated truths where life [con]fuses with art and art confuses reality" (694). In Loriga's case, art and life again become one and the same in his most recent novel *El hombre que inventó Manhattan* (*The Man Who Invented Manhattan*) (2004). Loriga lived in New York City for five years with his family and left shortly after the September 2001 terrorist attacks. *El hombre* takes place in Manhattan and presents itself at times as a real autobiography and, at others, as only an imaginary fantasy. Loriga assures us that the events are fiction and then suddenly insists they are not: "todas [las historias] son inventadas aunque muchas, la mayoría, son ciertas" (16) (all of the stories are invented although many of them, the majority, are true). This crossover between life and art has long been at the core of Loriga's literary project.

However, even though Loriga has capitalized on the Gen X image of literary rebellion and self-promotion, he has criticized the notion of a generation of writers: "lo de la generación X, Mañas y demás, creo que era muy artificial puesto que éramos gente que tenía muy poco que ver en lo literario y que además no teníamos ningún contacto personal" (2) (the generation X, Mañas and the rest, was very artificial, given that we were people that had little in common literarily and, furthermore, we didn't have any kind of personal contact) ("hombre"). Loriga compares his literary generation with what he considers the more legitimate Generation of 1927: "Existía un lugar de encuentro, era gente que se conocía . . . había un núcleo . . . cuando yo empecé a publicar no conocía de nada a ninguno de los escritores que luego me pusieron como compañeros de ruta y sigo sin conocerlos" (3) (there existed a common ground, they knew each other . . . there was a nucleus . . . when I started to publish I didn't know any of the writers that they later grouped me with and I still don't know them) ("hombre"). Other "members" of the Gen X group have expressed similar feelings of disengagement.

On January 15, 2004 at a roundtable discussion at the University of Valladolid, contemporary Spanish authors Juan Bonilla, Marcos Giralt Torrente, and Lucía Etxebarria raised the question: Was there ever a Generation X in Spain? Etxebarria confirms that the term originated with Douglas Coupland's book *Generation X: Tales for an Accelerated Culture* (Ferrari 259). Coupland describes a group of isolated and estranged young people living in the United States. They are satisfied to settle for a McJob, defined as undemanding employment that simply pays the bills (5). Coupland's benevolent Generation Xers have little to do with the violence, sexual promiscuity, and hard drug use characteristic of the Spanish Gen X.[3] The authors at the roundtable discussion conclude that there never was a Generation X in Spain. Etxebarria affirms that the current group of writers lacks a formal manifesto and they do not ascribe to a common literary legacy. She also suggests that publishers invented the term to sell certain authors, such as Mañas and Loriga (Ferrari 259). Juan Bonilla warns against confusing a historical generation with a literary group (260). He also points out that the contemporary writers grouped together as part of the Generation X never put forward the name to identify themselves, on the contrary, the label was forced upon them.

However, most critics will agree that the term Generation X accurately defines a group of Spanish writers and the literary spirit they embody. Loriga has said that "todos los escritores reniegan de ser metidos en una generación"

(4) (all writers refuse to be stuck in a generation) ("hombre") and perhaps it is the work of the critic and not the author to conceptualize literary movements. Nevertheless, I think it is important to address the issues brought up by the authors. Their reactions to the term reveal the fragile relationship between the author and the market. For these young writers working on a global stage dominated by the Internet, image is an intrinsic part of selling books. Perhaps the globalization of the Spanish book market and the immediate access to image via the internet can be considered additional characteristics of the Spanish Generation X. Commenting on current television production in Spain, Richard Maxwell observes: "cultural politics of nationality erupt onto the global grid of market culture" (271). Similarly, the specific traits of the Spanish Gen X movement give the authors a unique and marketable appeal to a global audience. They are at once Spanish (national) and international because they allude to British and American films, songs, and books in their works. The need to expand and clarify the term Generation X affirms its importance to the contemporary Spanish literary scene.

The historical relationship between television and the viewer also influences Spanish Gen X literature. As Barry Jordan points out, under Franco's dictatorship television programming as well as other media outlets were strictly controlled by the state and this "paternalistic legacy" would complicate later attempts to separate televised content from centralized state control (364). For example, the role of television during the transition to democracy was to "explain to the public the problems of the national economy (so as to avoid the association between democracy and economic instability, a serious problem in the early 1980's)" (367). Thus, television under Franco and during the transition was a tool of the state to convince the public of certain political ideologies. More recently, Spaniards have protested the lack of legislation controlling the amount of sex and violence on TV as well as the dominant foreign ownership of all Spanish mass media (Jordan 367; Bustamante 360).[4] We see in Loriga's work that television is not just a source of entertainment, but also a political tool that wields the power to influence and manipulate the public's worldview. Loriga's fiction seeks to deconstruct television's mediation between personal perspective and social reality. The contrast between the novel *Caídos del cielo* and the film *La pistola de mi hermano* stems from the relationship the reader/viewer establishes with the text. The novel presents a fast-paced narrative with jumps in location and time that require the reader to reorder the series of events. The narrative frenzy and chaos culminate in a scene on the set of a talk show that reveals the carnivalesque nature of television reporting. In the novel, the younger brother tells the story of how his older brother kills a security guard at a convenience store and then steals a car to escape from the law. In his haste to escape, the older brother speeds off with a young girl in the car. The narrator complains about how the media misrepresents his family but he can only speculate about what really happens. He pieces the story together through conversations with the girl only after his brother is shot and killed. The narrative perspective creates a source of doubt in the story, for readers do not have access to the main events. The young narrator must recreate them from the girl's recollections and bogus TV reports.

In the film, however, we follow the brother on his road trip and see the events unfold first hand. The element of doubt surrounding the younger brother's perspective is absent from the film. The camera work echoes the linear narrative and does not jump around frequently but is steady and focused. Loriga uses many single-shot scenes where the camera does not move but stays in one place, highlighting the importance of the dialogue. He does not cut from one speaker to the other in a traditional shot/reverse shot sequence but stays on one speaker while we hear the other's response off screen.[5] Loriga also uses slow motion at moments of high energy to underline emotional bonds instead of physical speed.

Loriga's movie creates a dialogue between television and film regarding violence in society. The story offers a glimpse into the startling manipulation of events through televised reporting and the alienation of misunderstood youth. Loriga questions the origins of violence in society: is violence produced by society or do individuals react violently to a society that alienates and degrades them? At one point in the film the main character has a brief but revealing conversation with the girl as they both watch a boxing match on TV:

—¿Crees que es culpa de la televisión?
—¿El qué?
—Todo.

(—Do you think television is to blame?
—For what?
—Everything.)

The girl does not respond, leaving the viewer to ponder the curt answer. Although the film does not exonerate the individual and blame television for "everything," the murderer in the story is portrayed as vulnerable, scared, and unable to understand his (or anyone else's) actions. Loriga juxtaposes brutal violence with adolescent awkwardness that leaves the reader/viewer wondering about the emotional price the individual must pay to fit in socially. He explores the mishandling of television that promotes sensationalism and creates a false reality while seducing viewers into believing in the power of violence.

Television newscasts edit and thus often falsify violent episodes in order to shock or at least impress the audience. TV automatically censors information with time limitations placed on news programs and talk shows as each story is carefully revised and packaged for immediate consumption. In this way events are "cut off from their antecedents and consequences" (Bourdieu 7). The factual information of any given event becomes less important than the dramatic rendering of that event that will stimulate and attract television viewers. Broadcasters show what they believe will reflect the general public's interest and "the television screen . . . becomes a sort of mirror for Narcissus, a space for narcissistic exhibitionism" (14). The simulated event is presented in a two-minute story on the evening news and "ultimately television, which claims to record reality, creates it instead" (22). Sharon Lynn Sperry has observed: "Television news is a blend of traditional, objective journalism and a kind of quasi-fictional prime-time story–telling which frames events in reduced terms with simple, clear-cut values" (131). Her assertion that television news is structured to complement the narrative shows framing the newscast reveals the implicit censorship involved in transmitting factual information, in short, fictionalized segments. Therefore, television is not a mediator between the human gaze and society (Navarro 3) but rather the images on television create a virtual reality. Loriga shows this process in the novel through the narrator's confusion and the process of fabricating misinformation becomes the axis of the narrative structure. The narrator grapples with his own perceptions of his brother, information from the girlfriend, and the many versions of his brother presented on TV.

In the novel, the young narrator criticizes the way in which the television press handles his brother's story. When a reporter asks him if his brother ever shot a gun at him he confides to the reader "los de la tele son la hostia" (15) (the people from TV are assholes). He also exclaims: "lo que me jodió es que los de la televisión dijeran que era marica sin conocerle" (16) (what pissed me off was that the people from television said he was a fag without knowing him). The TV reports invent a personality that has nothing to do with the older brother but attracts viewers. They create a sensationalistic story with an intriguing character hoping that viewers will follow the escapades of "el loco de la tele" (17) (the crazy guy from TV). On the other hand, the narrator feels privileged when "en el informativo semanal nos dedicaron casi media hora" (34) (we were on the weekly news show for almost a half an hour). The conditions and outcome of his brother's story gain importance with the amount of time televised. Therefore it seems logical to the younger brother that he and his mother make the requested television appearances.

The description of the narrator and his mother preparing for a talk show reveals the marketing strategy and general sensationalism that support "informative" shows. The show is called "Todos somos uno" (We all are one) suggesting the collective nature of the television experience. The "fabuloso mundo de la familia" (83) (fabulous world of family) extends beyond the studio to the household and includes the vast, faceless audience tuned in to the program. Cristina Moreiras mentions the "information invasion" that collapses the private and public spheres into one disorienting space. The television "obliga al sujeto a modificar radicalmente su concepción y, más importante aún, su experiencia del espacio y del tiempo, de lugar y de la historia, en fin, de la propia cultura" (200) (obligates the subject to radically modify her conception and, more importantly, her experience of space and time, of place and history, really of culture itself). Television allows the invasion of the private sphere by the public in a seemingly harmless way. But the images on TV do not faithfully represent the public sphere and in the novel the family's plight is embellished to incite the audience that ultimately ridicules the mother's testimony.

The narrator comments on the use of makeup that covers the physical ugliness of the presenter (Loriga 83) and how the makeup artists "me despeinaron un poco y me cambiaron la cazadora de mi hermano por una roja más vistosa" (84) (messed up my hair a little and changed my brother's jacket that I was wearing for a flashier red one). The presenter assures the audience that the narrator is wearing his brother's jacket, which we readers know is a lie, and the mother's desperate attempt to vindicate herself on television only provokes the crowd: "Mamá mientras tanto trataba de convencer a todo el mundo de que ella a pesar de todo era una buena mujer y de que yo era un buen chico y que lo de mi hermano era un caso aislado, pero nadie la creía. PORQUE TODOS SOMOS UNO" (84) (Mom tried to convince everybody that despite everything, she was a good woman and that I was a good boy and that my brother's case was an isolated incident, but nobody believed her BECAUSE WE ARE ALL ONE). The chanting crowd drowns out the mother's protests like a Greek chorus announcing the fall of the heroine. The calculated presentation strips the mother of an explanatory voice, for without her guilt the audience would have no scapegoat and no catharsis. The information presented by television journalism, according to Loriga, does not inform, but seduces in a dangerously mind-numbing way. The presentation is geared so that the viewer can actively participate in a virtual ritual of self-aggrandizement in Bourdieu's space of "narcissistic exhibitionism."

The collective agency of television produces an image of the assassin that mythifies his existence. He is labeled the "angel of death" by the press thus combining the beautiful and the morbid. His real identity becomes fluid and unimportant once the TV image takes hold. "The continual temporariness of identity has a corrosive effect: the search for identity results in the erasure of identity. Yet it is not an existential crisis. Identity may be fleeting but it is also instantly replaceable" (Klodt 51). The televised recreation of a particular identity replaces the brother's true identity. Even when the boy's futile escape from social structures is truncated and he is caught by the police and killed, the fabrication of the story continues to serve as a false referent that spurs on the fame of the girl and of his family.

Bourdieu points out that market-driven economics and competition push television journalism to the sensational, shocking, yet easily digestible bytes that will attract an audience. Today's "multichannel landscape is not a world of infinite diversity but rather a sophisticated marketplace that aims to attract demographic groups with spending power" (Spigel 16–17). Reality is sacrificed for a slick, sexy appearance (Bourdieu 19–20). When Loriga transformed his novel into a film, how could he at the same time present effectively these events and avoid the television excesses he deplored?

Not surprisingly, then, a slick, sexy seduction of the viewer is missing from the film. Given the opportunity to represent visually the talk show described in the novel, Loriga decides to resist the temptation of the visual and instead he makes a film that is poignant and visually poetic. He does not try to capture the fast pace of the verbal narrative but instead shoots a calm, understated film. The film lacks the expected rapid car chase and violent, chaotic editing that might portray the confusion at the store when the brother shoots and kills the security guard. Loriga shows that film is a narrative art and that the visual does not have to be the typical onslaught of information seen on television. His control of the images and calculated technique produce a slow pace that counters the television ethics he criticizes. Nevertheless, some television shows do have a slow pace and certainly many films contain high-speed car chases, so the opposition that Loriga sets up is not between television and film but rather the sedate filming style that he uses to tell a violent story stands out as an innovative choice.

Loriga achieves this through three fundamental camera techniques: single-shot scenes, pan, and slow motion.[6] Loriga uses single-shot scenes and pan shots frequently throughout the film while he uses slow motion sparingly. I will analyze scenes that demonstrate the importance of the camera as a tool of visual language that establishes mood in the film. Even though Loriga is dealing in a visual medium, he chooses not to exploit the visual in order to make a hyperbolic statement. Instead he explores the literary and poetic uses of image in order to complement and not simply reproduce his own literary work.

The talk show scene described in detail in the novel does not appear in the film. In fact the presence of television in the film is subtle at best. A television set appears in several scenes, most notably when the older brother and girl are talking in a motel room. They are not watching TV but the blue screen flickers as if it were a silent observer. At one point, we see a medium shot of the brother as he picks up a chair and bashes in the screen of the TV set. Just before he destroys it, the camera pans slowly to the girl asleep on the bed. The smooth camera movement suggests inclusiveness and we see the girl wake suddenly as the TV is destroyed. She runs to embrace the brother and thus closes the physical and emotional gap between them. The emotional symbolism of the filming is achieved through a medium shot that does not cut from one character to the other. This moment of rage and frustration reveals, according to Loriga, "el miedo que él tiene" (how afraid he is) and shows that the young assassin "en el fondo es un tío asustado" (Beilin 207) (deep down is just a scared guy). This intimate moment in the motel room is one of the few violent scenes in the film and Loriga chooses to eschew the obvious camera and editing techniques that would emphasize and exaggerate the power of the image. Instead of a tight close-up or a cut to the girl's startled reaction, his use of the pan shot at a distance removes us from the brother's outburst. When we see the girl jump up from the bed and embrace him we too can feel the need to accept and understand his frustration. We long for the close-up shot that will reveal to us his hidden emotions just as the girl longs to break through his stoic façade and understand his true feelings.

The single-shot scenes and pan shots give a smooth, seamless feel to the conversations in the film. Also, the single-shot scenes reveal the importance of the dialogue because the camera movement does not distract the viewer. In a sequence of single-shot scenes that take place in the motel room, the viewer is forced to concentrate on the dialogue for the lack of movement on the screen. The low light and stillness of the actors emphasize the focus on dialogue. These scenes create an intimate atmosphere and the two characters reveal innermost secrets about their pasts. The scenes include both characters; while one is talking the other is included in the frame and is completely focused on the speaker. In this way Loriga highlights the subtle art of listening, suggesting that we viewers take a cue from the camera's stillness and listen as well.

In the first scene of the sequence, the brother and the girl are watching boxing on TV. They sit at opposite ends of the screen facing the camera. The brother expresses his self-doubt and alienation from society when he asks her

"¿A veces no tienes vergüenza?" (Aren't you ashamed sometimes?) He confesses that his smile, the way he walks, even his hair embarrass him. The flicker of the TV illuminates their faces reminding us of its presence in the room and in their lives. The young man's self-consciousness is exacerbated by the glow of the television screen that often emits images impossible to emulate. The scene then cuts to another medium shot of the two characters sitting on the floor with the TV on in the background. Again, their conversation takes center stage as the girl explains her sexual adventures with a foreigner. In the next medium shot the girl is seated on the bed looking down as she explains a particularly strange and humiliating sexual experience she had and we see the brother in the background, watching and listening to her.

The girl clearly dominates the conversation and her revealing language takes the place of the anticipated sex scene. Even though they kiss passionately, he ends up masturbating alone in the bathroom. Through their words they become more intimate than they could through sex. The camera language creates an intimate feel as well; the frame encloses them both, tightening the claustrophobic space. Even in the short scene when the girl is washing her face in the bathroom, her voice continues in off as we see the brother through the bathroom door, sitting and waiting for her. They are always filmed in the same frame in a single shot. In this way, Loriga visually echoes their emotional solidarity by keeping them together in the same frame instead of cutting from one character to the other.

On the other hand, an earlier scene of the two brothers driving their mother's car reveals an interesting contradiction. This scene can be read as a foreshadowing of the danger that the brother will encounter when he steals a car and flees from the police after shooting the security guard. The boys ask their mother if they can borrow her car to go out for the day. As they leave the house she calls to her older son "Oye, tú, chico malo, conduce con cuidado" (Hey, you, bad boy, be careful driving). The scene cuts to the boy recklessly driving the mom's station wagon in an abandoned dirt lot. They turn fast corners and skid out of control. However, the driving scene is shot in slow motion with quiet guitar music and lilting female vocals. The scene of rebellion is transformed into a tender moment of sibling bonding. We see the car slowly spinning out of control and then the shot cuts to a front view of the brothers smiling, laughing, and having innocent fun. Of course this peccadillo will become even more poignant when at the end of their outing together the older brother will murder a stranger and eventually face his own death.

The relationship established early in the film between the brothers is highlighted in the car scene as the actions take back seat to the filmic technique.

The slow motion footage forces the viewer to concentrate on the facial expressions of the characters and injects the scene with nostalgia. The slow motion differentiates the scene from the rest of the film and heightens the sense of urgency since we know from the beginning that the older brother will die. The car ride is revealed as a special memory for the younger brother when we realize in a later scene that he has been relating to the police all the information we have been witnessing on screen. His version of the day's events leading up to the shooting includes this romantic notion of innocent rebellion with his older brother. Loriga clearly seeks to shed some positive light on the older brother. Despite his bad judgment in killing someone, he was a "normal" kid who enjoyed spending time with his little brother.

The juxtaposition of youth and corruption, of innocence and violence, lies at the heart of the film. In a revealing sequence, set to pulsating punk rock music, we watch the brother shoot the security guard, run out of the store, jump into the first car he sees, and speed away. A sudden cut in the music and image brings us back to the store where we see a small white dog splattered with blood tied to a colorful airplane ride. This abrupt cut to the blood-covered dog is a visual metaphor for the incongruity of violence and youth. The dog's oblivion to the situation symbolizes the innocence of the young and the blood on his white coat suggests society's inevitable violence. We see this dichotomy as well in the prodding police officer as he hounds the mother and younger brother. He claims that he does not want to hurt anyone but shoots the older brother anyway out of a sense of duty. In Loriga's work, institutions with power, such as television and the police, alienate and corrupt young people. He suggests that the innocence of youth does not stand a chance in the face of such social machines.

Nevertheless, Loriga is not the kind of author or filmmaker to preach to his public about the evils of corporate society. He includes violence in his works in order to explore human fascination with it. He claims: "Creo que la violencia es parte fundamental del ser humano" (Beilin 206) (I think that violence is a fundamental part of human beings). In the same vein, his criticism of television serves as a criticism of society's apathy toward violence in general. "La televisión no tiene culpa de nada. Es un espejo. La sociedad ve en la televisión lo que se merece" (206) (Television is not guilty of anything. It is a mirror. Society sees on television what it deserves). The novel and film make evident the fictional nature of many television newscasts and challenge accepted cultural expectations. Just as defenders of television assert that violent images on TV do not incite violence in the viewer but reflect the violence already established in society (Emmet, Corner), Loriga does not blame television for violence, but he does go to lengths to reveal the manipulative power of the image. John Corner defines the moving image as always edited and tailored to fit into the figuration and flow of television aesthetics (29).[7] Loriga extends this concept of flow to novel and film in which he creates an open dialogue between content, meaning.

Notes

1. Generation X writers from Spain were born in the 1960s and include in their works the absence of a notion of the historical, crime, unemployment, drug addiction, video culture, and a disenchanted world vision (de Urioste 456). The other foundational novel of the movement is *Historias del Kronen (Kronen Stories)* (1994) by José Ángel Mañas.

2. Loriga has published seven novels: *Lo peor de todo (Worst of All)* (1992), *Héroes (Heroes)* (1993) "El Sitio" Novel Award, *Días extraños (Strange Days)* (1994), *Caídos del cielo (Fallen From Heaven)* (1995), *Tokio ya no nos quiere (Tokyo Doesn't Love Us Anymore)* (1999), *Trífero (Trifero)* (2000), and *El hombre que inventó Manhattan (The Man Who Invented Manhattan)* (2004). Loriga also wrote and directed the film version of his novel *Caídos del cielo* titled *La pistola de mi hermano (My Brother's Gun)* (1997) and co-wrote the Pedro Almodovar film *Carne trémula (Live Flesh)* (1997). His script *El séptimo día (The Seventh Day)* was directed by Carlos Saura in 2003.

3. Santiago Fouz Hernández elaborates on the differences between Coupland's vision of the Generation X and Spanish narrative at the end of the twentieth century. Going one step further, Athena Alchazidu defines the Gen X in Spain as "neotremendismo" and convincingly ties it to mid-twentieth-century Spanish literature rather than to a foreign influence.

4. An example of the international influence on Spanish TV is the appointment of Maurizio Carlotti as director general of Telecinco in 1994 (Smith 17). He restructured the station and championed innovative programming that resulted in a series of prime time hit shows imitating US formats. See Smith's article "Quality TV?" for a more in-depth study.

5. Shot/reverse shot refers to the editing technique that creates a logical conversation in film. We see the speaker and then cut to the listener to see her reaction and response. Loriga often includes both conversing actors in a medium shot that reduces the editing or cutting of the film and creates a seamless shot.

6. A single-shot scene is when the entire scene takes place without a cut in the film. The camera stays in a fixed place and actors move in and out of the frame. A pan shot is a shot that pivots from left to right or right to left without the camera changing its position. For details on camera and editing techniques see Corrigan, *A Guide to Writing About Film*.

7. Corner explains the important "mobile concept of flow" (61) posited by Raymond
    Williams in his benchmark study *Television: Technology and Cultural Form.* Wil-
    liams sees all TV shows, news casts, commercials, etc. linked together to form mean-
    ing in a stylized sequence he calls flow instead of the static notion of individual pro-
    gram distribution.

Works Cited

Alchazidu, Athena. "Generación X: Una modalidad finisecular del tremendismo." *Etudes
romanes de Brno* 32.23 (2002): 99–108.
Beilin, Katarzyna Olga. "Ray Loriga: Dudas y sombras." *Conversaciones literarias con
novelistas contemporáneos.* Suffolk: Tamesis, 2004: 191–210.
Bourdieu, Pierre. *On Television.* 1996. New York: The New Press, 1998.
Bustamante, Enrique. "The Mass Media: A Problematic Modernization." Ed. Helen Gra-
ham and Jo Labanyi. *Spanish Cultural Studies: An Introduction.* New York: Oxford
University Press, 1995: 356–61.
Corner, John. *Critical Ideas in Television Studies.* Oxford: Oxford University Press,
1999.
Corrigan, Timothy. *A Short Guide to Writing about Film.* New York: Pearson Longman,
2004.
Coupland, Douglas. *Generation X: Tales for an Accelerated Culture.* New York: St.
Martin's Press, 1991.
Emmett, B.P. "Forward." *Violence on Television.* London: British Broadcasting Corpora-
tion, 1972: v–viii.
Ferrari, Enrique. "¿Hubo una generación X en España?" *Siglo XXI: Literatura y cultura
españolas* 2 (2004): 259–63.
Fouz-Hernández, Santiago. "¿Generación X? Spanish Urban Youth Culture at the End
of the Century in Mañas's/Armendáriz's *Historias del Kronen.*" *Romance Studies*
18.1(June 2000): 83–98.
Henseler, Christine. "Pop, Punk, and Rock and Roll Writers: José Angel Mañas, Ray
Loriga, and Lucía Etxebarria Redefine the Literary Canon." *Hispania* 87.4 (2004):
692–702.
"El hombre que inventó Manhattan." *Clubcultura* 22 June 2004.
<http://www.clubcultura.com/clubliteratura/rayloriga/ >.
Jordan, Barry. "Redefining the Public Interest: Television in Spain Today." Ed. Helen
Graham and Jo Labanyi. *Spanish Cultural Studies: An Introduction.* New York: Ox-
ford University Press, 1995: 361–69.
Klodt, Jason E. "'Nada de nada de nada de nada:' Ray Loriga and the Paradox of Spain's
Generation X." *Tropos* 27 (2001): 42–54.
Loriga, Ray. *El hombre que inventó Manhattan.* Barcelona: el Aleph Editores, 2004.
_____. *La pistola de mi hermano (Caídos del cielo)* 1995. Barcelona: Plaza y Janés,
1999.

Maxwell, Richard. "Spatial Eruption, Global Grids: Regionalist TV in Spain and Dialects of Identity Politics." Ed. Marsha Kinder. *Refiguring Spain: Cinema/Media/Representation*. Durham: Duke University Press, 1997: 260–83.

Moreiras Menor, Cristina. *Cultura herida: Literatura y cine en la España democrática*. Madrid: Ediciones Libertarias, 2002.

Navarro Martínez, Eva. "Una realidad a la carta: la televisión en algunas novelas de la última década del siglo XX." *Espéculo. Revista de estudios literarios* 25 (2003): 6 July 2004. <http://www.ucm.es/info/especulo/numero25/alacarta.html>.

Owen, Rob. *Gen X TV: The Brady Bunch to Melrose Place*. Syracuse: Syracuse University Press, 1997.

La pistola de mi hermano. Screenplay by Ray Loriga. Dir. Ray Loriga. Perf. Daniel Gonzáles, Nico Bidásolo, Karra Elejalde. Enrique Cerezo Producciones, 1997.

Rodríguez Marcos, Javier. "Entrevista: Ray Loriga. La literatura le da a la vida una lógica que no tiene." *El País.es* 31 enero 2004. 6 July 2004. <http://www.elpais.es/articuloCompleto.html?xref=20040131elpbabese> .

Smith, Paul Julian. "Quality TV? The *Periodistas* Notebook." *Contemporary Spanish Culture: TV, Fashion, Art and Film*. Cambridge: Polity, 2003: 9–33.

Sperry, Sharon Lynn. "Television News as Narrative." Ed. Richard Adler and Douglass Cater. *Television as a Cultural Force*. New York: Praeger Publishers, 1976: 129–46.

Spigel, Lynn. "Introduction." Ed. Lynn Spigel and Jan Olsson. *Television After TV*. Durham, Duke University Press, 2004: 1–34.

Urioste, Carmen de. "La narrativa española de los noventa: ¿Existe una generación X?" *Letras Peninsulares* 10.3 (1997–1998): 455–76.

Williams, Raymond. *Television: Technology and Cultural Form*. London: Fontana, 1974.

◆ **11**

Rocking around Ray Loriga's *Héroes*: Video-Clip Literature and the Televisual Subject

Christine Henseler

> *"Si pudiera vivir dentro de una canción para siempre todas mis desgracias*
> *serían hermosas."* (*Héroes* 127)

(If I could forever live within a song all my misfortunes would be beautiful.)

When *Héroes* appeared in 1993 with the image of Ray Loriga himself on its cover holding a bottle of beer, his long hair partly shading the provocative look in his eyes, many believed this new kid on the block was trying to buy into the recording business instead of navigating his way into the literary market.[1] Critics indeed confused his literary sensibility with the record-like design of the novel's cover, the intertextual references to the world of rock and roll, and the title of the book, taken from a David Bowie recording from 1977 by the same name. The permeating force of rock and roll on a textual and a paratextual level made some critics lose sight of the narrative's innovative quality and see in *Héroes* nothing more than a mediocre text with superb musical qualities, a novel that, according to one critic:

> carece de la elemental estructura interna, desarrollo narrativo, modulación de vo-
> ces, personajes y episodios que hacen de la novela lo que debe ser. Estamos más
> bien ante la llovizna de una conciencia rockera sensible, el pequeño infierno de un
> autor que puede ser letrista de rock de primer orden, pero que dista del hacedor de
> novelas medianamente profesional. (Dalmau)

(lacks the elemental internal structure, narrative development, modulation of voices, characters and episodes that turn a novel into what it should be. We are rather before the drizzle of a sensitive rocker consciousness, the small hell of an author who can be a first class rock writer, but who is far from being the producer of halfway professional novels.)

It is not enough to say that *Héroes* presents a rock and roll sensibility, that its chapters may be reduced to the lyrics of individual songs or that the entire novel may be equated to a rock and roll record. The text uses rock to produce a variety of temporal and spatial shifts that redefine the novel's cultural enterprise. Rock cannot be taken at face value in this novel, it must be recontextualized and examined within a variety of frameworks: a visual framework as performed by the character's dream sequences; a spatial framework that reduces his movements to his mind; a psychological framework of disengagement from reality; a temporal framework as defined by constant shifts between the past, present, and future; a cultural framework set in the globalized and capitalistic Spain at the end of the twentieth century; and a commercial framework that positions the individual and rock's subversive qualities against the communal and commercialized experience of the masses and the literary market itself.[2]

In *Héroes*, Loriga appropriates song lyrics to provide an audio-visual world in which the word moves beyond the written signifier to include a cultural present made up of the sounds of life's history to reflect, "the complex forms of incorporation and transformation that occur as specific cultural practices move between different configurations and domains of our lives" (Grossberg 177). *Héroes* appropriates rock and roll to construct a narrative subject identity that emulates the consumptive popular cultural reality of the 1990s. The text uses postmodern video-clip techniques to create a televisual subject who lives in a world of hyperappropriation where seemingly unrelated elements are remixed to produce new social meanings. *Héroes* emphasizes the idea proposed by Robert Goldman and Stephen Papson in relation to advertising that "texts become defined not so much by the stories they tell, but by the referential combinations they style" (93). In Loriga's novel, the use of video-clip techniques and intertextual references to rock and roll songs clash in their temporal and spatial re-appropriations and break through the static condition of the protagonist to present a mythical subject in motion.

The elevation of the subject to myth is not a foreign phenomenon to a generation of writers born between 1960 and 1975 who have matured in a relatively stable democracy, benefited from widespread technological transformations, and were absorbed by a "commodity culture [that] underscores the force of marketing factors and endows 'youth' and 'novelty' with extreme value" (Molinaro 302). Nina Molinaro explains that this generation, also referred to as the "novísimos narradores" (the newest narrators) or "los narradores surgidos de los noventa," (the narrators who emerged in the nineties) evinces five character-istics: an inclusion in the literary commercialization of "youth"; a rejection of uniformity and generational community; a reduction to the sub-group of writers called neorealists who "[emulate] the style and ideology of [North American] 'dirty realism'" (303); a professional production in a variety of literary genres; and a higher than usual inclusion of female authors (302–04). In the context of this volume, it is essential to underline the strong presence of the mass media, popular culture, and technology as sites of reference and reflexivity, of stylis-tic emulation, and of character identity development in their literary produc-tions. In the *oevre* of this generation it is therefore not surprising to find more intertextual references to North American films than to world literature, and the lyricism of Bob Dylan or Nirvana takes up more textual space than the poetry of Antonio Machado or Federico García Lorca. Thus, punk, grunge, and rock are transformed into stylistic literary approaches that meld with televisual sensitivities; they become linguistic sources of postmodern subversions that increase the commercial value of works by authors like José Ángel Mañas, Benjamín Prado, and Ray Loriga respectively. Like the proclamation of punk as an approach ridden of artificiality in José Angel Mañas's literary manifesto "El legado de los Ramones: literatura y punk" and its stylistic application in novels like *Historias del Kronen* or *Mensaka*, it becomes clear that it is not the music itself that makes Loriga's *Héroes* an innovative text, but the effect of the aural and lyrical rock culture as it melds with the stylistic results of the word.

The use of rock and roll references in Loriga's *Héroes* does not function as a subtext as much as a supertext, as a narrative that supersedes the main narrative thread and may be used, literally, to reread and interpret the charac-ter's life through each song's lyrics and each band's political and cultural re-percussions. Curiously, the rock references used in this text belong to a time set in the past, a North American and British tradition, including David Bowie, the Clash, John Lennon, Bruce Springsteen, and others, whose subversive musical and marketing productions of the 1970s and '80s may now be viewed as quaint, colorful, and somewhat amusing examples of past revolutionary expressions and iconic representations. Rock, whose subversive qualities have given way to far more contemporary means of contestation such as hip-hop, retains only a nostalgic memory of revolutionary ideals. From today's perspective, the music form serves less to comment on its social voltage in contemporary life than on its own construction as a sort of metafictional aural-narrative in which rock's effects are linked to its textual results. The self-reflexive products of rock's creations become apparent when the protagonist of *Héroes* explains why he always wanted to be a rock and roll star. The character says that he, "quería sentir cierto dolor extraño al que sólo las estrellas de rock and roll están expuestos y quería explicarlo todo de una manera confusa, aparentemente superficial, pero sincera, algo que sólo pueden apreciar los que han estado enganchados a la cadena de hierro y azúcar del rock and roll (19) (He wanted to feel this sort of odd pain that only rock and roll stars are exposed to and he wanted to explain everything in a confusing manner, seemingly superficial but sincere, something that only those who have been addicted to the chain of drugs and the sugar of rock and roll can understand). Drugs and rock and roll, or "rock" as drug, present this character with a very particular means of communal self-expression. The superficiality behind the confusion—fragmentation—and sincerity—lack of stylistic artificiality—demands that readers understand his cultural codes in order to appreciate his expressions of pain. Underlying this comment is also a punch at some members of the critical establishment whose attacks on the "superficiality" and "commercial selling-out" of Spanish Gen X texts disclose a disconnect to the cultural signifiers that infuse the stylistic and thematic modes of communication in new narrative novels. One cannot read *Héroes* through the same techniques that we have traditionally used to analyze a text by Cervantes or Unamuno. Critics have to reinvent themselves and integrate an entirely new set of signifiers—those born from the mass media—into their critical vocabularies and interpretive visions. They must, in this case, taste the sweet drug that is rock and roll.

Cristina Moreiras-Menor agrees that readers must suspend their disbelief concerning the definition of a written text and read *Héroes* "como si de una canción o un vídeo se tratase, en la medida en que éstos no sólo funcionan como referentes o como intertextos, sino como colonizadores del propio proceso literario de narrar una historia" (239) (as if we were dealing with a song or a video, in the sense that these do not only function as referents or intertexts, but as colonizers of the literary process of writing a story itself). The colonizing effect of the video-clip, made most famous through music television (MTV) but present today in everything from CNN News to advertising, best defines the narrative style and potential of Loriga's novel because the video-clip

> amplifies a quality that has always been operative in rock 'n roll: its status as an art between sense and nonsense, communication and noise, form and meaning. Already rock plays aurally on a dialectic in which words hover between sounds and semantics. Video music adds to this further difference in which the sense and

non-sense of words enters into a dialectic with the sense and non-sense of images: hence the possibility of a complex dialogism or polyphony. (Polan 52)

By living and re-living his life in his mind, the young protagonist-narrator creates a polyphonic framework in which fragments of dreams—spaces opened by songs—meet real life experiences from the past and where conversations with imaginary others allow for communal understanding in isolation. This new space suggests a common and generational experience (that of seeing the same television shows or hearing the same songs across the globe) at the same time that it highlights effects of commercial media (as we sit alone in front of a screen or react individually and emotionally to a tune). The mind thus becomes a space for personal formation where the linearity of the word cedes to the overlapping of visual and aural cultural images. The textual result is an automatic writing that jumps from one topic to another in a surrealist frustration of temporal and spatial juxtapositions. For the character in this novel to enter into a "video-clip consciousness," as one might call it, is to allow for a temporal eschewal from his socially imposed self and into an endless forray of selves as defined by the audio-visual means that most convincingly compose his musical repertoire of stars and angels.

If the contemporary subject, according to Moreiras-Menor, loses his or her sense of history and is thus denied a lineal representation of his self, deciding to reside in nonspace and nontime, it would make sense to find a story written in a style that emulates the psychological effects of such a (non)reality. Songs provide a personal space of development, redirected and infused with popular cultural signifiers that defy time as the protagonist internalizes his representation in aural or visual form. The need for spatial escape and self-explication through song is exemplified when the character admits to remembering the Sex Pistols better than he does his job. In particular, he remembers the song *Should I Stay or Should I Go* by the Clash. The protagonist's decision to stay or go is most closely related to his decision to leave the workforce and to lock himself in his room. The year is 2002, ten years after he has left his first voluntary imprisonment (during the Seville Expo of 1992) to attend to his brother who had lost an ear in an automobile accident. He answers the question, "should I stay or should I go?" by referring to another lyrical reference, *Johnny 99* by Bruce Springsteen. Here the protagonist of the song decides "to go," to act on his desperate situation by shooting a night clerk after he loses his job at an auto plant and finds himself in debt.[3] Sentenced to prison for 98 and one years, Johnny declares before court:

Now Judge, I got debts no honest man could pay
The bank was holdin' my mortgage and they was takin' my
house away
Now I ain't sayin' that makes me an innocent man
But it was more 'n all this that put that gun in my hand
Well, Your Honor, I do believe I'd be better off dead
And if you can take a man's life for the thoughts that's in his head
Then won't you sit back in that chair and think it over, Judge, one more time
And let 'em shave off my hair and put me on that execution line.

Faced with an existence behind bars, Johnny opts for total erasure so that he does not have to confront the memory of life's pressures and his own inability to meet them. Much the same, the protagonist of *Héroes* chooses temporary erasure from society because "estar mal, en cambio, es estar tranquilo como una fortaleza quemada en mitad de una guerra. Alejado de todos los retos, de todas las obligaciones" (139) (feeling bad, on the other hand, means feeling calm like a burnt fortress in the middle of a war. Distanced from all challenges and all obligations). He does not turn his life's despairs into criminal behavior, instead, he leaves his job and remains motionless in his inability to move his disjointed body anywhere but in his room and in his mind (his own private, yet endlessly open jail cell), leaving boredom, hopelessness, loneliness, and indifference outside.

The character first centers himself on a physical level in order for the mind to become a free space of lyrical composition and motion. He removes himself from the outside world and locks himself into a six-meter large, but unidentifiable room (readers cannot discern whether he is in his own house, a hospital room, or, for example, a prison cell). His room becomes a temporary hideout for a human being who has lost his path in the world and who is desperately seeking to return to a sense of self, a sentiment he describes when he says: "Si me preguntas a mí, te diré que no me gusta cómo están las cosas, pero tampoco tengo intención de entrometerme. Por ahora sólo quiero estar encerrado. No quiero volver al colegio de los idiotas, ni a la universidad de los idiotas, ni a la fábrica de los idiotas" (55) (If you ask me, I will tell you that I don't like the way things are, but I also don't have any intention of interfering. For now, all I want is to close myself in. I don't want to return to the school of idiots, nor the university of idiots, nor the factory of idiots). This space cuts him off from all communication to the outside world and functions to center him on a psychological level—"lo único que necesitaba era una habitación pequeña donde poder buscar mis propias señales" (15) (the only thing I needed was a small room where I could find my own marks); it becomes a realm outside of time and space where the linearity of past events is reorganized through the more synchronic and centering attributes of rock songs. The video-clip serves as a psychic metaphor for the audio-visual means of expression of the protagonist in his self-delineated space. On one hand, his retreat, escape, imprisonment, emphasizes a feeling of decenterdness and dissolution and indicates a recognition of an alienated and alienating society (Kaplan 47) that comes to the surface through repeated references to the violence, hatred, and ugliness that children and adolescents confront in the outside world. On the other hand, the protagonist's audio-visual escapes—the combination of songs and dreams—function, like video-clips, to "construct a brief 'centered' effect, intended to mediate the overall possibly unpleasurable decentering and to keep the spectator watching" (Kaplan 47). In the character's own words, songs provide a centering and controlling of emotions that allow you to "sentir lo mismo diez o doce veces, [y] tienes todas las sensaciones controladas como en uno de esos laboratorios en los que aíslan algún virus, tienes alguna sensación acorralada, [. . .] algo que puedes reconocer y que ya no se mueve. Y viene de una canción" (146) (feel the same ten or twelve times, [and] you have all the sensations controlled like in one of those labs in which they isolate some virus, you have some sensation cornered, something that you can recognize and that does not move. And it comes from a song). In music videos the 'centering' effect is produced by the song-image format and the constant return to the lip-synching face of the rock star who is being 'sold' in any particular video" (Kaplan 47). As such it is not surprising that the protagonist always wanted to be "una estrella de rock and roll" (19) (a rock and roll star) and that throughout the entire novel there is a confusion between the voice of the protagonist and that of the rock stars who "speak" to him either through songs, through questions, or through dreams. The rock and roll star becomes the ultimate visual icon of "togetherness"—or in the character's words, of angel status—and the most defining and stable factor of the narrative, that which "sells" him a better life and retains the hope for a better world while at the same time providing a scathing critique of human reality.

Several critics have pointed out that literature by neorealist writers of the 1990s, including Ray Loriga, José Ángel Mañas, Pedro Maestre, Juan Bonilla, Lucía Etxebarria, Gabriela Bustelo, and others, presents a social and personal disenchantment with life reminiscent of narratives by authors like Dennis Cooper, Douglas Coupland, Bret Easton Ellis and Evelyn Lau. Santiago Fouz-Hernández believes that beyond the apparent global quality of the mass media culture that is fictionalized by this group of writers, there is a "more persuasive common factor that they all seem to share located in the feelings of a generalized loss and confusion that is grounded in the *fin de siècle*" (95). Mark Allinson explains that at root of this sense of loss affecting Spain's youth is "the massive migration to the cities from the 1950s to the 1970s [that] created the conditions for a consumption-led popular youth culture with a diet of music, television, sport and fashion, and for authentic youth subcultures" (267). One factor that led to such conditions, says Allinson, was the university level education of most young people and the absence of abundant professional jobs that "deprived many [. . .] of the chance to live independent lives" (267). The result was a desire to escape from a social reality that was not fulfilling the needs of its inhabitants. On a historical level, this situation is expounded by a European-wide crisis that Cristina Moreiras-Menor describes in the following manner:

> España, junto a sus vecinos europeos, vive una permanente crisis surgida de los enormes cambios tecnológicos, de los continuos conflictos étnicos causados por olas de emigración hacia la vieja Europa, por los desastres ecológicos que se experimentan de modo casi apocalíptico, por la inestabilidad económica, por la confusión entre espacios privados y públicos y por el surgimiento de una intensa política de las identidades que impulsa en todas las esferas sociales la emergencia y representación de 'nuevas' subjetividades que hasta ahora no habían tenido espacio discursivo. Este contexto de crisis e incertidumbre, que privilegia al sujeto como consumidor y donde se dirimen importantes cuestiones sociales y culturales, resulta también en una transformación radical en los modos de pensar y en los modos de relación social. (68)

> (Spain, together with her European neighbors, lives in a constant crisis that evolved out of enormous technological changes, out of continuous ethnic conflics caused by waves of emigration to the old Europe, by ecological disasters that were experienced in an almost apocalyptic way, by economic instability, by the confusion between private and public spaces and by the appearance of an intense politics of identities that in all social spheres impulses the emergence and representation of 'new' subjectivities that up until now did not own any of its own discursive space. This context of crisis and uncertainty, which privileges the subject as consumer and where important social and cultural questions are poured out, also results in a radical transformation in the ways we think and in the modes of social relations.)

Moreiras continues to explain that this subject takes on one of two positions, or s/he violently rejects any sense of otherness and anti-nationalism, or the subject loses all sense of national historicity. In this era, individuals search for a global sense of well-being through media-events and they are informed and "connected" resulting in a sense of community and belonging. This virtual world, says Moreiras, is one in which all sense of time and space is lost and hegemony of the moment is essential (69).

The song lyrics in *Héroes* then functions to redefine the space in which subject identity is constructed and within which he presents a social critique of contemporay life in Spain. The protagonist finds, for example, that his college education provided him with nothing more than with the tireless, uninteresting, and menial job that is at the root of his dissatisfaction. He says:

> Antes tenía un trabajo. Me refiero a uno de esos trabajos que atan los días y los hacen iguales, como dos minutos sentados en el mismo banco son sólo uno. [. . .] El trabajo no era nada, sólo una especie de presión invisible. Una serpiente en el barro. Pero tampoco demasiado malo, ni demasiado duro, como mucho estúpido. (34)

> (Before I had a job. I mean one of those jobs that paralyze the days and makes them the same, like two minutes seated on the same bench are only one. [. . .] The job was nothing, only sort of an invisible pressure. A serpent in the mud. But also nothing bad, nor anything hard, just stupid.)

He presents his work as meaningless and he emphasizes the sense of futility and uselessness he feels toward his role in society: "Comprobé que la mayor parte de las luces se encendían y se apagaban sin contar conmigo. [. . .] Así que puse los dedos sobre los interruptores que podía controlar" (35) (I realized that most lights turned on and off without me [. . .] For this reason I put my fingers on the switches that I could control). He leaves his job and shifts his life into the opposite direction, into worlds where artistic modes of expression contribute to individual meaning-making and self-creation, modes of expression that he can totally control. Rock lyrics become a body of super-texts that allow him to critique certain social conditions while expressing very personal emotional states of being. For example, the lyrics of the Clash's song *Should I Stay or Should I Go* say the following:

> Darling you gotta let me know
> Should I stay or should I go?
> If you say that you are mine
> I'll be here till the end of time
> So you got to let me know
> Should I stay or should I go?
> Always tease tease tease
> Simpre—coqueteando y engañando

You're happy when I'm on my knees
Me arrodillo y estas feliz
One day is fine, next day is black
Un dias bien el otro malo
So if you want me off your back
Al detrás tuyo
Well come on and let me know
Me tienes que decir
Should I stay or should I go?
Puedo quedarme o puedo irme? [*sic*]

Extrapolating somewhat liberally, one could claim that the protagonist is metamorphosed into a female sex slave (of possibly Hispanic origin, therefore adding to her marginal status) on her knees before the institution of "Employment," critiquing work's power to erase individuals' agency, and emphasizing their unfulfilled promises. The title line, "Should I Stay or Should I Go," reminds "X", the nonface behind the labor workforce, of his state of feeling imprisoned yet wanting to escape, of feeling, every morning, before work, after a night out, on drugs, "desarticulado, como uno de esos muñecos del cuerpo humano en los que había que ir montando todas las piezas" (35) (disjointed, like one of those dolls of a human body to which one had to assemble all the pieces). He presents himself as a puppet on automatic, a man who has lost all sense of purpose, feeling, embodiment, and control.

This disembodied psychic state of the protagonist is reproduced on a stylistic level through disparate, sometimes even surreal dream structures that are propelled by rock and roll songs and artists. These sequences, or "miniclips," emulate music videos in the sense that they present "a chain of disparate images, which may involve the musical performers, but which stress discontinuities in space and time" (Kinder 3). These discontinuities are created through random uses of first and third person references and a seemingly uncontrolled overlapping of images and ideas. Case in point are not only the unrelated scenes presented in one minichapter after another (with ample blank space in between) or the seemingly unanchored questions that appear out of nowhere, but also those scenes where disparate news clips overlap to draw short narratives of confusing proportions, such as the consecutive scenes of the man who pulled a public telephone off its hook, the boy who tried to commit suicide, and the person who put a plow on his nose (121), all in seemingly logical order.

The dream "clips" in *Héroes* may be characterized by incoherence and boundlessness, since "the dreamer usually remembers specific images or scenes but no clear boundaries around individual dream texts, and [. . .] one never knows in advance which dreams or images will appear on the mind-screen" (Kinder 13). But they also function to anchor the book and highlight the character's psychological development. In the very first chapter of the novel, a third person character finds himself in Moscow where he remembers a photograph of Iggy Pop and David Bowie. He tries to find them, "pero no dio con ellos. Así que comenzó a angustiarse y se angustió tanto que se despertó" (11) (but he didn't find them. So he became anguished and so distressed that he woke up). Back asleep, his dream goes awry as he starts to kill everybody in his wake and turns into an old and tired man as he continues to search for the pop star. This dream comes full circle when in the second to last clip of the novel the narrator finally stumbles upon Bowie, his dream come true, "sentado debajo de un ángel de bronce. Sabía que estaría debajo de un ángel desde el principio, pero Berlín está lleno de ángeles" (179) (seated beneath a bronce angel. I knew he would be under an angel from the beginning, but Berlin is filled with angels). Transferred in time and space, the speaker finds the rock star in Berlin, the city to which Bowie himself moved "in 1977 [to] move away from the 'fast paced' self-destructive live-style [sic] in Los Angeles [and to] detoxify his body and his spirit" ("David") from alcohol and drugs. Once there, if we continue to psychic jump, the real David Bowie, according to one version of the story, saw two lovers kiss on opposite sides of the Berlin wall and wrote "'Heroes,' "a song [that] reflects two worlds and the clash between love and the gloom reality of The Wall" ("David"), and a song that perpetuates the clash between the liberating quality of an instance and the burden of history. The dream sequence comes full circle as the character may be interpreted to have reached a moment of clear confrontation with himself through his angel-guide Bowie, and with the Wall, a possible metaphor for the walls that separate the character from the outside world and from the "chica de pelo rubio" (blond haired girl) he so desperately wants to love.

In *Héroes*, not one but four walls contribute to the detoxifying adventures of this hero whose only wish is to find his angels and make love to his girl. The true gloom of his reality permeates the novel until the end when the readers are left with a sense of hope that the narrator will indeed leave his four walls and reintegrate himself into society. These hopes are underlined by the last "clip" of the novel that begins with the words: "A veces me imagino con una mujer y un niño corriendo por la casa. Un niño al que abrazar y dar besos, tan pequeño que todavía no está lleno de nada" (180) (Sometimes I imagine myself with a wife and a child running around my house. A little boy to hug and kiss, so small that he is not yet filled with anything). Adulthood becomes a state of congestion where the social impact of violence, death, hatred, mistrust, disappointment, and loneliness is intimately related to the growing up experience. This feeling of saturation becomes the defining characteristic of a human being who admits to feeling totally unanchored by the very end of the novel—"Me siento como un negocio que va cambiando de dueño" (180) (I feel like a business that constantly changes owners). His psychological need is such that in order to move beyond the ugliness of reality/his inner state of being, he must escape into songs. He must liken himself to a rock and roll star to avoid total contamination since, "Sentirte como Jim Morrison no te convierte en Jim Morrison, pero no sentirte como Jim Morrison te convierte en casi nada" (73) (to feel like Jim Morrison does not turn you into Jim Morrison, but to not feel like Jim Morrison turns you into almost nothing).

The rock and roll hero of *Héroes* not only appropriates the words and images of the rock world into his own system of signification but he himself enters the (commercial) consciousness of the many people who buy, read, and listen to the tunes of his life story and incorporate them into their own histories. The movement is multifold as reader/character/rock star constantly shift positions in their individual and collective borrowings and indirect exchanges. The protagonist's feelings of Angst—"Donde escondiste un diente hay ahora un tiburón" (48) (Where once you hid a tooth there is now a shark)—are often introduced through dialogues between himself and anonymous voices that may be conjectured to be that of rock and roll stars, individuals who can reside, like angels, above societies' demands and pressures. These voices trigger the narrator's thought processes at the beginning, middle and end of several chapters, or clips, with questions such as: "¿Qué hacías antes?" (34) (What did you do before?), "¿Qué es lo más triste que recuerdas?" (40) (What is the saddest that you remember?), or "¿Qué esperas de tus canciones?" (63) (What do you expect from your songs?), and provide one of three dialogic connections to a world in which he is alienated from other human beings. The second reference to an outside reader/spectator is that of an anonymous "you" in the singular and plural, referred to directly and indirectly (as others speak to him in the "you" form) when he shares his wisdom after having left his family and his schooling in order to be alone. He says: "No creas todo lo que te dicen, no creas nada de lo que te dicen. Si no te gusta esta fiesta no vuelvas por aquí. Yo podría transformarme en una estrella de rock and roll y desaparecer mientras te lo piensas" (49) (Don't believe everything they tell you, don't believe anything they tell you. If you don't like this party don't come back around here. I could transform myself into a rock and roll star and disappear while you think about it). With this piece of advice he not only invokes the readers' attention through a critical call of authorial subversion, but he also demands that we pay attention to the rapidly changing world, or party, in which he lives. His desire to disappear is in fact closely linked to the reality from which he is attempting to escape: "Claro que quiero ser tan rico como una estrella de rock and roll pero eso es por culpa del precio que le habeis puesto a las cosas" (48) (Of course I want to be as rich as a rock and roll star but that is because of the price you have placed on things). In a defiant stance he shifts his voice toward the readers, toward the potentially integrated members of society, and makes a scathing social commentary about the position of the individual within an economically and commercially dependent society.

The third reference to an outside reader/spectator/listener is that of the multiple references to song titles and names of rock stars sprinkled in the text, from "Light my Fire" by Jim Morrison (73) to Lou Reed's "Walk on the Wild Side" (87). These intertexts demand an audience who is familiar with the aural and verbal effects of songs that, curiously, span several generations and do not necessarily connect with the tastes and musical tradition of the 1990s' generation of teens, the generation most likely associated with the age group of the protagonist (presumably a young adult), thus creating a surprising disconnect between character, possible readers, and music. The disconnect may indeed provide another clue to the alienating force of today's social culture where "true" rock and roll stars find no space to exist. In order for the protagonist to find a place for pure embodiment he must appropriate a musical tradition before his time in order to be able to deal with his own more recent past in the present tense. This process of internalizing media images and songs from the world of rock and roll and combining them with private memories—"te dejaré estar en mis sueños si yo puedo estar en los tuyos" (12) (I will let you be in my dreams if I can be in yours)—to generate new fantasies and dreams, describes how "life" is no longer restricted to the recording or transmission of ideas, but is associated with whatever occupies the present consciousness of the spectator (Kinder 11). In this case the effect is a dissipation of temporal and spatial specificities to provide a very personal juxtaposition of cultural events.

The mind of the narrator functions similarly to a video camera, recording and retrieving one event after another in a reality televisual effect where pieces are not faithfully and beautifully edited together to provide a linear narrative, but where reality is filmed on the go, providing a fragmented or amateur-like home movie. In this home movie, the narrator also functions as producer and spectator of his own life, with the power to pause, fast forward, skip, rewind, or erase sections that he would like to see, not see, or forget. To become a spectator, he must be removed from the "action" and reside in his mind's eye. Here action takes the shape of a video-clip narrative whereby the character can remain physically motionlessness but move in time and space and "belong" to a storyline that will not push him out, as does real life, where, "Las cosas nunca te pasan a ti. Las cosas van demasiado rápido" (66) (Things never happen to you. Things happen too quickly). The screen of the video as a visual vehicle of self-expression presents an outlet for the personal reliving of sensations as it moves beyond memory and immediately re-embodies emotions in time. When compared to cinema, the video, explains the protagonist, allows for a very powerful outlet since:

> Antes cuando iba al cine, trataba de retener la sensación de Al Pacino durante mucho tiempo pero siempre se escapaba y lo que quedaba luego era el recuerdo de la sensación y eso ya no era lo mismo. Con el vídeo puedes tener la sensación aislada como un virus, y recuperarla siempre que quieras. Como el que se pone su sombrero favorito. Como las canciones. Puedes ponerte la sensación *Light my Fire* y salir a la calle. (73)

> (Before when I went to the cinema I tried to retain the sensation of Al Pacino for a long time but it always escaped me and what remained was the memory of a sensation and that is just not the same. With the video you can have the isolated sensation like a virus, and you can recuperate it whenever you want. Like a person who puts on his favorite hat. Like songs. You can put on the sensation of *Light my Fire* and go out into the street.)

His words echo those of Ann Kaplan in *Rocking Around the Clock* who in relation to the power of music videos explains:

> The movie screen harnesses the subject's desire in terms of subjection to a transcendental Subject, appearing momentarily to provide the longed-for plenitude, the television screen rather keeps the subject in the position of discovery of split subjectivity before the mirror and of the actual ensuing decenteredness. The TV screen's constantly changing "texts," of whatever kind, provide the constant promise of a plenitude forever deferred. (50)

The character in *Héroes* cannot keep up with the pace of life in his society, but he can manipulate and recover his own "texts" made up of images and song lyrics. His home video-clip allows him to become the center of his own show that he can, like television, turn on "at the flick of the switch" (Kaplan 28). By erasing any specific reference to family members and friends and not giving any specifics in regard to time, place, name, or physical features, he allows a space to open where he can eliminate any physical needs, elevate himself out of every day life, insert well-known faces of popular icons, and create an interpersonal connection with a wider community whose own pop cult family he shares and can realize. The audio-video format thus allows him to elevate himself into hero status by internalizing media images, combining them with private memories, and generating new fantasies and dreams. The video-clip becomes a vehicle of self-expression and of mental and ultimately physical transcendence as the protagonist decides to not leave the room, "hasta estar verdaderamente capacitado para engrosar las filas de los ángeles" (15) (until he is truly able to enter the ranks of the angels). Rock and its audio-visual and emotional manifestations thus functions in this novel as an actor, a mediator of temporal and spatial movement as well as a divider. What it divides is a physical, delineated and bound body, a metaphor for the effects of time on the self-definition of the character vis-à-vis societal expectations and trauma, and a fluid and continuously moving self that can rise above its own invisibility as (anti-) hero, and become a mythical subject in motion.

Héroes, far from being a superficial take on commercial life and art, presents a very serious commentary on the social effects and the emotional pain of a capitalist society emptied of anything but popular signifiers, signifiers that ironically provide the only means of salvation to the protagonist. As the quotation marks around the originally published song "Héroes" are removed in the title of the novel, its originally intended irony, "in which love rises above walls and conflict" ("David"), is replaced by a humorless take on the word, an imitation of the commercially constructed heroes that surround us on a daily basis. There where emptiness used to reside, is now a series of texts and images that span time frames, spatial frames, cultural frames, and visual and verbal frames. Collapsed in the hero image we now see three figures: the protagonist, the rock and roll star, and the author, and we hear echoing in our ears the lyrics of David Bowie, who sings: "I / I will be king / And you / You will be queen / Though nothing will / Drive them away / We can beat them / Just for one day / We can be Heroes / Just for one day." The use of the first person plural, "we", in "we can beat them" also includes the readers into a construction of heroism as we take up the novel and are asked to reevaluate the influence of audio-visual culture on our own reading habits and on the construction of our own identities.

Notes

1. *Héroes* is Ray Loriga's second book, after *Lo peor de todo* (1992). Subsequently he published *Días extraños* (1994), *Caídos del cielo* (1995), *Tokio ya no nos quiere* (1999), *Trífero* (2000), and *El hombre que inventó Manhattan* (2004).

2. I would like to clarify that while Cristina Moreiras-Menor has also studied the importance of the video-clip in relation to *Héroes*, she bases her study on the use of the video-clip as a stylistic source of imitation that turns the novel into a "video-text," and its role in the legitimation of literary value. What I am trying to do in this paper is to dig even deeper into the theoretical possibilities of the video-clip and to understand the ways in which *Héroes* functions as a video-clip on a multiplicity of spatial, temporal and psychological levels.

3. This scene calls to mind his novel *La pistola de mi hermano*, also known as *Caídos del cielo*.

Works Cited

Allinson, Mark. "The Construction of Youth in Spain in the 1980s and 1990s." *Contemporary Spanish Cultural Studies*. Ed. Barry Jordan and Rikki Morgan-Tamosunas. Oxford: Oxford University Press, 2000. 265–73.

Berland, Jody. "Sound, Image and Social Space: Music Video and Media Reconstruction." *Sound and Vision: The Music Video Reader*. Ed. Simon Frith et al. London: Routledge, 1993. 25–43.

Dalmau, Miguel. "Voces de una conciencia rockera." *El Mundo* 26 Nov. 1993: n.p.

"David Bowie Heroes." July 29th, 2004. <http://www.up-to-date.com/bowie/heroes>

Fouz-Hernández, Santiago. "Generación X? Spanish Urban Youth Culture at the End of the Century in Mañas's/Armendáriz's *Historias del Kronen*." *Romance Studies* 18 (2000): 83–98.

Goldman, Robert and Stephen Papsom. "Advertising in the Age of Accelerated Meaning." *The Consumer Society Reader*. Ed. Juliet Schor and Douglas Holt. New York: The New York Press, 2000. 81–98.

Grossberg, Lawrence. "Putting the Pop Back into Postmodernism." *Universal Abandon? The Politics of Postmodernism*. Ed. Andrew Ross. Minneapolis: University of Minnesota Press, 1998. 167–90.

Kaplan, Ann E. *Rocking Around the Clock: Music Television, Postmodernism, and Consumer Culture*. New York: Methuen, 1987.

Kinder, Marsha. "Music Video and the Spectator: Television, Ideology and Dream." *Film Quarterly* 38:1 (1984): 2–15.

Mañas, José Ángel. "El legado de los Ramones: punk y literatura." *Ajoblanco* 108 (1998): 38–43.

Molinaro, Nina L. "Facing towards Alterity and Spain's 'Other' New Novelists." *ALEC* 30.1.2 (2005): 301–24.

Moreiras-Menor, Cristina. *Cultura herida: literatura y cine en la España democrática.* Madrid: Ediciones Libertarias, 2002.

Polan, Dana. "SZ/MTV." *Journal of Communication Inquiry* 10–1 (1986): 48–54.

Part V
The Soundtrack of Gender: Violating Visions
 and the Psychological Power of Rock

◆ **12**

Watching, Wanting, and the Gen X Soundtrack of Gabriela Bustelo's *Veo Veo*[1]

Nina Molinaro

While the precise contours of Spain's Generation X remain hotly debated (and debatable)[2] critics on both sides of the Atlantic have been quick to seize upon a specific subset of the generational cohort in order to illustrate Peninsular youth culture. This group has been described as hard realists, neorealists, or even dirty realists.[3] Thus far most critical discussions of these writers have focused on novels by José Angel Mañas (and mostly his first novel) and Ray Loriga. The lone woman to be regularly admitted to the elite group is Lucía Etxebarria, who insists upon a feminine and feminizing vision of contemporary Spain, and whose considerable success hinges at least in part on her image management. Less well-known, Gabriela Bustelo articulates another feminine version of Generation X narrative. In particular, *Veo Veo* (1996)[4] her first novel, continues and tests Etxebarria's critique.

Like other Spanish Gen X novelists, Bustelo populates *Veo Veo* with twenty-something urban consumers who look to sex, drugs, and contemporary popular music for stimulation, signposts, and significance. As with Mañas's groundbreaking *Historias del Kronen* (1994), the action of *Veo Veo* is organized around the present-day nightclub scene in Madrid, and in both texts a first-person narrator/protagonist shifts from place to place in search of the next high. The two novels also insist upon referentiality, but *Veo Veo* teeters towards extravagance in its encyclopedic list of current films, actors, directors, TV shows, celebrities, Madrid landmarks, marketing icons, designers, and most importantly for my subsequent argument, recent popular music; in essence, the trauma of Bustelo's novel unfolds to a veritable panoply of musical references that largely point towards American and British pop music from the 1980s. Moreover, while *Veo Veo* shares with many other Gen X novels an exacting commitment to popular culture, Spanish and otherwise, unlike these other novels, Bustelo's text embeds the peripatetic journey of its female narrator/protagonist Vania Barcia within an elaborately articulated external threat that, in equal measure, propels the plot and the characters forward and resists narrative closure.[5]

Vania, whose identity is not revealed until mid-way through the novel, begins her odyssey (and, not coincidentally, the narration of her "talking cure") by consulting with an unnamed male psychiatrist, in order to dispel the overriding sense that she has acquired an unwelcome and unknown stalker. The unnamed psychiatrist prescribes a vacation and sends Vania on her way, but when she exits his office she finds that she is again being shadowed by her stalker. She immediately hires Peláez, a private detective, who subsequently discovers hidden microphones and two-way mirrors in her apartment, video recording equipment in the neighboring apartment, and a slew of videotapes that document Vania's most intimate moments in her bathroom and bedroom.

In response to proof that she is indeed being actively monitored by someone, Vania sets off on a two-week spree, which lasts almost the duration of the novel, through Madrid's fashionable (and not so fashionable) nightclubs, restaurants, and bars. In the process, she returns to former haunts, rekindles former friendships, and renews her former interest in alcohol and drugs. She also meets Ben Ganza, a mysterious Brazilian who unaccountably knows everyone she knows and shows up wherever she happens to be.

Predictably, the pair embarks on an extended seduction. Much less predictably, in the final twenty pages of the novel, Vania mistakes her lover for an intruder and shoots him dead with Peláez's gun. She then receives an anonymous letter that reveals Ben was in fact a jilted and vengeful ex-lover whom Vania had rejected several years prior to the narrative present. He had emigrated to Brazil, made his fortune, and undergone extensive plastic surgery after a motorcycle accident. When all the pieces of his plan were in place, he returned to Spain and, over the course of several years, thoroughly infiltrated her world.

When Vania learns the extent and depth of the conspiracy plot against her, she comes undone, buys her own gun, and returns to her apartment intent on committing suicide. At the last minute she instead turns the gun towards one of the two-way mirrors and unintentionally kills Peláez, who has been watching her with a video camera located on the other side of the mirror, in the adjacent apartment. Vania understandably panics, not so understandably returns to the office of the psychiatrist, and confesses everything. He convinces her to check into a "sanatorium" and drives her home to pack a suitcase. When they enter her apartment, however, they find no dead body, no broken mirror, no gun, and no evidence that any of the events from the previous two weeks have happened. After voluntarily spending several days heavily tranquilized at an unspecified mental institution on the outskirts of Madrid and meeting another patient whose history eerily resembles her own, she decides to return home. Vania opens the door of her apartment to the sound of the telephone ringing and when she answers, a male voice—the same male voice that has been calling throughout the novel—again asks for Soledad. The last line of the novel simulates the sound of an otherwise occupied telephone line, "Bip-bip-bip-bip. Bip-bip-bip. Bip-bip. Bip" (175).

Throughout her story, the narrator bolsters her waning self-confidence by listening to, remembering, and philosophizing about a musical soundtrack that includes more than thirty artists and/or songs largely taken from the 1980s era of rock, pop, jazz, and rhythm and blues.[6] In marked contrast to the visuality that initiates and sustains the threat and periodic reality of hypervigilance, the aurality of contemporary pop music appears to thwart the encroachment of unwanted visual attention, time after time returning the principal listener of the novel to sanity, coherence, and community. The pleasure of listening dominates Vania's experience and narrative, as music consistently trumps all other stimulants in the novel. At the level of textual structure, musical references also considerably outnumber allusions to other fields of cultural signifiers, such as film and literature, perhaps in order to bear witness to Will Straw's observation that "[m]usic is . . . among the most ubiquitous, easily ignored and trivialized of all cultural forms. . . . [M]usic seems to enter our ears uninvited, as 'something literally breathed into the body from the air.' This, too, is a way of 'consuming' music, alongside the more spectacularly obsessive ways which make music the centre of attention" (55).

Part of the allure of *Veo Veo* derives from the ways in which Bustelo successfully (re)creates a trail of musical consumption, not to mention a consumer of music, that traverses the continuum from unconscious absorption to outright obsession, and back again. Like most characters in Gen X narrative, Vania is first and foremost a consumer, and she habitually inflects her consumption with a sense of nostalgia, an attitude that she exhibits primarily through her idyllic recollection of recently past musical experiences and preferences. But Bustelo decisively situates her main character at the brink of physical, emotional, and even moral chaos by drawing a clear boundary between Vania's moderate (and moderated) habits of consumption before the action of the novel and her increasingly frenetic behavior throughout the two weeks that mark a literal return to sex, drugs, and rock & roll. Through her identification with popular music, and with particular kinds of popular music from a particular historical and cultural moment, Vania establishes an explicit connection to her own history, while also projecting an anachronistic sense of herself. In one sense the protagonist adheres to the youth cult of "vivir al día" (Allinson 266) (to live for the present day), but in another sense her return to hedonism is spectacularly signaled as a return, implicating her prior departure and, with it, her exile from the attitude of the truly young. Vania's narrative traces the paradoxical path of a subject who attempts to fully inhabit a present moment that is literally and figuratively shot through and through with her past. By the end of the novel, the only available future appears to be yet another return to the same.

Moreover, in a narrative text characterized by the protagonist's frequent invective directed to the lack of novelty available to her from the recycled cultural icons and events at hand, music extends to the novel's primary consumer the happy illusion of newness, difference, and revelation, via familiar and familiarly recuperated sounds. In short, music haunts *Veo Veo,* turning the narrator on by turning her (back) into a global user who learns anew that she must return to past pleasures in order to compensate for the failure and fear that characterize the uncontrollable circumstances of her present.[7] Music marks the time of those past pleasures. Significantly, the first musical reference, in the form of an epigraph taken from Lou Reed's "I'll Be Your Mirror," exceeds the formal confines of Vania's story: *"I'll be your mirror. / Reflect what you are in case you don't know"* (7, italics in the original).[8] The game between hearing and seeing, woven here and elsewhere in the novel into a romance-inspired idealistic fusion, begins with an explicit doubling[9] echoed in the title of the novel, between (male) seeing subject and (female) seen object, and the reader is strategically positioned between the two. The "use" of Lou Reed's music might appear to gesture towards cultural resistance, given Reed's longstanding association with the Velvet Underground, but because "I'm Your Mirror" features a delicate ballad organized around protective love, the gesture is withdrawn almost as soon as it appears.[10]

Early in the novel, while dancing to "temas todavía más antológicos" (75) (even more anthological topics), Vania herself links Lou Reed to The Rolling Stones, The Mammas and the Papas, and the Supremes (75), a relatively heterogeneous set of musicians who presumably have in common, at least within the context of *Veo Veo*, an iconic status, a certain interchangeability, and the ability to produce music that can be recycled into dance tracks. There is no cultural rebellion, typically associated with the pioneers of rock & roll, here or elsewhere in the novel, because the opportunity has long since passed, accompanied by Vania's youth. Popular music instead leads the way to cultural reappropriation and permits its listener to temporarily eclipse her current circumstances and imagine another time, place, and self. The soundtrack of the novel permits her to do something else and be someone else, and Reed's song sets the tone, the mood, and the relationship between consuming subject and consumed object. Given that *Veo Veo* explores the conflict between public and private, and the ways in which sensorial experience regulates both, it is not coincidental that music potentially occupies the space between the two, and that Vania uses music to bridge the gap. As Straw notes, music is "one of the most effective markers of public presence and social difference" (7). In a text regularly subjected to the partial perspective of an intensely solipsistic narrator, the initial appearance of Lou Reed's song suggests the public nature of intimacy and the private consequences of social difference.

Song lyrics notably inaugurate the novel, and songs constitute the primary musical medium of the text, whether they compel their listener to create a specific environment, conjure up pleasurable memories, and/or wax lyrical on the virtues of Music.[11] All of the aforementioned yield the same result: Vania feels emotional satisfaction and physical pleasure, she undergoes social connectedness, and she generally reassures herself that she is in control, even by being paradoxically out of control. All the uses to which music is subjected within the novel permit Vania to exert power over her narrative and her chronology, and to demonstrate agency and creativity in her life.

Control, at least for Vania, often resides in words about music. While she might want her listener to think otherwise, she is an explicitly verbal narrator, a woman who wants to be heard and even, as the novel moves forward, seen. It is telling that she consumes music by weaving song lyrics into the chronicle of her life. For example, during one of her trips by taxi to and from the many, seemingly interchangeable nightclubs (Amnesia, Archy, Café, Chusmi, Complot, Hispano, Joy, Pachá, Trainera and 42), the driver plays a song by American bluesman Robert Cray that includes the line "No hay nada como una mujer" (34) (there's nothing like a woman). After remarking on the enjoyment produced by hearing her preferred guitarist, she uses the song lyric to justify her negative conception of men, which flows from the singer to all men, and then to Ben Ganza, the current object of her sexual attraction. In a twist on Straw's suggestion that "Music compels us to judge the pleasure of others" (55), the character of Vania uses music to judge her own pleasure and desire in relation to the pleasure and desire of others, and she also exhibits her desires and pleasures, and her taste in music, up to the prospective assessment of her listener.

In a similar vein, during another evening on the club circuit, she asks the DJ to play "el tema que dice '¿Cómo puedes bailar cuando nuestras camas están ardiendo?'" (62) (the song that says 'How can you dance when our beds are burning?') (Midnight Oil's "Beds Are Burning"). Although the song was originally directed towards inciting civil resistance, in the novel the song serves only to supplement Vania's illusion that she can temporarily escape the confines of the material world: "Cuando yo cogía el ritmo de la música, me daba la sensación de ir al compás de la mismísima Tierra Madre. Me dejaba llevar de tal manera que perdía la noción de todo" (63) (When I got the rhythm of the music, it gave me the feeling of going to the beat of Mother Earth herself. I let myself go so far that I lost track of everything). Although she utilizes words to generate the sensorial connection, the song almost instantly "elevates" her into a state of imagined synthesis, a state to which she returns repeatedly via her musical memories.

She also uses contemporary popular music, and in particular the names of discrete musicians and songs, as a kind of shorthand reference system that positively marks her mood and her history. She happily sings along to La Unión's "Ella es un volcán" (25) (She's a Volcano) as a testimony to her own self-sufficiency, and thoughts of Rocío Jurado's "Como una ola" (27) (Like a Wave) accompany her anticipation of good whiskey and a vacation. When she hears Prince's "Little Red Corvette" during a taxi ride, she cannot help but hum and drum to "el ritmo más sesudo de nuestro siglo. La mente más cristalina y cachonda" (32) (the wisest rhythm of our century. The clearest and hottest mind). She listens to Mink Deville's "Spanish Stroll" (39) while driving the streets of Madrid and turns up an unnamed song by Ernie Isley to full volume in order to dance naked in her bathroom (60). The music of Teddy Pendergrass elicits feelings of gratitude, fortitude, and vitality (71), while she plays songs by Anna Domino, "la esperanza personificada" (79) (hope personified), in order to temporarily forget everything else. And at the height of her romance with Ben Ganza, she wants to buy flowers and play Nat King Cole (141).

In an alternative version of the same, Vania frequently returns to song lyrics in order to reify the intensity of her sexual attraction to Ben, a plot line that initially justifies her constant movement and eventually unravels, through the artificial appearance of a letter, to reveal that her stalker is in fact part of a much larger conspiracy designed to exact revenge upon Vania for her rejection, some years before, of a former lover, who just happens to be Ben Ganza, remade and unrecognizable. For example, she describes one of the frequent melodramatic scenes in which she and Ben exchange meaningful looks across a crowded room: "Le vi. Estaba de espaldas a mí, con la cabeza girada hacia atrás, en la misma postura que yo. Nos quedamos mirándonos, imantados. Intenté moverme, pero no podia. No podía hacer nada más que seguir mirando. . . . En ese momento lo supe. Supe que era verdad lo que cantaba Prince. 'Eyes never lie.' Los ojos nunca mienten" (65) (I saw him. He had his back turned toward me, with his head turned around towards me, in exactly the same position as me. Our eyes were glued to each other, like magnets. I tried to move, but I couldn't. I couldn't do anything but keep looking at him. . . . In that instant I knew. I knew that Prince told the truth when he sang 'Eyes never lie'). In an unconscious reversal of the epigraph, Vania literally mirrors her beloved, and, as happens repeatedly in her listening experience, succeeds in believing that she has transcended the present time and space. When she searches for the words to articulate her sensation, she finds a song lyric, which itself functions as shorthand for a mood. Only music, it would appear, can approximate the magnetic appeal that she and Ben seem to exert on one another.

On other occasions Vania employs music to synthesize negative perceptions and events. She refers to the title of Wings's "Live and Let Die" (1978) to capture the artificiality of Madrid's jet set, "un auténtico still life del paraíso postizo" (61) (an authentic still life of fake paradise). Mecano's "Me colé en una fiesta" (I gatecrashed a party) provides an apt description of her circumstances and humor when she finds herself naked in a swimming pool at a stranger's house party. The Doors's "The End" (1967) serves as the soundtrack for her aborted suicide attempt. And at the end of her stay in the sanitarium, Vania announces to her current psychiatrist, "Sí, doctor, aunque debo decirle que me apena enormemente no poder seguir una terapia con usted, pero ya se sabe, no siempre se consigue lo que se quiere, como dice Mick Jagger" (171) (Yes, doctor, although I should tell you that it saddens me greatly that I can't continue therapy with you, but, you know, like Mick Jagger says, you can't always get what you want). By ironically describing her situation against the chorus of the Rolling Stones's classic song, she distances herself from her listener, she exerts verbal (and emotional) oneupsmanship, and she suggests that she will, in fleeing from the psychiatrist and the institution, certainly be getting what she needs.

In equal measure, music is fused to Vania's memories, and she uses it to forget the present moment and remember her past. At the most obvious level of plot, she associates certain musicians, such as Fine Young Cannibals, with the initiation of friendships (42), some of which remain constant and some of which do not. In a larger sense, her entire re-visitation of the Madrid club scene recalls her uncontrolled habits prior to her year of abstinence, and then metonymically reminds her of her well spent (because misspent) youth. When she goes to the Sol nightclub, for example, she recollects better times and a more vibrant self: "En el Sol, que me conocía de arriba abajo, con todos sus entresijos, había visto y vivido las movidas más increíbles . . . . Además, se ligaba desaforadamente y ponían la buena música de toda la vida, Cars, Motels, Pretenders, no sé, esas canciones que uno quiere oír sin saberlo hasta que las oye" (74) (At Sol, which was absolutely familiar to me from top to bottom, with all its ins and outs, I had seen and lived the most incredible things . . . . Besides, we hooked up like crazy and they always played the great music of life, the Cars, the Motels, the Pretenders, I don't know, those songs that you want to hear without knowing it until you hear them). Sex and music, in her memory, complemented one another, even though she cannot quite remember (or does not want to) the names or the content of the songs. Desire, in her formulation, exceeds both language and knowledge, and resides squarely in the pleasures of listening.

Another example of this same move towards idealization occurs with Van Morrison's "The Mystery." The resident DJ offers to play a track from Morrison's recently televised live concert which, coincidentally, once again transports her beyond words. The lines, quoted in the text in Spanish, come from Morrison's "The Mystery": "Let go into the mystery / Let yourself go / There is no other place to be / Baby this I know" (72). This particular song inspires its listener to effusively elucidate the intangible value of music: "Hay canciones que se oyen una vez y se recuerdan siempre. A mí me ocurrió con aquella. Me parecía un mensaje de los cielos, codificado y sólo entendible para mí. El hilo invisible de melodía, letra y voz me producía ese cosquillero eléctrico en la nuca que me paralizaba de puro placer" (72) (There are songs that you hear once and remember forever, which is what happened to me with that one. It seemed to be a message from heaven, coded and only understandable to me. The invisible thread of the melody, lyrics, and voice gave me an electric tickle on my neck that paralized me with pure pleasure). In Vania's formulation, and as evidenced by the novel itself, music resists forgetfulness and proffers divine knowledge, translated into physical sensations. Over and over again the pleasures of listening far outweigh other kinds of potential and real pleasures.

Pleasure in *Veo Veo* is both public and private. While Vania spends most of the novel moving between public spaces (be they diurnal or nocturnal), when at home she inevitably listens to her favorite music in order to create a sense of nostalgia, on the one hand, and (re)capture a sense of timelessness, on the other.

One night, for example, she listens to Robbie Robertson's "Somewhere Down the Crazy River," the Motels's "Change My Mind," and Squeeze's "Cigarette of a Single Man" in succession and concludes that the best moments of her life, always past, were associated with a particular song: "Si me ponía a hacer zapping con mi vida, siempre había una banda Sonora. Siempre estaba la Música, la más abstracta de las artes, puesto que no es símbolo, como los demás, de nada real. Una melodía no representa nada, como la pintura, ni utiliza un lenguaje con significados, como la literatura. Para empezar, la música ni siquiera es corpórea. Es puro éter" (134) (If I started to flip through my life, there was always a soundtrack. There was always Music, the most abstract of all the arts, given that it isn't a symbol of anything real, like the other arts. A melody doesn't represent anything, unlike painting, and it doesn't use language with meaning, unlike literature. To begin with, music isn't even corporeal. It's pure aether). Listening to music, and more particularly to a series of favorite songs, engenders a "sublime connection" that rivals the individual components of the chain in both aesthetic value and transformative bliss. The narrator further differentiates between sound (la Música) (Music) and songs (la música cantada) (sung music) insofar as the latter takes her away from herself while the former permeates and transcends physical human existence.

But music, especially when it is condensed into a sound track, is an unavoidably temporal phenomenon and as such must come to an end. Vania eventually runs out of songs and into herself. When she kills Ben, or when she thinks that she kills him, her narrative and her life begin to vertiginously destabilize. She returns both literally and figuratively to the site of her original quest: a male authority figure to counteract the masculine desire that has, for better or worse, thus far controlled her. The last sounds, in the shape of a decreasing number of "bips," are not musical, or even verbal, but they do reinforce an endgame that even Vania's considerable repertoire of musical pleasures cannot contest. It seems only fitting that the repeated sounds fade and eventually disappear altogether, leaving nothing for Vania, and the reader, to listen to or for.

Notes

1. Thanks are due to Tony Molinaro who tracked down many of the musical references, made available several of the songs referred to in *Veo Veo,* and generously shared his vast knowledge of contemporary pop music.
2. I have in mind the discussion initially established during the latter half of the 1990s across the following series of articles and special issues: Toni Dorca's "Joven narrativa

en la España de los noventa: la generación X," Germán Gullón's "Cómo se lee una novela de la última generación (Apartado X)" and his introduction to the Destino edition of José Angel Mañas's *Historias del Kronen* (1994), Sabas Martín's "Narrativa española tercer milenio (guía para usuarios), " Noemí Montetes Mairal's "En el nombre de hoy," Carmen de Urioste's "La narrativa española de los noventa: ¿Existe una 'generación X'? Manuel Vázquez Montalbán's "La generación XYZ," in the March 1996 issue of *Quimera* devoted to "Narrativa española: Últimas tendencias," and the 1996 volume of *Insula* dedicated to "Narrativa española al filo del milenio."

3. Maria T. Pao also analyzes Mañas's *Historias del Kronen* as as an example of blank fiction, a term that may, I believe, usefully be extended to the works of other Spanish Gen X writers who choose realism as their dominant narrative strategy.

4. Gabriela Bustelo works as a professional translator and, in that capacity, has translated a number of children's books from the original English into Spanish. In addition to her translation of Kipling's 1894 classic *The Jungle Book* (published in Spain as *El Libro de la Selva* [Madrid: Anaya, 1995]), she has translated five installments of Beverly Cleary's "Ramona" series for young adults: *Ramona y su madre* (Madrid: Espasa, 1989), *Ramona y su padre* (Madrid: Espasa, 1989), *!Viva, Ramona* (Madrid: Espasa Calpe 1990), *Ramona empieza el curso* (Madrid: Espasa, 1993), and *Ramona la valiente* (Madrid: Espasa, 2000). To my knowledge, no critical studies have yet been dedicated exclusively to *Veo Veo*, although Toni Dorca incorporates Bustelo's novel into his discussion of Spain's Generación X and José María Izquierdo also mentions Bustelo in passing in his article on "Narradores españoles novísimos de los años noventa." Interestingly, Carmen de Urioste does not refer to Bustelo or *Veo Veo* in her 1997–1998 essay on Spain's Generación X, but she does include *Veo Veo* in her subsequent article on "Narrative of Spanish Women Writers of the Nineties: An Overview."

5. While it is not the primary focus of my argument, I would be remiss not to mention the richly textured parodic humor, concentrated in the self-consciously ironic tone, vocabulary, and discursive style of the narrator, that infuses the novel. Perhaps the most obvious source for this humor consists in the ways in which the novel translates the threat of visibility into an expanding dynamics of paranoia and elevates one woman's fear of being watched to the status of an immanent cultural phenomenon. Regarding the connection between humor and paranoia, in many ways *Veo Veo* represents both counter example and complement to Javier Tomeo's numerous narrative texts, such as *La agonía de Proserpina* (1993), in which masculinity expresses itself through excessive vigilance. We might in fact read Bustelo's text as a feminine response to the twisted ethics of masculine paranoia. See my article on *La agonía* for a further discussion of paranoia, masculinity, and visuality.

6. Vania names musical artists (or groups) and refers to song titles and/or lyrics in roughly equal measure. In some instances, a single line from a song lyric accompanies the name of a musician; in other instances, the musical reference features an oblique song lyric or series of lyrics; and on three occasions the protagonist mentions

a song title without the name of the artist. In chronological order, Vania incorporates the following musical references (I indicate information not included in *Veo Veo* parenthetically): lyrics from Lou Reed ("I'll Be Your Mirror)," "Ella es un volcán" (by La Unión), Rocío Jurado's "Como una ola," Prince's "Little Red Corvette," lyrics from Robert Cray's "Nothin' But a Woman," Mink Deville's "Spanish Stroll," FYC (Fine Young Cannibals), Ernie Isley, Wings's "Live and Let Die," a lyric from "Beds are Burning" (by Midnight Oil), Nina Simone's "My Baby Just Cares for Me," a lyric from Prince ("Slow Love"), lyrics from Van Morrison ("The Mystery"), Teddy Pendergrass, David Sanborn [sic], Mike River, the Cars, the Motels, the Pretenders, Steve Miller, Lou Reed, The Rolling Stones, the Mammas and Papas, the Supremes, a lyric from Mecano ("Me colé en una fiesta"), Anna Domino, Patricia Kraus, Leonard Cohen's "I'm Your Man," Robbie Robertson's "Crazy River" (the correct title of which is "Somewhere Down the Crazy River"), Martha Davis's "Change My Mind" (Martha Davis was the lead singer for the Motels), Guy Beart, Squeeze's "Cigarette of a Single Man," lyrics from George Michael 's "Faith," Nat King Cole, The Doors's "The End," "La vie en rose," and the title lyric from the Rolling Stones's "You Can't Always Get What You Want." Significantly, of the thirty-seven references, all but five are from U.S and British musicians, and of those five, only two, La Unión's "Ella es un volcán" and Mecano's "Me colé en una fiesta" correspond to the 1980s popular music scene in Spain.

7.   Although it is well beyond the scope of my current argument, the phenomenon of spectrality might well infuse, to a greater or lesser extent, all Generación X narrative. Jo Labanyi's Introduction to *Constructing Identity in Contemporary Spain* is especially suggestive in this regard; she theorizes that in contemporary Spain spectral traces of history and historical trauma unavoidably insert themselves into unconscious cultural memory such that it is possible to read modern Spanish culture as a ghost story (6). She further observes that "'Non-legitimate' forms of culture can be rendered 'ghostly' not just by being ignored, but also by being represented through ideological schemes that are those of 'legitimate' culture" (4). I would argue that this is precisely what happens in *Veo Veo* through the novel's schematization of popular music references. Following this line of thought, we also might read Bustelo's novel as an acute example of the conservative results of cultural hybridization, which Labanyi defines as "culture as a 'recycling' process in which nothing is lost but returns in new hybridized forms, adapting to changed circumstances" (12).

8.   Gabriela Bustelo follows the English-language text with a bracketed Spanish-language translation: "Seré tu espejo. / Reflejaré lo que eres, por si no lo sabes" (7). This is one of the few times that Bustelo includes both the English and the Spanish versions of a given song lyric. She is also inconsistent with English-language song titles; in some cases she gives only the original English-language title and in other cases she includes only the Spanish-language translation. In my essay I refer, unless otherwise noted, to the original versions of all song titles, whether they be in English, Spanish or, as is the case with "La vie en rose," French.

9. Doubling is also a crucial component of paranoia in general and gendered paranoia in particular, as I demonstrate in my article on Tomeo's *La agonía de Proserpina* (138–40).
10. "I'll Be Your Mirror" was originally performed by Nico and the Velvet Underground in 1967. The first recording of Lou Reed's solo version of the song occurred in 1974 on the *Perfect Night—Live in London* album. Bustelo includes three other salient, and in two cases iconic, songs that precede 1980: Wings's "Live and Let Die" (recorded in 1973 for the film by the same title and in 1978 on *Wings Greatest Hits*), Mink Deville's "Spanish Stroll" (from *Cabretta*, released in 1977), and The Doors's "The End" (from *The Doors*, 1967).
11. The one exception to this rule, and there are inevitably exceptions to all of Vania's rules, is David Sanborn, a jazz saxophonist. Tellingly, however, she does not actually listen or even talk about Sanborn's music; rather, she uses his album cover as a surface on which to arrange a line of cocaine.

Works Cited

Allinson, Mark. "The Construction of Youth in Spain in the 1980s and 1990s." *Contemporary Spanish Cultural Studies*. Ed. Barry Jordan and Rikki Morgan-Tamosunas. London: Arnold, 2000. 265–73.

Bustelo, Gabriela. *Veo Veo*. Barcelona: Anagrama, 1996.

Dorca, Toni. "Joven narrativa en la España de los noventa: la generación X." *Revista de Estudios Hispánicos* 31 (1997): 309–24.

Gullón, Germán. "Cómo se lee una novela de la última generación (Apartado X)." *Insula* 589–590 (1996): 31–33.

_____. "Introducción." José Angel Mañas. *Historias del Kronen*. Barcelona: Destino, 1998 [1994]. V–XXXIX.

Izquierdo, José María. "Narradores españoles novísimos de los años noventa." *Revista de Estudios Hispánicos* 35 (2001): 293–308.

Labanyi, Jo. "Introduction: Engaging with Ghosts; or, Theorizing Culture in Modern Spain." *Constructing Identity in Contemporary Spain*. Ed. Jo Labanyi. Oxford: Oxford University Press, 2002. 1–14.

Martín, Sabas. "Narrativa española tercer milenio (guía para usuarios)." *Páginas amarillas*. Madrid: Lengua de Trapo, 1997. IX–XXX.

Molinaro, Nina L. "Writing Masculinity Double: Paranoia, Parafiction and Javier Tomeo's *La agonía de Prosperpina*." *Anales de la Literatura Española Contemporánea* 24 (1999): 135–48.

Montetes Mairal, Noemí. "En el nombre de hoy." *Qué he hecho yo para publicar esto*. Ed. Noemí Montetes Mairal. Barcelona: DVD ediciones, 1999. 11–34.

Pao, Maria T. "Sex, Drugs, and Rock & Roll: *Historias del Kronen* as Blank Fiction." *Anales de la literatura española contemporánea* 27.2 (2002): 245/531–260/546.

Quimera 145 (1996): 35–48.

Straw, Will. "Consumption." In *The Cambridge Companion to Pop and Rock*. Ed. Simon Frith, Will Straw, and John Street. Cambridge: Cambridge University Press, 2001. 53–73.

Urioste, Carmen de. "La narrativa española de los noventa: ¿Existe una 'generación X'?" *Letras Peninsulares* 10.3 (1997–1998): 455–76.

_____. "Narrative of Spanish Women Writers of the Nineties: An Overview." *Tulsa Studies in Women's Literature* 20.2 (2001): 279–95.

Vázquez Montalbán, Manuel. "La generación XYZ." *Un polaco en la corte del Rey Juan Carlos*. Barcelona: Planeta, 1996. 360–86.

◆ **13**

Saved by Art: Entrapment and Freedom
in Icíar Bollaín's *Te doy mis ojos*

Linda Gould Levine

Much of the literary and cinematographic production of Spain's Generation X has been characterized by its nihilism, disengagement from an agenda for social and political change, dependence on the image as a basis for identity formation, and interest in representing different forms of popular culture, violence, and mass consumption (Moreiras Menor 188, 190). While the birth date of Icíar Bollaín (1967), scriptwriter and film director, coincides with that of members of the Generation X, her most recent film, *Te doy mis ojos* (2003), situates itself in a different ideological and esthetic terrain. Evoking the feminist concerns of a previous generation, it represents a successful attempt to use film as a medium for creating heightened public awareness about one of Spain's most serious social issues, domestic violence.

To the great surprise of the director herself, the film's disregard for conventional formulas of entertainment did not impede its acclaim at the 2004 Goya award ceremony in Madrid where it won seven awards, among them for best movie, director, script, sound, actor, actress, and supporting actress. Bollaín's eloquent acceptance speech was in consonance with the content of her film; she not only emphasized the need to cultivate freedom of expression in film making, but also paid tribute to the victims of domestic abuse, the Iraqi war, and ETA.[1] While her invocation of three disparate groups of Spaniards reflects her concern for social and political issues, Bollaín's approach to the pressing reality of domestic violence in *Te doy mis ojos* (Take My Eyes) transcends contemporary Spanish society. It offers her spectators a complex artistic and narrative structure that historicizes male power, privileges sixteenth and seventeenth-century painting as a mirror for the female protagonist's self reflection, recontextualizes classical mythology in the light of contemporary gender relations, and juxtaposes the invisibility of battered women in Spanish society with the visibility of female bodies in the paintings of Titian and Rubens.

This is not the first time that Bollaín has used her films to address issues related to women and their position in a patriarchal society that is simultaneously characterized by tremendous change and ingrained structures resistant to an egalitarian agenda for women and men. If, as critic Susan Martin-Márquez perceptively notes, Bollaín's "treatment of notions of home, of displacement, and of cultural differences" (257) is a central preoccupation in *Hola, ¿estás sola?* (Hi, Are You Alone?) (1995), and *Flores de otro mundo* (Flowers from Another World) (1999), these concepts evolve significantly in the nine-year period between her first film and *Te doy mis ojos*; most notably, the theme of domestic violence is more and more pronounced in each successive film. Reflecting what some critics consider a post-feminist mentality (Andrews and Brooksbank Jones, 235), *Hola, ¿estás sola?* portrays its marginal twenty-year-old protagonists, Niña and Trini, interpreted respectively by Silke and Candela Peña, in search of a new definition of home that replaces absent parents, maternal indifference, and patriarchal dominance with female bonding and amorous pairings with sensitive men. Bollaín skillfully juxtaposes two different models of gender and power relations through the harsh slap on the face Niña's father gives her when she challenges his concept of "normalcy" and the continually tender gaze of her Russian lover, Olaf, that illuminates her face and dispels sadness and loss.

While the bohemian Niña has the freedom to leave her paternal home and its explicit overtones of domination, Bollaín suggests in her second film, *Flores de otro mundo*, that marked economic and social disparities between men and women not only fuel domestic abuse but complicate for women the process of extrication. Problematizing the concept of "home" in a context of immigration, globalization, and the clash between such different "hybrid temporalities" as "the colonial time represented by the black female immigrants, and the time of the Spanish countryside represented by the mostly masculine community of Santa Eulalia" (Martín-Cabrera 48), Bollaín portrays the bolstering of patriarchal structures in Santa Eulalia through the town's "experiment" of importing women from Caribbean countries and urban settings to couple with or marry local men.

If in *Hola, ¿estás sola?* Olaf is seen as the mysterious "other," whose subjectivity is obscured by his limited command of Spanish but whose persona (and race) radiates a presence that impedes his reduction to ethnic clichés (Martin-Márquez 260, 261), the voluptuous Cuban immigrant Milady in *Flores de otro mundo*, interpreted by Marilyn Torres, is immediately stigmatized as the loose female or colonial version of the "wildly erotic black woman" (Martín-Cabrera 51), who is violently beaten by her older lover, Candelo, after she temporarily escapes to the city. If Milady's decision to leave Candelo and Santa Eulalia is initially complicated by her lack of resources, her status as lover and not wife, as well as the support she receives from her female friend, Patricia, interpreted by Lissete Mejía, facilitates her escape. Hence, despite the "pathologization of the black female body" in *Flores de otro mundo* (Martín-Cabrera 51), Bollaín allows for the recuperation of female autonomy and freedom from violent relationships steeped in ancestral traditions and stereotypes.

While *Hola, ¿estás sola?* and *Flores de otro mundo* focus on external and internal threats to the concept of home and introduce domestic violence as one of a myriad of topics relating to the complex portrayal of dislocation and change, Bollaín's social agenda in *Te doy mis ojos* is more textured; she grounds her film in a highly disturbing reality lived by women today at the same time that she examines compelling issues in art history across the centuries. Cultivating the primacy of the image that defines film as well as Generation X esthetics and values, she seamlessly weaves together images of domestic life as well as of art, and challenges her spectators to discover the relationship between the two. The lens of her camera, guided by a feminist sensitivity, is particularly adept in capturing the psychological drama involving her two protagonists, interpreted with great skill by actors Laia Marull and Luis Tosar. As her story unfolds, we witness how Pilar, whose eyes and being have been appropriated by her husband Antonio, discovers a new piece of herself while studying painting and mythology and explicating, as a volunteer tour guide, Titian's 1553 *Danaë*.[2] Her growing sense of self provokes, in turn, anger and fear in her husband, who feels threatened by the delight his wife finds in an image other than his own and by the sensual women in the paintings who are framed beyond his reach.

Jealousy and possession, art as simulacrum and sublimation of reality, scopophilia or the pleasure of looking versus surveillance, woman as subject and object of desire, Toledo as a site of exclusion and liberation, the husband as creator (Rubens) or destroyer (Antonio), and responses to art in the past and present are some of the themes called into question by this conflict. The result is a tightly-knit film that situates itself in the historical past and the present as well as in reality and representation, mythology and pathology, and entrapment and freedom, engaging the spectator both intellectually and emotionally. This essay reflects my fascination with the role of art as a catalyst for Pilar's liberation and re-vision of self and the suggestive reconfigurations of canonical thought that emerge from Bollaín's creative fusion of dominant male culture and marginalized female subjectivity.

The tense beginning of the film, highlighted with a haunting background music, proves easily identifiable to victims of domestic abuse. Pilar quietly wakes up her son, Juan, quickly gathers together some of their belongings, rushes out of their apartment, and catches a bus that takes them to her sister Ana's apartment in another part of Toledo. Unable to express the depth of her terror and fear to Ana (interpreted by Candela Peña), she breaks down only when she realizes that she has escaped from home still wearing her slippers. When Ana returns to Pilar's apartment to retrieve some of her clothes, Bollaín subtly introduces the metaphorical content of her film through concrete references that suggest the various meanings of the movie's title. The mirror in Pilar's house has been broken, the hospital records that Ana finds indicate that Pilar has loss of vision in one eye: during her nine-year marriage, she has indeed handed over her identity and sense of self to her husband.

As Bollaín develops the film through three different perspectives—Pilar's independent life as separated wife and mother and attendant in charge of selling tickets to the Church of Santo Tomé, Antonio's relationship with his therapist and group session and attempts to control his violence, and the reuniting of the two when Pilar moves back in and trains to be a tour guide—she cloaks each aspect of their individual and joint reality in an artistic subtext that offers a nuanced version of male dominance and power. Script writers Bollaín and Alicia Luna eloquently underscore this aspect of the film through their choice of Toledo as the setting for their story. By Bollaín's own account:

> . . . Toledo contaba mejor que cualquier diálogo todo ese peso histórico, de tradición, de cultura que tenemos todos detrás, el papel del hombre, el de la mujer. Cómo mencionar si no es con una imagen a tantos hombres poderosos, reyes, nobles, obispos y papas que desde los cuadros que cuelgan en la sala Capitular de la Catedral nos recuerdan quién ha tenido el poder durante siglos, quién ha decidido cómo se tenía que vivir. Y cómo se tenía que sufrir, como *la Dolorosa*, cabeza baja, lágrimas contenidas. (Bollaín, "Historia" 16)

(Toledo conveyed better than any dialogue the full historic weight of tradition, of culture that we all have behind us, the role of man and woman. How can you capture, if not through an image, the many powerful men, kings, nobles, bishops and popes whose paintings hang in the chapter house of the Cathedral, reminding us who had power for centuries, who decided how people had to live and how they had to suffer, like the *Dolorosa* with her bowed head and contained tears.)[3]

Hence, when Pilar first enters the Cathedral of Toledo where Ana works as a restorer, her eyes summarily peruse the portraits of the stern men that surround her but focus intensely on the only painting that features a woman and that Bollaín has mentioned, Luis de Morales's *Dolorosa*. If for art historians, Morales's painting is "a devotional image of profound and captivating dramatism" (Mena Marqués 74), for Pilar and Ana, it represents, instead, the plight of a woman who has "just realized she left home in her slippers."[4] Pilar's initial sense of identification with the woman behind the image and the survivor behind the icon becomes increasingly more complex and sophisticated as the film progresses and she is given the opportunity to train as a tour guide with her friends Lola and Rosa who work in the Museum of Santa Cruz in Toledo. She submerges herself in the world of art and mythology, studies the historical background and critical responses of art historians to selected paintings, and slowly finds a new voice and Foucauldian sense of authority as she enters the public arena of the museum, a "monument . . . to culture" (Feal 26) that infuses her with an empowerment missing from her role as wife and mother. Significantly, this part of the film is imbued with a continued air of tension as Pilar returns to Antonio believing that he has changed and hoping to restore her marriage much as Ana restores the sculpted figures in the interior of the Cathedral. She is also drawn to the strong sexual bond she shares with Antonio that is rekindled during their period of separation and that Bollaín films with exquisite sensitivity, framing the bodies of the two, and particularly Pilar's, as in a painting.

In this context, it is not difficult to understand Pilar's fascination with mythology and the paintings of Titian, an artistic world filled with the sensuality and vibrancy of the flesh that she experiences in her own life and must have found absent from El Greco's *Burial of the Count of Orgaz*, housed in the Church of Santo Tomé. By choosing Titian's *Danaë* as the focus for her apprenticeship as a tour guide, she, nonetheless, enters a historical and mythological world as filled with images of patriarchal power as those of the noble men whose paintings fill the Cathedral and who populate El Greco's masterpiece. Consider the following myth based on Ovid's *Metamorphoses* that Pilar relates in part to the public in Toledo who gathers around her and a slide of the Titian painting: Concerned about a prophesy predicting his death by a future grandson, King Acrisius of Argos locks his daughter Danaë in a bronze tower to impede her contact with men and possible impregnation. Undeterred by such a barrier, the God Jupiter transforms himself into a shower of gold, penetrates the tower, and seduces the princess with the golden coins that fall into her lap. In Titian's 1553 rendition of Ovid's tale, Danaë's nursemaid—or as Cathy Santore indicates, "procuress" (418)—looks on and gathers the golden coins while the princess seems lost in contemplation, her left hand subtly disappearing between her legs.

Given the impact that Ovid's tales have had on western literature and art, and the subsequent rewritings as well as visual representations of the Danaë myth, it is not surprising that the story has loaned itself to interpretation by male thinkers who have consistently condemned the young princess instead of the abusive male protagonists of the story. For St. Augustine, it illustrates "that female chastity is easily corrupted by gold" (Sluijter 15); for Boccaccio, it not only underscores female avarice, but also prostitution (Santore 413). Art historian Cathy Santore, reflecting on the long tradition of illustrations and paintings of Danaë that preceded and coincided with Titian's renditions of the popular myth, aptly concludes, "Danaë had become a symbol of mercenary love and everybody wanted a copy" (424).[5] This misogynistic view inevitably informed orthodox thinking in sixteenth-century Spain and most particularly "church doctrine which regarded antique subjects as a pretext for representing the naked body and thus arousing the baser instincts of the viewer" (Brown 211). Philip II, who commissioned the *Danaë* from Titian before he assumed the crown, and who owned six Titian mythological paintings or *poesie*, curiously reconciled his complex attitudes toward art and orthodoxy by imitating the behavior of King Acrisius, thereby blurring the boundary between myth and reality: He enclosed his *Danaë* as well as other Titian paintings in his private rooms in the Alcázar (fortress) of Madrid, safely guarded from the presence of women (Goldfarb 13) and the vigilant eyes of the upholders of the Inquisition (Mena Marqués 77).

In contrast to these varied male responses of condemnation and enclosure, Pilar's view of the *Danaë* is imbued with the full force of her passion for art and renewed sense of herself as a woman. It also resonates with echoes of Alicia's Ostriker's perceptive observations about women and myth. Pondering the potential of myth for creative women, Ostriker observes that while "at first thought, mythology seems an inhospitable terrain" that "belongs to 'high' culture and is handed 'down' throughout the ages by religious, literary, and educational authorities," it also represents the "quintessentially intimate . . . stuff of dream life, [and] forbidden desire" (316, 317). It is precisely this blend of culture and desire that accounts for the "double power" of myth (Ostriker 317), and that infuses Pilar's response to Titian's painting. Acknowledging Ovid's legacy and Titian's artistry, she penetrates the quintessentially intimate sphere of Danaë's being and celebrates her *jouissance* or sexual pleasure, her sense of self not just as object of Jupiter's desire, but as the subject of her own desire, albeit one molded by her creator. The commonplace view of Danaë as one of the "long series of seductive, sinful or fallen women which were such popular subjects in the sixteenth century" (Sluijter 16) is thus refreshingly replaced by Pilar's vindication of the sensual—not sinful—woman, as she declares, Danaë "está encantada de la vida, ¿no? Ella se entrega en cuerpo y alma a Júpiter . . . Al menos así la pintó Tiziano, con las piermas entreabiertas, ajena a lo que ocurre a su alrededor, sin oponer ninguna resistencia . . ." (121–22) (I think Danaë looks pretty happy, doesn't she? She gives herself in body and soul to Jupiter . . . At least that's how Titian painted her, with her legs open, oblivious to everything around her, without the slightest resistance . . .).

If this interpretation appears to spring from Pilar's own sense of sexual pleasure with Antonio—the glue that keeps their marriage together—her fascination with the young Danaë and her fusion of image and canvas suggest another level of identification reminiscent of her increasingly tense situation as abused wife who attempts to emerge from invisibility. Bollaín and Luna underscore this identification between Pilar and Danaë by indicating in their script: "Su rostro y el de la pintura tienen una expresión parecida" (122) (Her face and Danaë's have a similar expression). This mirror image, crystallized in the sensitive face of actress Laia Marull, is further reinforced as Pilar narra-tes Danaë's transit from isolation to public acclaim: "Algunos de sus dueños quisieron a Dánae así, como Júpiter, bien cerquita y en cambio otros hicieron como su padre, encerrarla para que no la viera nadie. Hubo un rey que incluso pensó en quemar el cuadro. Pero mira, no lo consiguió, y aquí está, a la vista de todos . . ." (122–23) (Some of her owners wanted to have *Danaë* close by, just like Jupiter. But others were like her father and locked it up so no one saw it. One king even thought of burning the painting. But as you can see, he didn't manage to, and here it is where everyone can see it . . .).

Once enclosed and invisible—a mythological version of the abused woman who cannot see herself or experience her autonomy—Pilar's Danaë emerges from the canvas as woman and survivor and metaphor for her own transit from invisibility to visibility.[6] By personalizing the myth and implicitly adding her own subjectivity to Titian's painting, Pilar avails herself of conflicting aspects of her identity that had previously remained separate: the victim of domestic abuse and the authorized tour guide. To this degree, her study of art and the *Danaë* is a holistic experience that is infused with sexual knowledge, artistic knowledge, and what Michel Foucault would call a form of "disqualified" or "subjugated knowledge" (81), that springs from her identity as battered woman but that is imbued with cultural value in Bollaín's film. This original blending of diverse perspectives stands in marked contrast to the monolithic commentaries on Danaë issued throughout the centuries. As such, it illustrates a new form of "revisionist mythmaking" or "hit-and-run attack" on "gender stereotypes" (Ostriker 318, 319) that is part of Bollaín's feminist agenda and creative rendering of art history, social reality, and identity formation in *Te doy mis ojos*. Underlying the potential of history, art, and myth as a catalyst for her protagonist's awakening, Bollaín suggests that Pilar's complex reading of Danaë is not merely limited to the world of the museum but extends to her home, empowering her to find her own voice much as she had intuited Danaë's.

At the same time, the film's challenge to canonical approaches to art is given additional texture as Bollaín examines the dichotomy between high art and pornography in western culture and raises the question of whether or not the two may simply be differentiated "in terms of the effects of the image or object on the viewer" (Nead 28). She introduces this concept through the play on words implicit in Pilar's description of Jupiter's "polvo de oro" (golden dust) and a subsequent observation made by a student in Pilar's tour. The student inquires about Danaë's reaction to Jupiter's "polvo" (dust or more colloquially, screw) and pointedly asks if Titian's painting was "un porno de la época" (121–22) (like pornography of the time). Pilar's response once again evokes contemporary ideas in feminist theory, most notably those of art historian Linda Nead, who challenges the canonical notion of viewing art as either a "quiet, contemplative pleasure" or an "incentive to action" (Nead 27). Validating once again her implicit belief that views on art must be inclusive rather than exclusive, Pilar suggests the breakdown in this either/or dichotomy as she playfully observes that Philip IV inherited the *Danaë* and placed it in the room where "echaba la siesta . . . la siesta o alguna otra cosa" (122) (he took a nap . . . a nap or something else). Contemplation and incentive to action seem to coexist in the King's private chambers, she suggests, as she not only questions rigid dichotomies in art history, but also makes allusions to sex that have dire consequences for her own life.

Bollaín creates the setting for this further level of interpretation by offering her viewing public a complex hall of mirrors in the *Danaë* scene: her spectators not only observe Pilar and the Titian painting, but also Antonio who surreptitiously observes Pilar explaining the *Danaë* to the museum goers who similarly observe her. Each separate viewing perspective plays havoc with the notion of art as contemplation versus art as arousal, while also implying the fusion and confusion of fear and desire, and reality and representation. Bollaín and Luna's script also suggests the difference between scopophilia and surveillance, two modes of looking that are captured in the film through close up shots that render Antonio's "anxious, dark" eyes (123) fixed on Pilar's "shining" ones (122).

As Antonio listens to Pilar's comments about Philip IV and witnesses her lively engagement with the painting and her public, he feels strongly incited to action and not contemplation. Entrapped in a paradigm of either/or that excludes the fusion of contemplation and arousal that Pilar acknowledges as part of an active (male) viewing experience, he becomes incapable of distinguishing between the image on the canvas and the image of his wife as spectacle exposed to her viewers. While he is unable to understand or intuit either the world of mythology or the complexity of Pilar's identification with Danaë, he nonetheless merges with the male figures in the Danaë story as his sense of possessiveness implicitly parallels that of kings Acrisius and Philip II and IV. Feeling both threatened and alienated by his wife's ability to master the discourse of high culture antithetical to his working class job, he subconsciously imitates Titian's "Jupiter Tonans" by creating an "atmosphere of dark foreboding" in their household (Panofsky 150). His fear of Pilar's infidelity and abandonment, and also of the loss of the treasures she gives him during their lovemaking that explain the title of the film—her nose, arms, legs, fingers, breasts, neck, hair, mouth, and eyes—inevitably leads him to lash out against her and annihilate her re-vision of self and autonomy.

Bollaín's textured presentation of Antonio's rage and narrow patriarchal mentality, a product of centuries of western culture and religious thought, is significantly clothed in the metaphor of art, despite his dislike of museums and high culture. In fact, an important part of the therapy he undergoes includes recording his emotions in a colored notebook, with yellow pages reserved for daily activities, green pages for the "good stuff," and red ones for "los malos rollos" (80) (bad stuff). Antonio's labored use of his notebook, and most particularly the red pages, is juxtaposed in the film with the paintings of Wassily Kandinsky that Pilar also explains in her tours in Toledo, leading this critic to wonder if there isn't an element of overly self conscious artistry on Bollaín's part in this segment of *Te doy mis ojos*. That said, it is interesting to note the symbolic value of colors in Kandinsky's world that relates most clearly to both Pilar and Antonio. As Pilar explicates one of Kandinsky's paintings to her tour and comments on the meaning of white, a color that represents "silence," her voice echoes with tinges of sadness as she also explains the meaning of violet, the color of "fear" (130). Antonio's world, in contrast, is dominated by the fiery color of red. Unlike Kandinsky who affirms that a certain "shade of red will cause pain and disgust through association with running blood" (Kandinsky 24), but who, nonetheless, experiments with multiple shades of the same color, Antonio is trapped in the monolithic realm of violence.

When he can no longer tolerate Pilar's increasing independence and friendship with Rosa and Lola, who encourage her to train with them to be tour guides in Madrid, he sabotages her maiden voyage to the capital and attempts to transform her into the very spectacle he feels she has made of herself in the museum. Once again, Bollaín infuses her characters' psychology and interactions with the metaphor of art as Lola, Rosa, and Pilar are seen through Antonio's eyes as a threatening version of the *Three Graces* painted by Rubens and reproduced in the book on Flemish masters that he gives her to make up for his bursts of anger. Art historian Erwin Panofsky has noted that the Three Graces "as a triad . . . retained, in one way or another, their old significance as a symbol of Friendship or Concord" (136); they also "represented the delight in living that produces art, dance, music, and love" (Monaghan 121). Given the bond that unites Bollaín's three women and their desire to offer their "Viaje por el arte con Rosa, Pilar y Lola" (101) (Rosa, Pilar and Lola's Guided Tours), it is not difficult to view the three, and most particularly, Rosa and Lola, as a modern day version of the mythological daughters of Zeus, transformed from Chastity, Beauty, Love and Pleasure (Panofsky 136) into a contemporary rendition of female savvy, wit, cynicism and earthiness.

If these associations are more apparent to Bollaín's informed spectator than to any of her characters and thus function as a marker of the film's complex structure, the parallels she suggests between the world of painting and her own film become even more steeped in art history when we consider that one of the *Three Graces* painted by Rubens is, in fact, a portrait of his second wife, Helena Fourment, whom he married when she was sixteen and he was fifty-six and whom he painted in countless nude and semi nude portraits in the ten years prior to his death. Unconcerned with the predominant Catholic morality in the Netherlands that discouraged the dissemination of "'indecent paintings' likely to compromise the virtue of maker, sitter, and viewer" (ThØfner 5), Rubens took pride in exhibiting the sensuality of his young bride and in celebrating in public "the licit sexual pleasures permitted to the married" by religious treatises of the seventeenth century (ThØfner 18).

In contrast to Rubens, Antonio regards the public exposure of his wife's sexuality much in the same manner as the reactionaries of Philip II's Spain or the misogynistic commentators of Danaë. Accordingly, he must punish her implied "indecency." His explosion of anger and inability to control it, despite all the strategies offered by his therapist, and his gradual and awaited transformation into a Jupiter Tonans who bursts forth without an accompanying shower of gold, create a dramatic climax that rivets Bollaín's spectators while providing additional mirror reflections on the role of art in her film. In an attempt to destroy the symbolic bond that unites Pilar with her friends and threatens his patriarchal control, Antonio tears out of her art book the painting of Rubens's *Three Graces* and casts it from the realm of high art to that of low art or popular culture as he confronts Pilar with the ripped up page and brutally inquires about Rubens' "gordas en pelotas" (naked fat ladies): "a ver, qué hacen, esta quién es, ¿la diosa de la menopausia que le toca el chichi a la diosa de la celulitis?" (143) (Come on, what are they doing, who's this one, the goddess of menopause who's feeling up the goddess of cellulite?).

This slippage from high to low culture and from sublime mythology to coarse physicality, as well as Antonio's inability to distinguish between reality and representation, a characteristic that appears in texts and films of Spain's Generation X (Moreiras Menor 221), are further intensified when he rips off Pilar's clothes and pushes her onto the balcony in only her bra, while screaming in jealous rage: ". . . ¿qué pasa, que aquí no hay público bastante . . . ? ¿O es que lo que te va es que te miren, que te miren el culo mientras hablas? Que te vean bien, de arriba abajo, cuánta más gente mejor, ¿verdad? ¿No es lo que te gusta? Pues venga, que te vea todo dios" (143–44) (. . . what's the matter? Aren't I enough of an audience for you . . . ? Isn't that what turns you on? What you like is being looked at, everyone looking at your ass while you talk. That's what you like, right?—everyone looking at your tits and ass. The more the better, right? Come on, let everyone take a look at you).

His furious attack not only reveals his insecurity and anger at Pilar's public success, but also suggests on a deeper level a concerted attack against art itself or rather, Pilar's passion for art. Once again, Bollaín avails herself of canonical ideas in art history to structure this sequence as she evokes the duality between "nude" and "naked" that art historian Kenneth Clark has discussed. Antonio unconsciously casts Pilar out of the realm of the sublime female nude, dressed in art, as Clark would say, and violently refashions her as naked, "huddled and defenseless" (Clark 23). His very act of denuding her, while aesthetically different from the sublime artistry of Titians and Rubens, nonetheless, bears the mark of male appropriation of the female body, although this time in the name of destruction rather than creation. Affirming himself as the aggrieved subject, he converts his wife into an object who is no longer the active spectator, but the denigrated "spectacle" consigned to the realm of "to-be-looked-at-ness"

(Mulvey 63), terrified and humiliated. Pilar's terror is expressively captured not only through her panic stricken look and desperate pounding on the balcony door, but also through her lack of control of her bodily functions. Urinating in distress, she is transformed into a symbol of what Julia Kristeva might call the state of "abjection" produced by the secretions and fluids that defile and defy "identity, system, order . . . positions, rules" (232). At the same time her trembling body painfully reminds us that there is nothing metaphorical about domestic violence and women stripped of their dignity and personhood.

And yet, on another level, there is, in fact, something very metaphorical in Bollaín's portrayal of Pilar as battered woman. If I return again to Kristeva's implicit critique of the notions of boundaries, and add Linda Nead's observation that for Kristeva, "power lies at the margins of socially constructed categories" (32), I offer the view that Bollaín's disturbing portrayal of Pilar represents a concerted attempt to erase fixed categories of canonical thought in art history and present other models of representation. Her graphic image of Pilar's naked and soiled body appears to illustrate what Nead calls "an engaged feminist practice" that "necessarily breaks the boundaries of the high-art aesthetic symbolized by the female nude" (33). By juxtaposing the ideal, that is the nude Danaë and the nude Pilar, beautifully framed after her love-making with Antonio, with the real or the naked Pilar, and inscribing both through the lens of her camera, she gives visibility to the canonical image and to the hidden one, assuring equal representation of both and authorizing again the subjugated and marginalized world of the battered woman.

The end of the movie loans itself to further reflections on the body and art, as Antonio tries to recapture Pilar's attention by inscribing on his own flesh rather than on the written page or Pilar's body, the full force of his desperation. However, his failed and pathetic suicide attempt has no affect on his wife. Broken down and battered, but fiercely determined, she leaves him with the help of her two friends and declares to her sister moving words that reinforce anew the movement from visibility to invisibility that has structured much of the metaphorical meaning of the film: "Tengo que verme . . . Tengo que verme . . . no sé . . . no sé quién soy, Ana . . . Llevo mucho tiempo sin verme" (155) (I have to see myself . . . I have to see myself. I don't know . . . I don't know who I am, Ana. I haven't seen myself in so long).

While the portrayal of female bonding and solidarity in *Te doy mis ojos* is implicitly dehistoricized and mediated by Bollaín's suggestive appropriation of painting and myth, it nonetheless evokes the model of support among women in *Hola, ¿estás sola?* and *Flores de otro mundo* that proved so crucial in Niña and Trini's journey from "home" and Patricia and Milady's sense of themselves as "flowers from another world." Curiously, the last scene in Bollaín and Luna's script version is noticeably different from the last scene of the film where Pilar leaves her apartment with Lola and Rosa, a female-centered rewriting of Ovid and Rubens's myth of Eurydice who finds her own path out of hell. In contrast, the script reinforces once again the role of art as a mirror through which Pilar regains her eyes and self. She is seen in the Museum of América in Madrid explicating to a group of children what appears to be Rubens's painting of Adam and Eve. Whereas she had previously attempted to give voice to the silent Danaë, she now engages in an even more active process of "revisionist mythmaking" as she declares: "Adán tiene una cara muy inocente, casi un poco tontorrón . . . , mientras que Eva, que es la tentadora, tiene todo más claro, ¿veis?" (158) (Adam has a very innocent face, even a little bit stupid . . . , while Eva, who is the temptress, really has things right. You see?). If each ending suggests an optimistic and perhaps unrealistic resolution to Pilar's failed marriage and abuse, they respond to the authors' attempt to write a script that fills in the gap between the initial moment of domestic abuse and the often inevitable and tragic end when the wife is killed (Bollaín, "Historia" 13). As actress Laia Marull herself suggested at the 2004 Spanish film festival in New York, if the film were real life, Antonio might well have followed his wife and killed her.

As much as *Te doy mis ojos* represents a creative fusion of disparate elements, the authors' process of writing the script similarly involved extensive research, not just on art history and the specific paintings featured in the film, but on the reality of battered women. By Bollaín's own account, she and Luna interviewed abused women, spent time with organizations that assisted victims of domestic violence, attended women's therapy groups, and visited police domestic rape divisions (Arnoldi). Their profound conviction that domestic abuse was not taken seriously enough in Spain and that there was a need to film a piece of the lives of the invisible women who suffered countless blows led them to the making of a movie whose social impact in Spain has been significant. As Bollaín has noted, *Te doy mis ojos* has not only won an award from an office for domestic violence in Spain, but "has also been used by many related groups from judges to women in therapy to all sorts of associations." Observing that "it can be hard sometimes for women to express in words what they have been through," she adds that the film has been of particular value to the police in training officers to demonstrate "greater sensitivity" when dealing with cases of abuse (Arnoldi).

As a further means of highlighting the social value of Bollaín's film, it is instructive to offer a brief reflection on two other films that have also addressed the issue of violence against women and that have similarly received acclaim in democratic Spain: Pedro Almodóvar's 1984 film, *¿Qué he hecho yo para merecer esto?* (What Have I Done to Deserve This?), and Alejandro Amenábar's 1996 film, *Tesis* (Thesis), the recipient of six Goya awards, including best picture. Despite major differences in their approach to cinematography and their narratization of Spanish society, all three films reveal their directors' desire to portray an endemic social problem through a heightened use of artifice and multiple means of representation, whether related to painting, art history, and mythology, as in Bollaín, or the blend of neo-realism, surrealism, melodrama, and other genres in Almodóvar (Triana-Toribio 228), or the dazzling multiplication of the concept of film and spectatorship in Amenábar's psychological thriller. While the marked presence of artifice does not dilute the social content of either *¿Qué he hecho yo . . . ?* or *Tesis*, and while both reveal female-centered plots which posit woman as "the identification figure throughout the film" (Smith 62), neither one suggests a feminist agenda for social change or a space for women outside of patriarchal control.

Consider first Almodóvar's film which portrays with simultaneously comic, poignant, realistic, and melodramatic overtones the plight of its exploited working-class protagonist, wife and mother Gloria, played with great skill by Carmen Maura. Increasingly trapped, exhausted, overworked, and abused by her authoritarian husband Antonio who demands from her countless domestic functions while he prepares for an affair with an old flame, she refuses to iron his shirt and cracks when he responds with a sharp blow. In a conscious nod to Roald Dahl and Alfred Hitchcock's "Lamb to Slaughter," a defiant Gloria summons the skills she has learned while cleaning a martial arts academy and watching a kendo class, and pointedly hits Antonio on the head with the ham bone she is preparing for dinner. Infinitely relieved at eliminating the oppressive "law of the father," and ridding herself of a marriage that gave her little satisfaction or comfort, Gloria, nonetheless, finds herself alone and rootless when her older son and mother-in-law depart from the city to make a new life for themselves in the country. Lest his movie end on a note of despair, Almodóvar saves Gloria from loneliness in the final scene when her teenage son, Miguel, who had abandoned the patriarchal home to live with his dentist-lover, returns home and declares, "This house needs a man."

It would indeed be a long stretch of the imagination to characterize Almodóvar's cinema in the vein of social realism given his penchant for pushing and transforming the limits of realism with his hybrid mixing of genres, ability to treat the bizarre and unusual with great naturalness, and multiple cultural and cinematographic references joined together in "a kind of pastiche," as Núria Triana-Toribio observes (227). Nonetheless, in a film such as *¿Qué he hecho yo* *para merecer esto?* that is grounded in the pressing context of female illiteracy and domestic servitude, the final undermining of the film's portrayal of Gloria's empowerment and the restoration of patriarchal order—a conclusion that one critic calls a "fairy tale ending" complete with the "tender reconciliation" of mother and son (Stone 128–29)—illustrates the articulation of an ideological message as mixed as Almodóvar's blending of different genres.

While it is possible to infer, as Paul Julian Smith notes, an "ironic" reading from the gay son's articulation of the discourse of the defunct heterosexual father, the fact remains that Gloria is confined at the end in a domestic space that doesn't allow for the expression of "female desire outside of patriarchy" (Smith 62). Violence is removed, but not the implicit structure of male domination that created it. By implicitly affirming the connection between female identity and motherhood, Almodóvar shifts his focus from a critique of gender inequality in marriage to mother-son bonding at the same time that he leads his spectators to envision the perpetuation of gender inequality in a different form. Thus, despite his female-centered plot, patriarchal values still occupy center stage and his film ultimately skews the "neo-realists'" sense of "ethical responsibility" for restructuring society (Smith 59).

The theme of violence within the home is replaced in *Tesis* with the portrayal of violence as an element that permeates society from top to bottom and that is intimately connected to a consumer market and audiovisual means of entertainment and information. Amenábar clearly offers a critique of the media's exploitation of violence through his characterization of film professor Jorge Castro, who views film as a money-making industry designed to give the public what it wants. Amenábar elaborates on this concept through his construction of a suspenseful plot centering on Angela, a university student portrayed by Ana Torrent, who is writing a thesis on audiovisual violence and who inadvertently stumbles upon a snuff film featuring the disappeared student, Vanessa. Aided by her friend, Chema, and despite great ambivalence, she is compelled to discover the young woman's murderer, and comes face to face with a sinister endeavor orchestrated by Professor Castro and his student, Bosco, to make money through the filming of female dismemberment. Continually integrating different levels of film or the act of filming and "camera presence" (Moreiras Menor 204) within his film, and juxtaposing the rational with the irrational, dream with fantasy, and approach/avoidance toward violence, Amenábar not only captures Angela's attraction toward Bosco and her desire to believe in his innocence, but also her fear that he is indeed Vanessa's killer.

Angela's subjectivity is revealed to the spectator through a series of superimpositions of film upon film which at times play havoc with psychoanalytic theories of "the way plot and camera place the female figure in situations of . . . voyeuristic punishment" (Gledhill 167). In one important sequence, we see Angela dreaming that she has been filmed; she wakes up and is terrified by the possible intrusion of a camera in her private domain. Leading the spectator to believe that Angela is now awake, Amenábar films Bosco entering her bedroom and slashing her throat while simultaneously kissing her and arousing her sexually. This initial sense of complicity between Amenábar's camera and the camera used in the snuff film is promptly undermined when it is revealed that the entire sequence is actually Angela's dream that Bosco has filmed her experiencing erotic desires while being mutilated. That is, through a dazzling multiplication of male camera gazes, Amenábar shifts the attention from suggesting a disturbing female rape fantasy to critiquing the imposition of a misogynistic male fantasy (Bosco's) on female unconscious.

As director, Amenábar continually works in this dualistic fashion throughout the entire film as he juxtaposes in horrific manner the cries of his victim, Vanessa, and the hesitant but courageous actions of his heroine, Angela, who winds up killing Bosco. Simultaneously foregrounding woman as victim and avenger in a split that is made whole in Almodovar's incorporation of both identities in Gloria, the end of his film features the fascination of male patients in a hospital with a television program's exposure of Professor Castro and Bosco's snuff film. Despite the "ethical" stance offered by the television commentator, the program nonetheless suggests the perpetuation of what feminist film theorists have called the "pleasures provided only for the male spectator" which implicate women once again as "spectacle," (Mulvey 63), and "objects, not subjects, of the gaze, their bodies eroticised and often fragmented" (Thornham 54). Thus, although Amenábar implicitly indicts a "sick" society that thrives on the consumption of violence (Moreiras Menor 261), his camera also privileges the dangerous union of Eros, Thanatos, and male pathos, leading this spectator to conclude that Bollaín offers a more consistent view than Almodóvar or Amenábar of film's responsibility to portray female subjectivity outside the boundary of Freudian thought or patriarchal confines.

As a postscript on *Te doy mis ojos*'s capacity as catalyst for social change, it must be noted that the Spanish Parliament approved in 2005 new legislation guaranteeing increased penalization for acts of violence against women, a political victory that confirms that the stories of invisible women have indeed become more visible. In its capacity as revisionist mythmaker, *Te doy mis ojos* also suggests the creation of a new mirror that reflects different and often antithetical images of women and that breaks down the countless binary oppositions that have informed and deformed discourses on culture, art, and gender roles. Clothing her cinematography in the finery of art, while fashioning her film much like a Titian "whose coloring breathes no differentially from flesh" (Sluijter 24), Icíar Bollaín achieves the delicate balance of creating a textured work that offers a naked look at domestic violence, a contribution to Spanish film that suggests the continued metamorphosis of gender relations in the twenty-first century.

Notes

1. Elsa Fernández-Santos's article, "El derecho y la libertad de expresión centró una ceremonia fría y tensa," reproduces Bollaín's comment and also discusses the political controversies surrounding the 2004 Goya awards and most particularly, Julio Medem's film, *Pelota vasca* (Basque Ball). ETA is the acronym for the radical separatist Basque nationalist movement, Euskadi ta Askatasuna (Basque Land and Liberty).

2. I refer here to the 1553 Danaë, commissioned by Philip II, to distinguish it from two other Titian Danaë paintings, the Naples *Danaë* of 1544 and the Vienna *Danaë* of 1554. While Panofsky (*Problems in Titian*) refers to the Prado painting as the *Danaë*, Brown (*The Golden Age of Painting in Spain*) calls it *Danaë and the Golden Rain*. This painting can be viewed at <http://www.spanisharts.com/prado/titian/htm>.

3. My own translation.

4. Icíar Bollaín and Alicia Luna, *Te doy mis ojos* (Guión cinematográfico), 49. All quotations from the film are taken from this screen play. The English translations I provide are primarily taken from the subtitles of the film, together with modifications I have made. I am particularly grateful to Gloria Waldman-Schwartz for her careful reading of this essay and assistance with translations and style, and to María José García Vizcaíno for her suggestions regarding translations.

5. Cathy Santore ("Danaë: The Renaissance Courtesan's Alter Ego") also highlights a notable exception to this harsh critique of Danaë. She observes, "Despite all this early condemnation of Danaë, in the middle ages there were some who managed to see her as a prefiguration of the Virgin Mary, since both Jupiter's golden rain and God's Holy Ghost caused a virgin's pregnancy." She subsequently adds that this interpretation was difficult to maintain, "for no classical source lauds the princess" (412–13).

6. There are many more implicit parallels between the Danaë myth and *Te doy mis ojos* that I mention briefly here. Bollaín and Luna include in their script a sequence omitted from the film that highlights the themes of male power and female greed suggested by canonical interpretations of the myth as well as Antonio's insecurity about his social class and financial status. Pilar recalls in a flashback how Antonio violently stuffed money in her mouth while screaming that he knew that the "princess" had told her mother that he didn't have enough money to give her (46–47). The conclusion of the Danaë myth also includes an interesting parallel with the title of Bollaín's film that

stresses again the importance of eyes and vision. Danaë's son, Perseus, who does inadvertently kill his grandfather, King Acrisius, also robs the eye of one of the Gray Women to gain their assistance in his plan to kill Medusa. Bollaín has indicated that the title of her film does not derive from mythology but from an African poem, where a young girl says, "Now I give you my eyes," a "romantic notion" that for Bollaín also "has a darker connotation" (Arnoldi). I am grateful to Andrew Levine for suggesting additional meanings of the Danaë myth as well as for offering invaluable observations about this essay.

Works Cited

Andrews, Margaret and Anny Brooksbank Jones. "Re-registering Spanish Feminisms." *Contemporary Spanish Cultural Studies*. Ed. Barry Jordan and Rikki Morgan Tamosunas. London: Arnold, 2000. 322–40.

Arnoldi, Matthew. "Hitting Back at Domestic Abuse: Spanish Writer-Director Icíar Bollaín Talks about Her Award-winning Film, 'Take My Eyes.'" <http://www.iofilm.co.uk/feats/interviews/i/iciar_bollain_take-my_eyes>.

Bollaín, Icíar and Alicia Luna. *Te doy los ojos*. Madrid: Colección Espiral, 2003. 19–159.

_____. "Historia de amor y maltrato." *Te doy mis ojos*. Madrid: Colección Espiral, 2003. 13–17.

Brown, Jonathan. *The Golden Age of Painting in Spain*. New Haven and London: Yale University Press, 1991.

Clark, Kenneth. *The Nude: A Study in Ideal Form*. New York: Doubleday & Co., Inc., 1956.

Feal, Rosemary Geisdorfer and Carlos Feal Deibe. *Painting on the Page: Interartistic Approaches to Modern Hispanic Texts*. Albany: State University of New York Press, 1995.

Fernández-Santos, Elsa. "El derecho y la libertad de expresión centró una ceremonia fría y tensa." *El País*, 2 February, 2004.

Foucault, Michel. "Two Lectures." *Power/Knowledge: Selected Interviews and Other Writings 1972–1977*. Trans. Colin Gordon, Leo Marshall, John Mepham, and Kate Soper. Ed. Colin Gordon. New York: Pantheon, 1980. 78–108.

Gledhill, Christine. "Pleasurable Negotiations." *Feminist Film Theory: A Reader*. Ed. Sue Thornham. New York: New York University Press, 1999. 166–79.

Goldfarb, Hilliard T. "Titian: *Colore* and *Ingegno* in the Service of Power." *Titian and Rubens: Power, Politics and Style*. Boston: Isabella Stewart Gardner Museum, 1998. 1–19.

Kandinsky, Wassily. *Concerning the Spiritual in Art*. Trans. and Intro. M.T.H. Sadler. New York: Dover Publications, Inc. 1977.

Kristeva, Julia. *Powers of Horror. The Portable Kristeva*. Ed. Kelly Oliver. New York: Columbia University Press, 1997. 229–63.

Martín-Cabrera, Luis. "Postcolonial Memories and Racial Violence in *Flores de otro mundo*." *Journal of Spanish Cultural Studies* 3.1 (2002): 43–55.

Martin-Márquez, Susan. "A World of Difference in Home-Making: The Films of Icíar Bollaín." *Women's Narrative and Film in Twentieth-Century Spain*. Ed. Ofelia Ferrán and Kathleen M. Glenn. New York: Routledge, 2002. 257–72.

Mena Marqués, Manuela B. "Titian, Rubens, and Spain." *Titian and Rubens: Power, Politics and Style*. Boston: Isabella Stewart Gardner Museum, 1998. 69–86.

Monaghan, Patricia. *The Book of Goddesses and Heroines*. New York: Elsevier-Dutton Publishing C., Inc., 1981.

Moreiras Menor, Cristina. *Cultura herida: literatura y cine en la España democrática*. Madrid: Ediciones Libertarias, 2002.

Mulvey, Laura. "Visual Pleasure and Narrative Cinema." *Feminist Film Theory: A Reader*. Ed. Sue Thornham. New York: New York University Press, 1999. 58–69. [Rpt. of 1975 essay]

Nead, Linda. *The Female Nude: Art, Obscenity and Sexuality*. London and New York: Routledge, 1992.

Ostriker, Alicia. "The Thieves of Language: Women Poets and RevisionistMythmaking." *The New Feminist Criticism: Essays on Women, Literature, and Theory*. Ed. Elaine Showalter. New York: Pantheon Books, 1985. 314–38.

Panofsky, Erwin. *Problems in Titian Mostly Iconographic*. New York: New York University Press, 1969.

Santore, Cathy. "Danaë: The Renaissance Courtesan's Alter Ego." *Zeitschrift für Kunstgeschichte* 54.3 (1991): 412–27.

Smith, Paul Julian. *Desire Unlimited: The Cinema of Pedro Almodóvar*. London: Verso, 1994.

Sluijter, Eric Jan. "Emulating Sensual Beauty: Representations of Danaë from Gossaert to Rembrandt." *Simiolus* 27.1–2 (1999): 4–45.

Stone, Rob. *Spanish Cinema*. Harlow, England: Pearson Education Limited, 2002.

Thofner, Margit. "Helena Fourment's *Het Pelsken*." *Art History* 27.1 (2004): IV, 1–33.

Thornham, Sue, ed. *Feminist Film Theory: A Reader*. New York: New York University Press, 1999.

Triana-Toribio, Núria. "*¿Qué he hecho yo para merecer esto?* (Almodóvar, 1984)." *Spanish Cinema: The Auteurist Tradition*. Ed. Peter William Evans. New York: Oxford University Press, 1999. 226–41.

◆ Afterword
The Moment X in Spanish Narrative (and Beyond)

Luis Martín-Estudillo

The convergence of preoccupations and narrative strategies which brought young authors such as Lucía Etxebarria, Ray Loriga, José Ángel Mañas, Benjamín Prado, and Roger Wolfe to the forefront of the Spanish literary panorama during the early- and mid-1990s was almost immediately used to promulgate the existence of a differentiated promotion of novelists. The creation of groups such as "Generation X"—echoing an earlier American phenomenon—usually responds to the commercial interests of publishers or to the pedagogical/taxonomical/critical efforts by academics. Both are legitimate, but none should cloud our understanding of a more complex reality. Thus, instead of a "Generation X," that particular junction of interests could be seen as a passing but significant moment in Spain's recent literary history. "Moment X," as I will call it, can be roughly identified with the 1990s, a period when these and a few other authors launched their aesthetic responses to the shock of a country which went from an instant of spectacular hype (which culminated with key international events hosted by Spain in 1992) to an almost immediate disillusionment marked by financial and political scandals and the growing sensation that what seemed to have become a dynamic society was, in fact, deepening its inequalities and creating new areas of exclusion. The aforementioned convergence between a few authors was to gradually disappear due to the predictable divergences which would progressively define their literary projects. This has resulted in a variety of narrative directions which I shall briefly exemplify toward the end of this afterword.

In order to situate Moment X in the cultural map of contemporary Spain, it may be useful to mention the kind of intellectual anchoring of the novelists in question. In his essay in this volume, Gonzalo Navajas invokes Jean-Paul Sartre's philosophy as embodied in his fictional character Roquentin to establish a comparative point of departure in his analysis of Generation X's approach to Western tradition. Roquentin negates such tradition after getting to know it, while Mañas's character Carlos (*Historias del Kronen*) despises it without having bothered to approach any of its major texts. Such lack of awareness of their cultural milieu and of their precedents, typical of some representative Moment X characters, leads to a "reduction of the self" viewed "as a fatal and unavoidable fact without the subject seemingly expressing its disagreement or protest" (7). This rejection of the cultural heritage left by their seniors is not accompanied by the construction of an alternative model which could fill the void left by that obliteration of tradition. Rather, it is marked by the adoption of elements that often originated in the mass-mediatic popular culture of English expression. Although some cryptic forms of knowledge are cultivated, the common approach to these cultural manifestations is to treat them as products for consumption (which is the case, for instance, of Vania in Gabriela Bustelo's *Veo veo*, as Nina Molinaro shows in her essay). Cultural products are to be accumulated and exhibited as signs of group inclusion/exclusion rather than approached critically by the processing of their messages.

Such a hermeneutic effort would imply a more sophisticated treatment of language than the one generally found in these narratives. What is seen by Navajas as linguistic economy, or by Cintia Santana (in this volume) as the literary recreation of marginal speech (*cheli*) in Moment X novels such as the widely discussed *Historias del Kronen*, may also be interpreted as a limit in the perception of the world and the ability to engage it in a fulfilling way. Besides a flexible and comprehensive notion of language, characteristic of the virtually immediate communicative exchanges of the Information Age (as Navajas sees it), this narrowing of the linguistic—and therefore, conceptual—horizon signals an inability to imagine possibilities which could influence reality beyond the presentness that frames the lives of these characters.

This presentness has something to do with the demise of utopian discourses that haunts late modernity. The noticeable solipsism and the absolute contemporaneity which regulate the lives of Moment X characters are the product of their unwillingness to play by the rules set by bourgeois society and to locate themselves within a net of non-fungible historical signifiers where their existence could acquire some degree of transcendence. Instead, they favor hedonistic and often self-destructive practices. Matthew Marr points in his essay to these characters' "excessive drinking and drug use as devices that contribute stylistically to a kind of accelerated narrative rhythm" (128) as he connects Mañas's first novel to Ernest Hemingway's *The Sun Also Rises* and interprets both works as a reaction against growing governmental control. For Navajas, such a lightening of being is seen "as a fatal and unavoidable fact without the subject seemingly expressing its disagreement or protest" (7). However, as Randolph Pope reminds us, the fictional universes of these novels find parallelisms in what is only a small fragment of contemporary Spain's social realities. Thus, the nihilistic hedonism of characters such as Carlos is alien to the growing number of young people who commit their time and energies to the causes of the myriad of NGOs which have appeared in Spain since the early 1990s, to the political activism of anti-militaristic *insumisos*, or to the alternative social options imagined by the squatter movement.[1]

For Navajas, *Historias del Kronen*'s Carlos and his friends are the victims of "the absolute lack of appeal of contemporary culture to the young generations" (14). One might wonder, however, if the passivity they show is actually conditioned by a scarcity of options, especially in the case of members of an economically privileged class such as Carlos himself, or the protagonist-narrators of *Mundo burbuja* (Bubble World, also by Mañas) and Loriga's *Lo peor de todo* (The Worst of All). The whining of so many of the characters in these novels ends up sounding rather frivolous when contrasted with a social background still troubled by different forms of more pressing misery: gender violence, unemployment, marginality, the hardships of immigration, etc., as Linda Gould-Levine and Cintia Santana appropriately point out in their respective essays. Thus, characters such as Carlos can be seen as upper-class youngsters who marginalize themselves because their interests do not coincide with those of their parents or many of their own friends. More importantly, they lack a vital project because—at least temporarily—they can afford not to have one. Their ennui and spleen are conveniently sponsored by parents who are afraid of repeating the oppressive patterns of the authoritarian society under which they suffered in their formative years.

Nevertheless, it is possible to point to a structurally conditioned reason for the self-alienation and apathy of Moment X characters. As Paul Begin reminds us in this volume, the high academic qualifications acquired by a large portion of Spanish youth (with levels of advanced education which compare favorably with most other countries in Europe) have not yet been paralleled by an improvement in employment and, consequently, with their expectations to meet the high standards of consumerism set by a rich Western society. Labor precariousness and other related problems such as the difficulties for emancipation from their parents' homes, which force many young Spaniards to delay their emancipation until their thirties, are a *Leitmotiv* in many of these novels. For the youngest members of the privileged social class portrayed in some of these works, these impediments to their independence may be the most striking features of what seemed to be the communal failure to consolidate the social and economic advances of the period which culminated with the 1992 Barcelona Olympics and Seville Universal Exhibition, and which in fact was, more probably, just the definite incorporation of the nation to the spectacles of the ultraliberal faction of late capitalism, with its growing social inequalities. To a certain extent, the protagonists of these narratives complain (but not necessarily protest) about the disruptions of a system which promises them more than what they actually receive, and not about the system itself and its inherent injustice, which of course affects many others in a much more dramatic way.

The social landscape of the 1990s was met with generalized fatalism within Spanish youth and also with the conformity of those among them who could afford to place themselves aside and look at it as if it were a mere TV show, and not a conditioning part of their existences. Ataraxic and abulic lives populate the pages of Moment X narrations, as if the end-of-the-century crises interrogated by their authors were somehow mirroring those *fin-de-siècle* characters imagined by Pío Baroja or José Martínez Ruiz (later to be known as Azorín) in novels such as *El árbol de la ciencia* or *La voluntad*. In both groups we can find characters who have in common their solipsism and inability to address their ennui through meaningful actions, but this problem is especially conspicuous in the case of our contemporaries, whose creators ponder in their novels if the subject is indeed freer in a society with almost countless options or if it is rather being obliterated in such a spectacle world of overwhelming, constant stimuli. However, in this society, like in most, there is always some room for different forms of agency and dissent, especially because its "structuring structures" (as Pierre Bourdieu calls them in his *Pascalian Meditations*) have flexible limits which can expand and thus normalize heterodox behaviors by assuming them as exceptions which confirm—and reassure—what is established as the "natural attitude" (Bourdieu 172). Such is the case, for example, of a few Moment X novels which present a reaction to the *statu quo* embodied in a runaway who hits the road with an inspiring rock'n'roll soundtrack, although the molds of the 'system' eventually prove to be inescapable, as Jorge Pérez shows us in his essay.

This volume analyzes successfully how Moment X narrators address their inevitable relationship with a mass-mediatic society (see Everly in this volume), but also their connections with the lettered world they encountered when they started publishing in the 1990s. Most of them were not breaking with tradition as radically as they may have thought, or, rather, as some interested parties presented them to the reading public. This is so, in part, because the rupture of tradition is often a mirage which involves a covert homage by a new writer to her/his predecessors. Moreover, many of the themes which characterize Moment X narratives were already in the work of authors with a longer trajectory such as Juan José Millás, as Samuel Amago shows, or Antonio Muñoz Molina and Manuel Rivas, as Elizabeth Scarlett demonstrates in her essay. The authors who were novel at that moment and their immediate predecessors shared not only certain preoccupations related to the social realities of 1990s Spain, but also many cultural references which configured their imaginaries.

In this sense, the powerful presence of foreign works of art (literature, cinema, and music) in these narratives has been rightly emphasized throughout the volume. Notwithstanding, and although this is a very relevant factor in the novels—one which contributes to place them in the wider net of a strongly Americanized global culture—it is important to remember that Spanish literature has gone through other recent periods of evident xenophilia. The fascination with mediated or artfully constructed images of other parts of the world and their cultural productions was a fruitful aspect of late-1960s and 1970s writing, most especially in poetry (with Guillermo Carnero, Pere Gimferrer, and Luis Antonio de Villena being clear examples of this approach). Perhaps the main differences can be found in the balance between high-brow and low-brow icons (with Moment X authors favoring the latter over the former) and the accessory use that those cultural elements had in Moment X, whereas for people such as Carnero and de Villena they often acquired a central position.

While cultural forms alien to the Hispanic tradition have been successfully processed and incorporated, there is something else which is radically *foreign* to many of the experiences narrated by these authors in their Moment X: the past. The simplification of reality implicit in the codes of mass-mediatic popular culture imposes a segregation from history, even if its models are usually nothing totally new. In a novel like Ray Loriga's *Tokio ya no nos quiere* (Tokio Does Not Want Us Any More), the ontological instability of the characters is tied to the annihilation of memory, a definite oblivion acquired through the use of a certain drug. In Álex de la Iglesia's *Payasos en la lavadora* (Clowns in the Laundry Machine), as Luis Martín-Cabrera notices in this volume, the main message is that "we have reached the end of the end." One might add that have only reached it once again, since the destructive, anti-past discourse of *Payasos*'s main character, the poet Satrústegui, is highly evocative of Filippo Marinetti's futurist invectives against the institutions that guard the cultural Archive. But, as Martín-Cabrera points out, Satrústegui's impulses have no finality, whereas the Italian modernist intended to substitute the Archive with a new set of works which were rejected by the artistic establishment at the time of his 1909 *Manifesto*.

I will insist now on the notion of a "Moment X" in contemporary Spanish narrative—rather than on the existence of an autonomous, cohesive "Generation X"— precisely on the basis of the diverging relationship with the past that this group of authors has developed since its emergence in the early 1990s. The works which initially put them on the literary map showed an "indifference to history" which has been mentioned by Navajas and Pope in this volume. Although this statement may be true of the inaugural novels of these authors, it often has to be nuanced—or plainly denied, as we shall see with Prado's latest novel, *Mala gente que camina* (Evil People Who Walk)—if we contrast it with their post-Moment X works.

The narrator of Mañas's *Mundo burbuja* (2001) is a writer who declares at the beginning of the novel that he writes out of boredom and a need for cash. Pressed for a new book, he flashes back to the world of the early 1990s, when he lived in a rich Madrid suburb and was enrolled (although mostly inactive) at a major university. The bulk of the text relates his experiences as an exchange student in Brighton and Grenoble with the agile style and the themes which characterize the author's texts: search for sex, drugs, music . . . in short, a very similar atmosphere to the one found in *Historias del Kronen*—Mañas's first book—and his subsequent works. Although the title of the novel points to the almost autarkic universe of the youth who populate it, the connection with its cultural and historical context is more explicit in *Mundo burbuja* than in Mañas's previous novels, as is apparent in the following fragment, which refers to the moment the narrator goes back to Spain definitively after his European adventure:

> En Madrid, ese verano, se notaba que el ambiente estaba cambiando. Se acababa la luna de miel con el consumismo democrático, y aunque la ilusión ochentera todavía daba sus últimos coletazos, entre la Expo y los Juegos Olímpicos, ya había nubarrones anunciando la tormenta política que se avecinaba con los grandes escándalos que cerraban la época socialista. (181)

(That summer in Madrid one could tell that the atmosphere was changing. The honeymoon with democratic consumerism was coming to an end, and, although the 1980s excitement was still alive with the [Seville Universal] Exhibition and the [Barcelona] Olympics, the clouds announcing the upcoming political storm with the great scandals which ended the socialist period were already in the sky.)[2]

To some extent, the novel is a biopsy of the emerging international affiliations formed among those Spanish youngsters who have had an opportunity to benefit from the new spaces created in Europe by political, educational and mediatic initiatives during the last couple of decades. Thus, Mañas effectively expands the geographical frame of his novelistic territory along with the widening of his subjects' horizons; however, the insistence on the same problematics and on the voice which conducts the narration almost falls in the formulaic, making us wonder if the author and the narrator of *Mundo burbuja* do indeed coincide in their motivations for writing.

For the most part, Mañas's project still falls within the scheme set by Henseler and Pope in their Introduction to this volume, where they notice that "by the late eighties a significant part of a new young society is not only enjoying different material conditions, political structures, and freedoms, but the luxury of forgetting the past and being able to concentrate in living an exuberant, consumerist, drug-imbued, sex-abundant life" (xiv). But it would not take long before such historical oblivion became a luxury which some of the narrators who protagonized Moment X could no longer afford. The pressures for the recovery of the experiences that the dictatorship tried to obliterate, and which during the transition to democracy were only partially vindicated (for the sake of national reconciliation), have grown stronger during the last few years. One can think of issues discussed recently such as the devolution of documents from the republican and civil-war periods to the Generalitat de Catalunya, the removal of Francoist symbols from public spaces, the research done on concentration camps, and the future of the *Valle de los Caídos* (Valley of the Fallen, the massive site of Franco's and José Antonio Primo de Rivera's tombs, built by political prisoners). The demands of several political and social groups have encouraged the center-left Socialist Party (governing since 2004) to prepare an Act For Historical Memory, which is to focus mainly on the official restitution of the memory of those who suffered different kinds of political repression by the regime, and which has proven to be an extremely complex and delicate issue, thus delaying its debate in the Spanish Parliament.

One of those sensitive issues, the case of the political prisoners' children who were separated from their parents and given to families akin to the dictatorship, is central to Benjamín Prado's novel *Mala gente que camina* (2006). Prado, whose first work of narrative (*Raro*, 1995) is studied in this volume as one of the seminal novels of the group of authors presented as Generation X (although he has repeatedly denied any kind of connection with most of them), is a good exponent of the search for a solid cultural ground where his characters could anchor themselves, rejecting that strong initial "presentness" typical of Moment X which I have discussed above. The key to his evolution has been a deepening in the historical mapping of his narratives: his novel *No sólo el fuego* (1999) already anticipated the deep historical preoccupation which is at the foundation of *Mala gente que camina*.

The title is taken from a stanza by Antonio Machado: "mala gente que camina/ y va apestando la tierra" (evil people who walk/poisoning the ground), which belongs to "He andado muchos caminos . . . ," a poem included in *Soledades, galerías y otros poemas* (Solitudes, galleries and other poems). The authorship of the quote is significant because Machado became one of the most prominent icons of the cultural opposition to the dictatorship, and Prado's novel is a fierce condemnation of the Franco regime. Machado's experience of the civil war included a well-known family drama: his eldest brother Manuel— another renowned poet and Antonio's close collaborator—happened to be on the rebels' side at the beginning of the conflict, and soon became one of Franco's propagandists. Their stories implicitly offer a powerful background for one of the main themes present in Prado's novel: the ethical implications of writing and, consequently, the role of the intellectual in times of crisis.

The first-person narrator Juan Urbano is an impending academic who combines his unsatisfactory position in a Madrid high school with his passionate research on the Spanish literature of the post-civil war period. While preparing a presentation on Carmen Laforet, he comes across *Óxido*, the only published (and now forgotten) novel of Dolores Serma, a fictitious writer whom Prado skillfully inserts in different quotes from real testimonials and essays on the period. Serma, who in the novel is described as a close friend of Laforet's and other literary figures, as well as a collaborator with some high-profile members of the regime, is still alive, but has lost her memory due to Alzheimer's disease. In Urbano's interpretation, her Kafkaesque novel is a denunciation of the government-supported theft of children from women punished by the regime for different kinds of connection to the defeated band. The researcher finally discovers that the Serma family had also been a victim of those atrocious policies.[3]

As Prado exposes through Urbano's conversations and research, some historical characters, such as the psychiatrist and prominent member of the

Francoist establishment Antonio Vallejo Nájera, theorized about the need to cleanse society by "quitándoles a sus hijos a los [according to Vallejo] 'débiles mentales', porque 'si militan en el marxismo, de preferencia, psicópatas antisociales, la segregación total de esos sujetos desde la infancia podría liberar a la sociedad de una plaga tan terrible" (137) ("taking their children away from the 'mentally weak,' for 'if Marxist militants are mostly antisocial psychopaths, the total segregation of those subjects from their childhood could set society free from such a terrible plague.") Tragically for many families, Vallejo Nájera's theories were put in practice by the regime during its early years and, later on, officially forgotten.

The issue of memory and the problematics which surround it is the thread that—more or less inadvertently—connects the main characters in the novel. For both Urbano and Dr. Natalia Estivel, memory is an essential part of their professional lives: he works with documents of the past, while she is a neurologist who deals on a daily basis with people who, as her mother-in-law Dolores Serma, have physically lost theirs. Serma's putative son, the lawyer and lawmaker Carlos Lisvano, prefers not to mess with the past: "es mejor no resucitar esas viejas historias. No nos conviene a nadie" (292) (it is better not to resuscitate those old stories. It does not benefit any of us). Thus, he symbolizes the official preference for a functional oblivion. Urbano's mother, who lived rather comfortably during the postbellum years, has somewhat ambivalent feelings toward her son's passionate endeavors, but she is always willing to revisit her past and discuss with him her own views and first-hand experiences as a regular citizen under Francoism.

What stands out from Prado's novel is the need to recover and protect the memories of those who had them silenced not only by Franco's authoritarian regime, but also by a democracy which, for the most part, decided that it was convenient to ignore a long history of crimes and oppression. The post-dictatorship establishment, represented in the book by Carlos Lisvano, opted to ratify a *statu quo* by which those responsible for atrocities such as the ones described in *Mala gente que camina* would die untouched by justice, just as the dictator did, even at the expense of the system's own stability: Carlos will emphatically try to ignore and hide his troublesome origins as the son of whom he always thought to be his aunt, Julia Serma. The novel is an exploration of the importance of remembering, or better, of *commemorating*: to remember along with others, collectively, reaching beyond one's own memories and thus knitting a dense net where we can place our existence and give it a meaning which would transcend the shallow presentness which characterized Spain's precipitated run to high modernity and, within it, Moment X.

From the growing interest in recent history apparent in wide sectors of Spanish society, it can be inferred that the moment has arrived for approaching the post-dictatorship ("transitional") moment in a truly critical way. For different reasons, the transition to democracy has been projected as a communal success for a number of years. It might be appropriate to analyze it also as a political arrangement produced mainly from above, one which did not provide closure to important issues and which consequently set a symbolic system which was far from satisfactory for many. This included the sacralization of different practices and pacts subscribed then (such as the Amnesty Act of October 15, 1977, which guaranteed the legal invulnerability of those who rebelled against the Republican government in 1936) and the consequent creation or consolidation of areas of exclusion. In this sense, some Moment X works—with their exploration of the shadows cast by the mainstream—can be read, as it is done in this volume, as a critical glance at the type of society built during those years. It is fortunate that some of the novelists who pointed to the dissonances of the new democratic system have found different ways to demonstrate that their repertoire is not limited to the same old songs of the 1990s.

Notes

1. Until the instauration of a professional army in Spain in 2001, a growing number of *insumisos* refused both serving in the military and completing the alternative social services mandated by the State, which they considered to be a punishment for their anti-militaristic stances (since for most of their existence such social services lasted longer than the military service) and which gave official status to unpaid work in a nation with a severe unemployment problem. They faced a sentence of two years, four months and one day in prison for this kind of civil disobedience. As for the squatter movement, it should be noted that in Spain it was much more politically sophisticated than in Britain (where it started), involving the organization of cultural centers in the "occupied" estates.
2. This and the other translations in this essay are mine.
3. The historical reality of these practices was brought to the general public's attention by a documentary titled *Els nens perduts del franquisme* (Francoism's lost children), which was produced by Catalan TV (TV3) in 2003. With a few exceptions, Prado does not give credit to the sources he used in the writing of his novel, which undoubtedly draws from a richness of historical research; hopefully this oversight will be mended in future editions with a bibliographical appendix.

Works Cited

Armengol, Montse, and Ricard Belis. *Els nens perduts del franquisme*. Televisió de Catalunya, 2003.

Baroja, Pío. *El árbol de la ciencia*. Ed. Pío Caro Baroja. Madrid: Caro Raggio y Cátedra, 1985.

Bourdieu, Pierre. *Pascalian Meditations*. Palo Alto, California: Stanford University Press, 2000.

Loriga, Ray. *Lo peor de todo*. Madrid: Debate, 1992.

_____. *Tokio ya no nos quiere*. Barcelona: Plaza y Janés, 1999.

Machado, Antonio. *Obras completas*. Ed. Oreste Macrì. Madrid: Espasa Calpe, 1988.

Mañas, José Ángel. *Historias del Kronen*. Barcelona: Destino, 1994.

_____. *Mundo burbuja*. Madrid: Espasa Calpe, 2001.

Marinetti, Filippo Tommaso. "Manifesto futurista." *Prosa e critica futurista*. Ed. Mario Verdone. Milan: Feltrinelli, 1973.

Martínez Ruiz, José. (Azorín). *La voluntad*. Ed. Antonio Ramos Gascón. Madrid: Biblioteca Nueva, 1997.

Prado, Benjamín. *Mala gente que camina*. Madrid: Alfaguara, 2006.

◆ Contributors

Samuel Amago teaches at the University of Notre Dame, where he is an Assistant Professor of Spanish and fellow of the Nanovic Institute for European Studies. He has published articles and lectured on contemporary Spanish fiction and cinema. His book, *True Lies: Narrative Self-Consciousness in the Contemporary Spanish Novel*, is forthcoming from Bucknell University Press. He is beginning a new project on transnational European cinema.

Paul D. Begin is Assistant Professor of Spanish at Pepperdine University (Malibu, California). His publications include articles on Luis Buñuel and Ángel Ganivet. He is currently researching the relationship between Anglo-American rock music and contemporary Peninsular narrative.

Kathryn Everly is Assistant Professor of Spanish at Syracuse University. Bucknell University Press published her book *Catalan Women Writers and Artists: Revisionist Views From a Feminist Space* in 2003. She has published on Mercè Rodoreda, Carme Riera, and Lucía Etxebarria among others in *Catalan Review, Letras Peninsulares*, and *Monographic Review* as well as in the collection of essays edited by Jacqueline Cruz and Barbara Zecchi published by Icaria in Spain *¿Evolución o involución? La mujer en la España actual* (2004).

Christine Henseler is Associate Professor of Spanish and Director of Latin American and Caribbean Studies at Union College. Her areas of specialization are contemporary Spanish narrative, women's studies, book publishing, visual culture, media and cultural studies, and Chicana literature and visual art. She has published several books and editions, including *Contemporary Spanish Women's Narrative and the Publishing Industry* (University of Illinois Press, 2003) and *En sus propias palabras: escritoras españolas ante el mercado literario* (Ediciones Torremozas, 2003). She is co-editor with Alejandro Herrero-Olaizola, of *Market Matters: Literary Commodities and Exchanges in Hispanic Publishing* (*Arizona Journal of Hispanic Cultural Studies*). She has authored a number of articles and interviews on contemporary Spanish literature and she is currently working on a book project on identity and technology in twenty-first century Peninsular literature.

Linda Gould Levine is Professor of Spanish and Chair of the Spanish/Italian Department at Montclair State University (New Jersey), where she has also directed the Women's Studies program. Her areas of specialization are contemporary Spanish literature and women writers from Spain and Latin America. She is the author of *Juan Goytisolo: la destrucción creadora* (Joaquín Mortiz, 1976) and two critical editions of Juan Goytisolo's novel, *Don Julián*, published by Cátedra in 1986 and 2004. She is also the author of *Isabel Allende*, a critical study of Allende's work (Twayne Publishers, 2002), co-author with Gloria Feiman Waldman of *Feminismo ante el franquismo: entrevistas con feministas de España* (Ediciones Universal, 1980), and co-editor with Gloria Feiman Waldman and Ellen Engelson Marson of *Spanish Women Writers: A Bio-Bibliographical Source Book* (Greenwood Press, 1993). She is also co-editor with Ellen Engelson Marson of *Proyecciones sobre la novela* (Ediciones del Norte, 1997), a collection of essays on the contemporary Spanish and Latin American novel. She has published articles on such contemporary Spanish and Latin American authors as Ana María Moix, Lidia Falcón, Esther Tusquets, Cristina Peri Rossi, Carmen Martín Gaite, Ana Rossetti, Paloma Díaz-Mas, Isabel Allende, and Juan Goytisolo, among others.

Matthew J. Marr is Assistant Professor of Spanish at the University of Illinois at Chicago. His most recent articles consider space and identity in the work of Esther Tusquets, humor and the deflation of the poetic ideal in verse by Roger Wolfe, and the post-punk aesthetic in José Ángel Mañas's *Historias del Kronen*. He is the author of *Postmodern Metapoetry and the Replenishment of* *the Spanish Lyrical Genre, 1980–2000* (2006), a book which examines the playful, theatrical, and comic reinvention of the poetic medium by such writers as Javier Salvago, Luis García Montero, Vicente Gallego, Felipe Benítez Reyes, and Carlos Marzal.

Luis Martín-Cabrera is Assistant Professor at UCSD (University of California, San Diego), specializing in transatlantic studies, twentieth-century Spanish literature, Spanish film, and Latin American Studies. He is currently working on a project based on the analysis of detective fiction during the post-dictatorship period in Spain and the Southern Cone. He has published articles on *El día de la Bestia*, the Zapatistas and the Latin American essay, and the representation of Caribbean immigrant women in *Flores de otro mundo*. He is also co-author of *Más allá de la pantalla: el mundo hispano a través del cine* (forthcoming), a textbook to teach Spanish through film.

Luis Martín-Estudillo is Assistant Professor of Spanish Literature at the University of Iowa. He has published several studies on Spanish literature and cultural history, including *Libertad y límites* and *Hispanic Baroques* (with Nicholas Spadaccini). His latest book is the forthcoming *La mirada elíptica: el Barroco en la poesía española contemporánea*. He is co-director of *Ex Libris: Revista de Poesía* and an Associate Editor of *Hispanic Issues*.

Nina Molinaro is Associate Professor of Spanish at the University of Colorado at Boulder and has served as Interim Director of Women's Studies at both CU Boulder and at the University of Akron. She has published a book on the fiction of Esther Tusquets and numerous articles on post-war peninsular literature, Hispanic women's literature and Spain's "Generation X." She is currently working on a book on ethics, gender and contemporary peninsular narrative.

Gonzalo Navajas is Professor of Modern Spanish Literature and Film in the Department of Spanish and Portuguese at UC Irvine. He is the author of many books and novels. His books on theory of modern literature and culture include *La modernidad como crisis*, *Más allá de la posmodernidad*, and *La narrativa española en la era global*. His latest novel is *La última estación*. He is a member of the editorial board of many journals, and he has been invited to teach and lecture at numerous national and international institutions

Jorge Pérez is Assistant Professor at the University of Kansas. He has forth-coming articles that deal with the negotiation between the local and the global in the works of Ray Loriga and Manuel Rivas, respectively. He is currently working on a book-length project with the tentative title of *Nomadic Culture: Mobile Identities in Post-Franco Spain*, which focuses on the notions of mobil-ity and displacement that permeate the cultural production of the post-Franco period.

Randolph D. Pope is Commonwealth Professor of Spanish and Comparative Literature at the University of Virginia, where he chairs the Department of Spanish, Italian and Portuguese. He has written three books, *La autobiografía española hasta Torres Villarroel, Novela de emergencia: España, 1939–1954*, and *Understanding Juan Goytisolo*. He has published numerous essays on Spanish and Latin American literature. He was for a decade the main editor for Peninsular literature for the *Revista de Estudios Hispánicos*.

Cintia Santana is Assistant Professor of Spanish at Claremont McKenna College. She specializes in contemporary Peninsular narrative, the relationship of politics and aesthetics, and questions of translation. While the burgeoning field of literary trans-Atlantic studies most often examines the relationship of Spanish literature with that of its former colonies, her current book project shifts the focus to Spain's literary exchanges with the United States.

Elizabeth Scarlett is Associate Professor of Spanish at the State University of New York at Buffalo. She has published a book, an edited volume, and many essays on Spanish literature and film. Her first book, *Under Construction: The Body in Spanish Novels*, was selected an Outstanding Academic Book of 1995 by *Choice*. She followed it with a volume co-edited with Howard B. Wescott, *Convergencias Hispánicas: Selected Proceedings and Other Essays on Spanish and Latin American Literature, Film, and Linguistics* in 2001. Her experience also includes travel-writing about Spain, Portugal, and Mexico through the *Let's Go* series, a Fulbright Teaching Assistantship in Southern France, and motherhood (Adrian and Sylvia).

◆ Index

Compiled by Eric Dickey

ABC Literario, 21, 22, 46
Acín, Ramón, 80
Adorno, Theodor, 14
Aerosmith (group); and "Dream On,"
　102
Alaska, 16, 17, 31n18, 103
Alberti, Rafael, xii
Alchazidu, Athena, 181n3
Allinson, Mark, 16, 28, 29n3, 191
Almodóvar, Pedro, xvii, 44, 93n4, 107,
　127, 230, 231; and *Carne Trémula*,
　107, 166n8, 181n2; and *Entre
　tinieblas*, 127; and *¿Qué he hecho yo
　para merecer esto?*; as domestic
　violence, 229
Althusser, Louis, 6
Amago, Samuel, xviii, 239
Amann, Elizabeth, 109n1
Amat, Nuria, 60
Amenábar, Alejandro, 122, 230, 231;
　and *Tesis* (film), 122; as domestic
　violence, 229–31
Anderson, Andrew, xxn1
Anderson, Perry, 94n8
The Animals (group), 98, 108
Anka, Paul, 16
Annesley, James, 128, 147n5, 147n6
Armendáriz, Montxo, 127; and *27
　Horas* 127

Arniches, Carlos, 39
Azevedo, Milton, 39, 52n5
Aznar, José María, 166n6

Baeza, José, 47
Bakhtin, M.M., 123
Balibar, Etienne, 6
Balzac, 25
The Band (group), 106
Baroja, Pío, xix, 39, 145, 146, 148n16,
　238; and *El árbol de la ciencia*, 238
Baroque, xii
Barthelme, Frederick, xvii
Bartolomé, Cecilia, 166n11; and
　Vámonos Bárbara (film), 166n11
Baudrillard, Jean, 86, 87
Beart, Guy, 213n6
Beat Generation, 127, 156
The Beatles (group), 64, 65, 103, 118;
　and "Day Tripper," 75n2; and
　"Dear Prudence," 103; and
　"Lucy in the Sky with Diamonds,"
　64, 75n2; and "Something in the way
　she moves," 118
Beattie, Ann, xvii
Begin, Paul, xvii, 237
Benet, Juan, 35
Benjamín, Walter, xiv, 11
Bermúdez, Silvia, 165n1

Bildungsroman, 87, 98, 124
"Blank Generation," 19
Blay, José, 46
Bloch, Ernst, 8
Blur (group), 25, 27; and "Country
    House," 25
Bogart, Humphrey, 25
Bollaín, Icíar, 216–20, 222–29, 231,
    232, 232n1, 232n4, 232n6; and
    Flores de otro mundo, 217, 227; as
    recuperation of female autonomy,
    218; and Hola, ¿estás sola?, 217,
    218, 227; and Te doy mis ojos, xx,
    216, 224, 227, 228, 231, 232n4,
    232n6; as domestic violence, 216–18,
    228, 232; as feminist agenda, 223
Bonilla, Juan, 35, 172, 190
Bordowitz, Hank, xxin5
Borges, Jorge Luis, 34, 49, 52n10, 68,
    69, 71
Bosé, Miguel, 103
Bourdieu, Pierre, 10, 176, 177, 238
Bowie, David, xv, 8, 62, 103, 107, 184,
    186, 194, 198
Brabazon, Tara, xxin4
Brando, Marlon, 160
Los Bravos (group), 16
British invasion, xv, xvii
Broyard, Anatole, 38, 51n4
Buford, Hill, 34, 37, 47, 50n2
Bukowski, Charles, 48, 49, 50n1, 52n9,
    79; and Erecciones, eyaculaciones,
    exhibiciones, 52n9; and Escritores de
    un viejo indecente, 52n9; and La
    máquina de follar, 52n9
Burdon, Eric, 98, 99; and "We Gotta Get
    Out of This Place," (song) 99
Bustelo, Gabriela, xx, 35, 190, 203–5,
    212n4, 213n8, 214n10; and Veo Veo,
    xx, 203, 205, 206, 207, 210, 211n1,

212n4, 212n5, 213n7, 236; as
    feminist narrative, 203, 204; as public
    and private space, 210

Calparsoro, Daniel, 166n8; and Ausentes
    (film), 166n8
The Cambridge History of Spanish
    Literature, xiii, xxn2
Los Canarios (group), 99
Cánovas, Rodrigo, 92n2
Cañeque, Carlos, xviii, 60, 62, 66, 68,
    69, 72–74; and Conductas desviadas,
    60; and Conversaciones sobre
    Borges, 60; and Dios en América, 60;
    and Muertos de amor, 60, 68; and El
    pequeño Borges imagina el Quijote,
    60; and El pequeño Borges imagina
    la Biblia, 60; and Quién, 60, 61, 66,
    68–70, 72, 73
Capa, Robert, 17, 18, 30n5
Capanaga, Pilar, 44
Capone, Al, 140
Cardwell, Richard, xiii
Carlotti, Maurizio; as director general of
    Telecinco, 181n4
Carnero, Guillermo, 239
Carroll, Traci, 67, 73; and Beavis and
    Butt-Head (film), 67; and Mystery
    Science Theater 3000 (film), 67
The Cars (group), 210, 213n6
Carver, Raymond, xvii, 34, 36–40, 43,
    45, 46, 48–50, 50n1, 51n4, 79, 128,
    147n6; as Carver Country, 40; and
    Catedral, 34, 38, 39, 45; and Quieres
    hacer el favor de callarte, por favor?,
    46; and What We Talk About When We
    Talk About Love, 38
Casarieglo, Martín, 78
Casavella, Francisco, 35
Castillo-Puche, José Luis, 148n16

Cela, Camilo José, xix, 35, 145
Cercas, Javier, 74
Cervantes, Miguel de, xv, 71, 187; and
    Don Quixote de la Mancha, xv, xix,
    9, 99
Cervera, Rafa, xvii
Chambers, Iain, 49
Cioran, Emile, 8, 72
Clapton, Eric, 103
Clark, Kenneth, 226
The Clash (group), 15, 25, 107, 186,
    188, 192; and "Should I Stay or
    Should I Go," 188, 192, 193
Cobain, Kurt, xvi, 159, 160
Cocker, Joe, 103
Cohan, Steven, 163
Cohen, Leonard; and "I'm Your Man,"
    (song) 213n6
Colgrave, Stephen, xvii
Compte, Auguste, 92n2
Cooper, Dennis, 128, 190
Corner, John, 180, 182n7
Coupland, Douglas, 18, 20, 21, 24,
    30n9, 30n12, 52n8, 181n3, 190
Cray, Robert, 207; and "Nothin' But a
    Woman," (song) 213n6
Cuadros, Ricardo, 92n2
The Cure (group), 44, 102, 126

Dante, 72
Dardis, Tom, 142, 147n8
Davis, Martha; and "Change My Mind,"
    (song) 213n6
De la Iglesia, Alex, 81, 84, 86, 93n4; and
    Acción Mutante, 93n4; and *8000
    Balas*, 93n4; and *La comunidad*,
    93n4; and *Crimen perfecto*, 93n4;
    and *El Día de la bestia*, 93n4; and
    Payasos en la lavadora, xviii, 81, 87,
    90, 93n4, 239, 240; as high/low

culture art, 82–85, 92; and *Perdita
    Durango*, 93n4
De Quincey, Thomas, 127; and
    *Confessions of an English Opium
    Eater*, 127
Dean, James, 160
Death and the Maiden, 99
Deconstruction, 13
Debord, Guy, 87
Dee Dee Ramone, 25
Deleuze, Gilles, 164
Delibes, Miguel, 35
Depech Mode (group), 44, 126
Derrida, Jacques, 6, 33
Deverson, Jane, 18
Diego, Gerardo, xxn1
Dirty Realism, xvii, 30n12, 34–38, 47,
    48, 50n1, 50n2, 51n3, 51n4, 128,
    147n6, 186; as class difference, 36,
    42, 45–47
Djos, Matts, 133, 143, 148n11
Domino, Anna, 208, 213n6
The Doors (group), 98; and
    "The End," 209, 213n6, 214n10
Dorca, Toni, 61, 211n2, 212n4
Driver, Jim, xxiin8
Dúo Dinámico (group), 16
Dylan, Bob, xv, xxin5, 10, 62, 107, 157,
    186

Easy Rider (film), 160
Echevarría, Ignacio, 21, 43
Eliot, T.S., 25, 26, 126
Ellington, Duke, 25
Ellis, Bret Easton, xvii, 21, 30n12, 47–
    49, 50n1, 79, 127, 128, 147n6, 190;
    and *American Psycho*, xvii, 21, 122;
    and *Less than Zero*, xvii, 21, 30n12,
    127, 147n6; and *Menos que cero*, 47
ETA, 50, 121, 216, 232n1

Etxebarria, Lucía, xi, xvi, 30n10, 30n12, 35, 60, 62, 68, 73, 74, 98, 102, 107–9, 127, 172, 190, 203, 235; and *Amor, curosidad, prozac y dudas*, xi, 63; and *Beatriz y los cuerpos celestes*, 63, 68, 102, 103, 105
European Community, 138
Evans, Hill, 71
Everly, Kathryn, xix, 239
Existentialism, 13

Faulkner, William, 40
Fernández Porta, Eloy, 78
Fernández-Santos, Elsa, 232
Feyerabend, Paul, xxin6
Film noir, 97
Fine Young Cannibals (group), 209, 213n6
Fitzgerald, F. Scott, 147n4; and *The Great Gatsby*, 147n4
Folkart, Jessica, 104
Ford, Richard, 37, 38, 41, 46; and *Ladrón de cuarteles*, 46; and *Rock Springs*, 37, 46; and *Tres rosas amarillas*, 46
Fortes, José Antonio, 50n1, 94n7
Foucault, Michel, 223
Fouz-Hernández, Santiago, 52n8, 121, 124n2, 181n3, 190
Franco, Francisco, xiii, xxin2, 16, 23, 29, 102, 127, 137, 148n12, 154, 162, 170, 173, 241–43
Frere-Jones, Sasha, 62
Freud, Sigmund, 116, 117, 120, 123, 124n1, 231; and *Civilization and its Discontents*, 116
Frith, Simon, 29
Frost, Linda, 167n12
Fuentes, Eugenio, 166n11; and *Venas de nieve*, 166n11

Fukuyama, Francis, 83
Fussell, Paul, 25, 26

Gabinete Caligari, 43
García Lorca, Federico, xii, 25, 186
García Márquez, Gabriel, 40
García-Posada, Miguel, 46, 80, 94n7
García Vizcaíno, María José, 232n4
Generation of 98, xii, xiii, 121
Generation of 27, xii, xiii, xxn1, 121, 172
Generation of 1950, xiii
Generation of 1968, 73, 136
Generation of 1970, xiii
Generation X, xii, xiii, xiv, xviii, xix, xx, 6, 9-11, 13, 15–22, 25–29, 30n5, 30n12, 34, 59, 60, 67, 78–81, 97–99, 101, 102, 104, 105, 107–9, 116, 121, 127–29, 136, 137, 145, 147n6, 155, 165, 165n3, 170–72, 186, 187, 203, 205, 213n7, 216, 226, 235, 236, 240, 242; as aesthetic, 61, 68, 74, 218; as blankness, 18, 19, 22; as dissolution of the self, 11; as film, xii; as globalization, 173; as humanist tradition, xii, 5, 14; as minimalist culture, 9-11, 30n12, 36, 47, 50n2, 51n4; as "pact of forgetfulness," xiv; as punk, 15–19, 22, 24–29, 61, 186; as reductionism of time, 6, 7; as rejection of the past/history, xiv, xv, 6, 10, 14, 116, 181n1, 239, 240; as rejection of society, xvi, 61; as road rock 'n' roll novel, xix, 153–55, 161–65; as "sex, drugs and rock & roll," xii, xiv, xv, xvi, xviii, xxin6, xxin7, 3, 16, 35, 59, 60, 62, 68, 71, 74, 79, 98, 109, 120, 203, 206; as television (as political tool and entertainment), xix, 170, 171, 173, 175–78, 180; as video-clip, xx, 187; as visual media, 11, 12

Generation X (group), 18; and "Wild Youth," 18, 19; and "Your Generation," 18
Generation Y, 101
"Generational method," 79, 80, 92n2
Gilchrist, Ellen, 37
Gimferrer, Pere, 239
Giralt Torrente, Marcos, 172
Girard, René, 117
Goethe, 2
Goic, Cedomil, 92n2
Goldman, Robert, 185
Góngora, Luis de, xv
Goñi, Javier, 46; and *El Urogallo*, 46
González, Felipe; and socialist administration, 156
Goody, Jack, 39
Gopequi, Belén, 35
Gould-Levine, Linda, xx, 237
Goytisolo, Juan, xi, xiv, xv, xviii, xix, 35, 59, 127; and *Count Julián*, xv; and *La reivindicación del Conde Julián*, 59
Gracia García, Jordi, xxin2, 35, 73
Gramsci, Antonio, xvii
Granta, 34, 36–38, 41, 42, 45–48, 50n2, 51n3
Grassian, Daniel, xii
Green Day (group), xxiin7
Griggers, Cathy, 167n12
Grossbert, Lawrence, xvii, 28, 155
Guatari, Felix, 164
Guerra, Juan, 166n6
Gullón, Germán, 30n12, 42, 50n1, 94n7, 212n2
Guzmán, Almundena, 127

Hall, David, 49
Hamblett, Charles, 18, 23, 30n9, 30n12, 52n8

Haynsworth, Leslie, xxiin7
Hebdige, Dick, 15
Hegel, Friedrich, 5
Hell, Richard, 19
Hemingway, Ernest, xix, 38, 49, 126, 128, 129, 132, 133, 142, 145, 146n1, 146n2, 147n6, 147n8, 148n16; and *The Sun Also Rises*, 126, 128, 129, 131–33, 140, 142–44, 146, 146n2, 148n9, 237; as protest against American prohibition, 140–42
Hendrix, Jimi, 160
Henseler, Christine, xx, 61, 108, 171, 241
Henson, Jim, 17
Hermoso, Miguel, 166n11; and *Fugitivas*, 166n11
Herralde, Jorge, 49
High Sierra (film), 25
Hitchcock, Alfred; and "Lamb to Slaughter," 229
Holquist, Michael, 123
Holtz, Geoffrey, xviii
Honey, 51n3
Hooper, John, 16, 29n2, 137, 138, 148n12
Horkheimer, Max, 14
Hornby, Nick, 50n2
Howe, Irving, 39
Huerga, Manuel; and *Antártida* (film), 165n2

Idol, Billy, 18
Iglesias, Eduardo, 35, 165n3; and *Aventuras de Manga Ranglan*, 165n3; and *Por las rutas los viajeros responden a las plegarias*, 162, 165n3; and *Tormenta Seca*, 162, 165n3
Indurain Eraso, Carmen, 167n12

Interrante, Joseph, 156
Iron Maiden (group), 100, 101
Isley, Ernie, 208, 213n6
Izquierdo, José María, 212n4

Jagger, Mick, 107, 209
James, Tony, 18
Jameson, Fredric, 83, 84
Janowitz, Tama, 46, 48
Jímenez, Juan Ramón, xii, xv; and
    Entre visillos, xi, xv
John, Elton, 106
Johnny Guitar (film), 25
Jordan, Barry, 173
Jurado, Rocío; and "Como una ola,"
    (song) 208

Kafka, Franz, 49, 52n10, 62, 66; and
    Metamorphosis, 66
Kandinsky, Wassily, 225
Kaplan, Ann; and Rocking Around the
    Clock, 197
Keitel, Harvey, 161
Kerouac, Jacques, 79, 127, 160; and
    On the Road, 127, 160, 166n7
"The Kids Are Alright," (song) 102
King, Carole, 99; and "You've Got a
    Friend," (song) 99
King Cole, Nat, 208, 213n6
Klodt, Jason, 61
Knickerbocker, Dale, 75n3
Kraus, Patricia, 213n6
Kristeva, Julia, 227
Kuhnheim, Jill, 165n1

Labanyi, Jo, 213n7
Laderman, David, 167n12; and rock 'n'
    road movie, 153, 154
Lang, K.D., 103

Langa Pizarro, M. Mar, 50n1
Lau, Evelyn, 190
Lazarillo de Tormes, 34
Leavitt, David, 46, 48, 49
Lefebvre, Henri, 158
La lengua de las mariposas (film), 100
Lennon, John, 106–8, 160, 186
Lennox, Annie, 103
Levine, Andrew, 233n6
Lewis, John, 25
Lipovetsky, Gilles, 78
Lipsitz, George, 159
Loriga, Ray, xi, xvi, xix, 6-8, 11, 21, 22,
    30n10, 30n12, 34–36, 39, 43, 45, 60,
    65, 71, 73, 74, 78, 80, 97, 107–9,
    127, 160, 166n9, 170–72, 174, 177,
    179, 181, 181n5, 186, 187, 190, 203,
    235; as deconstruction of television,
    173, 180; as visual and verbal
    language, 170, 171, 174–78, 180; and
    Caídos del cielo, xix, 22, 30n10, 154,
    160, 171, 173, 181n2, 199n1; and
    Días Extraños, 22, 30n14, 166n8,
    181n2, 199n1; and El hombre que
    inventó maniatan, 166n8, 171, 181n2,
    199n1; and Héroes, xi, 8, 11, 22,
    30n14, 43, 107, 166n8, 171, 181n2,
    184, 185, 187, 189, 192, 194, 195,
    197, 198, 199n1; as intertextual
    references, 185, 186, 196; rock as
    spatial and temporal shift, 185, 192,
    198; as video-clip, 185, 188, 190,
    193, 194, 196–98, 199n2; and Lo
    peor de todo, xi, 15, 21, 22, 24, 25,
    27, 30n14, 34, 36, 166n8, 170,
    181n2, 199n1, 237; as nihilism, 24;
    and La pistola de mi hermano, xix,
    154, 159–63, 166n8, 166n8, 166n9,
    171,173, 181n2, 199n3; as violence

and youth, 180; and *Tokio ya no nos quiere*, 7, 65, 166n8, 181n2, 199n1, 239; and *Trífero*, 166n8, 181n2, 199n1

Lost Generation, xix, 127, 129, 140, 147n6

Love, Courtney, 30n10

Luna, Alicia, 232n4

Lyotard, Jean Francois, 84, 92

Machado, Antonio, xii, 186, 242

Machado, José, 35; and *A dos ruedas*, 154, 155, 157, 158, 160, 162, 163, 165n5; as grunge culture, 159; as the "Spanish Dream," 159; and *Grillo*, 166n5

Machado, Manuel, xii

Madonna, 103

Madrid, Juan, 60, 74; and *Días contados*, 74

Maestre, Pedro, 35, 190

Magrinyà, Luis, 35, 48; and *Belinda y el Monstruo*, 48

Mainer, José Carlos, xiv

Mamá (group), 31n18

The Mammas and the Papas (group), 206, 213n6

Manuel, Víctor, 157

Mañas, José Ángel, xi, xvi, xix, 3, 5-7, 11, 30n10, 30n12, 34–36, 39, 43–45, 60, 66, 68, 71, 73, 74, 78, 80, 98, 104, 107–9, 115, 121, 127, 128, 132, 135, 136, 138, 140, 142, 143, 145, 146, 172, 186, 190, 203, 235, 241; and *Ciudad rayada*, 3, 9, 165n3; and *Historias del Kronen*, xi, xvii, xviii, xix, 5-7, 13, 30n10, 34, 36, 43–45, 52n8, 66, 68, 70, 71, 73, 75n4, 105, 115, 117, 118, 121–23, 124n2, 128, 129, 131, 133, 140, 146, 147n6,

165n3, 186, 203, 212n2, 236, 237, 240; as "blank fiction," 128, 147n5, 181n1, 212n3; as countercultural protest novel, 140; as generational differentiation, 135, 136, 142; and *Mensaka*, 165n3, 186; and *Mundo burbuja*, 237, 240, 241; and *La soledad era esto*, 60–63, 66; and *Sonko 95*, 165n3

Marcus, Millicent, 154

Marías, Javier, 35

Marlowe, Phillip, 26

Marr, Johnny, 105

Marr, Mathew, xix, 147n6, 237

Marsé, Juan, xiv

Martín, Annabel, 105

Martín, Sebas, 212n2

Martín-Cabrera, Luis, xviii, 239, 240

Martín Gaite, Carmen, xi, xviii, 59; and *El cuarto de atrás*, 59

Martín-Márquez, Susan, 217

Martín Rojo, Luisa, 44

Martínez Cachero, José María, 78–80, 92n2

Martínez de Pisón, Ignacio; and *Carreteras secundarias*, 162

Marx, Carl, 5

Marzal, Carlos, 127

Masoliver, Kosián, 52n7

Masoliver Ródenas, Juan Antonio, 50n1

Mason, Bobbie Ann, 36–38, 42, 51n3, 52n7; and *Feather Crowns*, 51n3; and *In Constant Flight*, 51n3; and *In Country*, 51n3; and *Love Life*, 51n3; and *Shiloh and Other Stories*, 51n3, 52n7

Matute, Ana María, 35

Mauri, Antonio, 52n7

McCartney, Paul, 75n2

McInerney, Jay, 46–49; and *Luces de neón*, 47

Mecano (group), 209; and "Me colé en una fiesta," 209, 213n6

Medem, Julio; and *Pelota vasca* (film), 232n1

Mendoza, Eduardo, 60, 74

Metallica (group), 132

Michael, George; and "Faith," (song) 213n6

Midnight Oil (group); and "Beds are Burning," 213n6

Millás, Juan José, xviii, 35, 60, 62, 65, 66, 68, 73, 74, 75n1, 239; and *Dos mujeres en Praga*, 60

Miller, Henry, 159; and *Tonto, muerto, bastardo e invisible*, 65, 75n3

Miller, Steve, 213n6

Mink Deville (group); and "Spanish Stroll," 208, 213n6, 214n10

Modernism, xiii

Molina, Antonio, 99

Molinar, Nina, xx, 122, 186, 236

Molinaro, Tony, 211n1

Moment X, 235, 236, 238–44; as cultural ignorance and rejection, 236; as self-alienation, 237

Monk, Thelonious, 25

Monroe, Marilyn, 71

Montero, Rosa, 62, 74, 97; and *Te trataré como a una reina*, 97

Montetes Maizal, Noemí, 212n2

Moore, Susanna, 128

Moreiras Menor, Cristina, 50n1, 79, 80, 92n1, 176, 187, 188, 191, 192, 199n2

Morrison, Jim, 98, 99, 108, 195, 196; and "Light My Fire," (song) 196, 197; and "Riders on the Storm," (song) 99

The Motels (group), 210, 213n6; and "Change My Mind," 211

Movida, 16, 17, 23, 24, 29n1, 29n4, 43, 45, 124, 136

MTV, 103, 187

Muffs (group), 25

Múgica, Daniel, 35, 127

Muñoz Molina, Antonio, xviii, 35, 60, 62, 74, 97, 98, 102, 105, 107–9, 239; and *El invierno en Lisboa*, 97; and *El jinete polaco*, 98, 99, 101–3, 105, 107, 109

Nabokov, Vladimir, 159

Nacha Pop (group), 31n18

Navajas, Gonzalo, xvi, 116, 236, 237, 240

Nead, Linda, 223, 227

Neumeister, Sebastian, xxin6

Nevermind (album), 20, 117, 159

Nietzche, Friedrich, xxin6, 12, 13, 72; and *The Birth of Tragedy*, 164; and *The Genealogy of Morals*, 12

Nirvana (group), xv, xxiin7, 20, 21, 25, 27, 30n10, 105, 106, 117, 119, 157, 159, 160, 186; and "Something in the Way," 117, 118; and "Smells Like Teen Spirit," 21, 159

Novela negra (noir novel), 97

October, Gene, 18

O'Hara, Craig, xvii

Oleza, Joan, 50n1

The Orb (group), 103, 104

Ordovás, Jesús, 16

Ortega, Antonio, 42

Ortega y Gasset, José, xii, xiii, xiv, xviii, xxn2, 79, 93n3, 145; and *El tema de nuestro tiempo*, 79, 93n3; and *En torno a Galileo*, xiii

Ostriker, Alicia, 221
Ovid, 220–22, 228; and *Metamorphoses*, 220
Owen, Rob, 170

Pacino, Al, 197
Panofsky, Edwin, 225, 232n2
Pao, María, 61, 121, 122, 147n5, 212n3
Papas (group), 206
Papson, Stephen, 185
Paraíso (group), 31n18
Parálisis Permanente (group), 105
Paris, Texas, 166n9
Pasco, Allan, 99, 109
Pearl Jam (group), 62, 157; and "Alive," 157
The Pegamoides (group), 31n18
Pendergrass, Teddy, 208, 213n6
Peña-Ardid, Carmen, 165n4
Pérez, Jorge, xix, 238
Pérez Galdós, Benito, xv, 39; and *Fortunata y Jacinta*, xv
Pertierra, Tino, 35
Pet Shop Boys (group), xxin4
Peterson, Julius, 79
Phillips, Jayne Anne, xvii, 37, 38, 42, 47, 51n3; and *Black Tickets*, 51n3; and *Fast Lanes*, 51n3; and *Machina Dreams*, 51n3; and *Shelter*, 51n3
Pink Floyd (group), 157
Pirandello, Luigi, 11
The Pistols (group), 19, 27
Pitt, Brad, 163
The Pixies (group), 62
Platas Tasende, Ana María, 50n1
Poe, Edgar Allan, 98
Poesía española: Antología 1915-1931, xxn1
Pop, Iggy, 103, 194

Pope, Randolph, xix, 237, 240, 241
Powell, Bud, 25
Pozo, Raúl del, 45
Prada, Juan Manuel de, 35
Prado, Benjamín, 15, 25, 26, 30n12, 34, 35, 39, 45, 50n1, 78, 186, 235, 243, 244n3; and *Mala gente que camina*, 240, 242; as recuperation of memory, 243; and *No sólo el fuego*, 242; and *Nunca le des la mano a un pistolero zuedo*, 15, 25, 26; and *Raro*, 27, 34, 35, 50n1, 242
Pratt, Marie Louise, 52n5
Pressley, Elvis, 16
The Pretenders (group), 210, 213n6
"Pretty Vacant," (song) 18, 19
Prince, 208, 209; and "Little Red Corvette," (song) 208, 213n6; and "Slow Love," (song) 213n6
Prodigy (group), 103
Proust, Marcel, 11

Radio Futura (group), 31n18
Rae Hark, Ina, 163
The Ramones (group), 15
Real Academia Española, 43
Realism, xii
Realismo sucio, 34–40, 48–50, 107; as *cheli*, 43–45, 49, 51n3; as class difference, 36, 42; as orality, 42, 43
Reality Bites (film), 65, 73
Rebein, Robert, 50n2
Rebel Without a Cause (film), 160
Redding, Otis, 99; and "My Girl," (song) 99
Reed, Lou, 98, 99, 196, 206, 207, 213n6, 214n10; and "I'll Be Your Mirror," (song) 206, 213n6, 214n10; and "Walk on the Wild Side," (song) 99, 196

R.E.M. (group), xxiin7, 62
Retratista, Ramiro, 99
Rico, Eugenia; and *Los amantes tristes*,
  166n10; and *La edad secreta*, 154,
  161–64, 166n10; as masculine
  dominant society, 162, 163; and
  Muelles de Madrid, 166n10; and
  La muerte Blanca, 166n10; and
  La paz y la palabra, 166n10; and
  Que la vida iba en serio, 166n10; and
  Sobre raíles, 166n10
Riera, Miguel, 45
Ríos, Miguel, 157; and "El blues del
  autobus," (song) 157
Rivas, Manuel, xviii, 60, 62, 74, 98–100,
  102, 109, 110n2, 239; and "El míster
  & Iron Maiden," 100–102; and *¿Qué
  me quieres amor?*, 100, 101; and
  "Solo por ahí," 101
River, Mike, 213n6
Robertson, Robbie; and "Crazy River,"
  (song) 213n6; and "Somewhere
  Down the Crazy River," (song) 211
Robinson, Tom, 29n4
Rock 'n' roll; as anti-Franco protest, 97;
  as disenchantment, 98; as dissidence,
  97, 108
Rodríguez-Pazos, Gabriel, 146n2
Rolling Stone, xvi, 103
The Rolling Stones (group), 157, 206,
  209, 213n6; and "You Can't Always
  Get What You Want," 213n6
Romanticism, xii
Romeo, Félix, 35
Los Ronaldos (group), 105
Rotten, Johnny, 16, 19, 26, 28
Ruiz Carnicer, Miguel Ángel, xxin2
Russell, Bertrand, 18
Russo, Richard, 36, 37

Salinas, Pedro, 92n2
Sanborn, David, 213n6, 214n11
Sánchez Ferlosio, Rafael, xi, 39; and *El
  Jarama*, xi, 105
Santana, Cintia, xvii, 30n12, 236, 237
Santos, Care, 30n10; and *La muerte de
  Kart Cobain*, 30n10
Santote, Cathy, 221, 232n5
Sanz Villanueva, Santos, 94n7
Sartre, Jean-Paul, xvi, 3; as humanism 4,
  5, 6, 236; and *La nausée*, 3
Saura, Carlos; and *El séptimo día*,
  166n8, 181n2
Savater, Fernando, 72
Scarlett, Elizabeth, xviii, 239
Schwartz, Jeffrey, 141, 148n14
Scout, Ridley, 163; and *Thelma and
  Louise*, 161, 163,166n12; as
  empowerment of women, 163
Senabre, Ricardo, 42
The Sex Pistols (group), 15, 25, 26, 28,
  29, 107, 188
Shamen (group), 103
Shlovski, 9
Simone, Nina; and "My Baby Just Cares
  for Me," (song) 213n6
Siniestro Total (group), 31n18, 105
Smith, Carter, 148n13
Smith, Kevin, 73; and *Clerks*, 73
Smith, Patti, 25
Smith, Paul Julian, 230
Solomon, Claire, 92n1
Sonic Youth (group), 25, 157, 160
Spanish Civil War, xiii, xiv, 100, 171
Spengler, Oscar, xxin6
Sperry, Sharon Lynn, 175
Spires, Robert, 59, 74, 105
Springsteen, Bruce, 107, 186, 188
Squeeze (group); and "Cigarette of a
  Single Man," 211, 213n6

Stanton, Harry Dean, 166n9
Stewart, Miranda, 43, 44, 52n5
Stiller, Ben, 65
Stone, Oliver; and *Natural Born Killers* 160; and *Straight-Jacket* 25
Straw, Will, 110n4, 205, 207
Streisand, Barbara, 103
Sullivan, Chris, xvii
The Supremes (group), 206, 213n6
Surrealism, xii
Szatmary, David, 30n5

Tallent, Elizabeth, 36–38, 42, 51n3; and *Museum Pieces*, 51n3; and *Time with Children*, 51n3
Tasende Platas, Maria, 42
Tatum, Art, 25
La Terremoto (group), 16
The The (group), 105, 117; and "Giant," 115, 117, 119
Thurmaier, David, 165n1
Tillman, Lynne, 128
Tomeo, Javier, 212n5; and *La agonía de Proserpina*, 212n5, 214n9
Torrecilla, Jesús, 166n11; and *En la red*, 166n11
Torrente Ballester, Gonzalo, 35
Tos (group), 31n18
Towe, John, 18
Townshend, Pete, xvi
Traugott, Elizabeth, 52n5
Triana (group), 16
Triana-Toribio, Núria, 229
Trías, Eugeni, 8,
Trudgill, Peter, 40
Trueba, David, 78; and *Cuatro amigos*, 162
Tyler, Steven, 102
Tyras, Georges, 50n1

U2 (group), 62
Übermensch, 13
Ulrich, John, 18, 26
El Último de la Fila (group), 16
Umbral, Francisco, 43-45
Unamuno, Miguel de, xii, 8, 11, 27, 71, 72, 187; and *Niebla*, 27
La Unión (group); and "Ella es un volcán," 208, 213n6
Urioste, Carmen de, 50n1, 212n2, 212n4
Urrutia, Jorge, 165n4

V-Effekt, 9
Valderrama, Juanito, 99
Valis, Noel, 108
Valle Inclán, José María del, xviii
Valle-Inclán, Ramón María del, xii
Vallejo Nájera, Antonio, 243
Van Morrison, 210, 213n6; and "The Mystery," (song) 210, 213n6
Vattimo, Gianni, 7, 8
Vázquez Montalbán, Manuel, 35, 45, 74, 80, 91, 212n2; and *El estrangulador*, 74
Vega, Garcilaso de la, xvi
The Velvet Underground (group), 25, 98, 206, 214n9
Vicious, Sid, 15, 22, 24, 26-28, 31n15
Vilarós, Teresa, xxin2, xxin3, 155
Villena, Luis Antonio de, 239
Virgil, 72
The Voidoids (group), 19
Voltaire, 3

Waldman-Schwartz, Gloria, 232n4
Watt, Ian, 39
Waugh, Patricia, 73
The Wild One (film), 160
Williams, Joy, 37
Williams, Raymond, 182n7

Willis, Sharon, 167n12

Wings (group), 209; and "Live and Let Die," 209, 213n6, 214n10

Wolfe, Roger, 35, 39, 43, 48, 49, 50n1, 127, 145, 235; and *El índice de Dios*, 43; and *Quién no necesita algo en que apoyarse*, 49

Wolff, Tobias, xvii, 34, 36–38, 42, 47; and *De regreso al mundo*, 34

Wood, Grant, 37; and *American Gothic*, 37

Wurtzel, Elizabeth, 21, 30n12; and *Prozac Nation*, 21, 30n12

Young, Neil, 62, 160; and *Sleeps with Angels* (album), 160

Zenner, Otto, 99

VOLUMES IN THE HISPANIC ISSUES SERIES

33 *Generation X Rocks: Contemporary Peninsular Fiction, Film, and Rock Culture,* edited by Christine Henseler and Randolph D. Pope

32 *Reason and Its Others: Italy, Spain, and the New World,* edited by David Castillo and Massimo Lollini

31 *Hispanic Baroques: Reading Cultures in Context,* edited by Nicholas Spadaccini and Luis Martín-Estudillo

30 *Ideologies of Hispanism,* edited by Mabel Moraña

29 *The State of Latino Theater in the United States: Hybridity, Transculturation, and Identity,* edited by Luis A. Ramos-García

28 *Latin America Writes Back. Postmodernity in the Periphery (An Interdisciplinary Perspective),* edited by Emil Volek

27 *Women's Narrative and Film in Twentieth-Century Spain: A World of Difference(s),* edited by Ofelia Ferrán and Kathleen M. Glenn

26 *Marriage and Sexuality in Medieval and Early Modern Iberia,* edited by Eukene Lacarra Lanz

25 *Pablo Neruda and the U.S. Culture Industry,* edited by Teresa Longo

24 *Iberian Cities,* edited by Joan Ramon Resina

23 *National Identities and Sociopolitical Changes in Latin America,* edited by Mercedes F. Durán-Cogan and Antonio Gómez-Moriana

22 *Latin American Literature and Mass Media,* edited by Edmundo Paz-Soldán and Debra A. Castillo

21 *Charting Memory: Recalling Medieval Spain,* edited by Stacy N. Beckwith

20 *Culture and the State in Spain: 1550–1850,* edited by Tom Lewis and Francisco J. Sánchez

19 *Modernism and its Margins: Reinscribing Cultural Modernity from Spain and Latin America,* edited by Anthony L. Geist and José B. Monleón

18 *A Revisionary History of Portuguese Literature,* edited by Miguel Tamen and Helena C. Buescu

17 *Cervantes and his Postmodern Constituencies,* edited by Anne Cruz and Carroll B. Johnson

16 *Modes of Representation in Spanish Cinema,* edited by Jenaro Talens and Santos Zunzunegui

15 *Framing Latin American Cinema: Contemporary Critical Perspectives,* edited by Ann Marie Stock

14 *Rhetoric and Politics: Baltasar Gracián and the New World Order,* edited by Nicholas Spadaccini and Jenaro Talens

13   *Bodies and Biases: Sexualities in Hispanic Cultures and Literatures,*
     edited by David W. Foster and Roberto Reis
12   *The Picaresque: Tradition and Displacement,* edited by Giancarlo Maiorino
11   *Critical Practices in Post-Franco Spain,*
     edited by Silvia L. López, Jenaro Talens, and Dario Villanueva
10   *Latin American Identity and Constructions of Difference,*
     edited by Amaryll Chanady
 9   *Amerindian Images and the Legacy of Columbus,*
     edited by René Jara and Nicholas Spadaccini
 8   *The Politics of Editing,* edited by Nicholas Spadaccini and Jenaro Talens
 7   *Culture and Control in Counter-Reformation Spain,*
     edited by Anne J. Cruz and Mary Elizabeth Perry
 6   *Cervantes's Exemplary Novels and the Adventure of Writing,*
     edited by Michael Nerlich and Nicholas Spadaccini
 5   *Ortega y Gasset and the Question of Modernity,* edited by Patrick H. Dust
 4   *1492–1992: Re/Discovering Colonial Writing,*
     edited by René Jara and Nicholas Spadaccini
 3   *The Crisis of Institutionalized Literature in Spain,*
     edited by Wlad Godzich and Nicholas Spadaccini
 2   *Autobiography in Early Modern Spain,*
     edited by Nicholas Spadaccini and Jenaro Talens
 1   *The Institutionalization of Literature in Spain,*
     edited by Wlad Godzich and Nicholas Spadaccini